THE RISE OF ENVIRONMENTAL LAW IN THE REPUBLIC OF TRINIDAD AND TOBAGO

BY

RAJENDRA RAMLOGAN

"*When I have to, I'll run; when I can, I'll fight, but whatever I do, I'll not quit. It ain't because I have more nerve than the next man, it's just that I'm not very smart.*"

—Words quoted by Tell Sackett in the book *The Sackett Brand* by Louis L'Amour

"*Es mejor morir de pie que vivir de rodillas*" (Words attributed to Emiliano Zapata)

All proceeds from the sale of this book are for the use and benefit of the Management Society of the University of the West Indies (MSU).

Cover Picture of Sea Side Scenery Reproduced with Permission from Nadir Ali

Cover Picture of Fish Kill Reproduced with Permission from Fishermen and Friends of the Sea

ISBN: 978-1-54395-532-3

This book is dedicated to the following persons:

To Friends that endured: *Sally, Indra, and Manohor*
To Friends that rose from the ashes: *Michael, Adrian, and Lionel*
To Family that never doubted: *Krishna, Rohenee, Rehana, Renuka, Krishendath, and Reanne*

TABLE OF CONTENTS

TABLE OF CASES

TABLE OF STATUTES

LIST OF TABLES

LIST OF ACRONYMS

AWNC	Asa Wright Nature Centre
CEC	Certificate of Environmental Clearance
EIA	Environmental Impact Assessment
EMA	Environmental Management Authority
FFOS	Fishermen and Friends of the Sea
GNI	Gross National Index
IMA	Institute of Marine Affairs
MOWT	Ministry of Works and Transport
NGC	National Gas Company of Trinidad and Tobago Limited
OECD	Organization for Economic Corporation and Development
PAPWT	Pointe-a-Pierre Wildfowl Trust
PURE	People United Respecting the Environment
TEWs	Trini Eco Warriors
THA	Tobago House of Assembly
TOR	Terms of Reference
TT	Republic of Trinidad and Tobago
TTCRA	Trinidad and Tobago Civil Rights Association
TTFNC	Trinidad and Tobago Field Naturalists' Club
UNCHE	United Nations Conference on the Human Environment
UNFCC	United Nations Framework Convention for Climate Change
UNDP	United Nations Development Program
UNEP	United Nations Environmental Program
USA	United States of America
UWI	The University of the West Indies

CHAPTER 1

THE PRELUDE

The ascendancy of modern man has been accompanied by leaps in both scientific and technological developments that accelerated man's triumph over nature. Modern man conquered the land with modes of motorised transport, the air with supersonic aircrafts, and some even ventured into outer space. Nuclear energy was harnessed, albeit initially for destructive purposes. Chemical and biological agents were manipulated to enhance growth rates of plant and animal life and thereby increase food supplies, and to control pests. Mechanisation became the order of the day as society progressed, replacing direct human effort. It became possible to enhance human longevity and reduce rates of mortality, causing demographical increases worldwide. Human cloning and genetic manipulation to produce the perfect human have left science fiction and entered the realm of the foreseeable reality. Man strode into the digital era, marking yet another fascinating step forward; meetings can now be held while sitting at opposite ends of the globe. The dream of the hologram, a feature of Star Trek fantasy became reality in the posthumous performance of Tupac.

Development of any type, generally comes at a price and the developed world has recognised that technological advances can result in unanticipated adverse effects on the ecosystem. Gaia is threatened as never before. The United Nations Conference on the Human Environment of 1972 (UNCHE), held in Stockholm, was the first initiative to raise awareness of the environment on a global level. Unfortunately, it is only when the threat of danger is imminent or has already taken effect that any type of action is initiated. Human nature has shown time and again that the curative approach is preferable to the preventative approach, as the technocrats and scientists who assisted in the creation of the problem became essential components of the solution.

An example of such an issue would be the early discovery in 1974 by scientists Molina and Rowland, that the ozone layer was subject to depletion. The depletion was caused by anthropogenic factors, such as the production and emission of chlorofluorocarbons (CFC's) and other Ozone Depleting Substances (ODS) into the atmosphere. It only assumed international importance following the discovery of a large stratospheric ozone hole over Antarctica in 1984 by British Antarctic Survey scientists, Joseph Farman, Brian Gardiner, and Jonathan Shanklin. A decade had elapsed before people began to fully appreciate the gravity of the situation. The ozone layer is extremely important, as it acts as a natural filter against excessive ultraviolet radiation. Greater exposure to ultraviolet light increases the risk of skin cancer, eye cataracts and sunburn. It has also been said to be responsible for reduced crop yields, weakening the body's immune system and damaging the very fibre of human life – DNA.

One of the emerging dimensions to the environmental debate is the need to understand the magnitude of acts of environmental degradation in developing countries and the resulting attitude of governments in these countries. The construction of the Tehri Dam in India is expected to be completed in 2019[1], despite the fact that it has been opposed by a wide cross section of society due to it being built in an ecologically fragile area, which also happens to be earthquake-prone. Thousands of families will be displaced, yet this project conceived as far back as 1949 and in the face of widespread protest, has seen the Indian government proceed with a typical "business as usual attitude."[2]

The Three Gorges Dam, the world's largest hydroelectric project and a symbol of China's growing global technological ascendancy, was pursued with ruthless vigour in the face of domestic and international concerns over its safety as well as threats to the environment. In 2011 at the time of

---

1 https://ejatlas.org/conflict/tehri-dam-and-hydropower-plant

2 Shaukat Hassan, *Environmental issues and security in South Asia* (published 1991, Oxford: Nuffield Press)

certification of the dam's array of generators as suitable for hydroelectric generation, the final step in a contentious 19-year effort to complete the project, it was observed that the project was troubled by urgent pollution and geologic problems.[3]

THE PLIGHT OF DEVELOPING COUNTRIES

Considering the consequences of environmental damage to the global village due to the increased interdependency of nations, the quality of the partnership offered by the developing world in the environmental struggle becomes significant. Sociologically, environmental protection in the developing world is vastly different from that found in the developed world as a consequence of their differing needs. Environmental protection receives little attention in the developing world, as urgent issues, such as, *inter alia,* the reduction of poverty, improved health care and infrastructural development must be addressed. The relationship between development issues and environmental protection is such that one will, more often than not, be achieved at the expense of the other. There is often conflict and it is usually the environment that becomes the hapless victim. It can be argued that developed countries have reached a stage of development where they can seek to deal with "low priority" issues, such as the protection of the environment, whereas developing countries are still in the preliminary stages of development and wish to deal with more "high priority" topics, such as building economic and social infrastructure. This is concisely summarised by Grant, who states that:

> *While the forms of Northern interests were on issues of population, marine pollution and the rapid depletion of natural resources, the South emphasized development, stressing the need to address the inequities of the international economic system, especially in terms of trade, technology transfers, aid flows as*

3 Micheal Wines, *China Admits Problems With Three Gorges Dam*, New York Times (19 May 2011) <http://www.nytimes.com/2011/05/20/world/asia/20gorges.html>

well as the eradication of poverty.[4]

The United Nations Development Programme (UNDP) has noted that developing countries are being left behind in the human development journey.

> *Given that broader context, the Report then raises two fundamental questions: who has been left out in progress in human development and how and why did that happen. It emphasizes that poor, marginalized and vulnerable groups—including ethnic minorities, indigenous peoples, refugees and migrants—are being left behind furthest behind...The top 1 percent of the global wealth distribution holds 46 percent of the world's wealth. Inequalities in income influence inequalities in other dimensions of well-being, and vice versa.*[5]

It has further been pointed out by UNDP that the environment is paying the price for such inequality and the burden is being unevenly shared.

> *The environmental costs to developing countries are staggering. Every year, 24 billion tonnes of fertile soils are lost to erosion, and 12 million hectares of land are lost to drought and desertification, affecting the lives and livelihoods of 1.5 billion people. Desertification could displace up to 135 million people by 2045. Biodiversity is below safe levels across more than half the world's lands. Every year, 300 million tonnes of plastic are manufactured, but only 15 percent is recycled, leaving 46,000 floating pieces of plastic per square mile of ocean. But this is a minuscule fraction of the total amount of waste held in the seas, which affects nearly 700 marine species. In 2012 an estimated 8.4 million people died from air, water or land pollution. At least 6.5 million people a year are believed to be dying from air pollution, with many more injured. The cost of air pollution in welfare losses has been estimated at $5 trillion, 60 percent of which is in developing regions. About 2.7 billion people still depend on wood or waste fires that cause indoor air pollution, affecting women and children the most. Indoor air pollution leads to around 3.5 million deaths a year. Forests and trees provide vital resources to 1.3 billion people, and in developing countries, forest*

---

4 Cedric Grant, *Environmentalism, Development and Integration: The Caricom Dimension'*(December 1998) Beyond Law 6:20, 175

5 UNDP, *Human Development Report 2016*, p.7

income is second only to farm income among rural communities. Between 60 million and 200 million indigenous peoples rely on forests for survival. Acting as the lungs of the world, forests also slow climate change, and acting as carbon sinks, they increase resilience. Yet in tropical countries the annual net forest loss is 7 million hectares—the size of Ireland. pg.139 Water stress is a major challenge affecting more than 4 billion people worldwide.pg 140 The combined effects of growing populations, rising incomes and expanding cities will cause the demand for water to rise exponentially, while supply becomes more erratic and uncertain. Water is becoming scarcer in the Arab States and in the African Sahel, where it is already in short supply, and may start disappearing in Central Africa or East Asia, where it is currently abundant. These regions could see declines of as much as 6 percent of GDP by 2050 because of water-related impacts on agriculture, health and income. In 2012 more than 80 percent of the world's primary energy supply came from fossil fuels, and only 16 percent came from renewable energy. In 2015 fossil fuels accounted for 55 percent of global energy investment, and today fossil fuel companies benefit from global subsidies of $10 million a minute. The world has the resources, the technology and the expertise to overcome human deprivations. And the notion of sharing prosperity gives us hope that we are ready to tackle human deprivations together 1 billion people worldwide lack access to electricity. By 2040 the planet's energy system will need to serve 9 billion people, and much of the energy will have to be renewable. Climate change will aggravate land degradation—especially in drylands, which occupy 40 percent of global land area, are inhabited by some 2 billion people and support half the world's livestock. By 2030 climate change is expected to cause an additional 250,000 deaths a year from malaria, diarrhoea, heat stress and malnutrition.pg 146 The poorest people are more exposed than the average population to climate-related shocks and are at high risk of floods, droughts and heat waves; crop failures from reduced rainfall; spikes in food prices after extreme weather events; and increased incidence of diseases after heat waves and floods. Poor people are also more exposed to higher temperatures and live in countries where food production is expected to decrease. If climate-smart action is not taken now, more than 100 million additional people could be living in poverty by 2030. pg147 Climate change can have the most disastrous effects on indigenous peoples, who rely more on natural resources and agriculture[6]

A projected sea related impact is the proliferation of tropical storms. It is likely that as oceans warm-up, storms will increase in intensity and regular-

---

6 UNDP, *Human Development Report 2016*, p.38-39

ity. As noted by Meade:

> *Since hurricanes began to be recorded and classified, in 1851, thirty-three storms have reached Category 5 strength in the Atlantic, according to Michael Lowry, a visiting scientist at the University Corporation for Atmospheric Research, in Boulder, Colorado. Two of those tore through the Caribbean within the last two weeks. Data compiled by Weather Underground shows that in only twelve hours Hurricane Maria strengthened from a Category 2 hurricane to a Category 5. When the storm made landfall in Dominica, on Monday, it unleashed a-hundred-and-seventy-five-mile-per-hour winds on the island of seventy thousand people.[7]*

The most ambitious attempt to deal with climate change due to anthropogenic forces emerged in the Paris Accord that builds upon the United Nations Framework Convention for Climate Change (UNFCC). On the UNFCC website, it is noted that the Paris Accord achieved the threshold level for entry into force on 5 October 2016, before the people of United States of America (USA) catapulted Donald Trump on the global environmental stage. It is observed that the "Paris Agreement's central aim is to strengthen the global response to the threat of climate change by keeping a global temperature rise this century well below 2 degrees Celsius above pre-industrial levels and to pursue efforts to limit the temperature increase even further to 1.5 degrees Celsius. To reach these ambitious goals, appropriate financial flows, a new technological framework and an enhanced capacity building framework is to be put in place, thus supporting action by developing countries and the most vulnerable countries, in line with their own national objectives." Donald Trump, in typical cavalier fashion to the dismay of the rest of the world, quickly indicated a desire to revisit the commitment of the USA to the Paris Accord.

Unsurprisingly, at the time when world leaders should have been listening with bated breath, Donald Trump, along with many other leaders left the United Nations General Assembly at a meeting held on September 2017, in

---

7 Natalie Meade, *Eden Is Broken: A Caribbean Leader Calls for Action on Climate Change*, The New Yorker (24 September 2017)

the aftermath of Hurricane Maria prior to a speech delivered by the Prime Minister of Dominica, Roosevelt Skerrit. The vicissitudes inherent in the destructive path carved by Maria, led to a plaintive epicedium contained in language reflecting national grief. As reported by Meade,

> To deny climate change is to procrastinate while the earth sinks; it is to deny a truth we have just lived. It is to mock thousands of my compatriots who in a few hours without a roof over their heads will watch the night descend on Dominica, in fear of sudden mudslides . . . and what the next hurricane may bring.....My fellow-leaders, there is no more time for conversation. There is little time left for action. While the big countries talk, the small island nations suffer. We need action and we need it now.[8]

Skerrit reminded the world that many developing countries with no impact on global warming are the unwitting recipients of its consequences.

> We as a country and as a region did not start this war against nature. We did not provoke it.... We do not pollute or overfish our oceans. We have made no contribution to global warming that can move the needle. But yet we are among the main victims.[9]

It must be noted, however, that inadequate resources resulting from the development/environment debate in the developing world leaves much to be desired vis-à-vis the existing legal and institutional framework for the protection of the environment. The domestic regimes of many developing countries all show that despite the existence of legislation, protection of the environment remains on the back burner largely as a result of a lack of financial, human, research and mechanical resources. This book will involve an examination of the journey of one developing country in managing its environment from a legal, institutional and policy perspective. It is not however, an attempt to offer a panacea for developing countries as it relates to the concerns of environmental matters but to illustrate the use of judicial mechanisms to protect the environment.

---

8 Ibid.
9 Ibid.

TT BACKGROUND AND HISTORY

TT is an independent nation comprising two islands situated at the south-ernmost point of the Caribbean archipelago, a chain of islands stretching from Florida in the USA to Venezuela in South America and enclosing the Caribbean Sea. Trinidad is the larger of the two islands with one thousand, eight hundred and sixty-four (1,864) square miles and lies just seven miles (7) from the Venezuelan coast, whereby Trinidad is separated from the Venezuelan Coast by way of the Gulf of Paria, one of the finest natural harbours in the world. Tobago is twenty (20) miles north-east of Trinidad. A central chain of mountains, called the Main Ridge, extends nearly two thirds of the length of the island from its north-eastern tip, the highest point being five hundred and sixty-seven (567) metres. The Main Ridge comprises many ridges and conical hills which form attractive valleys through which numerous streams run to the sea. The south-west-ern tip, Crown Point, is low-lying coral limestone, and off the coast there is a coral lagoon bounded by the beautiful Buccoo Reef. There are several smaller islands around the coast of TT which are ideal reserves for wild life. Most notable of these is Little Tobago, a sanctuary for the world-fa-mous "Bird of Paradise". Tobago was initially isolated and unknown to Europeans for many decades after the discovery of Trinidad. The island was visited by the English captain Robert Dudley in 1596 but remained uninhabited until 1632 when a party of about two hundred (200) New Zealanders was sent there by a company of Dutch merchants. For the next two hundred (200) years, the island changed hands among the Dutch, the English and the French, all rival colonists. In 1763, Tobago was ceded to Britain, then captured by the French in 1781 and recaptured by the British in 1793. After again changing hands several times, the island was ceded to Britain in 1814 by the Treaty of Paris. On 6 April 1889, Trinidad and Tobago became united as one territory due to the insistence of the British Government, whereby Tobago became a ward of the colony of Trinidad and the finances of the two islands were merged.

TT follows the Westminster model of government and upholds the tra-ditions of parliamentary democracy inherited from Britain. The country gained independence in 1962 and became a Republic in 1976. It is a member of the British Commonwealth. Legislative power lies with the House of Representatives with forty-one (41) elected members, and the Senate comprising thirty-one (31) members appointed by the President, sixteen (16) on the advice of the Prime Minister; six (6) on the advice of the Leader of the Opposition; and nine (9) by the President as Independents. Executive power lies with the Prime Minister and his/her Cabinet, which is appointed from Members of Parliament. Tobago has its own elected House of Assembly (THA) responsible for the administration of the island, and the implementation of policies which are referred by Parliament. The President of TT is elected for a five-year renewable term by an Electoral College consisting of members of the House of Representatives and the Senate. The Judiciary is independent of the Government and this is guaranteed by the Constitution which provides for the entrenched protection of fundamental human rights and freedoms.

ECONOMIC PROFILE OF TRINIDAD AND TOBAGO

TT is a developing country designated as an upper middle income country which is rich in natural resources, especially oil and natural gas. With a Gross National Income (GNI) Per Capita, Atlas Method, of US$16,240.00, it is twice the average GNI Per Capita, Atlas Method for Latin America and the Caribbean which stands at US$8,272.00.[10] TT is ranked 11th by the World Bank on a GNI per capita basis for countries outside the high-income definition of the World Bank. TT has always had a largely natural resource based economy, as illustrated by its dependence on sugar in an earlier era, and then on oil and natural gas. Hydrocarbon development in TT dates back a long time. In 1867, the first oil deposits were discovered by the Paria Petroleum Company in Aripero in South Trinidad.[11] The first oil well, however, was drilled by the Merrimac Oil Company of the USA at La Brea in 1857. By the 1920s, some forty (40) oil companies operated in TT.

---

10 http://wdi.worldbank.org/table/WV.1 (2016 Figures)

11 http://www.energy.gov.tt/our-business/oil-and-gas-industry

The peak in petroleum production in 1978 encouraged exploration, which resulted in the discovery of significant gas reserves. Natural gas, which hitherto had been treated as a nuisance product and flared, began to assume an economic significance of its own. Gas is used as the petrochemical feedstock in the production of ammonia, methanol and urea, and provides an energy source for non-energy products such as steel, and other minor manufactured products. With eleven (11) ammonia plants and seven (7) methanol plants, TT is a major world exporter of ammonia and methanol, according to IHS Global Insight (2013).[12] Government policy has led this twin island nation to become a major global exporter of liquefied natural gas. Natural gas is, in fact, the key driver behind the current intensive industrial sector development and expansion programme. Moreover, the energy sector of TT accounts for around thirty-four point nine percent (34.9%) of the country's gross domestic product.

A major development of the natural gas industry was the liquefaction of natural gas for export to various destinations around the world. Atlantic LNG Company of Trinidad and Tobago, the operator of a four-train liquefaction facility located at Point Fortin on the southwest coast of Trinidad, and one of the largest exporters of LNG in the world, produces liquefied natural gas (LNG) from natural gas delivered from fields in and around TT.[13]

---

12 http://www.energy.gov.tt/our-business/oil-and-gas-industry/
13 https://www.atlanticlng.com/our-business/overview

ENVIRONMENTAL ISSUES CONFRONTING TRINIDAD AND TOBAGO

TT sits on the continental shelf of South America, separated by only twelve (12) kilometres from Venezuela. Both islands are therefore geologically part of the mainland, with evidence indicating that Trinidad was only recently separated, about 11-15,000 years ago. This recent parting of the islands over very small distances locates TT in the same bio-geographic region as tropical coastal South America. The biodiversity of TT as seen in Table 1.0 is the most diverse of the islands in the Caribbean archipelago due to the continental origin of the islands which therefore provides TT with a rich tropical South-American natural heritage. [14]

TABLE 1.0 BIOLOGICAL DIVERSITY[15]

Major Group	Number of Species
Vascular Plants	2160
Birds	450
Mammals	95
Reptiles	85
Snakes	55
Amphibians	30
Freshwater fishes	45
Marine fishes	354
Butterflies	600
Nematodes	200-300

Based on its economic profile which is anchored in the hydrocarbon sector and its rich biological diversity, it is hardly surprising that TT is confronted by numerous environmental challenges. As noted by the UNDP:

Environmental degradation remains a major issue for Trinidad and Tobago. The country experiences many environmental problems, from flooding, widespread pollution of its waterways and coastal areas, illegal dumping, deforestation, excessive soil erosion,

---

14 http://tt.biosafetyclearinghouse.net/0003.shtml

fisheries and wildlife depletion. As a Small Island Developing State (SIDS), Trinidad and Tobago is highly vulnerable to natural disasters like tropical storms, earthquakes, floods and droughts, as well as climate change and sea levels rising.[15]

Added to the list of environmental woes identified by the UNDP is air pollution, reflecting a heavily industrialized and motorized society with non-existent landfills leading to a waste disposal nightmare.

THE RISE OF ENVIRONMENTAL AWARENESS IN TRINIDAD AND TOBAGO

Science

One of the important factors in the rise of environmental awareness is the growing role of science in shaping human understanding on environmental issues. It is largely agreed that the impetus for changing human behaviour quite often has its genesis in science. The role of science in solving the world's environmental problems has evolved over the years and has become a critical factor in addressing the threats to the environment.

In TT, the role of science is slowly building impetus in addressing environmental problems. This is not to say, however, that science has completely ignored the environment. There are organizations that have been developed in TT whose aim is to bring to light the importance of having a society that is environmentally and socially responsible, healthy, and prosperous which seeks to improve the quality of life. The Institute of Marine Affairs (IMA) is an example of an organization that has certainly harnessed scientific resources to better understand the threat of pollution and development projects to the marine environment and has continuously engaged in the conducting of studies and generation of data with respect to marine issues.

In April 2012, Cabinet appointed a Steering Committee to develop an Inte-

---

15 http://www.tt.undp.org/content/trinidad_tobago/en/home/ourwork/environmentandenergy/in_depth.html

grated Coastal Zone Management Policy Framework, Strategies and Action Plan for Trinidad and Tobago. The Steering Committee was appointed for two years with the IMA as Chair. The IMA has also been instrumental in introducing a new technology aimed at detecting the levels of pollution in the sea and its potential impact on aquatic life and the surrounding ecosystem. The Water Quality Monitoring Buoy, which was made possible through a collective effort between Microsoft Caribbean and its partners on the project, the IMA, Fufitsu Caribbean and Digicel,[16] will provide early detection of environmental incidents such as fish kills and oil spills and further, will provide a significant boost for underwater quality testing in TT.

Scientific research faces numerous challenges, not least funding. Christopher Dally, lecturer in the Civil and Environmental Engineering Department of The University of the West Indies (UWI), stated that it could be difficult to get funding because there is no real profit to be made from doing research and so, it is difficult to get private investment. He suggested that students be funded through a national or regional science board that has the long-term interest of society at heart. It also must have full governmental support but at the same time, be independent of political influence.

Individual researchers and scientists such as Professor Hamid Farabi, Professor Julien Kenny (deceased), Dr. Mike Oatham and others from UWI, St. Augustine, have written extensively on the various threats to the environment posed by anthropogenic factors. Thus, the contributions of individual scholars and institutional efforts have introduced a scientific approach to environmental issues and create a greater awareness of the threats confronting TT.

Media and Film

The media is an important player in raising environmental sensitivity. TT is certainly experiencing change in this area, and within the last decade, the

---

16 Rajiv Jamar Alim, *Sinking into Paradise: Climate Change Worsening Coastal Erosion in Trinidad* (UNDP, 19 November 2015)

role of the media has gathered increased significance. While the broadcast media has no regularly scheduled environmental programmes, it is usual for radio stations and television stations to investigate and comment on environmental issues. For example, Mark Bassant, a Senior Investigative Reporter, covers several major issues concerning the environment in both print and broadcast format.

The print media, in particular, has witnessed some improvement in the coverage of environmental issues. However, understanding by the general media personnel of the complexity of environmental issues is limited. This is further compounded by the fact that few reporters have a background in science or technology. With limited staff, it is not feasible for the media to devote one reporter to environmental topics; as a result, reporters deal with several issues together with the environment. However, reporters such as Robert Clarke, Kim Boodram, Mark Meredith and Shaliza Hassanali have distinguished themselves with journalistic investigation of environmental issues.

Within recent times, there continues to be improvement in environmental reporting, as there has been an allocation of column space dedicated to highlighting environmental issues. This has made way for professionals in the field to write and help bring awareness to the current issues affecting the environment. Heather Dawn Herrera and Marc De Verteuil are examples of professionals who regularly contribute articles in the written media on environmental matters.

As expected in the world of social media, providers such as Instagram, Twitter and Facebook are proving invaluable in raising environmental awareness. Social media represents a digital revolution which has given access to a huge amount of information at our fingertips. People throughout the world are searching for answers on the internet and are connecting to each other, forming a virtual community through these social networks online. Social sites offer brilliant opportunities to even create environmental awareness which is critical to preserving the environment and in turn ensuring a sustainable future. Fishermen and Friends of the Sea (FFOS), a non-governmental organization (NGO) has successfully used social media to reach the population of TT and beyond. The mainstream media has also embraced the virtual world to disseminate news pertaining to the environment.

An emerging factor in enhancing environmental awareness is the use of the film media. Sustain T&T, an NGO, has been instrumental in hosting an annual Environmental Film Festival. Further, in conjunction with the IMA, Sustain T&T has produced the films "The Bottle," and, "Nature Man" to bring these issues to light.[17]

Education

Education is also responsible for the recent upsurge in environmental consciousness. Education has been identified by environmentalists as the key to rescuing the environment[18] as there is a need to make known the inherent relationship between man and the environment. Accordingly, education must lead the way in nurturing a more responsible attitude towards the environment. In TT, the education system is being revamped with the hope of incorporating environmental education into the curriculum. However, the heavy reliance on textbooks, note taking and regurgitation of information with very little critical thinking and linking of related concepts and ideas is not conducive to teaching environmental material, which is of itself, very dynamic and encourages or even requires personal interaction with the material.

Environmental education is part of the primary school curriculum of TT.[19] At the primary school level in TT there is more emphasis on tradi-

---

17 *All About the Environment,* Trinidad and Tobago Newsday (21 October 21, 2017) http://newsday.co.tt/2017/10/21/all-about-the-environment

18 Joan Ferreira, *Advocacy of Environmental Journalism - The EMA's Experience,* (Paper presented at the CPACC Media Conference, 27-28 April 2000, Ambassador Hotel, Port of Spain, Trinidad, 2000), 3.

19 Armstrong, Hyacinth G., *Environmental education in Tobago's primary schools: a case study of coral reef education* (Revista de Biología Tropical, 2005) 53(Suppl. 1), 229-238. Retrieved 16 March 2018, from http://www.scielo.sa.cr/scielo.php&pid=S0034-77442005000300028&lng=en&tlng=en.

tional subject areas such Social Studies, Mathematics, Language Arts and Arts and Crafts, which do little to introduce students to environmental issues in TT.[20] However, in an effort to address these shortcomings, the Division of Curriculum Development in the Ministry of Education has sought to incorporate environmental concepts into the Science and Social Studies syllabi. In recent times there has been some effort to bring some improvement at the primary school level. As such, staff from the Buccoo Reef Trust, an NGO based in Tobago, facilitated a pilot program which taught students from fifteen (15) primary schools about coral reefs, using interactive tools and hands-on methods. The pilot program ran over an eight (8) week period with prepared lessons being taught every two (2) weeks and student evaluations taking place once before the first lesson and once after the last lesson, and further supplemented with a field trip to a coral reef ecosystem. Despite several challenges that were faced in the implementation process, the overall outcome of the pilot program was successful. Teachers and students reacted positively to the information that was being shared, thereby reinforcing the effectiveness of using a dynamic, active method of teaching to advance environmental education.

Environmental issues are currently part of the geography syllabus in secondary schools and elements are further being introduced in chemistry, biology and principles of business. At the advanced level in secondary schools, environmental sciences have been incorporated into the syllabi of geography, chemistry, biology and physics. Over forty (40) students received open Scholarship in Environment Studies in 2017. Two (2) of the more prestigious denominational schools in Port of Spain have established laboratories and classes solely for environmental sciences. A major study conducted by Rawatee Maharaj-Sharma stated:

> *In a study in Trinidad and Tobago involving 176 secondary school students aged 15-17 years, it was found that 90% of the group had a good working knowledge about environmental issues. More students from rural schools were*

---

20 Ibid.

found to be personally aware of specific environmental issues in their communities, while more urban students indicated that they had done something tangible about one or more environmental issues. The students were surveyed by way of a 2-sectioned attitudinal-based opinionnaire, which gauged general knowledge and awareness in the first section and students' responsiveness in the second section. The results showed the while both urban and rural students were highly aware of environmental issues, rural students were slightly more responsive to these issues. A small percentage of students in this work were found to have a weak knowledge base about environmental issues, were generally indifferent to environmental issues within their communities, and had never been involved in any initiative on environmental matters.[21]

At the tertiary level, environmental studies can be found at state funded institutions throughout TT. At UWI, offerings now include a BSc Environmental Science and Sustainable Technology (Special), BSc Major in Environmental Science and BSc Biology with Specializations. There are also M.Phil. and Ph.D. programmes in Environmental Biology. At the College of Science, Technology and Applied Arts of Trinidad and Tobago, the Department of Environmental Studies offer many undergraduate Associate and Bachelor of Science degrees in environmental related fields. Another state funded institution engaged in offering environmental programmes is the Cipriani Labour College where students can pursue an Associate of Science Degree in Environmental Management. Additionally, there are tertiary institutions offering degrees in association with non-TT universities such as the School of Business and Computer Science which offers a Bachelor of Science in Occupational Safety, Health and Environment. Finally, the University of Southern Caribbean, a private partially funded university, offers a Bachelor of Science in Biology which covers environmental components.

A related aspect of education is the number of environmental books being published in TT. Today, the emphasis is mainly on biological resources but the upsurge in publications is most noteworthy. These books include Donna

---

21 Rawatee Maharaj-Sharma, *Awareness of and Responsiveness to Environmental Issues: Views from Secondary School Students in Trinidad and Tobago* (2015) Caribbean Curriculum Volume 23, 79-97

Spencer's "Our Marine Heritage", Joy Rudder's "Our Native Land", Julian Duncan's "A Guide to Wild Flowers of Trinidad and Tobago", Julian Kenny's "Views from the Ridge" and "Views from the Bridge", Victor Quesnel's "Trees", Hans Boos's "Snakes", Julie Morton's "The Magical Mystical Ibis", and Richard Laydoo's "A Guide to the Coral Reefs of Tobago". Thus the literature on environmental issues specifically pertaining to TT is becoming more abundant and available for public perusal, allowing for greater sensitivity to environmental issues.

Environmental Events

While there have been no spectacular events affecting human life and biological diversity of the magnitude of Bhopal, Chernobyl and the Exxon Valdez spill, TT has had its fair share of environmental disasters, such as oil spills, on both land and sea. On 19 July 1979, the largest tanker oil spill thus far took place off the coast of Tobago. About 2.2 million barrels of crude oil were spilled after a collision between the Atlantic Empress and the Actaeon Captain. Having taken place off the coast of a developing country, it is hardly surprising that very little is known about the environmental consequences of this disaster.

In the past decade, the marine waters of TT have been subject to severe assaults through numerous offshore oil spills especially in South Trinidad that adversely affected residents living along the coastline, especially fishermen. Indeed, in 2013, the Petroleum Company of Trinidad and Tobago Ltd. recorded eleven (11) oil spills in ten (10) days.[22] It is hardly surprising that reports of oil spills and subsequent clean-up operations are often accompanied by graphic imagery of dead fish floating in the sea and littering the shoreline.

An equally distressing environmental event is the almost annual burning of the Beetham Landfill (generously called a landfill). The screaming headline

---

22 Sean Douglas, *11 Oil Spills in 10 Days,* Trinidad and Tobago Newsday (31 December, 2013) http://archives.newsday.co.tt/2013/12/31/11-oil-spills-in-10-days/

in 2015 tells it all:

> *After fire at Beetham landfill Smoke covers city again- Business owners and people working in Port-of-Spain once again were bracing for the worst yesterday after the capital became engulfed in smoke due to a fire at the Beetham landfill.[23]*

The fire occurred an hour after workers of the Trinidad and Tobago Solid Waste Management Company Limited ended their third consecutive day of protest. However, the workers maintained they did not start it.

The occurrences of these environmental events, although unfortunate, have made citizens become more aware of the importance of their environment.

The Role of Non-Governmental Organizations

The Global Perspective

Non-Governmental Organizations (NGOs) are generally defined as privately run organizations dedicated to advancing the cause of a particular group or issue. A historical review of the evolution of NGOs shows that they can be categorized into six (6) main types. First, there are welfare and relief agencies. Second, there are technical innovation organizations that implement their own projects in order to pioneer or improve approaches to problems. Third, there are public service contractors, or NGOs funded from official sources, which work closely with governments in tasks such as the implementation of components of official programs. Fourth, there are popular development agencies involved in activities like self-help programs and social development in general. Fifth, there are grassroots developmental organizations whose objectives are shaping a popular developmental process; contained in this category are mainly NGOs located in the developing world and drawing their membership from the poor and oppressed. Finally, there are advocacy groups and networks that are primarily engaged in lobbying and educational activi-

---

23 Rachael Espinet, *After fire at Beetham landfill Smoke covers city again*, Trinidad and Tobago Guardian, (23 April 2015) http://www.guardian.co.tt/news/2015-04-23/after-fire-beetham-landfill-smoke-covers-city-again

ties. Environmental NGOs normally fall into this latter category.[24] However, as will later be shown, their role has been steadily evolving, thereby making this straightforward categorization of limited use.

NGOs have proved to be a major contributor to the global upsurge in interest in environmentalism. Environmental NGOs appeared as early as 1865 with the formation of the Commons, Open Spaces, and Footpaths Preservation Society in the United Kingdom (UK). The latter campaigned strenuously for the preservation of land for reasons of amenity, particularly in urban areas.[25] However, there can be no doubt that the last quarter of the 20th century and the start of the 21st century have witnessed an explosion in the number of environmental NGOs.

Environmental NGOs do not necessarily, collectively endorse any single philosophy and accordingly, their views and commitments are not homogeneous. This being the case, their objectives and manifestos for action also vary. Some NGOs work closely with official agencies and are quite often referred to as sell-outs by those who are committed to a more radical agenda because they see officialdom as part of the threat against the environment. There are also cultural differences between NGOs and these differences are reflective of the North-South division. Many NGOs in the developing world have their origins in political, social justice and human rights challenges, while, in the developed world, NGOs like Greenpeace were started for the purpose of opposing nuclear activities.[26]

The organizational cultures of NGOs vary as well. Some can be extremely bureaucratic, as are many large corporations, while others reflect the flexibility typically associated with NGOs. Not only do NGOs differ with respect to their own cultures and philosophies, but they

---

24 J. Clark, *Democratising Development: The Role of Voluntary Organizations* (London: Earthscan, 1991) 40-41.

25 J. McCormick, *The Global Environmental Movement: Reclaiming Paradise* (London: Belhaven Press, 1992), 5.

26 Ibid at [7-8]

also vary in terms of name recognition and the general social view of the acceptability of their mission in their home countries. Many NGOs in the developing world struggle to maintain their existence and must often confront hostile officials. Their situations are therefore markedly different from those of NGOs in the developed world, a fact which has led them to develop organizational cultures suited to operating under siege.[27]

Additionally, some environmental NGOs do not necessarily start off as environmental groups, but may subsequently embrace such objectives. An example of this can be seen with the growth of the Chipko movement in India. This group initially represented a protest by hill people concerned about logging activities that affected their livelihood. It later grew into a major NGO, operating across India and articulating environmental policies designed to protect and conserve the forest and its resources from the actions of man.[28] Further, some NGOs pursue activities that are of an environmental nature, when their larger purpose is not an exclusively environmental one.

Today, NGOs are receiving unprecedented recognition worldwide as efforts are being made to further integrate them into the formal structure of national and international power. It has come to be understood that NGOs offer knowledge, skills, and a non-bureaucratic approach to problem solving and grassroots perspectives that enable them to be more effective than official agencies in implementing projects or the communication of ideas.[29] This role gives them more significance in the developing world and has led to the call for NGOs to occupy a more pivotal role in global governance.[30] Yet, while there may be justification

---

27 Ibid at [8-9]

28 S.R. Bowlby & M.S. Lowe, *Environmental and Green Movements* in Environmental Issues in the 1990s, ed. A. M. Mannion & S. R. Bowlby (Chichester: John Wiley & Sons, 1992), 171.

29 Commission On Global Governance, *Our Global Neighbourhood* (Oxford: Oxford University Press, 1995), 33.

30 Ibid at [34]

for euphoria at the recognition of NGOs in helping in the building of a better global village, certain problems still remain to be addressed.

As environmental NGOs are being urged to embrace officialdom and join mainstream activities, there is a danger in their forming alliances with official agencies. These organizations are known for their flexibility and willingness to experiment and adapt to non-hierarchical values, and their emphasis on forging partnerships based on mutual values and re-spect for the community within which they work. Working with official agencies can therefore lead any organization to assimilate its collective values and work habits, such as aloofness, inflexibility, bureaucratic meth-odology and a pre-occupation with centralization and control.[31]

Moreover, NGOs have been successful because of their grassroots ap-peal, and it is precisely this, which may be compromised by heightened interaction with governments and official agencies.[32] NGOs are also presently being seduced by the large sums of money being made avail-able to them in exchange for working with official entities, and are therefore also touting a new professionalism. However, environmental problems in developing countries are largely the result of official prac-tices and policies, and working together with their perpetrators is a task fraught with risk. The grassroots supporters on which NGOs have been built may also come to feel increasingly isolated in the face of such an arrangement, and the net effect could be the loss of status on the part of the NGO itself.

Accepting funds from official agencies can, in most instances, only lead one to engage in activities consistent with the objectives of the funders, even though they may not be consistent with what is right for the environment. This situation has emerged in India, where some NGOs have agreed to assist in the re-settlement of people displaced by the Narmada Dam, the construc-tion of which has been opposed by other NGOs on the grounds that it is

---

31 M. Edwards & D. Hulme *Scaling-Up the Development Impact of NGOs: Concepts and Expe-riences* (London: Earthscan, 1992), 16.

32 Ibid at [14]

likely to cause environmental damage. The activities of the NGOs working with the Indian government in a related re-settlement program have been frowned upon by NGOs who oppose the construction of the dam altogether, a fact which only further evidences the real pressures such organizations face. Another criticism levelled against NGOs is the lack of any concerted attempt to evaluate the effectiveness of their work. Their successes are well documented, especially as they have proved astute at attracting media coverage; however, their failures often go unnoticed.

At times, the media are not inclined to probe NGOs due to the fear of a popular backlash. NGOs are currently attracting unparalleled amounts of funding from private benefactors, corporations to international agencies, and there is therefore an even greater need to evaluate their activities so as to ensure accountability and transparency. The number of NGOs operating in the developing world has grown exponentially in recent years, and these organizations are benefiting tremendously from monies donated by major corporations, particularly, multinationals. Yet, there is very little documentation as to the effectiveness of the use of such monies in promoting a better environment. Until their projects and undertakings are properly evaluated on a regular basis, NGOs will continue to make unchecked mistakes and in some instances, cause greater harm than good.

As mentioned, many environmental NGOs are moving from mere rhetoric to actual implementation of projects that are generally helpful to the environment. This has been the rationale for their participating in some debt-for-nature swaps. Such projects are highly laudable, but they can also have dubious consequences. Having a piece of forest set aside in exchange for repayment of external debt is only the beginning of a conservation exercise. Above all, the designated piece of land must be monitored to ensure that it remains unexploited. Such monitoring is, however, frequently left to governmental bodies that are already under-manned, under-financed and sometimes corrupt. In other words, putting money on the line for a conservation project may be admirable, but the project may ultimately be unsuccessful due to lack of awareness of its long-term implications.

Generally, NGOs have been accused of portraying the developing world in a manner that does not do justice to the dignity and pride of the people of these nations. In order to raise funds in the developed world, spectacular images are flashed across the media screens, images designed to loosen wallets. Furthermore, some NGOs engage only in high profile activities and ignore many basic environmental problems that affect the people of the developing world. Moreover, NGOs from the developed world are often criticized for embracing environmental causes that are of interest or marketable to consumers in the developed world. Biological diversity, deforestation and global warming are, for example, high on their agendas, but life threatening problems such as the quality of indoor air, sanitation and water remain largely ignored.

Despite the criticisms that can be levelled against NGOs, there is little dispute over the positive role they have played in moving environmentalism to centre stage in the global village, and in ensuring that the environment is not forgotten in the debates on how best to forge an international community, sensitive and alert to the needs of the developing world.

The TT Perspective

In TT as in most countries, NGOs play different roles in the development of a culture of environmentalism. Accordingly, there are NGOs that are dedicated to specific environmental concerns and raising awareness of those concerns within the society. An example of such an NGO is the Pointe-a-Pierre Wildfowl Trust (PAPWT) which has been in existence for over 50 years. PAPWT is highly respected for its work with birds, ecosystems and climate change. In 1977/78, PAPWT initiated the first Environmental Education audio-visual program in schools throughout TT. Four years later, PAPWFT introduced Nature & Wildlife Photography to the public of TT. PAPWT in 1982, presented the First Environmental Education Curriculum for schools to the Minister of Education of the Government at that time. In 1983, PAPWFT Trust initiated a Hands-On Environmental Education program for primary and secondary schools which include outdoor field work; pond-dips; leaf & feather labs. The same year,

24

PAPWFT also designed the first Sea Turtle Recovery Plan for TT which included: patrolling beaches, tagging turtles and carrying out the first aerial surveys of nesting turtles on the East & North-western coasts of Trinidad. In 1985, PAPWFT initiated Turtle Patrols at Matura beach as part of an outreach environmental education program for secondary school students. PAPWFT has also played a role in promoting international issues and in 1989, PAPWFT introduced education on Climate Change in PAPWFT's school and community programs. The year 1993, saw PAPWFT successfully lobbing the Government of TT to accede to the *Ramsar Convention*, an international treaty for the conservation and sustainable use of wetlands.[33]

Another NGO with largely an environmental specific pro-active agenda is Nature Seekers. During the decades of the 1970's and 1980's, the high slaughter rates of egg-bearing female turtles created sufficient national concern to designate the nesting beach in Matura a *Prohibited Area* under the *Forests Act Chap 66:01*[34] in 1990 from 1st March to 31st August inclusive. As a result, the Wildlife Section of the Forestry Division engaged the Matura community in consultation to find a solution to this national problem. This integrated approach taken by the Wildlife Section of the Forestry Division and the community prompted a tour guide-training course which created awareness among community participants of the natural environment and the need to use it wisely for the benefit of the community. It is from this training course that participants decided to stay together to form a nature-based group which was subsequently named "Nature Seekers." Initially the majority of the community rejected this conservation strategy due to the fact that some villagers believed that the prohibition of the beach would curb their use of the beach. The Forestry Division later made the beach accessible to the community with the acquisition of a free permit. Nature Seekers was now trusted with the responsibility to provide regular patrols to protect the turtles and to ensure they nested successfully. The government was so motivated by the efforts of the community that

---

33 https://www.ramsar.org/wetland/trinidad-and-tobago
34 *Forests Act Chap 66:01*

they commissioned the group members to perform beach patrols and to provide a tour guide service to visitors who purchased permits to visit Matura Beach during the nesting season. Over the years this project demanded a tremendous commitment from Nature Seekers and it needed an all-night, every night attention for six (6) months every year since 1991. During this time the activities of Nature Seekers attracted and transformed eight (8) poachers and children of poachers into conservationists. Today, Nature Seekers is proud that the community is the nucleus of the leadership and management of this project. This uniqueness embraces the community as the main catalyst in the decision making process. It allows the community based organization to decide what should happen in the community regarding the protection of the natural resources with the technical advice and guidance from the Forestry Division and other important stakeholders. This involvement developed the initiatives of Nature Seekers to work towards the protection and conservation of the leatherback turtles and at the same time reduced the slaughtering of turtles on land from 30% to 0%.[35]

The Asa Wright Nature Centre (AWNC),[36] one of the first nature centres to be established in the Caribbean, also provides an environmental service within the context of a specific goal. The AWNC is an NGO established in 1967 by a group of naturalists and bird-watchers to "protect part of the Arima Valley in a natural state and to create a conservation and study area for the protection of wildlife and for the enjoyment of all". Comprising nearly 1,500 acres of mainly forested land in the Arima and Aripo Valleys of the Northern Range, the AWNC's properties is retained under forest cover in perpetuity, to protect the community watershed and provide important wildlife habitat. The Centre's main facilities are located on a former cocoa-coffee-citrus plantation, previously known as the Spring Hill Estate. This estate has now been partly reclaimed by secondary forest, surrounded by impressive rainforest, where

---

35 http://www.natureseekers.org/about/history/
36 http://asawright.org/

some original climax forest on the steeper slopes have a canopy of 100-150 feet. The whole effect is one of being deep in tropical rainforest."[37]

The Trinidad and Tobago Field Naturalists' Club (TTFNC) is perhaps the oldest NGO in TT. It is dedicated to the general environmental objective of the natural heritage. The TTFNC was founded on 10th July 1891 but lapsed into inactivity in 1907. The TTFNC "was reactivated in 1924 and, except for a short period of inactivity from 1948-1953, has remained active since then." The TTFNC was later incorporated by an Act of Parliament (Act No. 17 of 1991). The TTFNC conducts an annual program of monthly meetings, lectures and field trips for the enjoyment and edification of its members. The mission of the TTNFC is to "foster education and knowledge on natural history and to encourage and promote activities that would lead to the appreciation, preservation and conservation of our natural heritage."[38]

Some NGOs have been formed to pursue a specific environmental concern that may be impacting on the society. In the 2000s, with the announced plan of the then government of TT, to pursue economic diversification through the establishment of aluminium smelters, Smelta Karavan, an NGO, was formed to advocate through public education, resistance and judicial activism the rejection of aluminium smelters. The membership of Smelta Karavan was drawn from persons with a sufficient interest in its objectives and persons who may be directly and adversely affected by the establishment of proposed aluminium smelters. Smelta Karavan launched a successful judicial challenge of the granting of the Certificate of Environmental Clearance (CEC) by the Environmental Management Authority (EMA) to Alutrint Limited for the establishment of an aluminium smelter at La Brea (See, *Smelta Karavan v Environmental Management Authority, Alutrint Limited (Interested Party) and the Attorney General of Trinidad and Tobago).*[39]

TT has also seen the emergence of NGOs with a more radical and di-

---

37 Ibid.

38 http://ttfnc.org/about-the-club/

39 CV 2007–02257

rect approach to environmentalism. One such NGO is Trini Eco Warriors (TEWs). TEWs started in 2010 and its mission included using tools such as video and photography to help in fulfilling its role as one of the leading local forum on environmental awareness and advocacy. TEWs has taken a "hands on" approach to environmentalism and has now become known for bringing into sharp focus environmental issues that negatively impact on the environment of TT.

Another interesting NGO is the Trinidad and Tobago Civil Rights Association (TTCRA) which was incorporated in March, 2003 as a non-profit organization and prior to and since its incorporation, the TTCRA has been involved in social humanitarian work to promote the economic and social rights of the citizens of TT. The TTCRA, with the support of one of the leading legal practitioners in TT, Ramesh Lawrence Maharaj, has engaged in extensive judicial activism including environmental related matters. Indeed, TTCRA also opposed the establishment of aluminium smelters in TT (see *Trinidad and Tobago Civil Rights Association v Environmental Management Authority, Alutrint Limited (Interested Party) and the Attorney General of Trinidad and Tobago*,[40] and was successful together with Smelta Karavan and People United Respecting the Environment (PURE) (see *People United Respecting the Environment and Rights Action Group v Environmental Management Authority, Alutrint Limited (Interested Party) and the Attorney General of Trinidad and Tobago*,[41] in overturning the decision of the EMA to grant a CEC to Alutrint Limited for the establishment of an aluminium smelter facility in La Brea, South Trinidad.[42]

---

40 HCA No. S1070 of 2005

41 CV 2007–02263

42 Dean-Armorer J delivered a main judgment in *People United Respecting the Environment v Environmental Management Authority, Alutrint Limited (Interested Party) and the Attorney General of Trinidad and Tobago* and subsequently delivered another judgment in *Trinidad and Tobago Civil Rights Association v Environmental Management Authority, Alutrint Limited (Interested Party) and the Attorney General of Trinidad and Tobago and Smelta Karavan v Environmental Management Authority, Alutrint Limited (Interested Party) and the Attorney General of Trinidad and Tobago*. This judgment endorsed the judgment in *People United Respecting*

By far, FFOS is the NGO with the longest history of judicial activism on behalf of the environment. The judicial landscape on environmental law is dominated by legal proceedings pursued by FFOS. This is in addition to its strong public awareness and advocacy program on environmental causes. This group was formed in 1996 out of an interest in fishing and at that time was known as the North Coast Fishermen. The group functioned as an unincorporated body from 1996 until 2000. From its inception the group was formed as a community based initiative which patterned itself on the United Nations model of focal point leader networks. The group organised meetings with fishing communities all along the North Coast. Those North Coast meetings quickly expanded to include other fisher communities from the Gulf of Paria, and the North East Trinidad, all of whom shared concerns with the consequences of the unsustainable and poorly regulated shrimp trawl sector. The group met with over eighty (80) community based representatives from twenty-six (26) coastal communities throughout TT and at one of these meetings, in November 1996, the group adopted the name "Fishermen and Friends of the Sea". The chief objectives of FFOS became:

(a) *Fostering public awareness of the developmental challenges facing underprivileged communities and the environment;*

(b) *Initiating positive actions in order to influence the activities of those perceived as contributing to the demise of the environment and human communities;*

(c) *Influencing the positions adopted by the Government of TT with regard to environmental management and sustainable development according to the intention embodied by the Environmental Management Act;[43]*

(d) *Developing its capability to engage in projects designed to protect the integrity of the environment;*

(e) *Adocating for careful, precautionary, and sustainable development which is*

---

the Environment v Environmental Management Authority, Alutrint Limited (Interested Party) and the Attorney General of Trinidad and Tobago.

43 *Environmental Management Act, Chapter 35:05.*

mindful of the needs of human and biological communities who are without a voice;

(f) *Conducting outreach programmes and campaigns to educate the public on the importance of their participation in the public consultation process and to promote a better pubic understanding of the new environmental regime which was designed to protect communities and ecosystems from improperly planned, poorly regulated developments which have irreversible negative long term impacts,*

(g) *Building alliances with national, regional and international NGOs that share its objectives; and*

(h) *Ensuring that new developmental projects are mitigated according to the best scientific standards and in accordance with the Environmental Management Act.*

FFOS, over the past two decades, broadened its sustainable development/ environmental activities to assist communities lacking the financial, human and technological resources to deal with environmental and social issues affecting the economy, health and safety of communities. FFOS has advocated the urgent addressing of domestic, industrial and sewage waste contamination, polycyclic aromatic hydrocarbon contamination of the Gulf of Paria, siltation, overfishing, monofilament fishing, long-lining, shrimp trawling, deforestation, mangrove removal, and a wide range of planning issues which were negatively impacting rural communities throughout TT. Indeed, FFOS was commended by a prominent government economic advisor for its judicial activism in the correct application of the polluter pays principle in TT. According to Terrence Farrell,

> *the Fishermen and Friends of the Sea…must be complimented for sticking to its guns on this important issue and getting the right outcome. Our society is the better for it.*[44]

NGOs have received praises from the highest office of TT, that is, the of-

---

44 Terrence Farrell, 'Bad Economics, poor public policy, poor judicial review' *Trinidad and Tobago Express* (03 December 2017) 11

fice of the former President, Anthony Carmona.

> *In Trinidad and Tobago, we have many labouring in the trenches to ensure a viable and sustainable ecological patrimony for our generations to come. I can recall the passionate writing of Heather Dawn Herrera, and the committed Journalists Paolo Kernahan and Robert Clarke and of course I cannot forget two prime activists in the form of Molly Gaskin, (Curator and Founder of the Pointe-a-Pierre Wild Fowl Trust, the second in the world that celebrated its 50th anniversary late last year) and Gary Aboud, Corporate Secretary of Fishermen and Friends of the Sea (FFOS). Ms. Molly Gaskin and her team have put in a significant amount of work into replenishing different species at The Wild Fowl Trust, our Scarlet Ibis, the Black-Bellied Whistling Tree Duck, Wild Moscovies and the blue and gold Macaws. This breeding programme has improved the survival of animals in the wild and has increased their populations because they are kept safe and away from easy access by humans. Their efforts in research, breeding and translocation of endangered waterfowl and wetland birds is truly commendable, praiseworthy and an inspiration to us all. Ladies and Gentlemen, it is no longer about protecting man from beast but rather about protecting the beast from man. The roles have now been reversed. The team led by Molly Gaskin and Ms. Carolyn Sheppard have opened their doors to pre-schoolers, secondary schools and even tertiary educational institutes who wish to take a lesson out of the traditional classroom setting. At the Wild Fowl Trust, biology and environmental studies come alive and education no longer has to be static. Experiments are conducted and learning becomes easier when students immerse themselves in nature. The Trust continues to be the preferred choice of teachers when it comes to school based assessments as students can conduct their experiments in a peaceful, serene environment.*

Factors Affecting the Work of NGOs in TT

(i) Funding

Civil society in TT faces tremendous challenges in the environmental decision-making process. By far, the greatest challenge is the availability of funding to oppose decisions both through the public education and mobilization process and in the Courts. Most environmental NGOs struggle financially and very often the major NGOs accept funding from the private sector, which can then lead to conflict with their advocacy activities.

An example of this potential conflict can be seen in the operations of PAPWT, an NGO headed by one of the foremost environmentalists in TT, Molly Gaskin. PAPWT is set in the middle of an industrial estate owned by the State-owned Petroleum Company of Trinidad and Tobago Limited ("PETROTRIN"). PAPWT has acknowledged receiving funding from entities such as British Gas (Trinidad), Carib Glassworks, National Gas Company of Trinidad and Tobago Limited, Nestle and PETROTRIN.[45] It is questionable whether an NGO receiving such extensive funding from corporate sponsors can undertake the challenges of dealing with environmental decision-making, especially in situations where its sponsors may be involved. NGOs need funds to survive and pursue their environmental agenda; unfortunately, however, satisfying this need from corporate funding may lead to an undermining of the ability of the NGO to pursue environmental advocacy fearlessly and without favour.

The funding struggle is not helped by the fact that TT is generally a country where awareness of environmental issues is now growing. Membership in civil society, especially those who are strong advocates of environmental causes and who wish to challenge the State through litigation, tend to be limited. For example, FFOS' core activities are conducted by one individual. Similarly, Smelta Karavan, an NGO formed to oppose the construction of aluminium smelters in TT, had its mandate driven in large part by a few individuals. This attitude in TT is not unusual and the lack of involvement in a more radical environmental agenda translates into an unwillingness to contribute financially to public interest environmental litigation. On the other hand, in developed countries, groups such as Friends of the Earth and Greenpeace are often in a position to attract continuous funding at all levels of society. This therefore creates a significant barrier to some civil societies launching public interest environmental litigation in developing countries.

---

45 http://www.trinwetlands.org/

(ii) Limited Recourse to Technical Assistance

Effective public interest environmental litigation often hinges substantially on the ability of civil society to present their legal position within a sound scientific and technical standpoint. TT is a relatively small country with a population just in excess of one million people. Scientific and technical professionals are not in abundance and those that are present are very often engaged in earning their livelihood from work within the corporate sector. Therefore, it is not easy to attract technical and scientific assistance to support public interest environmental litigation. The struggle to provide technical and scientific support for public interest environmental litigation has involved few local scientists, such as Dr. Ahamad Khan, Dr. Peter Vine and Cathal Healy-Singh. One promising development in the drive to obtain scientific and technical assistance has been the work of Environmental Law Alliance Worldwide operating out of the USA. This group has started to provide scientific and technical assistance to aid the challenges by civil society through public interest litigation to question approvals granted by the EMA. In the case of *Trinidad and Tobago Civil Rights Association v Environmental Management Authority, Alutrint Limited (Interested Party) and the Attorney General of Trinidad and Tobago*,[46] Staff Scientist, Mark Chernaik, of Environmental Law Alliance Worldwide submitted a written expert affidavit on behalf of the claimants in this matter. Environmental Law Alliance Worldwide provided assistance also in the case of *Fishermen and Friends of the Sea v Environmental Management Authority, Ministry of Works and Transport (First Interested Party) and KALL Company Limited (Second Interested Party)*[47] where in the preparatory work for the filing of a judicial review claim for the grant of a CEC by the EMA for the construction of a highway in close proximity to the Aripo Savannas, a designated sensitive area with designated sensitive species, technical expertise was provided by Dr. Heidi Weiskel. The need to source external technical

46 CV 2007-02272
47 CV 2017-03452

resources at a minimal cost leads to delay in preparation of environmental litigation which often involves the review of extensive technical documents including Environmental Impact Assessments (EIAs).

(iii) Litigation Resources

A major issue affecting the work of NGO's in TT has been the cost of litigation and access to expert attorneys. Very often, the planning agencies that are being judicially reviewed have access to state funding that allows for legal representation at the highest level. In addition, the company that benefited from the planning approval more often than not, will join the litigation as an interested party. In **People United Respecting the Environment and Rights Action Group v Environmental Management Authority, Alutrint Limited (Interested Party) and the Attorney General of Trinidad and Tobago,**[48] **Trinidad and Tobago Civil Rights Association v Environmental Management Authority, Alutrint Limited (Interested Party) and the Attorney General of Trinidad and Tobago**[49] and **Smelta Karavan v Environmental Management Authority, Alutrint Limited (Interested Party) and the Attorney General of Trinidad and Tobago,**[50] the regulatory body, the EMA, had a full team of legal officers which also included the services of a Senior Counsel (the equivalent in the English legal system to a Queen's Counsel). Additionally, Alutrint Limited, the developer, engaged its own Senior Counsel and the Attorney-General of TT also decided to appear in the matter through Senior Counsel. All three entities also had available copious support resources in the form of junior attorneys. Smelta Karavan and TTCRA were represented by Senior Counsels while PURE was represented by two junior attorneys.

The 2017 matter of **Fishermen and Friends of the Sea v Environmental Management Authority, Ministry of Works and Transport (First Interested Party) and KALL Company Limited (Second Interested Party),**[51]

---

48 CV 2007-02263
49 CV 2007–02272
50 CV 2007-02257
51 CV 2017-03452

demonstrates the hardship of obtaining legal representation. In TT, *pro bono* legal services is quite limited, particularly in the environmental field, and this is especially when most environmental litigation involves multiple state parties where lucrative legal briefs are obtained due to access to almost unlimited funds by state entities. NGOs are not as fortunate and are forced to search extensively for *pro bono* or limited fees legal services. This search for legal resources also contributes to the delay in filing legal proceedings by NGOs challenging environmental decisions.

(iv) Intimidation

Engaging in public interest environmental litigation can be dangerous in the Caribbean as TT has recently acquired a strong reputation for violence. According to Carmen Sanchez*:*

> *With a steady rise in violent crime including an alarming increase in homicides, Trinidad and Tobago has overtaken Jamaica as the "murder capital of the Caribbean"..... According to the Economist, the English-speaking Caribbean, which extends from the Bahamas in the north to Trinidad & Tobago in the south, averages 30 murders per 100,000 inhabitants per year, one of the highest rates in the world. By comparison, the murder rate in both Canada and the UK is about two per 100,000. With 550 homicides in 2008, Trinidad and Tobago has a rate of about 55 murders per 100,000 making it the most dangerous country in the Caribbean and one of the most dangerous in the world.[52]*

Indeed there is already a history of an environmental consultant being murdered in Trinidad and Tobago. As reported in 1996:

> *A prominent Trinidad businessman has been charged with murder in the death of Bryan Hobbs, an environmental consultant from Dania. Jai Ramkissoon, 54, appeared before a magistrate in Port of Spain, Trinidad's capital, Wednesday morning. The murder charge carries the penalty of death by hanging in Trinidad. Police said Ramkissoon and Hobbs quarrelled before Hobbs was shot twice in the abdomen and abandoned on a rural road in eastern Trinidad. He*

---

52 Carmen Sanchez, *Trinidad & Tobago Now Murder Capital of the Caribbean,* Eturbo News (18 June, 2009

died in the hospital on Monday.[53]

The situation is exacerbated when there are allegations of complicity by law enforcement officers with respect to illegal activities that adversely impact on the environment. In TT, illegal quarrying has been blamed for many environmental problems and according to one journalist, the situation of possible police complicity has led to an all pervading sense of fear descending on those that are willing to confront the issue:

The scent of danger is getting too overbearing for many of the handful of house-holders in Runway Drive, off Mausica Road, Arima, within earshot of Piarco International Airport. In fact, residents in the 23 or so households in Runway Drive are seriously contemplating selling the houses they've occupied for years and taking up residence elsewhere. In the wake of the Sunday Guardian's exclusive report on December 20 of illegal quarry operators raking millions from seven massive construction material sites at Runway Drive while polluting the nearby Caroni Arena water treatment plant, residents have decided to come out in the open with their complaints....In that December 20 report, Enill's right-hand man, Minerals Division Director, Richard Oliver, had told the Sunday Guardian, based on information received, that illegally quarried material mined in Matura and Vega de Oropouche was being washed at Runway Drive and sold cheaply, and that Environmental Management Authority (EMA) security officers had executed a raid at two storage sites and arrested and charged several people. Oliver had expressed fears for the safety of his staff and for his own safety because the illegal operators were being hit in the pockets to the tune of millions of dollars. But he vowed to curtail operations at another five storage sites and avert the threat of further pollution to WASA's biggest water treatment plant from the gravel washing exercise. It entails washing the offending mud into the Carapo River which takes it to the treatment plant a kilometre away... Householders told of seeing marked police vehicles with senior officers from Eastern and Northern Divisions entering Runway Drive several times a month, then speeding back out. They speak in hushed tones, too, of marked EMA security vehicles visiting Runway Drive and exiting the area in haste. And they say that in addition to

---

53 Staff Report, *Murder Suspect Charged*, Sun Sentinel (18 April 1996)http://articles.sun-sentinel.com/1996-04-18/news/9604180157_1_trinidad-ramkissoon-chicken-farm

fast becoming a dumping ground for hazardous substances, which posed a further threat to the WASA plant, there is a growing atmosphere of violence about the quarrying retailing operations....Retired school principal, Farouk Khan and his wife, Afreen I Mohammed-Khan, an attorney,... unlike the neighbours, they are not afraid to speak out....Khan, 48, who is now a community liaison officer with a prominent Opposition MP...deemed it time to take a stand.... "Inside here is a law unto itself. People talk a lot of gun talk. These people have a lot of contacts. They deal with people in high places. It seems they know anything they do they can get away with it," declared a bitter Khan. He said he often saw law officers in Runway Drive. "They stare me down. I know that stare...[54]*

The few environmentalists prepared to confront the Government on decisions adversely affecting the environment have faced threatening circumstances. The attacks on local environmentalists have now attained the status of actual physical violence being inflicted on the few members of civil society prepared to confront the State decision-makers. Dr. Peter Vine was reportedly physically manhandled in front of the media and the editor of a national daily newspaper, Raffique Shah, has expressed strong sentiments as to the lack of action by the police authority on the matter.

Vine, who is known for dramatizing his protests, had a fishing vessel take him close to a barge being used by the surveyors. He then jumped off the pirogue, swam to the barge, and was actually helped aboard by one employee (video footage would show this). Once on-deck, he appeared to be pleading with the eight-or-so men on board, to abandon their work... Suddenly, one goon grabbed Vine in a most vicious manner. Clearly a bigger man than the activist, he shoved, pushed and finally threw Vine overboard the tug.... What that goon did was assault Vine, not only with battery (as the law would say), but with anger that oozed from his quivering frame. To date, although the brutal assault was captured on video, no action has been taken by the police against the perpetrator.[55]

---

54 Peter Balroop, *Million-dollar illegal quarry operation...a threat to Mausica residents*, Trinidad and Tobago Guardian (1 February 2010) http://m.guardian.co.tt/archives/business/business/2010/01/31/million-dollar-illegal-quarry-operation-threat-mausica-residents

55 Raffique Shah, *A Goon Attacks a Vine*, Trinidad and Tobago News Blog (24 February 2008) http://www.trinidadandtobagonews.com/blog/?p=452.

In a protest led by FFOS and other fisher folk groups, with respect to the claimed failure for ensuring proper environmental impact assessment of offshore seismic activities, violence erupted. As reported by Mark Fraser:

A stand-off between protesting fisher folk and police at the Port of Spain Waterfront yesterday led to two supporting activists and a fisherman being arrested. This is the latest and most dramatic instalment in a series of planned protests by the fishing community, as they attempt to get the Government to regulate seismic testing by energy companies in local waters. This type of testing uses dynamite or air guns underwater, in the search for and assessment of oil and gas reserves with the use of soundwaves. Detained by police yesterday were Gary Aboud, head of Fishermen and Friends of the Sea (FFOS), environmentalist Cathal Healy-Singh and La Brea fisherman, Wayne Henry...They bore placards calling on the Government and Prime Minister Kamla Persad-Bissessar to lay down the law on energy companies that have, for decades, conducted seismic underwater tests without being required to provide an Environmental Impact Assessment (EIA) or apply for a Certificate of Environment Clearance (CEC). The proceedings became heated when the gathering was refused police permission to march outside the Parliament Chamber, where they wanted to "knock on the door," Aboud said, as a symbolic gesture of their requests to the Government. The police refusal to allow the entire group to do so and subsequent orders that the gathering disperse, led to a hand-on-shoulder human barricade being formed and the group's staunch refusal to leave. After some time of bandying between the police, Aboud, Healy-Singh and several other protesters on the front line, Aboud turned to the crowd and for the third time that day, began to sing the National Anthem. The crowd joined him, causing a policeman in the lead to move into the crowd and attempt to pull Aboud out. Henry surged forward, calling out to the policeman to leave Aboud alone. This led to an immediate attempt by the police to subdue Henry and they tried to drag out of the crowd to handcuff him, Aboud and others held on to his body. Aboud was then dragged off Henry and tackled to the ground. Henry, who was standing, handcuffed, had his feet kicked out from under him by a police officer and was also taken, face down, to the ground. Aboud crawled forward and draped himself on Henry, both still singing the national anthem. More protesters, including Healy-Singh, threw themselves on Henry and Aboud, who was by then close to tears and calling out to Henry as his "brother", pleading with the police to release the 43-year-old fisherman....Following were

Aboud and Healy-Singh, who were also then arrested and shoved into the back of a waiting police vehicle.[56]

It is becoming increasingly clear that the few members of civil society prepared to confront the State on environmental issues are not receiving the level of protection that ought to be present in a country with the democratic credentials of TT.

(v) Risk of Costs and Bankruptcy

In the case of **Fishermen and Friends of the Sea v Environmental Management Authority and BP Trinidad and Tobago LLC (Interested Party)**,[57] the EMA sought to drive a dagger into public interest litigation in TT by recovering costs from the unsuccessful litigation launched by FFOS. While seeking recovery of legal cost was in itself legally justifiable, attempts to hold directors personally liable for the legal costs could only have been intended to destroy future attempts at the initiating public interest litigation by environmental NGOs. Despite judges in the various stages of **Fishermen and Friends of the Sea v Environmental Management Authority and BP Trinidad and Tobago LLC (Interested Party)**[58] acknowledging the environmental pedigree of FFOS as a bona fide public spirited organization, the EMA still sought to argue that the organization was a façade for private individuals, namely its directors, by seeking to have the directors of FFOS pay legal costs associated with the unsuccessful litigation in **Fishermen and Friends of the Sea v. Environmental Management Authority and BP Trinidad and Tobago LLC (Interested Party)**.[59] Justice Pemberton in this case, saw through this thinly disguised attempt by a statutory body to quell any future attempts at challenging its decisions in very clear language.

---

56 Mark Fraser, *Activists, fisherman arrested in protest*, Trinidad and Tobago Express (12 November 2013)

57 HCA No. 1715 of 2002.

58 Ibid.

59 Ibid.

Pemberton J:

[1] The Claimant is a company duly incorporated under the Laws of Trinidad and Tobago. The Defendants are the Environmental Management Authority and BP Trinidad and Tobago LLC.

[2] Fishermen and Friends of the Sea (FFOS) unsuccessfully challenged the decisions of the Environmental Management Authority (EMA) and BPTT all the way to the Privy Council. Suffice it to say that the Privy Council ordered the FFOS to pay costs. These costs were taxed by the Registrar and by Allocator of 25th September 2003 the quantum of costs was notified to the parties.

[3] There has been no movement by FFOS to pay these costs. The EMA, in order to recover its costs filed an application for the directors of FFOS to pay the costs.

[4] The sole issue for my determination therefore is whether the directors of FFOS should be made to satisfy the Costs Order directed to the FFOS by the Privy Council.

[24] Thirdly, that FFOS was a "facade simply set up for the convenience of Gary Aboud and other members ..." There is no evidence to back up what clearly amounts to statements of opinion and not evidence to which any weight can be attached by the court. Even if the court were to grant the Order, who among the other directors should be named? There is no assistance or guidance on this issue and it seems that too much of this application has been left to the Court's fancies. I decline to accept this invitation to proceed on a frolic of my own with no directions.

[25] This is in stark contrast to evidence of Mr. Beddoe, a director of FFOS. "FFOS has always operated on a very limited budget. We have never asked our membership to pay fees. Our greatest resource has always been volunteerism. Over the years we have managed to attract a wide range of persons who were able to provide us with scientific advice, technical assistance, administrative and management assistance, fishery expertise as well as legal advice.

[26] In addition, I accept that Fishermen and Friends of the Sea was a body satisfying the "public interest" component of the JUDICIAL REVIEW ACT. This is acknowledged and I daresay accepted by all concerned including

the Defendants at every juncture of these proceeding. It would be foolhardy of this Court at this late stage to accept a proposition stating otherwise.

(vi) Facilitating Judicial Scrutiny of Environmental Decisions: Public Interest Litigation

A necessary element in environmental democracy is an ability to engage in judicial contest as part of the strategy to ensure that environmental decision-making properly considers issues that are important to the public. Challenging the State is most often undertaken by the NGOs on behalf of members of the public. The genesis of public interest litigation lies in *Section 5 of the Judicial Review Act.*[60]

> *5(1) An application for judicial review of a decision of an inferior court, tribunal, public body, public authority or a person acting in the exercise of a public duty or function in accordance with any law shall be made to the Court in accordance with this Act and in such manner as may be prescribed by rules of court.*
>
> *(2) The Court may, on an application for judicial review, grant relief in accordance with this Act—(a) to a person whose interests are adversely affected by a decision; or (b) to a person or a group of persons if the Court is satisfied that the application is justifiable in the public interest in the circumstances of the case...*
>
> *(6) Where a person or group of persons aggrieved or injured by reason of any ground referred to in paragraphs (a) to (o) of subsection (3), is unable to file an application for judicial review under this Act on account of poverty, disability, or socially or economically disadvantaged position, any other person or group of persons acting bona fide can move the Court under this section for relief under this Act.*

The *Judicial Review Act*, by virtue of *Section 5(2)(b)*, expressly provides for public interest litigation and has been used so far mainly in environmental matters brought by civil society. The Government of TT in 2005 moved swiftly to limit public interest litigation. The *Judicial Review (Amendment) Bill 2005* ("the Bill") was introduced by the Government in Parliament in 2005 with the express aim of limiting the categories of persons who might apply for judicial review by repealing *Section 5(2)(b) of the Judicial Review Act*

---

60 *Judicial Review Act, Ch.7:08.*

which vests jurisdiction in the Court to deal with public interest litigation. It is interesting to note that the Bill came quickly after the conclusion in 2004 of *Fishermen and Friends of the Sea v Environmental Management Authority and BP Trinidad and Tobago LLC (Interested Party).*[61] Due to the proroguing of Parliament in September 2005, the Bill effectively lapsed;[62] however, during the time between the laying of the Bill in Parliament and when it lapsed, a challenge launched by the TTCRA attacked the decision of the Government to remove public interest litigation. In a matter filed by the *Trinidad and Tobago Civil Rights Association v Attorney General of Trinidad and Tobago,*[63] Justice Gobin in her decision on the challenge, noted:

> *"I consider that the role of the bona fide public interest litigant in a relatively young democracy such as ours is critical to the maintenance of the rule of law. This is more so at a time when for the most part the population is crippled and consumed by fear for personal safety, protection of family and property. When in this environment there are still to be found persons who are genuinely public-spirited who can emerge out of the State of paralysis to act with the intention to promote the rule of law, they ought to be encouraged. If they are shut out either on technicalities by judges or by overstepping of the executive, we may as well pave the road to tyranny. The public interest litigant is the watchdog that may yet prove to be more valuable to us as a society than the one that actually barks."*

The decision of Justice Gobin was reversed at the level of the Court of Appeal in the case of the *Attorney General of Trinidad and Tobago v Trinidad and Tobago Civil Rights Association.*[64] According to Warner JA:

> *33. Public interest litigation in its purest form entered the Indian judicial process in a bout the year 1970. The disenchantment with the formal legal system's impact on the underprivileged led to the development of the jurisprudence of public interest litigation.*

---

61 PCA No.30 of 2004

62 L.N. No. 219 of 2007

63 HCA No. S1070 of 2005

64 CA No. 149 of 2005. There has been no further attempt to re-introduce the Bill in Parliament.

34. The genesis of that class of litigation is explained in the case of Guruvayur Devaswom Managing Committee and another v C K Rajan and others [2003] INSC 375 (14th August 2003)The Courts exercising their power of judicial review found to its dismay that the poorest of the poor, deprived, the illiterate, the urban and rural unorganized labour sector, women, children, handicapped by 'ignorance, indigence and illiteracy' and other down trodden have either no access to justice or had been denied justice. A new branch of proceedings known as 'Social Interest Litigation' or 'Public Interest Litigation' was evolved with a view to render complete justice to the aforementioned classes of persons. It expanded its wings in course of time. The Courts in pro bono public granted relief to the inmates of the prisons, provided legal aid, directed speedy trial, maintenance of human dignity and covered several other areas. A balance was, therefore, required to be struck. The Courts started exercising greater care and caution in the matter of exercise of jurisdiction of public interest litigation. The Court insisted on furnishing of security before granting injunction and imposing very heavy costs when a petition was found to be bogus. It took strict action when it was found that the motive to file a public interest litigation was oblique."

35. In Canada, the concept of public interest standing originated in such cases as Thorson v Canada (Attorney General), [1975] 1 S.C.R. 138, Nova Scotia (Board of Censors) v McNeil, 1975 CanLII 14 (S.C.C.), [1976] 2 S.C.R. 265, Canada (Minister of Justice) v Borowski, 1981 CanLII 34. (S.C.C.), [1981] 2 S.C.R. 575 and was further explained in Finlay v Canada (Minister of Finance), 1985 CanLII6 (S.C.C.), [1986] 2 S.C.R. 607. It originated to allow individuals to sue to prevent illegal government action, or the operation of invalid legislation, even though the litigants could not demonstrate that they had a private right that was being interfered with, or that they were suffering damage peculiar to themselves, different from that of the public generally. (See Maurice v Canada Minister of Indian Affairs and Northern Development 1999 Can LII 9147).

36. Public interest legislation was introduced in this jurisdiction by the Judicial Review Act 2000. Standing, though relaxed after the decision in IRC v National Federation of Self Employed and Small Business 1982 A C 617 is still a prerequisite. An applicant does not need to show a direct financial or legal interest to succeed, but must show a sufficient interest.

37. Counsel for the respondent's arguments that the Bill prohibits public interest litigation are self-defeating when viewed against the background of the authorities he cited. These authorities demonstrate that claimants of limited means as well as other activists do have access to the courts. (See R (Corner House) v Trade Secretary of State for Trade and Industry – claimants were an educational research and campaign organization; [2005] 1 WLR 2600 and R v Lord Chancellor ex parte Child Poverty Action Group 1998 2 ALL ER 755 – applicants were a registered charity whose objects included promotion of action for relief of poverty among children; R (on the application of England) v Tower Hamlets London Borough Council and others 2006 EWCA – claimant an active campaigner for the industrial heritage of Tower Hamlets. The respondents cannot therefore complain that the bill if enacted would prevent them from setting foot in the 'court room door'. (See Matthews v Ministry of Defence (2003) 2 WLR 135 Paragraph 29.)

38. The protection of the law that the respondents enjoyed was the right to apply to a court for such remedy (if any) as the law of Trinidad and Tobago gives to them.

39. In the result, I have found no violation of threatened violation of the respondents' constitutional rights. The appeal is therefore allowed and the decision of the judge is set aside.

The decision of the Court of Appeal suggested that the Court seemed inclined to adopt the position that while the Bill may have the effect of limiting the statutory right to public interest litigation, this right existed independent of the Bill in the judicial practice of TT.

(vii) Delay

As observed, NGOs struggle to find the technical and legal resources to launch challenges against decisions by the EMA that may impact adversely on the environment. Judicial review challenges must be initiated promptly but no later than three months from the date of the decision being challenged. When there is a failure to act promptly and no later than three months from the date of a decision, the Court may use its discretion to grant or refuse leave for judicial review.

Judicial Review Act, Section 11 provides:

11(1) An application for judicial review shall be made promptly and in any event within three months from the date when grounds for the application first arose unless the Court considers that there is good reason for extending the period within which the application shall be made.

(2) The Court may refuse to grant leave to apply for judicial review if it considers that there has been undue delay in making the application, and that the grant of any relief would cause substantial hardship to, or substantially prejudice the rights of any person, or would be detrimental to good administration.

(3) In forming an opinion for the purpose of this section, the Court shall have regard to the time when the applicant became aware of the making of the decision, and may have regard to such other matters as it considers relevant.

(4) Where the relief sought is an order of certiorari in respect of a judgment, order, conviction or other decision, the date when the ground for the application first arose shall be taken to be the date of that judgment, order, conviction or decision.

In the first major environmental litigation initiated in TT, the Court ruled that from first instance to the Privy Council, leave would be refused in the application for judicial review filed by FFOS on the basis that the application for leave was filed five months from the date of the decision in question [**Fishermen and Friends of the Sea v. Environmental Management Authority and BP Trinidad and Tobago LLC (Interested Party)**].[65] The struggle to file for judicial review within the permitted time and the discretion in the Court to refuse leave for judicial review came in sharp focus in a matter where FFOS filed five days after expiration of the three month period from the date of the decision by the EMA [**Fishermen and Friends of the Sea v. Environmental Management Authority, Ministry of Works and Transport (First Interested Party) and KALL Company Limited (Second Interested Party)**].[66] Justice Ramcharan refused leave on the basis of delay for judicial review, the matter was ap-

---

65 PCA No. 30 of 2004

66 CV 2017-03452

pealed to the Court of Appeal which on a preliminary hearing continued an injunction initially granted by Justice Ramcharan and decided to have the refusal for leave determined by a full panel of the Court of Appeal [*Fishermen and Friends of the Sea v. Environmental Management Authority, Ministry of Works and Transport (First Interested Party) and KALL Company Limited (Second Interested Party)*] as per Rajkumar JA.[67] The Court of Appeal sitting as a full panel, upheld the decision of Justice Ramcharan on the basis that there was undue delay by FFOS in bringing the judicial review application and that granting leave in the absence of promptitude and outside the three month statutory period for bringing an action from the date of the decision would substantially prejudice the rights of the third party contractor and be contrary to the principle of good administration.[68] The decision of the TT courts was upheld by the Privy Council.

Fishermen and Friends of the Sea (Appellant) v Environmental Management Authority and others (Respondents), [2018] UKPC 24

Lord Carnwath

21. ...It is satisfied that where, as here, the proceedings would result in delay to a project of public importance, the courts were right to adopt a strict approach to any application to extend time. It was unnecessary to show specific prejudice or hardship to particular parties. There was no such competing public interest in the Abzal Mohammed case, which concerned a challenge by a police officer to an individual decision of the Police Service Commission. However, in considering whether there is good reason to extend time, there may, as Mr Knox QC for the Authority accepts, be some overlap between sections 11(1) and (2), so that the issues including the relative merits of the applicant's case, and any prejudice, public or private, may be taken into account in the overall balance....

30. The Board would add one comment on the appellant's reliance on its status

---

67 Civ Appeal No. P050 of 2018

68 Civ Appeal No. P050 of 2018. See also, **Virgin Islands Environmental Council v. The Attorney General and Quorum Island BVI Limited, BVIHCV2007/0185.**

as a public interest litigant. This is undoubtedly an important role, which is recognised in section 7 of the Judicial Review Act ("Leave of Court in public interest"). However, this is not in itself a reason for applying the delay rules with less rigour, particularly where, as here, there are strong competing public interests on the other side...

32. The Board doubts that it is appropriate to apply stricter standards to public interest litigators than to others, and it recognises the need to take account of the limited resources that may be available to them. However, it agrees that full weight must be given to all aspects of the public interest, that respect must be paid to the time-limits laid down by the rules, and that the real substance of the complaint should be identified with reasonable precision at an early stage. The latter is important both for the court, and in fairness to the respondent who is entitled to know the case against him so that he can respond to it. It was unfortunate that the court in this case was faced with no less than 14 grounds of challenge, which themselves differed significantly from the four points identified in the Pre-action letter, and of which only two have been found to have weight by any of the seven judges who have considered the matter.

The Role of the Corporate Sector

The business sector in TT has played a growing role in developing environmental awareness through Corporate Social Responsibility (CSR) programs. In a 2007 Report, "Mapping Corporate Social Responsibility In Trinidad & Tobago Private Sector and Sustainable Development" that reviewed investment by the private sector in social and environmental initiatives, it was observed that the:

private sector plays an important role in the provision of social and environmental programmes in the country. Per annum, the companies in the sample spent over TT$ 54 million on external social and environmental programmes over the period 2001-2006, which is between 2% and 4% of the annual expenditure of the Government on social and developmental programmes over the past few years. This highlights the important role the private sector plays, not only as a consumer, but also as a promoter of national development.[69]

---

69 www.tt.undp.org/content/dam/trinidad_tobago/docs/.../CSRMappingReport.pdf

Many corporate citizens incorporate environmental concerns in their values. The National Gas Company of Trinidad and Tobago Limited (NGC) is one such company that boasts that its business model is an expression of its corporate values and comprises voluntary activity – in cash or in kind – beyond commercial and legal obligations that contributes to the economic, social and environmental sustainability of the communities in which it operates. The support of NGC ranges from developing programmes to partnering with and sponsoring the initiatives of hundreds of non-governmental and community-based organisations through grants and contributions.[70] The Unit Trust Corporation of Trinidad and Tobago launched the UTC Foundation and after inwards in 2017 intending to nurture the development of environmental citizenship.[71] Some corporate citizens such as Atlantic LNG Company of Trinidad and Tobago articulates a vision of striving to achieve sustainable development by practising responsible environmental stewardship and minimising adverse impacts to the environment through the optimal use of resources by recycling and reduction of waste and emissions.[72] BP Trinidad and Tobago has taken a leadership role in environmental awareness through education and has launched a successful Schools' Environmental Awareness Competition.[73] Other corporate entities engage in pro-active environmental activities such as coastal clean-up. In 2013 Employees of TATIL showed their support for the local leg of 2013 International Coastal Cleanup by working with other affiliated companies to assist with clean-up efforts at Caura River.

---

70 https://ngc.co.tt/corporate-social-responsibility/

71 https://www.ttutc.com/corporation/corporate-social-responsibility.htm

72 https://www.atlanticlng.com/96-sustainability/our-sustainability-commitment

73 https://www.bp.com/en_tt/trinidad-and-tobago/media/media-releases/bptt-energises-environmental-awareness-in-students-.html

UNDERSTANDING THE LEGAL AND INSTITUTIONAL BACKGROUND TO ENVIRONMENTAL MANAGEMENT IN TRINIDAD AND TOBAGO

THE ROLE AND CHALLENGES OF LEGISLATION IMPACTING ON THE ENVIRONMENT

It is becoming increasingly apparent that developing nations are important players in the emergence of environmental problems, while at the same time being significant victims to the consequences of such problems. Accordingly, it is vital that the status of environmental legal regimes in developing countries be assessed both in terms of the presence of adequate legal norms and enforcement of said legal norms.

Apart from the *Environmental Management Act,* as depicted in Table 2.0, there are over one hundred pieces of legislation touching and impacting on the environment. These laws or appropriate sections were not revoked with the enactment of the *Environmental Management Act* and are therefore still necessary in understanding the environmental legal regime of TT.

TABLE 2.0 ENVIRONMENTAL SECTOR SPECIFIC LEGISLATION	
AIR POLLUTION	
	Motor Vehicles and Road Traffic Regulations, made pursuant to the Motor Vehicles and Road Traffic Act (rev. 1980), Regulation 38, Rule 13
	Motor Vehicles and Road Traffic (Amendment) Act, No. 25 of 1997, Sections 14 and 100.
	Welfare Regulations made pursuant to the Factories Ordinance (1950), Regulation 3
	Public Health Ordinance (1950), Sections 69, 54(1)(f), 70(1)(m) and Public Health (Streets and Buildings) Bye Law 25
	Standard Act No. 18 of 1997, Sections 15(1), 24(5), 25(1) and 34(1)
	Section 4 (2) of the Trade Ordinance No. 19 of 1958– Used to put on the negative list for importation goods that impact on the Ozone layer
	Customs Act, Ch. 78:01, Section 44
	Consumer Protection and Safety Act (1985), Sections 21(1) and 22(3)
	Municipal Corporations Act, Section 221(1)
	Petroleum Act, Sections 29 (1)(j) and 91. Regulation 43(s) of the Petroleum Regulations
	Town and Country Planning Act (rev. 1980), Second Schedule, Part II.
	Mines Regulations made pursuant to the Mines, Borings and Quarries Act, Regulation 2
	Cremation Act (rev.1980), Sections 4(1) and 8(1)
	Gas Cylinders (Use, Conveyance and Storage) Act (rev.1980), Section 2

TABLE 2.0 ENVIRONMENTAL SECTOR SPECIFIC LEGISLATION	
	Drilling Regulations made pursuant to the Mines, Borings and Quarries Act (rev.1980), Regulation 18
	Tobago House of Assembly Act No. 40 of 1996, Section 25 (1)
	Civil Aviation Order LN 91 of 1995 Section 55
	Environmental Management Act, Ch.35:01, Sections 49, 50 and 51. Air Pollution Rules and Air Pollution (Fees and Charges) Regulations
HAZARDOUS SUBSTANCES	
	Pesticides and Toxic Chemicals Act (1979)
	Fertilisers and Feeding Stuffs Act (rev. 1980),Sections 4, 5, 8 and 9
	Trade Ordinance No. 19 of 1958
	Explosives Act (rev.1980) Sections 4(1,) 35(1), 36(1) and 39. Importation, Storage etc. of Dynamite Regulations, Regulation 6
	Tobago House of Assembly Act No. 40 of 1996, Section 25 (1)
	Mines, Borings and Quarries Act (rev. 1980) Section
	Environmental Management Act, Ch.35:01, Sections 59,and 60
BIOLOGICAL DIVERSITY	
Fauna	
	Mongoose Act, Section 2(1)
	Animals (Diseases and Importation) Act, Sections 14(1) and 15(1)
	Dogs Act, Section 3(1)

TABLE 2.0 ENVIRONMENTAL SECTOR SPECIFIC LEGISLATION

	Control of Importation of Live Fish Act, Sections 2(1) and 3
	Fisheries (Conservation of Marine Turtles) Regulations (1994) Sections 4, 8 and 9
	Protection of turtle and turtle eggs Regulations, Sections 2 and 3
	Beekeeping and Bee Products Act, Section 9, Regulations 23 and 24
	Anatomy Act, Section 4(1)
	Tobago House of Assembly Act No. 40 of 1996, Sections 25 (1)
	Territorial Sea (Amendment) Act No. 22 of 1986 Section 6A(1).
	Conservation of Wildlife Act Sections 3 (2) and 5(1). Regulations 6,7 10, 11, 18, 19 and 24
	Marine Areas (Preservation and Enhancement) Act, Sections 3(1), 6(1)
	Summary Offences Act, Section 16
	Zoological Society of T&T Act, Section 4
	Environmental Management Act, Ch. 35:01, Sections 41 to 44. Environmental Sensitive Species Rules
Flora	
	Marine Areas (Preservation and Enhancement) Act, Sections 3(1) and 6(1)
	Forests Act, Sections 4, 5, 6, and 23
	Summary Offences Act, Sections 19, 21 and 25
	Town and Country Planning Act, Section 20(1)
	Malicious Damage Act, Sections 17 and 19

TABLE 2.0 ENVIRONMENTAL SECTOR SPECIFIC LEGISLATION	
	State Lands Act, Section 6(1)
	Plant (Export) Prohibition) Act, Section 3
	Plant Protection Act, Sections 3(1),5(1), 6(1), 7(1), 8(1) and 15(1). Regulations 9, 10 and 11
	Protection of New Plant Varieties, Section 3
	Cocoa (Import and Export) Act, Section 3
	Exportation of Fruit Act , Sections 8 and 10(1)
	Tobago House of Assembly Act No. 40 of 1996, Section 25 (1)
	Environmental Management Act, Ch.35:01, Sections 41, 42, 43 and 44. Environmentally Sensitive Species Rules
Land/Forests	
	Agricultural Fires Act, Sections 17 (1), 18(4), 19, 22, 23(2), 26, 29 (1), 30 (a), 32 and 33(2)
	Sawmills Act, Sections 2, 4, 5, 7, 9 and 11
	Forests Act, Sections 2, 4(1) and 8. The Felling of Trees (Permits) (Private Land) Rules, 2000 and, LN No. 309 and LN No.310 of 2000
	Malicious Damage Act, Section 17
	Chaguaramas Development Authority Act, Sections 14 (3) (b) and 21(1)
	Slum Clearance and Housing Act, Sections 4(a) 10(1)(a) and 11(2)
	Town and Country Planning Act, Sections Section 5, 8 and 20(1),
	Asphalt Industry Regulation, Section 10. Regulation 4
	Agricultural Development Bank Act, Section 6

TABLE 2.0 ENVIRONMENTAL SECTOR SPECIFIC LEGISLATION	
	Agricultural Small Holdings Tenure Act, Sections 2(1), 9(1)(b) and 38(2)(g)
	Litter Act, Ch. 30:52, Sections 2(1) and 3(1)
	Public Health Ordinance, Section 36(1) and Section 37(2
	Petroleum Act, Sections 16 and 29(1)(j). Regulation 42(2)(h) of the Petroleum Regulations and Regulation 11 of the Petroleum (Testing, Storage, etc.) Regulations
	Pipelines Act, Section 4(1)
	State Lands Act, Section 6(1) and 25
	Agricultural Contracts Act, Section 25
	Disaster Measures Act, Sections 2(1) and 3
	Drilling Regulations made pursuant to the Mines, Borings and Quarries Act (rev.1980), Regulation 18(1) and 20(4)
	Minerals Act, Sections 10, 14(1), 20(1), 21(1), 43 (1), and 44
	Regularisation of Tenure Act, Section 25(1)
	Tobago House of Assembly, Section 25 (1)
	Trinidad and Tobago Electricity Commission Act, 33, 34, 37, 38 and 99
	Environmental Management Act,, Sections 41, 42, 43 and 44. Environmentally Sensitive Areas Rules
Wetlands	
	Malaria Abatement Act, Sections 4, 5, 9and 10(1)
	Regulation 42(2)(c) of the Petroleum Regulations
	Drilling Regulations 20(4) made pursuant to the Mines, Borings and Quarries Act (rev.1980)
	Municipal Corporations Act, Section 232(I)

TABLE 2.0 ENVIRONMENTAL SECTOR SPECIFIC LEGISLATION		
	Marine Areas (Preservation and Enhancement) Act, Sections 3(1) and 6(1).	
	State Lands Act, Section 6(1)	
	Forests Act, Section 2	
	Tobago House of Assembly Act No. 40 of 1996, Section 25 (1)	
	Litter Act, Ch. 30:52, Sections 2(1) and 3(1)	
	Environmental Management Act,, Sections 41, 42, 43 and 44. Environmentally Sensitive Areas Rules	
Coral Reefs		
	Marine Areas Preservation and Enhancement Act, Section 2 and 3	
	Environmental Management Act,, Sections 41, 42, 43 and 44. Environmentally Sensitive Areas Rules	
WATER		
Freshwater		
	Petroleum Act, Sections 29(1)(j). Petroleum (Pollution Compensation) Regulations made pursuant to Section 29 (1)(j) of the Petroleum Act, Regulations 3 and 4. Regulation 42(2)(c) of the Petroleum Regulations. Regulation 11 of the Petroleum (Testing, Storage, etc.)	
	Litter Act, Ch. 30:52, Sections 2(1),3(1) and 4	
	Second Schedule, Part IV, Clause 8 of the Town and Country Planning Act	
	Malaria Abatement Act, Sections 4, 5, 9, 10(1)	
	Dry River Act, Sections 2 and 9	

TABLE 2.0 ENVIRONMENTAL SECTOR SPECIFIC LEGISLATION

	Waterworks and Water Conservation Act , Sections 15(1) and 18(1). Regulation 7 of the Water Improvement Area (Caroni Irrigation), Regulation
	Water and Sewerage Authority Act, Sections 42, 51(1) and Section 53(1). Byelaws have been made to prevent pollution of two water systems, the Courland Waterworks and the Quare River of Valencia. These are known as the Prevention of Water Pollution (Quare River and Valencia) Bye Laws respectively.
	Highways Act, Section 36(3)
	Public Health Ordinance, Sections 36(1), 37(2), 54(1)(c), 55A 55E(1), 56C, 57(1), 60F, Section 60I, 68(1), 70(1)(j), 80, 89(1), 90 and 92
	Summary Offence Act, Sections 72 and 73
	Municipal Corporations Act, Sections 145, 170(1) and 232(e)
	Drilling Regulations made pursuant to the Mines, Borings and Quarries Act (rev.1980), Regulation 20(4)
	Tobago House of Assembly Act, Section 25 (1)
	Environmental Management Act Ch35:01, Sections 52, 53 and 54
Marine	
	Oil Pollution of Territorial Waters Act, Sections 2(2 and Section 3(1)
	Fisheries Act, Sections 3 and 4,
	Control of Importation of Live Fish Act Section 2
	Summary Offences Act, Section 18
	Municipal Corporations Act, Section 232(f) and (I)
	Archipelagic Waters and Exclusive Economic Zone Act, Sections 12 (2), 19, 21, 22, 24 and 32

TABLE 2.0 ENVIRONMENTAL SECTOR SPECIFIC LEGISLATION	
	Petroleum Act, Section 29(1)(j). Regulation 42(2)(c) of the Petroleum Regulations. Regulation 9 of the Petroleum (Testing, Storage, etc.) Regulations
	Continental Shelf Act, Sections 3, 7(1) and 13
	Motor Launches Act, Section 4
	Harbours Act, Sections 21 and 24
	Marine Areas (Preservation and Enhancement) Act, Sections 3(1) and 6(1)
	Tourist Board Act, Sections 2, 10, and 16(1)
	Port Authority Act, Sections 8(1)(a) and 75(3)(a)(iii)
	Shipping Act, Sections 316 and 335(1)
	Chaguaramas Development Authority Act, Section 14 (3)(b)
	Carenage Pier Act, Section 3
	La Brea Jetty and Tramway Act, Section 3
	Caribbean Fisheries Training and Development Institute Act, Section 4
	Carriage of Goods by Sea Act, Schedule, Article 3(1)
	Litter Act, Ch. 30:52, Sections 2(1) and 3(1)
	Drilling Regulations made pursuant to the Mines, Borings and Quarries Act, Regulations 20(4) and 21
	Tobago House of Assembly Act, Section 25 (1)
	Three Chains (Tobago) Act, Section 2
	Public Health Ordinance, Section 70(1) and (2)
WASTE	
Hazardous	

TABLE 2.0 ENVIRONMENTAL SECTOR SPECIFIC LEGISLATION

	The Town and Country Planning Act (rev. 1980), Class IV (2) of the attached Schedule of the Town and Country Planning (General Development) Order
	Pesticides and Toxic Chemicals Act, Section 12(1). Regulation 4(1) of the Pesticides (Registration and Import Licensing) Regulations (1986) and Regulation 16(1) of the Pesticides (Licensing of Premises) Regulations (1986)
	Quarantine Act, Ch. 28:05, Section 4(1) (a)
	Customs Act, Ch. 78:01, Section 44
	Trade Ordinance, Section 4 (2)
	Drilling Regulations made pursuant to the Mines, Borings and Quarries Act (rev.1980), Regulation 18
	Petroleum Act, Regulation 43(s) of the Petroleum Regulations
	Tobago House of Assembly Act, Section 25 (1)
	Environmental Management Act, Ch. 35:01. Sections 55, 56, 57 and 58
Non-Hazardous Waste	
	Litter Act, Ch. 30:52, Sections 2(1) and 3(1)
	Public Health Ordinance, Sections 54(1)(o), 57D, 57E, 58A, 59C, 59E, 60A, 64), 67 and 141
	Municipal Corporations Act, Sections 136 and 232(j)
	Petroleum Act, Section 26(2)(d)
	Second Schedule, Part IV of the Town and Country Planning Act
	Water and Sewerage Act, Sections 62.
	Factories Ordinance, Section 5
	Highways Act, Sections 47(c) and 54(1)

TABLE 2.0 ENVIRONMENTAL SECTOR SPECIFIC LEGISLATION	
	Regulations 20 and 33 of the Airports Authority Regulations, made pursuant to the Airport Authority Act.
	Advertisements Regulation Act, Sections 3 and 6
	Country Markets Act, Section 4(1)
	Demolition of Unsafe Structures Act, Section 3(1)
	Disposal of Uncleared Goods Act, Sections 6 and 7
	Tobago House of Assembly Act, Section 25 (1)
	Environmental Management Act, Ch. 35:01. Sections 55, 56, 57 and 58
NATURAL AND CULTURAL HERITAGE	
	Friends of Mr. Biswas of Trinidad and Tobago (Incorporation) Act
	Municipal Corporations Act, Sections 132, 232 (f) and (I)
	Advertisements Regulation Act, Sections 3 and 6
	Burial Grounds Act, Regulation 13
	San Fernando Recreation Ground Act, Section 4
	State Lands Act, Section 6(1)
	Botanic Gardens Act, Section 4(1). Regulations 9, 10 and 13 of the Botanic Garden Regulations
	Malicious Damage Act, Sections 6 and 33(1)
	Protection of Wrecks Act, Section 3(1)
	National Trust of Trinidad and Tobago Act, Sections 5 and 27
	Recreation Grounds and Pastures Act, Sections 2(1) (2) and 3
	Forests Act, Section 2

TABLE 2.0 ENVIRONMENTAL SECTOR SPECIFIC LEGISLATION

	Town and Country Planning Act, Section 20(1). Second Schedule, Part IV, Section 5 of the Town and Country Planning Act
	Tobago House of Assembly Act, Sections 21 (2)(f) (o) and (u), 25 (1)
	Queen's Park Act, Section 2(1)(2)
	Tobago House of Assembly Act, Fifth Schedule
	Litter Act, Ch. 30:52, Sections 2(1) and 3(1)
NOISE	
	Municipal Corporations Act, Section 221(1)
	Air Navigation and Aerodromes Ordinance (1950), basically provides for English Air Navigation laws between 1920 and 1949 to be applicable to T&T. Section 41(1) of the Civil Aviation Act 1949(UK)
	Civil Aviation Order LN 91 of 1995 Section 80 and Section 41(2) of the Act as set out in Schedule 2 to the, 1949 (Overseas Territories) Order 1968
	Airports Authority Act, Section 43(1)(c)
	Maxi Taxi Act, Sections 2 and 12A (1)
	Theatres and Dancehall Amendment Act, Section 4C(1)
	Summary Offences Act, Sections55(1), 63, 64 (1), 64 (2) (a), 99, 100, 120 and 121(1)
	Motor Vehicles and Road Traffic Regulations, Regulation 38, Rule 12(1). Regulations 28(j) 43 and 49
	Public Health Ordinance, Section 69
	Tobago House of Assembly Act, Section 25 (1)
	Environmental Management Act, Ch. 35:01, Sections 49, 40, 51. The Noise Pollution Rules and the Noise Pollution (Fees and Charges) Regulations

TABLE 2.0 ENVIRONMENTAL SECTOR SPECIFIC LEGISLATION	
GENERAL PLANNING	
	Regulation 4(1) and Class IV of the attached schedule of the Town and Country Planning (General Development) Order made pursuant to the Town and Country Planning Act (1980)
	Environmental Management Act, Ch. 35:01, Sections 35, 36, 37, 38, 39 and 40. Certificate of Environmental (Designated Activities) Order, Certificate of Environmental Clearance Rules and Certificate of Environmental (Fees and Charges) Regulations

Delays in Assenting to Laws

An interesting facet of the environmental legal regime of TT has been the reluctance to enforce laws that have already been passed in the House of Parliament. Of much importance in TT is the protection of local flora, having regard to its considerable biological diversity and the value of the range of species in sustaining the faunal community. In 1940, the *Plant Protection Ordinance* was passed to provide for the prevention, eradication and control of diseases and pests affecting plants. This law, while serving an important function, was considered to be unsatisfactory in light of new biological developments. Efforts were therefore made to modernise the law and this was done by way of the passage of the *Plant Protection Act*[74]. Yet, for reasons unknown, this law only became effective in 1997 when it received presidential assent.

Another example of the apathy in bringing laws into force can be found in the passage of the *National Trust of Trinidad and Tobago Act*.[75] This law, passed in 1991, was intended to serve many important environmental functions, including listing and protecting property, in terms of natural beauty and biological diversity. However, this important piece of legislation which

---

74 *Plant Protection Act, Chap 63:56*

75 *National Trust of Trinidad and Tobago Act, Chap 40:53.*

was intended to fill a gap with regard to preservation of property of natural and cultural interest only came into force in 2000.

Special Problems Associated with the Use of Provisions for Making of Regulations

While it is felt that a sufficient number of laws exist in TT to protect the environment, an additional dimension to the perception of the adequacy of laws lies in the making of regulations or the use of existing legal norms to create more effective legal powers in the fight against environmental abuse. The second column of Table 3.0 is dedicated to the listing of the particular provisions in various pieces of legislation on environmental protection in TT that may be used for the passage of regulations. It is accurate to say that most of the laws are worded in a general manner, with the intent being the passage of regulations to provide for specificity. This method of passing legislation can be used successfully to update laws and stipulate new standards as may be required by changing modern conditions. Unfortunately, it would seem as though there is a reluctance to use such regulatory powers and this has resulted in some laws being largely unenforceable. Indeed, in the case of over 80 percent of the laws in Table 3.0, the regulatory powers inherent in the laws had not been exercised either at all or for any environmental purpose. The failure to exercise regulatory powers is readily apparent in a review of the work of enforcement agencies.

TABLE 3.0 LAWS, REGULATIONS AND ENFORCEMENT AGENCIES IN TRINIDAD AND TOBAGO		
Laws	Regulatory Power	Enforcement Agency
Advertisements Regulations	Section 6	Municipal Corporations
Agricultural Development Bank Act	Section 49(1)	Agricultural Development Bank
Agricultural Fires Act	Section 36	County Fire Control Officer
Agricultural Small Holdings Act	Section 57	Agricultural Tribunals
Airports Authority Act	Section 43(1)	Airports Authority

TABLE 3.0 LAWS, REGULATIONS AND ENFORCEMENT AGENCIES IN TRINIDAD AND TOBAGO

Air Navigation and Aerodromes Ordinance	---	Airports Authority
Animals (Diseases and Importation) Act	Section 15(1)	Chief Technical Officer (Agric.)
Archipelagic Waters and EEZ Act	Section 32	Coast Guard, Fisheries, Harbour Master, Customs Officer, Police
Aviation Act	---	Airport Authority
Asphalt Industry Regulation	Section 6(1)	Ministry of Energy
Beekeeping and Bee Products	Section 9	Inspector of Apiaries
Botanic Gardens Act	Section 4	Superintendent of Public Gardens
Burial Grounds Act	Section 4(1)	Municipal Corporations
Chaguaramas Development Authority Act	Section 28	Chaguaramas Develop. Authority
Cocoa and Coffee Industry Act	Section 9(1)	Cocoa & Coffee Industry Board
Condominiums Act	Section 40	Land Commission & Land Registrar
Conservation of Wildlife Act	Section 24(1)	Chief Game Warden
Consumer Protection & Safety Act	Section 29(1)	Director of Consumer Guidance
Constitution	---	Private actions
Continental Shelf Act	Section 13	Ministry of Energy
Control of Importation of Live Fish Act	Section 2(1)	Customs
Customs Act	Section 44	Customs
Dogs Act	Section 18	Municipal Corporations

TABLE 3.0 LAWS, REGULATIONS AND ENFORCEMENT AGENCIES IN TRINIDAD AND TOBAGO

Dry River Act	Section 9	Municipal Corporations
Employment of Women (Night) Act	Section 8	Police
Environmental Management Act	Section 96(1)	Environmental Management Authority
Factories Ordinance	Sections 33 & 68	Safety & Welfare - Factories Inspectorate; Sanitary - Municipal Corporations
Fertilisers and Feeding Stuff Act	Section 8(1)	Chief Analyst
Fiscal Incentives Act	Section 31(1)	Ministry of Finance
Fisheries Act	Section 4	Fisheries Division (Agriculture)
Laws	Regulatory Power	Enforcement Agency
Foreign Investment Act		
Forests Act	Sections 2 & 23	Conservator of Forest
Harbours Act	Section 63(1)	Harbour Master
Highways Act	Section 149	Highways Authority & Municipal Corporations
Hotel Development Act	Section 44	Ministry of Finance
Laws	Regulatory Power	Enforcement Agency
Housing Act	Section 74	National Housing Authority
La Brea Jetty and Tramway Act	---	Lake Asphalt of Trinidad and Tobago Ltd.
Lime Oil Act	...	...
Litter Act	Section 24(1)	Police & Public Authorities
Malaria Abatement Act	Section 10(1)	Municipal Corporations
Malicious Damage Act	---	Police

TABLE 3.0 LAWS, REGULATIONS AND ENFORCEMENT AGENCIES IN TRINIDAD AND TOBAGO		
Marine Areas (Preservation) Act	Section 6	Ministries of Agriculture & Foreign Affairs
Masters and Servants Ordinance		
Maxi Taxi Act	Section 13(1)	Licensing Authority
Mongoose Act	---	Chief Technical Officer (Agric.)
Mines, Borings and Quarries Act	Section 25	Mines & Quarries - Factory Inspectorate: Borings - Chief Petroleum Officer
Motor Launches Act	Section 15(1)	Harbour Master
Motor Vehicles and Road Traffic Act	Section 100	Licensing Authority
Municipal Corporations Act	Section 221	Municipal Corporations
National Agricultural & Marketing and Development Corp. Act	Section 31(1)	NAMDC
National Trust of Trinidad and Tobago Act	Section 30	National Trust of Trinidad and Tobago
Oil Mining Act	---	Chief Petroleum Engineer
Oil Pollution of Territorial Waters Act	---	Harbour Master
Oil and Water Board Ordinance	Section 57	Oil and Water Board
Pesticides and Toxic Chemicals Act	Section 12(1)	Pesticides & Toxic Chemicals Board
Petroleum Act	Section 29(1)	Ministry of Energy
Pipelines Act	---	Municipal Corporations & Commissioner State Lands
Plant (Export Prohibition) Act	Section 3	Customs

TABLE 3.0 LAWS, REGULATIONS AND ENFORCEMENT AGENCIES IN TRINIDAD AND TOBAGO

Plant Protection Ordinance	Section 15	Plant Protection Officers
Plant Protection Act	Section 17	Plant Quarantine Service
Laws	Regulatory Power	Enforcement Agency
Port Authority Act	Section 75	Port Authority
Protection of Wrecks	Section 3(1)	Police
Public Health Ordinance	---	Ministry of Health Authority / Municipal Corporations
Quarantine Act	Section 4(1)	Quarantine Authority
Recreation Ground & Pastures Act	Section 4	Municipal Corporations
Sawmill Act	Section 11	Conservator of Forests
Shipping Act	Section 406	Division of Maritime Services
Slum Clearance and Housing Act	Section 43(1)	National Housing Authority
Standards Act	Section 33	Bureau of Standards
State lands Act	Section 4(3)	Commissioner of State lands
Sugar Industry Control Board Act	Section 15(1)	Sugar Industry Control Board
Summary Offences Act	---	Police
Territorial Sea Act	---	Police, Customs, Coast Guard
Trinidad and Tobago Export Development Act	Section 23	Trinidad and Tobago Export Development Corp.
Trinidad and Tobago Free Zones Act	Section 14	Trinidad and Tobago Free Zones Co. Ltd.
Tobago House of Assembly Act	---	Tobago House of Assembly

TABLE 3.0 LAWS, REGULATIONS AND ENFORCEMENT AGENCIES IN TRINIDAD AND TOBAGO		
Tourism and Industrial Development Company of Trinidad and Tobago Ltd. Act	---	TIDCO
Trade Ordinance Act	4(1)	Competent Authority
Town and Country Planning Act	Section 89	Town & Country Planning Division
Water and Sewerage Act	Sections 50, 51 & 84	Water & Sewerage Authority
Water Works & Conservation Act	Section 15	Irrigation Officer, Minister of Public Utilities, Competent Authority
Zoological Society of Trinidad and Tobago Act		

While in some instances the absence of regulations has proved problematic in TT, in others, the presence of regulations that have not been adjusted to the passage of time have been equally unsatisfactory. For example, the bulk of regulations made under the *Fisheries Act* to deal with equipment for fishing purposes were originally promulgated in 1926. Unfortunately, a large percentage of the equipment identified in the regulations are no longer made or used. Further, no efforts have been made to exercise the existing regulatory power to repeal what can only be described as archaic regulations, and implement more appropriate ones. The failure of the law to deal with more contemporary fishing equipment has meant that the Fisheries Division is often without recourse when certain modern equipment inimical to the interest of fish stock conservation is used.

It is important to examine the changes made by the *Environmental Management Act* in response to the lethargic approach to regulation making in TT. This is of course due to the wide-ranging regulatory power for the protection of the environment included in the *Environmental Management Act*.

EMA Regulations

(i) Certificate of Environmental Clearance

Sections 35-36 of the Environmental Management Act

35(1) For the purpose of determining the environmental impact which might arise out of any new or significantly modified construction, process, works or other activity, the Minister may by Order subject to negative resolution of Parliament designate a list of activities requiring a certificate of environmental clearance (hereinafter called "Certificate").

(2) No person shall proceed with any activity which the Minister has designated as requiring a Certificate unless such person applies for and receives a Certificate from the Authority.

(3) An application made under this section shall be made in accordance with the manner prescribed.

(4) The Authority in considering the application may ask for further information including, if required, an environmental impact assessment, in accordance with the procedure prescribed.

(5) Any application which requires the preparation of an environment impact assessment shall be submitted for public comment in accordance with section 28 before any Certificate is issued by the Authority.

36. (1) After considering all relevant matters, including the comments or representations made during the public comment period, the Authority may issue a Certificate subject to such terms and conditions as it thinks fit, including the requirement to undertake appropriate mitigation measures. (2) Where the Authority refuses to issue a Certificate, it shall provide to the applicant in writing its reasons for such action.

The process of implementing the CEC process started with the designation of activities requiring a CEC in the *Certificate of Environmental Clearance (Designated Activities) Order*[76] as amended. This was done

---

[76] *Certificate of Environmental Clearance (Designated Activities) Order, 2001 (L.N. No. 103 of 2001)*

together with *the Certificate of Environmental Clearance Rules*[77] and the *Certificate of Environmental Clearance (Fees and Charges) Regulations.*[78]

(ii) Protected Areas

Sections 41-43 of the Environmental Management Act

41(1) The Authority may prescribe in accordance with section 26(e) the designation of a defined portion of the environment within Trinidad and Tobago as an "environmentally sensitive area"…, requiring special protection to achieve the objects of this Act.

(2) For the purpose of subsection (1), designation shall be made by Notice published in the Gazette.

42. In pursuance of section 41(1), the Notice shall include— (a) a comprehensive description of the area…to be so designated; (b) the reasons for such designation; and (c) the specific limitations on use of or activities within such area… which are required to adequately protect the identified environmental concerns.

43. Any designation of an "environmentally sensitive area"…— (a) may permit the wise use of such area…and provide for the undertaking of appropriate mitigation measures, but shall not otherwise be deemed to authorise or permit any activity not previously authorized or permitted with respect to such area…and (b) shall only require compliance with the specific limitations on use or activities specified in the designation.

In 2001, the *Environmentally Sensitive Areas Rules*[79] came into force and since then, areas have been designated as environmentally sensitive areas, albeit at a relatively sluggish pace.

- *The Environmentally Sensitive Area (Matura National Park) Notice*[80]

- *The Environmentally Sensitive Areas (Nariva Swamp Managed Resource*

---

77 *Certificate of Environmental Clearance Rules, 2001 (L.N. No. 104 of 2001)*

78 *Certificate of Environmental Clearance (Fees and Charges) Regulations (L.N. No. 91 of 2001)*

79 *Environmentally Sensitive Areas Rules (L.N. No. 37 of 2001)*

80 *Environmentally Sensitive Area (Matura National Park) Notice (L.N. No. 323 of 2004)*

Protected Area) Notice[81]

- *The Environmentally Sensitive Areas (Aripo Savannas Strict Nature Reserve) Notice[82]*

(iii) Protected Species

Sections 41-43 of the Environmental Management Act

41(1) The Authority may prescribe in accordance with section 26(e) the designation of...any species of living plant or animal as an "environmentally sensitive species", requiring special protection to achieve the objects of this Act.

(2) For the purpose of subsection (1), designation shall be made by Notice published in the Gazette.

42. In pursuance of section 41(1), the Notice shall include— (a) a comprehensive description of the...species to be so designated; (b) the reasons for such designation; and (c) the specific limitations on use of or activities...with regard to such species which are required to adequately protect the identified environmental concerns.

43. Any designation of... "environmentally sensitive species"— (a) may permit the wise use of...species and provide for the undertaking of appropriate mitigation measures, but shall not otherwise be deemed to authorize or permit any activity not previously authorized or permitted with respect to such...species; and (b) shall only require compliance with the specific limitations on use or activities specified in the designation.

With the coming into force of the *Environmentally Sensitive Species Rules*,[83] several species have been designated as environmentally sensitive.

- *Environmentally Sensitive Species (Manatee), Notice[84]*

---

81 *Environmentally Sensitive Areas (Nariva Swamp Managed Resource Protected Area) Notice (L.N. No. 334 of 2006)*

82 *Environmentally Sensitive Areas (Aripo Savannas Strict Nature Reserve) Notice (L.N. No. 152 of 2007)*

83 *Environmentally Sensitive Species Rules (L.N. No. 63 of 2001)*

84 *Environmentally Sensitive Species (Manatee), Notice (L.N. No. 123 of 2005)*

- *Environmentally Sensitive Species (Pawi), Notice[85]*

- *Environmentally Sensitive Species (White-tailed Sabrewing), Notice[86]*

- *Environmentally Sensitive Species (Ocelot) Notice[87]*

- *Environmentally Sensitive Species (Golden Tree Frog), Notice[88]*

- *Environmentally Sensitive Species (Leatherback Turtle), Notice[89]*

- *Environmentally Sensitive Species (Loggerhead Turtle), Notice[90]*

- *Environmentally Sensitive Species (Green Turtle), Notice[91]*

- *Environmentally Sensitive Species (Hawksbill Turtle), Notice[92]*

- *Environmentally Sensitive Species (Olive Ridley Turtle), Notice[93]*

- *Environmentally Sensitive Species (Scarlet Ibis) Notice[94]*

(iv) Noise Pollution

Sections 49-51 of the Environmental Management Act

49(1) The Authority shall, as soon as practicable after the commencement of this Act, investigate the environment generally and such premises and vehicles as it thinks necessary for the purpose of— (a) ascertaining the extent of... noise pollution and the significant sources of pollutants which by their release

---

85 *Environmentally Sensitive Species (Pawi), Notice (L.N. No. 124 of 2005)*

86 *Environmentally Sensitive Species (White-tailed Sabrewing), Notice (L.N. No. 125 of 2005)*

87 *Environmentally Sensitive Species (Ocelot) Notice (L.N. No.31 of 2013)*

88 *Environmentally Sensitive Species (Golden Tree Frog), Notice (L.N. No. 32 of 2013)*

89 *Environmentally Sensitive Species (Leatherback Turtle), Notice (L.N. No. 88 of 2014)*

90 *Environmentally Sensitive Species (Loggerhead Turtle), Notice (L.N. No. 89 of 2014)*

91 *Environmentally Sensitive Species (Green Turtle), Notice (L.N. No. 90 of 2014)*

92 *Environmentally Sensitive Species (Hawksbill Turtle), Notice (L.N. No. 91 of 2014)*

93 *Environmentally Sensitive Species (Olive Ridley Turtle), Notice (L.N. No. 92 of 2014)*

95 *Environmentally Sensitive Species (Scarlet Ibis) Notice (L.N. No. 143 of 2018)*

cause or contribute to such pollution; and (b) characterizing or describing that pollution.

(2) The Authority shall cause a register of...Noise pollutants to be maintained as prescribed by Rules, which shall contain data identifying the quantity, conditions or concentrations relevant to the identification of each pollutant.

(3) The Authority shall develop and implement a programme for the management of such pollution which shall include the registration and further characterization of significant sources of any ongoing or intermittent releases noise pollutants into the environment.

50(1) The Authority may require and grant permits to authorize any process releasing air pollutants subject to such terms and conditions as it thinks fit...

51(2) No person shall emit or cause to be emitted any noise greater in volume or intensity than prescribed in Rules made under section 26 or by any applicable standards, conditions or requirements under this Act.

The *Noise Pollution Control Rules*[95] and the *Noise Pollution Control (Fees) Regulations*[96] now regulate the emission of noise in TT.

(v) Air Pollution

Section 49-51 of the Environmental Management Act

49(1) of the Environmental Management Act - The Authority shall, as soon as practicable after the commencement of this Act, investigate the environment generally and such premises and vehicles as it thinks necessary for the purpose of— (a) ascertaining the extent of air...pollution and the significant sources of pollutants which by their release cause or contribute to such pollution; and (b) characterizing or describing that pollution.

(2) The Authority shall cause a register of air...pollutants to be maintained as prescribed by Rules, which shall contain data identifying the quantity, conditions or concentrations relevant to the identification of each pollutant.

---

95 *Noise Pollution Control Rules (L.N. No. 60 of 2001)*

96 *Noise Pollution Control (Fees) Regulations (L.N. No. 51 of 2001)*

(3) The Authority shall develop and implement a programme for the management of such pollution which shall include the registration and further characterization of significant sources of any ongoing or intermittent releases of air…pollutants into the environment.

50(1) The Authority may require and grant permits to authorize any process releasing air pollutants subject to such terms and conditions as it thinks fit.

(2) The terms and conditions of a permit may relate to the design, construction, operation, maintenance and monitoring of the facility and processes releasing air pollutants.

(3) A person shall apply to the Authority for the grant of an Air Pollution Permit in accordance with the form as determined by the Authority.

51(1) No person shall release or cause to be released any air pollutant into the environment which is in violation of any applicable standards, conditions or permit requirements under this Act.

Two decades of the coming into force of the *Environmental Management Act*, regulations were finally made to address this critical area of concern for the well-being of the environment in TT through the *Air Pollution Rules*[97] and the *Air Pollution (Fees) Regulations.*[98]

(vi) Water Pollution

Section 52-54 of the Environmental Management Act

52(1) The Authority shall, as soon as practicable after the commencement of this Act, investigate the environment generally and such premises and vehicles as it thinks necessary for the purposes of— (a) ascertaining the extent of water pollution and significant sources of water pollutants; and (b) characterizing or describing that pollution.

(2) The Authority shall cause a register of water pollutants to be maintained as prescribed by Rules, which shall contain data identifying the quantity, conditions or concentrations relevant to the identification of each pollutants.

---

97 *Air Pollution Rules (L.N. No. 12 of 2015)*
98 *Air Pollution (Fees) Regulations (L.N. No. 13 of 2015)*

(3) The Authority shall develop and implement a programme for the management of such pollution which shall include the registration and further characterization of significant sources of any ongoing or intermittent releases of water pollutants into the environment.

53(1) The Authority may require and grant permits to authorize any process releasing water pollutants subject to such terms and conditions as it thinks fit.

(2) The terms and conditions of a permit may relate to the design, construction, operation, maintenance and monitoring of the facilities and processes releasing water pollutants.

(3) A person shall apply to the Authority for the grant of a water pollution permit in accordance with the form as determined by the Authority.

54. No person shall release or cause to be released any water pollutant into the environment which is in violation of any applicable standards, conditions or permit requirements under this Act.

A decade after the enactment of the *Environmental Management Act*, the environmental legal regime for addressing water pollution was made effective through the Water Pollution Rules,[99] *Water Pollution (Amendment) Rules*[100] and *Water Pollution (Fees) Regulations.*[101]

Main Outstanding EMA Subsidiary Legislation

There are still major areas of environmental concern where subsidiary legislation is still outstanding, despite the fact that the *Environmental Management Act* was enacted over 20 years ago.

(i) Record Keeping and Monitoring

Sections 47-48 of the Environmental Management Act

(47) The Authority may, as prescribed by Rules, require any person who releases a pollutant from any premises or vehicle, or who engages in the handling of

---

99 *Water Pollution Rules (L.N. No. 230 of 2001)*
100 *Water Pollution (Amendment) Rules (L.N. No. 112 of 2006)*
101 *Water Pollution (Fees) Regulations (L.N. No. 142 of 2001)*

any hazardous substance, on a one-time or periodic basis to— (a) sample and analyse such pollutant or hazardous substance, or material which has become contaminated with such pollutant or hazardous substance, for specified constituents or characteristics; (b) install, use and maintain such monitoring equipment, and implement such environmental audit procedures, as may be specified in any permit or licence issued pursuant to this Act; (c) establish and maintain records regarding such sampling, monitoring and environmental auditing activities; (d) establish and maintain records regarding pollution control equipment on the premises (including exception. co-ordination. appeal. record-keeping and monitoring requirements, records on control equipment parameters, production variables and other indirect data when direct monitoring is not required); (e) submit reports and compliance certifications; and (f) provide such other information as the Authority may require.

48(1) Where an application is made under section 50(3), 53(3), 57(4) or 60(2) for the grant of a permit or licence under section 50(1), 53(1), 57(1) or 60(1), respectively, and the Authority requires further information for the purpose of dealing with the application, the Authority may require the person to provide results of research or analysis to be undertaken by such person.

(2) The Authority may, as prescribed by Rules, revoke, suspend, vary or cancel any provision in such permit or licence where the Authority determines such action is necessary.

(3) Any conditions imposed in respect of a permit, or a revocation, suspension, variation or cancellation takes effect when notice is served on the holder of the permit or such later time as the Authority may direct in the notice.

(4) Any such revocation, suspension, variation or cancellation of a permit or licence shall be capable of appeal to the Commission by the permit or licence holder.

(ii) Wastes

Sections 55-58 of the Environmental Management Act

55(1) The Authority shall, as soon as practicable after the commencement of this Act, investigate the environment generally and such premises and vehicles as it thinks necessary for the purposes of— (a) ascertaining the volume and nature of wastes which are handled and disposed into the environment; and (b) identifying and characterizing the different categories and the significant sources of such wastes. Water pollution permits. Prohibiting water pollution.

(2) The Authority shall develop and implement a programme for the management of such wastes which may include the registration and further characterization of significant sources of wastes being disposed into the environment.

56. The Authority shall as soon as practicable after the commencement of this Act, submit to the Minister a programme to define those wastes which should be deemed "hazardous wastes", to establish requirements for the handling and disposal of hazardous wastes, to establish appropriate standards and design criteria for hazardous waste-handling and disposal facilities, and to establish licensing and permitting requirements with respect to such wastes.

57. (1) The Authority may require and grant a permit to authorize any person's waste disposal activities, or licences for the operation of any waste-handling facility, subject to such terms and conditions as it thinks fit.

(2) The terms and conditions of a licence under this section may relate to the design, construction, operation, maintenance and monitoring of any waste-handling facility.

(3) The terms and conditions of a permit under this section may relate to a person's handling of any waste.

(4) A person shall apply to the Authority for the grant of such licence or permit as prescribed by Rules.

58. No person shall handle or dispose of any waste or hazardous waste in a manner which is in violation of any applicable licence, permit, standards, conditions or requirements under this Act.

(iii) Hazardous Substances

Sections 59-60 of the Environmental Management Act

59. The Authority shall, as soon as practicable after the commencement of this Act, submit to the Minister a programme for the designation of specific hazardous substances and performance standards and procedures for the safe handling of such hazardous substances.

60(1) After final designation of such specific hazardous substances and the establishment of the performance standards and procedures under section 26, a person shall not handle, or cause to be handled by any other person through contract, agreement or other arrangement, any hazardous substance except in accordance with— (a) such performance standards and procedures; or (b) a licence or permit granted by the Authority.

(2) A person shall apply to the Authority for the grant of a licence or permit as prescribed by Rules.

(iv) Accidental Spills or Releases

Section 61 of the Environmental Management Act

61(1) As soon as practicable after the commencement of this Act, and thereafter as appropriate, the Authority shall investigate and designate categories of circumstances involving accidental spills or other releases of pollutants, or other incidents with respect to hazardous substances, which may present a risk to human health or the environment.

(2) The designation of such categories by the Authority shall be submitted for public comment in accordance with section 28.

(3) After the final designation of any categories under this section, any person in charge of any premises or vehicle shall, as soon as he has knowledge of a release or other incident referred to in this section associated with such premises or vehicle, notify the Authority of such release or incident and provide to the Authority— (a) a brief description of the release or incident; (b) an assessment of any damages or potential risks to human health or the environment associated with the release or incident; (c) a description of the response measures taken and to be taken to address and otherwise mitigate damages or contamination resulting from the release or incident.

(4) The Authority shall investigate and evaluate any such release or incident as it thinks fit, and may— (a) respond to the release or incident as authorized under section 25; and (b) develop and implement appropriate environmental programmes, standards, conditions, permits, licences or requirements designed to avoid such releases or incidents in the future.

Legal Language: Vagueness or Absence of Specific Standards and Unusual Hardship

The presence of law is one aspect of an environmental legal regime but the ability to use this law effectively may pose a more difficult challenge, as in some instances the language used in legislation can impose severe constraints on those responsible for implementing and enforcing the law. This has certainly been apparent in the environmental legal regime of TT. The issue of vagueness has led to reluctance on the part of some agencies in enforcing important pieces of legislation. The problems associated with the vagueness or absence of specific standards and unusual hardship in the environmental legal regime has been somewhat alleviated by subsidiary legislation made under the *Environmental Management Act*. Starting with the implementation of the CEC process, there are defined conditions for engaging in certain designated activities that encompass a wide range of environmental impacts *Certificate of Environmental Clearance (Designated Activities) Order, Certificate of Environmental Clearance Rules*, and the *Certificate of Environmental Clearance (Fees and Charges) Regulations)*. Specifically subsidiary regulations with precise standards and enforcement protocols have been established through the *Air Pollution Rules*, the *Water Pollution Rules* and the *Noise Pollution Rules*.

Lack of Appropriate Sanctions

Another setback faced by enforcement agencies is based on the absence of sanctions at a level that would render breaches of environmental laws quite undesirable. It would appear that in TT, it is more cost effective to break the law and pay a fine than to take steps to desist from breaching laws applicable to environmental protection. The low financial penalties for breaches of the law have contributed to the lack of enthusiasm on the part of agencies for bringing court actions in order to have these said laws enforced. Indeed, many governmental entities have cited the lack of punitive sanctions as the major cause for the lethargic approach to enforcement. This situation, however, is somewhat addressed by the *Environmental Management Act*.

Civil Remedies

The *Environmental Management Act* provides for civil enforcement by the EMA when there is breach of an environmental requirement as defined in *Section 62 of the Environmental Management Act*.

> *62. For the purposes of this Part and Part VIII, "environmental requirement" means the requirement upon a person to— (a) comply with the procedures for the registration of sources from which pollutants may be released into the environment; (b) comply with the procedures and standards with respect to permits or licences required for any person to install or operate any process or source from which pollutants will be or may continue to be released into the environment; (c) provide in a timely manner complete and accurate information in any required submission to or communication with the Authority or in response to any inspection or request for information by the Authority; (d) refrain from any unauthorized activities impacting on the environment in an "environmentally sensitive area" or with respect to an "environmentally sensitive species"; (e) comply with the performance standards, procedures, licensing or permitting requirements established for the handling of hazardous substances; (f) apply for and obtain a Certificate of Environmental Clearance; (g) comply with the conditions and mitigation measures in any such certificate; Environmental requirements; (h) comply with the procedures and standards with respect to the periodic or continual monitoring of pollution or releases of pollutants or conditions required under a permit or license; (i) provide timely and accurate notification with respect to an accidental or unauthorized release of a pollutant or other incident with respect to a hazardous substance; (j) control the release of pollutants in such a manner as to comply with any permit or license granted under section 50(1), 53(1), 57(1) or 60(1); (k) submit timely payment of required fees or charges payable to the Authority; and (l) comply with all other procedures, standards, programmes and requirements in such a manner as may be prescribed by Rules or Regulations.*

Sections 63-68 of the Environmental Management Act set out the procedures to be followed by the EMA in addressing the breach of an environmental requirement.

> *63(1) Where the Authority reasonably believes that a person is in violation of an environmental requirement, the Authority shall serve a written notice of violation (hereinafter called "Notice") on such person in a form determined by the Board,*

which shall include— (a) a request that the person make such modifications to the activity within a specified time, as may be required to allow the continuation of the activity; or (b) an invitation to the person to make representations to the Authority concerning the matters specified in the Notice within a specified time.

(2) Where a matter specified in the Notice may be satisfactorily explained or otherwise resolved between the person and the Authority— (a) the Authority may cancel the Notice or dismiss the matters specified in the Notice; or (b) an agreed resolution may be reduced in writing into a Consent Agreement.

64. The Authority may issue an Administrative Order under section 65 where the person— (a) fails to make representations to the Authority within the time specified in the Notice; or (b) is unable to resolve with the Authority all matters specified in the Notice.

65(1) An Administrative Order served by the Authority shall, where appropriate— (a) specify details of the violation of one or more environmental requirements; (b) direct the person to immediately cease and desist from the violation or specify a date for coming into compliance; (c) direct the person to immediately remedy any environmental conditions or damages to the environment arising out of the violation or specify a date by which such remedial activities shall be completed; (d) direct the person to undertake an investigation regarding any environmental circumstances or conditions within such person's responsibility or control, including any release of a pollutant into the environment or the handling of any hazardous substance; (e) direct the person to perform any monitoring or record-keeping activities which may be required under section 47; (f) include a proposed administrative civil assessment made by the Authority; (g) direct a person to comply with any other requirement under this Act.

(2) Directives contained in an Administrative Order served upon a person shall be deemed final and conclusive after the expiry of twenty-eight days, unless within such period the person— (a) appeals the Administrative Order to the Commission; (b) reaches an agreement with the Authority which is reduced in writing into a Consent Agreement; or (c) obtains an extension of time from the Authority which is confirmed in writing.

(3) Any Administrative Order shall contain a notice advising of the matters in

subsection (2).

66(1) For the purposes of sections 65 and 81(5)(d), the Authority or the Commission may make an administrative civil assessment of— (a) compensation for actual costs incurred by the Authority to respond to environmental conditions or other circumstances arising out of the violation referenced in the Administrative Order; (b) compensation for damages to the environment associated with public lands or holdings which arise out of the violation referenced in the Administrative Order; (c) damages for any economic benefit or amount saved by a person through failure to comply with applicable environmental requirements; and (d) damages for the failure of a person to comply with applicable environmental requirements, in an amount determined pursuant to subsections (2) and (3).

(2) In determining the amount of any damages to be assessed under subsections (1)(c) and (d), the Authority or the Commission shall take into account— (a) the nature, circumstances, extent and gravity of the violation; (b) any history of prior violations; and (c) the degree of wilfulness or culpability in committing the violation and any good faith efforts to co-operate with the Authority.

(3) The total amount of any damages under subsection (1)(d), shall not exceed— (a) for an individual, five thousand dollars for each violation and, in the case of continuing or recurrent violation, one thousand dollars per day for each such Administrative civil assessment instance until the violation is remedied or abated; or (b) for a person other than an individual, ten thousand dollars for each violation and, in the case of continuing or recurrent violations, five thousand dollars per day for each such instance until the violation is remedied or abated.

67(1) The Authority may file any Consent Agreement or final Administrative Order and an application for enforcement with the Commission.

(2) Where an Administrative Order contains a proposed administrative civil assessment, that assessment is not enforceable until such time as the Commission makes an Order determining the amount of such assessment.

68. Whenever the Authority reasonably believes that any person is currently in violation of any environmental requirement, or is engaged in any activity which is likely to result in a violation of any environmental requirement, the Authority may in addition to, or in lieu of, other actions authorized under this Act— (a) seek a restraining order or other injunctive or equitable relief, to prohibit the continued violation or prevent the activity which will likely lead to a violation; (b) seek an order for the closure of any facility or a prohibition against the continued operation of any processes or equipment at such facility in order to halt or prevent any violation; or (c) pursue any other remedy which may be provided by law.

In the absence of resolution of a breach of an environmental requirement, the EMA has taken action to have the Environmental Commission determine whether or not there is the existence of such a breach.

Environmental Management Authority v Michael Trestrail [102]

Facts: Micheal Trestail is the owner of a parcel of land located at Mal D. Estomac Baby, North Coast Trinidad. Trestail commenced development work on the land including clearing, grading, excavating and filling without first applying for and obtaining a Certificate of Environmental Clearance. Such activities are designated activities under the Certificate of Environmental Clearance (Designated Activities) Order and required a Certificate of Environmental Clearance. Trestrail was served with a Notice of Violation but continued the activities.

Held: Environmental Commission

In conducting the above mentioned activities without having applied for or obtained a CEC, the Court holds that the Respondent has been in violation of an environmental requirement as per Section 62(f) of the EM Act in that he failed to apply for an obtain a certificate of environmental clearance pursuant to section 35(2) of that Act for the conduct of certain designated activities.

The EMA cannot however issue a Notice of Violation and an Administrative Order without having a reasonable basis for issuing the Notice of Violation in the first instance. In such a case, the EMA can be liable for malicious prosecution by civil suit in the Supreme Court.

Learie Neale v Environmental Management Authority [103]

Facts: Learie Neale, a self-employed mechanic operating a small automotive repair garage, claimed that an administrative order was made against him without his knowledge and that subsequently, an application was made to the En-

---

102 EAA 002 of 2011
103 CV 2014-03449

vironmental Commission to enforce such an order. The enforcement proceedings were discontinued against Learie Neale on the date of hearing and the EMA was ordered to pay his costs. Learie Neale filed an action in the Supreme Court claiming damages, inclusive of exemplary and aggravated damages for malicious prosecution for the wrongful issue of proceedings by the Defendant pursuant to Section 67 of the Environmental Management Act.

Held: Rahim J

Firstly, this court is of the view that this court is bound by the dicta of Their Lordships given by way of majority judgment in Crawford. It is clear to this court that the law under consideration is that which is of equal applicability to this jurisdiction, namely the availability of a remedy for the tort of malicious prosecution in relation to proceedings brought by officers of the state against members of the public to whom they owe a duty to act fairly and in accordance with the principles of natural justice. In that regard this court is duty bound to apply the dicta set out by Mendonca JA in Goodridge v Nagessar supra, that decisions of the Privy Council on appeals from other jurisdictions are binding on this Court where the issue of law is the same before this Court as it was before the Privy Council and there is nothing to suggest that the law in this jurisdiction is any different. Similarly, in this case, the law under consideration is that of applicable principles in relation to the common law principles of the tort of malicious prosecution which principles are in large measure no different from that which obtains in the Cayman Islands.

Secondly, this court agrees with the submission of the Claimant that as the tort of malicious prosecution is based on an abuse of the coercive powers of the state, the tort ought to apply as much to civil as to criminal proceedings. An improper and wrongful motive lies at the heart of the tort of malicious prosecution in civil cases as it does in criminal cases. In this case, the Act confers powers on the EMA to make Administrative Orders and to enforce those orders in the absence of the individual subject to the order. Of course there are safeguards provided within the legislation but for the purpose of ascertaining the applicability of the tort in this case, the court has given weight to the fact that the powers conferred unto those who are entrusted with performing the obligations and duties provided by the Act are coercive in nature.

Thirdly, in the court's view, there appears to be no other effective remedy available to the Claimant to right the wrong of the improper and wrongful use of the pow-

ers given to the Authority under the Act. In that regard this court does not agree with the submission of the Defendant that the Commission or Environmental Court, being a superior court of record, is empowered to in similar manner to the High Court to award compensation to the Claimant for the wrong. To so do would be to derogate from the statutory remit and jurisdiction granted to the Environmental Court by virtue of the Act. In so far as the Environmental Court is a court of superior record, it cannot be reasonably argued that the court is vested with the jurisdiction to make awards of compensation for abuse by the Authority of the process set out by the Act. In fact, the Defendant admits in submissions that the Act is patently silent on the ability to award aggravated or exemplary damages for wrongs of that nature.

100. In relation to the Defendant's submission that the Court of Appeal is vested with the jurisdiction to hear and determine appeals from the Environmental Court, this argument in the court's view collapses on itself, the Environmental Court having no jurisdiction to award damages for the abuse of the process set out in the Act to ensure compliance with environmental standards by officers employed with the Authority.

101.This court has also considered the remedy of Judicial Review and its applicability and considers that the Environmental Court, is not an inferior tribunal and it is doubtful whether its decisions fall to be judicially supervised by the High Court in respect of its decisions, except where statute so provides.

102. In the event, the proper forum in which to seek redress would be to invoke the jurisdiction of the High Court. In the words of the majority of the court in Crawford, where there is a wrong there should be a remedy unless there is compelling justification to deny such a remedy. There is no such justification in this case. As a consequence, this court finds that a claim for malicious prosecution in relation to enforcement proceedings brought under the Act is actionable in law.

273.The court is of the view that there was an absence of an honest belief in the merits of the case as Inspectors were sent subsequently as if to embark on a mission to justify that which had already been instituted. It is passing strange that most of the evidence from the Inspectors in this case relate to matters which occurred after the decision to institute proceedings were taken and carried out. Coupled with the fact of non-production of the report of Ms. Alexander by any of the witnesses, serious doubts have been raised in the court's mind as to the whether an honest belief was held by Ms. Alexander when she instituted proceedings against the Defendant and the court is satisfied that she did not hold such a belief. The evidence of Ms. John-Roopnarine-singh, that she Ms. John- Roopnarinesingh was satisfied rings hollow in the absence of the report of Ms. Alexander.

274. The court therefore finds that in this case malice is to be inferred from the absence of reasonable and probable cause and from lack of evidence of an honest belief held by Ms. Alexander. There shall therefore be judgment for the Claimant for malicious prosecution with damages to be assessed and prescribed costs quantified by a Master on a date to be fixed by the court office.

Criminal Sanctions

The *Environmental Management Act* has brought to the forefront, the use of criminal sanctions to address environmental crimes by establishing penalties that can act as an effective deterrent to anthropogenic conduct that harms the environment. Evidently, this is a major departure from other legislation.

Section 70 of the Environmental Management Act

70(1) Any person who through the release or handling of any pollutant or hazardous substance, or the arrangement for another person through any contract or other agreement to release or handle any pollutant or hazardous substance, knowingly or recklessly endangers human life or health, commits an offence, and is liable on conviction on indictment, to a fine of one hundred thousand dollars and imprisonment for two years.

(2) Any person who knowingly or recklessly undertakes or conspires to allow any activity in an "environmentally sensitive area" or with respect to an "environmentally sensitive species" designated under section 41, which may have an adverse impact on the environment within such area or on such species, commits an offence and is liable, on conviction on indictment, to a fine of one hundred thousand dollars and imprisonment for two years.

(3) A complaint for any offence under this section shall be made within three years from the commencement of this Act, or from the time when an action giving rise to such offence is first discovered by the Authority.

(4) For the purposes of this section, endangerment of human life or health means placing one or more persons in danger of death or serious bodily injury, including unconsciousness, extreme pain, or physical or mental impairment.

(5) Any action under this section may be in addition to any other action taken by the Authority under this Part.

Section 71 of the Environmental Management Act that addresses criminal liability also contemplates criminal conduct by body corporates.

(71) Where a violation of any environmental requirement has been committed by a person (other than an individual), any individual who at the time of the violation was a director, manager, supervisor, partner or other similar officer or responsible individual, or who was purporting to act in such capacity, may be found individually liable for that violation if, having regard to the nature of his functions in that capacity, the resources within his control or discretion, and his reasonable ability to prevent the violation— (a) the violation was committed with his direct consent or connivance; or (b) he, with knowledge, did not exercise reasonable diligence to prevent the commission of the violation.

The sad reality is that since its enactment in 1995, prosecution of environmental crimes only first made a limited appearance in 2018, with the enforcement of regulations made under the *Environmental Management Act* to protect the Scarlet Ibis, one of the national birds of TT. This is despite the acknowledged fact of many environmental crimes being committed in TT in areas such as water, noise and biological diversity.

INSTITUTIONAL CHALLENGES

One aspect of the environmental legal regime of TT is the method for creating enforcement agencies. TT's legal structure for the protection of the environment appears somewhat chaotic. The authority for each agency to act is derived strictly from the statute providing its power. A review of the environmental legal regime for TT as identified in Table 3.0 identifies around 50 government related agencies that are involved in activities, which in varying degrees, may impact on the protection of the environment. These agencies can be placed into several broad categories.

First, there are government ministries that are directly responsible for taking action pertaining to the environment as specified by legislation. Second, there are departments of government. Third, there are statutory bodies. Fourth, there are incorporated companies, established by law, whose shareholdings are owned by the government and are described as independent of governmental control despite the fact that the government appoints the governing boards. Finally, there are the municipal corporations made up of the elected local government officials which also perform certain environmental functions under several laws.

Insufficient Resources

The most debilitating problem confronting enforcement agencies with responsibility for the environment in TT is the lack of access to sufficient resources, the most important being financial resources. This lack of adequate financial resources can be correctly interpreted as being the root of all difficulties with human, mechanical, technical and research resources.

In TT, in the year 2000, the Government announced the imposition of a new tax called a Green Fund Levy. According to *Section 62 (1) of the Finance Act*:[104]

> *62(1) With effect from 1st January, 2001, there shall be levied and paid to the Board of Inland Revenue a tax at the rate of 0.1 per cent to be known as a Green Fund levy on the gross sales or receipts of a company carrying on business in Trinidad and Tobago, whether or not such business is exempt from the business levy..*

The Green Fund Levy was placed in a special fund for environmental purposes as seen in *Section 65 of the Finance Act*

> *(65) Notwithstanding section 29(2), a fund to be known as the Green Fund is hereby established for the purposes of this Part. 66. The purposes of the Green Fund are— (a) to enable grants to be made to community groups and organizations primarily engaged in activities related to the remediation, reforestation and conservation of the environment; (b) to undertake or do all such things as are incidental or*

---

104 *Finance Act, No. 91 of 2000.*

conducive to the attainment of the purpose referred to in paragraph (a).

The *Green Fund Regulations*[105] were made in 2007 to provide the specific legal framework for the actualization of the Green Fund. The Green Fund can be accessed by a body incorporated by statute other than the *Companies Act*; or a body incorporated as a non-profit company under the *Companies Act*; or a non-governmental organization registered with the Ministry with responsibility for community development or the THA which is engaged in activities related to the remediation, reforestation and conservation of the environment. As an example of how the EMA can access the Green Fund, it received TT$68,545,511.00 for the Nariva Swamp Restoration, Carbon Sequestration and Livelihoods Project.[106]

The *Environmental Management Act* also provides for environmental funding through the establishment of an Environmental Trust Fund to finance the operations of the EMA as seen in *Sections 72-73 of the Environmental Management Act.*

> *(72) There is hereby established an Environmental Trust Fund which shall be used to fund the operations of the Authority and for other purposes authorized under this Act....*

> *73(1) Five members of the Board of Directors of the Authority (other than the Managing Director) shall be designated by the President to act as Trustees for the Fund and shall be responsible for its administration.*

With the availability of these two different mechanisms, the operations of the EMA ought to be well funded, however, this would not appear to be the case. The Environmental Trust Fund, which is specifically for activities including the funding of the operations of the EMA, has failed to capture the level of investment to make the EMA self-sufficient. Accordingly, reference ought to be made to *Section 74 of the Environmental Management Act.*

> *(74) The resources of the Fund shall consist of— (a) such amounts as may be appropriated annually or for special purposes by Parliament for the use and operations of the Authority; (b) such amounts which the Authority may collect as pay-*

---

105 *Green Fund Regulations (L.N. No. 34 of 2007)*

106 www.un.org/esa/forests/pdf/facilitative-process/tt/Laydoo-TT-Green-Fund.pp

ments for services rendered, fees due regarding permits, applications or licenses un-
der this Act, fees due for the review and processing of applications for a Certificate
of Environmental Clearance and any environmental impact assessments required
under section 35, fees charged for the reasonable cost of providing environmental
information to interested persons, or fees due from the users of properties under the
administration and control of the Authority; (c) such amounts which are provided
to the Authority or the Government of the Republic of Trinidad and Tobago by
foreign States, international organizations, multilateral or bilateral lending agen-
cies, private individuals, foundations, corporations or other entities to further the
objects of the Act and the National Environmental Policy under section 18; (d)
such amounts borrowed by the Authority consistent with section 77; and (e) any
other sums or amounts to which the Fund may make a lawful claim.

An important source of funds contemplated by *Section 74 of the Environ-mental Management Act* relates to amounts provided through grants from internal and external sources. However, funds where the trusteeship resides in government appointees, such as the Environmental Trust Fund has traditionally experienced difficulties in attracting grants due to a perception that there may be a lack of objective oversight.

In turn, the Green Fund although being funded through the Green Fund Levy and accessible to the EMA, is not accessible for funding the general operations of the EMA. Therefore, the ideal situation for the funding of the operations of the EMA, is to have the Green Fund Levy paid into the Environmental Trust Fund and to expand the oversight of the Environmental Trust Fund to include a broader range of representatives from the private sector and NGOs.

Multiplicity of Enforcement Agencies

The second most critical factor confronting enforcement agencies in TT lies in the sheer number of enforcement agencies. This creates problems associated with multiple agencies, such as overlapping jurisdiction, independence syndrome and lack of proper co-ordinating of the work of enforcement agencies.

Table 3.0 provides a list of all the enforcement agencies established by various pieces of legislation. The total number of agencies with environmental enforcement functions is approximately 50. Theoretically, overlapping jurisdiction should not prove problematic by itself, as it should afford greater scope for environmental protection. However, the result has not always been satisfactory. What has emerged is an informal rationalization of activities that has not managed to serve the interest of the environment.

The *Environmental Management Act* clearly considered the problem of multiple enforcement agencies whereby the EMA was mandated to address this problem through the execution of Memoranda of Understanding. *Section 32 of the Environmental Management Act* states,

> *32(1) The Authority shall, not later than three months after the commencement of this Act, initiate consultation with the other governmental entities performing various environmental management functions, with the objective of formulating memoranda of understanding or other arrangements between the Authority and such other governmental entities, which shall establish the mechanisms for coordination across jurisdictional lines and provide for the implementation of integrated environmental management programmes.*

The EMA has made great strides in this area and many governmental entities have executed memoranda of understanding with the EMA.

Multiplicity of Environmental Policies

Prior to the preparation of the National Environmental Policy (NEP 1998) by the EMA (now replaced by the NEP 2018), there is very little evidence of enforcement agencies taking steps to prepare specific environmental policies. This general absence of environmental policies at the level of agencies accounts, in part, for the attitude towards environmental protection. However, as illustrated in Table 4.0, the last two decades have seen an explosion in the preparation of official policies touching on the environment. It is becoming increasingly common for different governmental entities to produce specific policies to address their respective environmental agenda. While this trend may appear laudable, such policies have no force of law and would appear to be largely cosmetic.[107]

---

107 Environment Specific Policy refers to a policy that deals with a component(s) of the

TABLE 4.0 NATIONAL POLICIES ON THE ENVIRONMENT OR IMPACTING ON THE ENVIRONMENT		
Policy Description[110] (Whether Environment Specific or Industry Specific or Incidental	Environmental Component	Name of Policy
Environment Specific	General	National Environmental Policy
Environment Specific	General	Working for Sustainable Development in TT
Environment Specific	Biological Diversity	Biodiversity Strategy and Action Plan for Trinidad and Tobago
Environment Specific	Biological Diversity	National Wildlife Policy
Environment Specific	Biological Diversity	National Protected Areas Policy
Environment Specific	Biological Diversity	National Wetlands Policy
Environment Specific	Air Pollution	National Climate Change Policy
Environment Specific	Air Pollution	Strategy for the Reduction of Greenhouse Gas (GHG) Emissions
Environment Specific	Air Pollution	Framework for Development of a Renewable Energy Policy
Environment Specific	Freshwater	National Integrated Water Resources Management Policy
Environment Specific	Freshwater	Water Resources Management Strategy

environment. Industry Specific policies are intended to provide guidelines for the management of a particular sector and the environmental challenges pertaining to that sector. Incidental policies deal with non-environmental issues but contain objectives that have environmental implications.

TABLE 4.0 NATIONAL POLICIES ON THE ENVIRONMENT OR IM-PACTING ON THE ENVIRONMENT		
Environment Specific	Marine	National Integrated Coastal Zone Management Policy
Environment Specific	Marine	Integrated Coastal Zone Management Draft Policy Framework
Environment Specific	Waste	National Waste Recycling Policy
Environment Specific	Hazardous Substances	Stockholm Convention on Persistent Organic Pollutants-National Implementation Plan
Environment Specific	Land	National Action Programme to Combat Land Degradation in Trinidad and Tobago
Industry Specific	Tourism	Ecotourism Policy
Industry Specific	Tourism	Trinidad and Tobago Tourism Master Plan
Industry Specific	Tourism	National Tourism Policy
Industry Specific	Mining	White Paper on National Minerals Policy
Industry Specific	Waste Disposal	Scrap Metal Policy
Industry Specific	Yachting	Draft Yachting Policy
Industry Specific	Marine/ Hydrocarbon	National Oil Spill Contingency Plan
Industry Specific	Fishing	National Fisheries Policy
Incidental	Disaster Management	Comprehensive Disaster Management Policy Framework for Trinidad and Tobago
Incidental	Disaster Management	Preliminary Vulnerability Index of Trinidad and Tobago

TABLE 4.0 NATIONAL POLICIES ON THE ENVIRONMENT OR IMPACTING ON THE ENVIRONMENT		
Incidental	Agriculture	National Food Production Action Plan
Incidental	Development	Medium Term Policy Framework 2011-2014
Incidental	Development	The Comprehensive Economic Development Plan, 2013-2017
Incidental	Gender	National Policy on Gender Equality and Development
Incidental	Planning	National Physical Development Plan of Trinidad and Tobago 1984
Incidental	Planning	National Spatial Development Strategy
Incidental	Planning	North East Tobago Management Plan
Incidental	Health	National Health Service Plan and Policy

Notwithstanding the rapid preparation of a wide range of environmental impacting national policies, the main policy for protection of the environment remains the NEP. The EMA is required by *Section 16 (1) (a) of the Environmental Management Act, "to— (a) make recommendations for a National Environmental Policy"*. The exact procedure for establishment of the NEP. The EMA is laid out in *Section 18 of the Environmental Management Act.*

> *18(1) In furtherance of section 16(1)(a), the Board shall prepare and submit to the Minister, not later than two years after the commencement of this Act or such other time as the Minister may direct by Order, recommendation for a comprehensive National Environmental Policy (hereinafter called "the Policy") in accordance with the objects of this Act including— (a) incorporation into the Policy of provisions which seek to encourage the establishment of institutional linkages locally, regionally and internationally to further the objects of this Act; (b) an analysis of the legislative, regulatory and practical issues impacting upon the*

development and successful implementation of the Policy; and (c) a programme for promoting the Policy and seeking an effective commitment from all groups and citizens in the society to achieve the stated objectives in the Policy.

(2) In preparing its recommendations as provided in subsection (1), the Board shall develop and submit to the Minister a report which may— (a) describe the general environment and environmental conditions within Trinidad and Tobago; (b) specify the general environmental quality objectives to be achieved and maintained under the Policy; (c) describe the ecological and other balances required to be maintained for the conservation of natural resources and protection of the environment; (d) specify the elements or areas of the environment which require special protection; (e) identify specific beneficial uses of the environment to be permitted or protected by the Policy; (f) describe the indicators, parameters or criteria which will be used in measuring environmental quality; and (g) establish a programme by which the environmental quality objectives, balances, beneficial uses and protections referred to in the foregoing paragraphs are to be achieved and maintained.

(3) After considering the recommendations and report developed by the Board, the Minister shall cause a draft of the Policy to be— (a) prepared by the Board; and (b) submitted for public comment in accordance with section 28.

(4) After considering the public comments received on the draft Policy, the Board shall submit a revised draft Policy to the Minister for approval.

(5) The Policy may be revised from time to time in accordance with the procedures specified in this section.

(6) The Minister shall, within one month of the approval of any policy submitted under subsection (4), cause the policy to be laid in Parliament.

The NEP was established to ensure that all branches of government give due consideration to the sustainable environment before any major action transpires and aims to achieve sustainable environmental development for the present and future generations. This national policy encourages productive harmony between man and the surroundings, thereby eliminating intentional damage to the ecological environment. The NEP fosters excellent action that protects, restores and enhances natural resources.

What is unique about the NEP is that it has the force of law and must be adhered to by all governmental entities including the EMA.

Section 31 of the Environmental Management Act

(31) The Authority and all other governmental entities shall conduct their operations and programmes in accordance with the National Environmental Policy established under section 18.

In *Fishermen and Friends of the Sea v. The Minister of Planning, Housing and the Environment*,[108] Lord Carnwath in upholding the polluter pays principle as enshrined in the NEP stated: *"In Trinidad and Tobago an attempt has been made to tackle such questions in a more methodical way through the statutory National Environmental Policy ("the NEP") as applied to charges for licenses, and, in the context of water pollution, through the Water Pollution Management Programme ("the WPMP").*

Lax Attitude and Corruption

The effectiveness of enforcement agencies is also undermined by certain attitudes and behaviours towards environmental protection as manifested in the form of a generally lax attitude towards enforcement of the law, corruption and ignorance of the law. Regarding the lax attitude among enforcement agencies towards enforcement of laws impacting on the environment, this can be illustrated in the case of biological control. The Wildlife Division would appear to follow a procedure of almost exclusively checking to see whether a specie is on the international list of endangered species prior to importation, with almost no further investigation to determine the effect of the introduction of that specie in TT. Evidently, this can have far reaching implications for the native biological diversity.

In terms of corruption, there have been numerous allegations of corruption by officers of the agencies which may be instrumental in non-enforcement of relevant laws. The agencies, in which corrupt practices are believed to be prevalent, are unfortunately some of the more important ones, including Town and Country Planning. These allegations must be assumed to be unfounded as there has been no proof of misconduct. Nevertheless,

---

108 PCA No. 0028 of 2016

the lingering allegations are disturbing. According to the Attorney General of TT in 2017:

> *Al-Rawi said this was a reality. But the AG made it clear that the majority of law enforcement officers went above and beyond the call of duty, adding that allegations of corruption existed across all levels of the protective services. "Our country has for many years been treating with allegations of corruption throughout the public service and in the Police Service." Al-Rawi told the T&T Guardian before he spoke at their official opening of the Al-Hikmat Office for the Caribbean and South America at the Central Warehouse Complex in Charlieville. "We have heard of corruption in the Licensing Division, Immigration Division, Customs, TTPS (T&T Police Service), TTDF (T&T Defence Force (but I am not for one moment pouring scorn on the many excellent people that do work in these positions. "But in so far as the allegations, there must be a system for analysis and treating with this," Al-Rawi said.[109]*

Delays in the Justice System

A common complaint by enforcement agencies is the delays in the justice system. Because of manpower constraints and low penalties, there are a great deal of cynicism toward enforcement of the many environmental laws that are being breached. As an example, in 2006, a Cedros fisherman was charged with bringing into TT two hundred birds infected with the bird flu virus. The matter against the fisherman was dismissed but subsequently appealed by the State. A retrial was ordered and it was only on 7 December 2017 that the fisherman was convicted. It took over a decade for this matter to be concluded.[110]

Executive Lobbying

TT, as noted in its economic profile, is the host of numerous multinationals, particularly in the energy sector. These corporations are often head-

---

109 Geisha Kowlessar, *Cooked cops a real problem,* Trinidad and Tobago Guardian (2 April 2017) http://www.guardian.co.tt/news/2017-04-02/crooked-cops-real-problem

110 *Fisherman fined $10,000 for smuggling 200 sick birds,* Trinidad and Tobago Guardian, 8 December 2017, A 10.

quartered in the developed world where high standards of behaviour with respect to environmental issues are well established. Many multinationals operating in TT are quite proud to publicly proclaim their environmental pedigree, however, at times, these corporations may contribute to the low environmental standards in TT.

The issue of pressure being placed on the EMA, mainly due to the actions of large businesses, is one that has been articulated both in the Courts of TT and in the public domain. In *Fishermen and Friends of the Sea v. The Environmental Management Authority and Atlantic LNG Company of Trinidad and Tobago (Interested Party)*,[111] the applicant for judicial review raised the issue of unfair political action. This case queried a letter from the Chief Executive Officer of ALNG to Dr. Ken Julien, who at that time was the Chairman of the Cabinet-appointed Standing Committee on Energy. It was argued on behalf of FFOS that this letter was an attempt by ALNG to have the EMA approve the project without properly considering same. ALNG has many shareholders BP plc, BG Group, Repsol YPF, Suez LNG, and the National Gas Company of Trinidad and Tobago.[112] However, the Court was clear that there was no evidence to suggest that Dr Julien did anything on behalf of ALNG with respect to this letter. Indeed, Justice Stollmeyer noted in the judicial review decision:

> *In support of these submissions, FFOS relied upon the chronology of events, discussions and the correspondence which led up to the grant of the CEC, together with the other evidence in the case to show that the grounds upon which it seeks judicial review have been established. The EMA vigorously denied these allegations. Mr. Martineau submitted that there was not one hint of evidence of delegation or surrender. In fact, he submitted, the evidence pointed to exactly the opposite. ALNG had complained to Dr Ken Julien that EMA's consideration of the matter was time consuming and excessive.*

The Chairman of the EMA has made a plaintive cry against pressure from what he deems "big business".

Chairman of the Environmental Management Authority, Dr. John Agard, on

---

111 H.C.A. Cv. 2148 of 2003

112 See http://www.atlanticlng.com/sections.aspx?sid=2.

Thursday said the authority is pressured by big business to back off on enforcing its policies. "Frequently no one will be happy... but it is an odd situation and we have to be dispassionate" he told journalists at an EMA seminar on environmental journalism at the EMA's Elizabeth Street, St. Clair, offices. "It is very stressful around here because industry believes that the EMA is giving them a hard time. I would be bold enough to say that one of the stresses of a regulatory organization is you end up pleasing no one.[113]

THE ROLE OF THE COMMON LAW

Nuisance

The common law remedy of nuisance is a long-standing legal principle that can afford some relief in certain circumstances from environmental harm. It must be noted that the common law remedy of nuisance was not abolished by the enactment of the *Environmental Management Act*, and therefore operates in tandem with the *Environmental Management Act*.

"A private nuisance may is any activity or state of affairs causing a substantial and unreasonable interference with a claimant's land or his use or enjoyment of that land."[114] There are three kinds of interest 'which nuisance law affords protection: the protection of land per se; the protection of the use of land; the protection of the enjoyment of the land. In each case, the damage must always be referable to the land, and not merely chattels which happen to be on the land".[115]

Wilton Innis (Plaintiff) v Guyana Telephone & Telegraph Company Limited (Defendant)[116]

Facts: The plaintiff who resides at 49 Melanie Damishana, East Coast Demerara claim damages in nuisance as a result of damage he says he suffered as a result of the operation of a generator which was operated by the defendant and which was located a few feet from his home. The defendant denied the plaintiff's

---

113 Jada Loutoo, *EMA cries pressure from big business,* Trinidad Guardian (31 May 2003)
114 Christopher Witting, *Street on Torts,* (13th Edition, Oxford University 2013) 410
115 Ibid.
116 (2012) 1998 No. 392/W (GY)

claim and put him to strict proof of the damage claimed and stated that its generator was placed there to facilitate the provision of telephone service to the area. The defendant pleaded that it provided a telephone service to the community including the plaintiff in the Melanie Damishana area and that it had permission from the Local Democratic Council to locate its facility, an International Outside Plant Access Cabinet, on the Council's Property.

Held: George J

Despite my finding that the major claims of the plaintiff have not been proven, I, however, do accept the plaintiff's evidence that he owns the premises where he lives and that in the period leading to the filing of this action the defendant's generator did emit noise (though there is no evidence of the level or degree of noise in the period leading up to and at the filing of this action) that there was smoke from the exhaust of the generator and that his curtains were dirtied often by the smoke. The plaintiff did not testify how, if at all, the noise affected him personally and I have given my findings that the plaintiff has not proven that the smoke affected him personally. The issue therefore is whether what the plaintiff has actually proven can amount to nuisance so as to make the defendant liable in damages...

This may be a case of private nuisance however, for as Prof Kodilinye has stated (p 193 – 194) "the law of private nuisance has been designed to protect the individual or occupier of land from substantial interference with his enjoyment thereof."...

"The main problem in the law of private nuisance is in striking balance between the rights of the defendant to use his land as he wishes as the right of the plaintiff to be protected from interference with his enjoyment of his land. In order to strike this balance, two main requirements have been developed: the injury of interference complained of will not be actionable unless it is (a) sensible (in the case of material damage to land); or (b) substantial (in the case of interference with enjoyment of land); the defendant will not be held liable unless his conduct was unreasonable in the circumstances.

Sensible material damage

'Sensible material damage' means damage (a) which is not merely trifling or minimal; and (b) which causes a reduction in the value of the plaintiff's property...

Substantial interference with enjoyment of land

Where an action in nuisance is founded on interference with enjoyment of land, such as where a plaintiff complains of inconvenience, annoyance or discomfort caused by the defendant conduct, the interference must be shown to be substantial." (Emphasis mine.)

In Winfield & Jolowicz on Tort by WVH Rogers . . . the learned author has this to say on the issue of damage:

"In the case of a private nuisance, however, although it is said that damage must be proved, the law will often presume it . . . This inference appears to apply to any nuisance where the damage is so likely to occur as to be superfluous to demand evidence that is has occurred. The inference cannot be made if the discomfort is purely personal, for personal sensitivity to smells, smoke and the like varies considerable and it is only fair that evidence of substantial annoyance should be required." (Emphasis mine.)

Another issue that is relevant in this case is the reasonableness of the defendant's conduct. Professor Kodilinye has this to say at pp 196 – 197 on this and the related issue of utility of the defendant's conduct.

"Reasonableness of the defendant's conduct: Whether the plaintiff claims in respect of injury to property or in respect of interference with enjoyment of land, the primary question in any action in private nuisance is: 'Was the defendant's activity reasonable according to the ordinary usages of mankind living. . . in a particular society? There are no precise criteria for determining this question; all depends upon the circumstances of the individual case. However, a number of factors have been taken into account in determining this issue. . ."

The factors to which reference has just been made are identified by Professor Kodilinye as follows:

(1) locality, (2) utility of the defendant's conduct, (3) the plaintiff's abnormal sensitivity, (4) the defendant's malice, and (6) the duration of the harm...

Mr. Trotman cited the Canadian case of Suzuki v Munroe 2009 BCSC 1403 (CanLII) where at para 36 Verhoeven J cited the Supreme Court of Canada decision of St Lawrence Cement Inc. v Barrette 2008 SCC 64 (CanLII) at para 77 where it was stated as follows:

At common law, nuisance is a field of liability that focuses on the harm suffered rather than on prohibited conduct. Nuisance is defined as unreasonable interference with the use of land. Whether the interference results from intentional, negligent or non-faulty conduct is of no consequence provided that the harm can be characterized as a nuisance. The interference must be intolerable to an ordinary person. This is assessed by considering factors such as the nature, severity and duration of the interference, the character of the neighbourhood, the sensitivity of the plaintiff's use and the utility of the activity. The interference must be substantial, which means that compensation will not be awarded for trivial annoyances.

In this case, the plaintiff lived in the community of Melanie Damishana. No description of the community was given e.g. whether it was residential, farming, industrial or mixed, though I gathered from the evidence that there were residences nearby. . . there is no evidence that the facility was unlawfully placed where it was located. Be that as it may, even it if had been proven that permission was sought from and granted by the local government authority, this would not mean as I said that the defendant would not be liable in nuisance once proven. Given my finding that based on the plaintiff's evidence he has proven that the generator did emit noise and that there was smoke from the exhaust of the generator which dirtied his curtains, the questions is – has the plaintiff proven that he suffered "sensible material damage" or "substantial annoyance"?...

And in Greenidge (supra) while it was agreed that it was not a defence for the defendant to say that it had obtained permission to erect and operate its power generation facility, it was found by the court that permission to operate a facility did not exempt the company from proceedings in nuisance and that "the law has always insisted that an owner of property cannot use his property unreasonably and it is an unreasonable use of property to cause substantial damage to another." . . . Further. . .

"The law of nuisance does not allow as a defence that the place is a convenient or suitable one for committing the nuisance of that the business or operations causing the nuisance is useful to persons generally in spite of the annoyance to the plaintiff. It is likewise no defence to say that the best known means have been taken to reduce or prevent the nuisance complained of or that the cause of the nuisance is the exercise of a business or trade in a reasonable and proper manner. Moreover, the fact

that an area is an industrial one does not rule out the possibility of an actionable nuisance on the ground of excessive noise."

In this case, the facility was used to provide telephone service to Melanie Damishana and the surrounding community. In the context of reasonableness of the defendant's conduct, there is no evidence to support a conclusion that by placing the facility in that particular location and by having an automatic generator to power it when there were power outages the defendant was acting unreasonably. This is not a case where the defendant was acting out of malice or spite, in which case nuisance would be actionable. And "some consideration [can] be given to the fact that the offensive enterprise is essential and unavoidable in the particular locality, like a coal mine, quarry or some public utility or service. . . While this latter sentence would be relevant to this case as the telephone service provide by the defendant to the community may be considered essential, in appropriate cases, despite the necessity of the conduct, the fact that conduct associated with a defendant's enterprise is so offensive as to cause proven substantial damage then the nuisance would be actionable and liability would follow.

In this case, however, at the end of the day what the plaintiff has actually proven is very limited; no serious material or substantial damage or substantial annoyance has been proven and I am constrained to hold that the plaintiff's case has to be dismissed.

(i) Air

Air pollution is an area where the remedy of nuisance has been pursued as evident in the case of ***Point Lisas Industrial Port Development Corporation Limited v. Arcelor Mittal Point Lisas Limited.***[117] In this case, it was claimed that Arcelor Mittal Point Lisas Limited, as the operator of an industrial plant producing iron and steel which included loading at its own port, of *inter alia*, Direct Reduced Iron which it produced for export, and the storage on site of a waste product – slag, in breach of its covenant in its tenancy agreement, caused a nuisance which affected the landlord and other tenants.

---

117 CV 2015- 00712

Rajkumar J

7. Whether the claimant has established that the defendant's operations produced effluent dust which was emitted to surrounding areas?

I find that it clearly has, repeatedly within the Limitation period, while its plants were in operation.

1. If so whether such effluent dust emissions (solid particles) in breach of covenant contravene the World Bank, (and therefore the World Health Organization's standards which it adopted), for operations of the iron and steel industry.

I find that since the Defendant's plant ceased operation it is not producing PM10 effluent emissions in breach of covenant. The defendant accepts that the Claimant has been able to establish, on a balance of probabilities, that the PM10 concentrations at three sites of the Defendant's premises, matching a Slag yard source, exceeded World Bank guidelines in 2012 and were therefore in breach of covenants 4(10) and 4(17) of the Deed of Lease. Given that on resumption of its operations there is real likelihood of a continuation of excessive emissions of visible dust, and the fact that while the defendant's plant was operating in 2012 there were occasions of excessive PM 10 concentrations detected in ambient air at its own sites, an injunction is necessary to restrain the possibility of emissions of either type of dust, PM10 dust or otherwise. With respect to the slag piles the evidence is that they currently are not a source of excessive P10 particulate emissions since the defendant's plants ceased operating.

1. Whether the Defendant was responsible for the production of effluent dust emissions which constitute or constituted a nuisance in breach of covenant which unduly interfered with the claimant in the comfortable and convenient enjoyment of its property and in particular its port, or unduly interfered with the claimant's tenants in the comfortable and convenient enjoyment of their property.

I find that it clearly was so responsible, repeatedly, within the Limitation period, while its plants were in operation. I find that this has been established sufficiently conclusively to justify the grant of an injunction to restrain any such future dust emissions.

1. Whether the Defendant was responsible for the production of effluent dust emissions which constitute or constituted a nuisance in breach of covenant which caused or contributed to damage to the claimant's equipment and machinery.

I find that a causal link has not been established on the expert scientific evidence between the damage and loss with respect to the claimant's equipment and machinery, and dust which has as its source the operations of the defendant, including its melt shop, its slag piles, or its loading operations.

1. Whether the claimant established its case on the pleadings that the defendant's operations produced DRI dust or particulate matter that: -

a. Constituted a nuisance generally, and / or

b. Caused damage to its equipment and machinery.

I find that the claimant has established that the defendant's operations produced DRI dust and particulate matter that constituted a nuisance generally to the Claimant and its tenants by unduly interfering with the claimant and its tenants in the comfortable and convenient enjoyment of property.

I do not find however that it has been established on the scientific evidence on a balance of probabilities that any damage to the claimant's equipment and machinery, even that caused by abrasion or corrosion, was attributable to dust having as its source any of the defendant's operations or loading processes.

The common law remedy of nuisance was also pursued in a case involving noxious fumes.

Stanley Ryan and Athena Ryan v Petroleum Company of Trinidad and Tobago Limited[118]

The appellants live at Hickling Village, Fyzabad. Across the road from their house is an abandoned oil well 'FZ 94'. This abandoned oil well is some forty yards away from their house and it sits on land under the control of the respondent. The appellants alleged that toxic emanations from this well and/ or its environs which are under the control of the respondent have caused them to suffer injury to their health and loss to the value of their property. The appellants

118 CA S-012 of 2011

sued the respondent for this injury and loss which they contended was caused by the negligence of the respondent. Further and/or alternatively the appellants contended that the abandoned oil well was the source of a nuisance for which the respondent was liable.

Smith JA (Majority Judgment)

55. The trial judge correctly accepted a quote from Clerk and Lindsell on Torts which reflects the law on a claim in respect of this type of nuisance, namely: 'A nuisance of this kind, to be actionable, must be such as to be a real interference with the comfort or convenience of living according to the standards of the average man'.

56. In this case the facts relied on to prove nuisance were the same facts relied on to prove negligence.

57. The trial judge relied on his earlier findings of fact to conclude that the appellants had failed to establish that the hydrocarbon emanations were sufficient to cause substantial discomfort or interference with the appellants' comfort. Hence the claim in nuisance failed. As I have indicated before, the appellants did establish that the hydrocarbon emissions were of such a nature as to cause substantial discomfort or interference with their health and comfort. Hence they are also entitled to succeed on the claim for nuisance.

The majority decision of the Court of Appeal of TT was overruled by the Privy Council in ***Petroleum Company of Trinidad and Tobago Limited v Stanley Ryan and Athena Ryan.***[119]

(ii) Noise and Vibration

As expected, the issue of noise dominates the legal landscape in the application of the common law remedy of nuisance. In ***Rasheed Ali v Super Industrial Services Limited and the Attorney General of Trinidad and Tobago***,[120] the Claimant's house was a two storey dwelling structure made of concrete. In or around the end of January 2004, the Defendant began rehabilitative road work. It was claimed that during the execution of the

---

119 2017 UKPC 30
120 CV 2006-02256.

road work, the Defendant caused or permitted such noise and vibrations to arise from their said works which in turn, created a nuisance for the Claimant.

Held: Rahim J

74. The relevant principles are set out in Clerk & Lindsell on Torts 19th edition paragraph 20-11 under the rubric standard of comfort as follows :

"A nuisance of this kind, to be actionable, must be such as to be a real interference with the comfort or convenience of living according to the standards of the average man. (An interference which alone causes harm to something of abnormal sensitiveness does not of itself constitute a nuisance. In practice the general application of the concepts of foreseeability and reasonable user may have rendered the notion of abnormal sensitivity less significant in modern law, although it is submitted that it remains useful as a guideline when applying those broad concepts in particular cases. ...When it is said that a householder is entitled to have the air in his house untainted and unpolluted by any acts of his neighbour, that means that he is entitled to have "not necessarily air as fresh, free and pure as at the time of building the plaintiff's house the atmosphere then was, but air not rendered to an important degree less compatible, or at least not rendered incompatible, with the physical comfort of human existence". Moreover, the discomfort must be substantial not merely with reference to the claimant; it must be of such a degree that it would be substantial to any person occupying the claimant's premises, irrespective of his position in life, age, or state of health; it must be "an inconvenience materially interfering with the ordinary comfort physically of human existence, not merely according to elegant or dainty modes and habits of living, but according to plain and sober and simple notions among the English people". ...It is not necessary to prove injury to health. Indeed, it seems that no regard should be had to the needs of insomniacs or invalids."

75. In this regard, the evidence from the Claimant and at least one of his supporting witnesses, Basdeo Bocal was that the vibrations caused by the piling were significant, resulting in the vibration of the entire house and the movement of furniture, wares, pictures and ornaments. There was also some breakage of glass as a consequence. Not only did this occur during the daytime but also during the night. According to Bocal, the piling went late into the night at times and it affected his ability to sleep. It is to be noted that the Claimant was in the later part of his years at the time. So that there was significant vibration from the planting of ninety beams over at least a five-day period according to the evidence of the defence witness Chatergoon.

76. This amounts, in the view of this court, to an inconvenience materially interfering with the ordinary physical comfort of human existence, not merely according to elegant or dainty modes and habits of living.

77. Further, this type of damage or result would certainly have been reasonably foreseeable by the Defendant having regard to all the circumstances in which this construction was taking place and the close proximity of the houses.

78 In the result the court finds that the Claimant is entitled to be compensated under the head of Nuisance for the excessive noise and vibration to his property.

(iii) Light

The common law remedy of nuisance has also been pursued in cases of interference with access to lights as in **Irma George v William Thomas and Claire Thomas**[121]

Facts: The Plaintiff seeks damages for obstructing the access of light to her premises situate at No. 169 Kitchener Avenue, Barataria (No. 169). She claims that between May 1989 and August 1990 the Defendant erected a wall on the western side of the Plaintiff's dwelling house thereby impeding the flow of light through the Plaintiff's windows. The Defendants deny the erection of a wall during the aforesaid period and maintain that the said wall was erected in 1974 with the Plaintiff's consent. The Defendants contend further that certain renovation works undertaken by the Plaintiff herself diminished the flow of light to her premises.

Held: Tiwary-Reddy J

27. The House of Lords considered the extent of the right to light acquired by the user in Colls v Home and Colonial Stores Ltd [1904] AC 179 and established the basic principle that the measure of light to which right is acquired, of which it has to be seen whether there is such diminution as to cause nuisance, is the light required for beneficial use of the building for any ordinary

---

121 HC 502 of 1994

purpose for which it is adapted. Per Lord Davey at page 204:

"According to both principle and authority, I am of the opinion that the own-er or occupier of the dominant tenement is entitled to the uninterrupted access through his ancient windows of a quantity of light, the measure of which is what is required for the ordinary purposes of inhabitancy or business of the tenement according to the ordinary notions of mankind, and that the question for what purpose he has thought fit to use the light or the mode in which he finds it convenient to arrange the internal structure of his tenement does not affect the question."

28. In Allen v Greenwood [1980] Ch. 119 at 134-135 Buckley L.J deduced from the decision in Colls v Home and Colonial Stores Ltd (supra) that:

"...the amount of light to which a dominant owner is entitled under a prescriptive claim is sufficient light, according to the ordinary notions, for the comfortable or beneficial use of the building in question, again according to the ordinary notions, for such purposes as would constitute normal uses of a building of its particular character. If the building be a dwelling house, the measure must be related to reasonable standards of comfort as a dwelling house. If it be a warehouse, a shop or a factory, the measure must be related to reasonable standards of comfort or beneficial use (for comfort may not be the most appropriate test in the case of such a building) as a warehouse, a shop or a factory as the case may be."

29. The decision in Colls v Home and Colonial Stores Ltd (supra) further made it clear that the nature and extent of the prescriptive right to light acquired by user was not altered by the Prescription Act 1832, (identical to the Prescription Ordinance Chap. 5 No. 8) which was only concerned with the conditions or length of user. At page 183 Lord Halsbury L.C stated:

"The statute literally construed by the use of the words 'the light' would mean all the light which for twenty years has existed in the surroundings of the ten-ement which has enjoyed it; yet, singularly enough there has been a complete uniformity of decision upon the construction of the statute that it has made no difference in the right conferred, but is only concerned with the mode of proof; ...

30. The learned authors of Unlawful Interference With Land: Elvin & Karas (2002) at paragraph 2-117 page 241 stated that a right to light is not lost by the rebuilding or structural alteration of the dominant building. However, an alteration in the dominant building cannot increase the burden upon the servient land and the right of the dominant owner to light will be determined by reference to his entitlement as if the dominant building had been left unaltered, unless a prescriptive right is claimed in respect of the dominant building in its altered state.

31. In Ankerson v Connelly [1907] 1 Ch. D 678, the Defendants pulled down their building No. 172 and rebuilt upon the site and some adjoining land a much larger building. The Defendant attempted to preserve his ancient lights but he raised the east wall between the yard and the plaintiff's land and left in it a small window to the shed and two other apertures to give light to the yard and indirectly the windows. The yard, however, was otherwise entirely covered in a structure of some kind being built over it so that all the light was shut out from the ground floor windows except what passed through these apertures in the east wall. In May 1905 the Plaintiff placed hoardings 8 feet high on their own land, which prevented any access to light to the small window and the other two apertures in the new wall. The defendant removed the plaintiff's hoardings and the plaintiff sought a declaration that the defendant was not entitled to any easement over the plaintiff's land for light and air in respect of any of the windows or openings or otherwise.

32. At first instance Warrington J gave judgment for the plaintiffs. He held that the defendant had increased the burden on the plaintiff's land, but that he no longer had any right, which could be enforced, and consequently the plaintiffs were entitled to the declaration they claimed. On Appeal Cozens-Hardy M.R. held, affirming the judgment of the lower court, that:

"I think the learned judge was right in saying that what the defendant had done had substantially destroyed all the lights in the house so that it was a case of de minimis which was left. The mere fact that there might be a little trace of light coming through the portion of the old openings was not of such a nature as to entitle the defendant to an injunction.

33. In News of The World Limited v Allen Fairhead and Sons Limited [1931] 2 Ch. D 402, the court held that an owner of ancient light cannot so diminish his ancient light area as to increase the burden on the servient tenement. At pages 406

— 7 Farewell J said:

"If the plaintiff pulls down the building with ancient light windows and erects a new building totally different in every respect, but having windows to some extent in the same position as the old windows, he cannot require the servient owners to do more than see that the ancient lights, if any, to which he is still entitled are not obstructed to the point of nuisance."

34. In H.C.A. No.14 of 1992 *Zorina Garib and Sobaida Singh v Len Seepaulsingh (Garib)* the Plaintiffs were leasehold owners of premises situated at 149 Western Main Road, St. James, which they purchased in 1973. They lived in the upper storey of the premises and let the ground floor for commercial purposes. The Defendants resided next door at 151 Western Main Road. The Plaintiffs claimed that in 1992 the Defendants completed the extension of their building by two storeys and substantially diminished the Plaintiffs' access to light and ventilation.

35. For three apertures on the western wall of the upper storey of 149, requiring the Plaintiff to use artificial lighting throughout the day. The Plaintiff claimed an entitlement to the use of light and air pursuant to section 3 of the Prescription Ordinance Chap 5 No. 8. Warner J held that the evidence revealed the Plaintiff's culpability in the reduction of light to their own premises as a consequence of previous alterations to 149. She said at page 10:

"Although the owner of a dominant tenement does not lose or restrict his right to light by non-user, or by not using the full measure of light which the law permits, in my view, the fact that the plaintiff has tinted the windows, blocked up the decorative bricks with sheets of ply-board and installed an air conditioning unit thereby increasing the burden on the servient tenement must be relevant in determining whether she has proved an obstruction, amounting to an actionable nuisance. …It therefore seems clear to me that if the plaintiffs are complaining that the quantity of light which comes to the windows of their dwelling house has been diminished, some indication as to whether living has been made less comfortable must be determined by examining what they have voluntarily done to the property- by their deliberate acts they have excluded light and air."

36. In the instant case the dominant tenement has increased the burden on the

servient tenement by undertaking substantial renovations to No. 169. These included the addition of two bedrooms, one of which was constructed next to the original bedroom used as a sewing room. Further the Plaintiff subsequently constructed a covered walkway, which extended the Plaintiff's roof on the western side up to the Defendants' wall. The Plaintiff admitted that the two pieces of galvanize which she had erected on her side of the Defendants' raised wall, reached the height of the Defendants' card-cutting room.

37. From the foregoing authorities it is clear that while a right to light is not lost by the rebuilding or structural alteration of the dominant building, such changes cannot increase the burden on the servient owner. The right of the Plaintiff to light will be determined by reference to her entitlement as if the dominant building had been left unaltered from 1972.

38. Once it has been established that the dominant owner has a right to light the question is whether the interference with that right is so substantial as to amount to a nuisance. In Colls v Home and Colonial Stores Limited (supra) Lord Lindley noted at page 210:

"But the question to be decided is not how much light is left, but whether the plaintiff has been deprived of so much as to constitute an actionable nuisance."

And at page 186 Lord McNaughten said:

" 'It is not sufficient' as Lord Hardwicke observed in Fishmongers' Co. v East India Co. 'to say it will alter the plaintiff's lights ...The law says it must be so near as to be a nuisance.'

Further, at page 187 Lord McNaughten approved as the test the jury direction of Chief Justice Best in the case of Back v Stacey (1862) 2 C. & P 465:

"Chief Justice Best told the jury, who had viewed the premises that they were to judge rather from their own ocular observation than from the testimony of any witnesses, however respectable, of the degree of diminution which the plaintiff's ancient lights had undergone. It was not sufficient to constitute illegal obstruction, that the plaintiff had, in fact, less light than before; nor that his warehouse, the part of his house principally affected, could not be used

for all the purposes to which it might otherwise have been applied. In order to give a right of action, and sustain the issue, there must be a substantial privation of light, sufficient to render the occupation of the house uncomfortable, and to prevent the plaintiff from carrying on his accustomed business (that of a grocer) on the premises as beneficially as he had formerly done. His Lordship added that it might be difficult to draw the line, but the jury must distinguish between a partial inconvenience and a real injury to the plaintiff in the enjoyment of the premises."

In Garib (Supra) Warner J applying Colls v Home and Colonial Stores Limited (Supra) said at page 8:

"Does the interference amount to an actionable nuisance? In other words, there must be substantial interference with the plaintiffs' use and comfortable enjoyment of their premises according to the usages of ordinary persons in the locality of Western Main Road St. James, in the City of Port of Spain."

39. In the instant case, the Plaintiff and her witnesses testified that the Defendants' raised wall ultimately caused the Plaintiff's sewing room to further darken and it became hot. The Plaintiff consequently reduced sewing in the room. In Colls v Home and Colonial Stores Limited (supra) Lord McNaughten, adopting the test in Fishmongers' Co. v East India Co, cautioned that in determining whether the interference constitutes a nuisance the court must distinguish "between a partial inconvenience and a real injury to the plaintiff in the enjoyment of the premises." In Garib (supra) Warner J. held that the extent to which the plaintiff's own actions diminished light to their premises was relevant in establishing nuisance.

40. It is submitted therefore that in the circumstances of the case, the Plaintiff has failed to show an obstruction of light by the Defendants amounting to an actionable nuisance.

Relationship Between Breach of Environmental Management Act and Common Law Principle of Nuisance

If there is a breach of an environmental requirement under the *Environmental Management Act*, an aggrieved party can proceed by means of direct private party action under *Section 69 of the Environmental Management Act* to enforce the *Environmental Management Act* and its subsidiary legislation. However, where the breach of an environmental requirement is attached to a common law claim of nuisance, then an aggrieved party can pursue a claim for nuisance at the Supreme Court without getting entangled in an issue of jurisdiction with the Environmental Commission. This is due in part to the non-abolition of the common law remedy of nuisance with the enactment of the *Environmental Management Act* and the limitations of available remedies as seen in Chapter 10 dealing with the Environmental Commission.

Ahmad Mohammed and others v Ameer Mohammed and AM-COWELD Engineering Services Limited[122]

Facts: The claimants have brought a claim in private nuisance against the defendants Ameer Mohammed and his limited liability company, AMCOWELD Engineering Services Limited. The claimants are owners of several parcels of land that form part of a neighbourhood that they informally call "Ali Rahaman Road". The neighbourhood is situated off Calcutta No. 2 Main Road in Freeport. All the lots in the neighbourhood form part of two larger parcels of land out of which they were created. The developer of this neighbourhood, Mr Ali Mohammed Rahaman, is the second claimant. He is the grandfather of the first defendant. The road leading into the neighbourhood off Calcutta No. 2 Main Road is named after him, and, it seems, the neighbourhood takes its name from the name of the road. The claimants either own land or have constructed dwelling houses in the neighbourhood, and in particular, on Ali Rahaman Road itself. The parties in this action are all related. The second defendant, a limited liability company, is owned and operated by the first defendant. The nub of the claim is that the defendants' use of their property for industrial activities creates disturbance and discomfort for the claimants that amount to nuisance. The claimants are seeking: (a) a declaration that the defendants by themselves, their servants and/ or workmen or otherwise howsoever are not entitled to use or permit or invite any persons to use Ali Rahaman Road otherwise than for the passage of light motor vehicles to get to their dwelling house; (b) an injunction restraining the defendants whether by themselves, their servants and or agents and or workmen from using Ali Rahaman Road otherwise than for the passage of light motor vehicles to get to their dwelling house; (c) an injunction restraining the

---

122 CV 2008-01297.

defendants from continuing their acts of nuisance against the claimant; and (d) damages and costs.

Held: *Aboud J*

5. Sometime in June 2007 the first defendant, although he had no approval for an industrial building, was granted a Certificate of Environmental Clearance by the Environmental Management Authority. The CEC required that the defendants consult with and seek the approval of the Couva/Tabaquite/Talparo Regional Corporation with regard to the establishment and design of an approved access road to the defendants' parcel of land via Ramkalia Road. Ramkalia Road adjoins the second defendant's premises in the neighbourhood. The second defendant is said to have breached the CEC since it has failed to consult with and seek the approval for the alternate access road. The defendants use the Ali Rahaman Road as a private road for the commercial purposes of their business. As a result, since April 2006 the claimants say they have experienced considerable inconvenience, loss and damage by the passage of the defendants' equipment and the activities being carried out.

7. From and since April 2006 the defendants are alleged to have wrongfully caused the emission, from their heavy vehicles and equipment, quantities of noxious smoke, fumes, vapours and gases which spread and diffuse themselves into and upon the dwelling house and property of the claimants and pollute the air. Prior to and after the issuance of the CEC, and in breach of it, the defendants openly carry on sandblasting activities contiguous to and upwind of the dwelling houses and property of the claimants.

8. The defendants are also alleged to carry on spray painting activities outside of the spray painting room as a result of which spray painting emissions spread and diffuse themselves into and over and upon the claimants' dwelling houses and property. The claimants' say that their dwelling houses and property have been rendered unhealthy and uncomfortable to live in and that they and their families have suffered great discomfort, inconvenience, disturbance and upset and have suffered loss and damage.

9. It is alleged that the defendants are in breach of the CEC having failed to enclose and utilise sound and noise reducing apparatus in all their noise generating equipment. They have also failed to ensure that cleared areas and stockpiled areas are watered regularly at least three times per day so as to alleviate the impact of dust on the air quality and public health of the claimants.

10. The activities of the defendants are said to gravely affect the claimants' health and enjoyment of their premises and unless restrained by an injunction the defendants will continue to and threaten to continue their acts of nuisance against the claimants.

27. According to Clerk and Lindell on Torts, 20th Ed., a private nuisance may be and usually is caused by a person doing, on his own land, something which he is lawfully entitled to do. His conduct only becomes a nuisance when the consequences of his acts are not confined to his own land but extend to the land of his neighbour by:

1) Causing an encroachment on his neighbour's land, when it closely resembles trespass;

2) Causing physical damage to his neighbour's land or building or works or vegetation upon it; or

3) Unduly interfering with his neighbour in the comfortable and convenient enjoyment of his land.

28. The case before me falls into the third category of nuisance. This form of nuisance involves interference with the enjoyment of land. The authors describe this category as, "the personal inconvenience and interference with one's enjoyment, one's quiet, one's personal freedom, anything that discomposes or injuriously affects the senses or the nerves."

29. The authors of Winfield and Jolowicz on Tort, 18th ed. have written:

"Generally the essence of a nuisance is a state of affairs that is either continuous or recurrent, a condition or activity which unduly interferes with the use or enjoyment of land. It is not necessary that there be any physical emanation from the defendant's premises. Noises and smells can be nuisances, but so, it seems can be otherwise inoffensive businesses. The mere presence of a business is not, however, a nuisance. Not every slight annoyance is actionable. Stenches, smoke, the escape of effluent and a multitude of different things may amount to a nuisance in fact but whether they constitute an actionable nuisance

will depend on a variety of considerations, especially the character of the defendant's conduct, and a balancing of conflicting interests."

30. As mentioned earlier there is no absolute standard to be applied. It is always a question of degree whether the interference with comfort or convenience is sufficiently serious to constitute a nuisance. The acts complained of as constituting the nuisance, such as noises, smells or vibration, will usually be lawful acts which only become wrongful from the circumstances under which they are performed, such as time, place, extent or the manner of performance. The ordinary domestic use of premises cannot therefore constitute a nuisance, even though interference with the enjoyment of neighbouring premises is caused, if that interference results solely from construction defects for which the defendant is not responsible. It is the responsibility of the court to strike a balance between the right of the defendant to use his property for his own lawful enjoyment and the right of the claimant to the undisturbed enjoyment of his property.

31. In determining whether an act constitutes a nuisance the circumstances of the case ought to be considered. This would include the time of the commission of the acts complained of, the place of its commission, the manner of committing it and the effects of its commission. The authors of Clerk and Lindell, supra, at para 20-11, p. 280 say:

"The discomfort must be substantial not merely with reference to the claimant; it must be of such a degree that it would be substantial to any person occupying the claimant's premises, irrespective of his position in life, age or state of health; it must be an inconvenience materially interfering with the ordinary comfort, physically, of human existence, not merely according to elegant or dainty modes and habits of living, but according to plain and sober and simple notions among the English people."

32. The character of the neighbourhood is vital in considering the standard of comfort or convenience or living of the average man. In the landmark case of Sturges v Bridgman (1879) LR 11 Ch. D 852 Thesiger LJ reasoned that what constitutes reasonable use of one's property depends on the character of the locality and that it is no defence that the plaintiff came to the locality and met the nuisance. If the locality has been traditionally used for a particular purpose not amounting to public nuisance, then an action in private nuisance would likely fail. Thesiger LJ said: "Whether anything is a nuisance or not is a question to be determined, not merely by an abstract consideration of the thing itself, but by reference to its circumstances; what would be a nuisance in Belgrave Square would not necessarily be so in Bermondsley; and where a locality is devoted to a particular trade or manufacture carried on by the traders or manufacturers in a particular and established manner not constituting a public nuisance, Judges and juries would be justified in finding, and may be trusted to find, that the trade or manufacture so carried on in that locality is not a private or actionable wrong."

33. The cases of Wood v Conway Corporation (1914) 2 CH 47 and Halsey v Esso Petroleum Co Ltd (1961) 2 ALL ER 145 are instructive on the issue of actionable nuisance.

a. *Wood v Conway Corporation: The English Court of Appeal upheld the High Court's decision restraining the defendants from carrying on works because it amounted to a nuisance. The defendants were owners of a gasworks undertaking for the supply of gas. In 1912, the defendant extended its operations. The defendant, in execution of its statutory powers, discharged noxious fumes and smells over the plaintiff's land. The plaintiff applied to the court for an injunction to restrain the defendants from carrying on or permitting to be carried on upon their gasworks the business or undertaking of manufacturers of gas so as or in such a manner as by the discharge of noxious or offensive fumes or vapours to cause a nuisance or injury to the plaintiff's property or to the plaintiff or his family. The court agreed that the gasworks discharged over the plaintiff's property caused a serious, growing and permanent injury to the plaintiff's premises; that the injury being of a continuous nature it was impossible to measure the damage thereby occasioned with any certainty; and the plaintiff was therefore entitled to the injunction he asked for.*

b. *Halsey v Esso Petroleum Co Ltd: the plaintiff occupied a house in an area zoned for residential purposes. The defendant operated an oil distributing depot at adjoining premises which were situated in an area zoned for industrial purposes. The defendants' depot dealt with fuel oil in its light, medium and heavy grades, the oil being pumped from river tankers on to the depot and from the depot into road tankers. The plaintiff complained that the defendant's chimneys emitted acid* *smuts containing sulphate which damaged the paint work of his car and his clothes when he hung them out to dry. The depot emitted a pungent and nauseating smell which went beyond a background smell and was more than would affect a sensitive person, but the plaintiff had not suffered any injury to health from the smell. During the night there was noise from the boilers which at its peak caused windows and doors in the plaintiff's house to vibrate and prevented the plaintiff from sleeping. The defendants had attempted to reduce this noise by soundproofing the walls of the boiler house but it remained and it was more than trivial. Further during the night shift from 10:00 pm to 6:00am there was noise from road tankers which arrived and left the depot at points close to the plaintiff's house. The noise from the tankers was made partly on the public highway and partly in the depot itself. The court found that the defendants were liable to the plaintiff for*

(1) emission of acid smuts, (ii) in respect of nuisance by smell because the smell emanating from the defendant's premises amounted to a private nuisance, notwithstanding that there was no proof of injury to the plaintiff's health, for injury to health was not a necessary ingredient in the cause of action for nuisance by smell, (iii) in respect of private nuisance by noise from boilers and the road tankers when in the depot, in either instance at night, because the noise was an inconvenience which materially interfered with the ordinary physical comfort of human existence according to plain, sober and simple notions among ordinary people, such as the plaintiff living in that particular part of Fulham, (iv) for the noise from road tankers at night on the public highway (a) as a public nuisance since the concentration of moving vehicles in a small area of the public highway caused special damage to the plaintiff whom it affected more than the ordinary members of the public (b) as a private nuisance, since the noise was directly related to the operation of the depot and it was not a prerequisite of private nuisance that the matter complained of emanated from the defendant's land so long as it affected the plaintiff's property and in the present case the noise from the highway materially interfered with the plaintiff's enjoyment of his house.

34. As pointed out earlier, this is a case of nuisance whereby one party is alleged to be unduly interfering with the comfortable and convenient enjoyment of his neighbour's land. The claimants have presented that the defendants engage in the following activities:

1) Industrial activities on the defendants' land along Ali Rahaman Road;

2) The passage and re-passage of heavy vehicles and equipment which generate noise, noxious fumes, vibration and cause damage to Ali Rahaman Road and discomfort to the home owners.

3) The obstruction of Ali Rahaman Road by the parking of heavy trucks and equipment and the cars of employees and customers

These activities were said to have interfered with the claimants' use and enjoyment of the land in the following ways:

a) These activities emitted offensive, noxious smoke, fumes, vapours and gases which polluted the air. They also produced noxious, dirty or sooty matter which spread and diffused itself over the dwelling houses and lands of the claimants;

b) They caused excessive noise from the said activities which were made by the cranes, trucks, forklifts, welding plants, generators and compressors which were used for steel fabrication and for spray painting;

c) They produced intensive lighting which was maintained by the defendants on their premises during the nights. This resulted in the surrounding areas of the claimants' homes to be brightly lit which adversely affected their sleep, studies and family life.

35. The defendants have not disputed that they are conducting industrial activities on their lands along Ali Rahaman Road. The cross examination of the first defendant and his witnesses proves that the defendants have established an industrial business and, save for sandblasting (which was halted as a result of the 2009 consent order), do in fact conduct the activities complained of. I cannot agree with the proposition that, because it does not emanate from the defendants' land, the nuisance created by the passage and re-passage of heavy vehicles and equipment along the Ali Rahaman Road cannot in law be attributed to them. In Halsey v Esso Petroleum Co Ltd, supra, the court found that the noise generated by trucks as they entered and left a depot amounted to a nuisance, even when the trucks were driving along a nearby public road. Knight Bruce VC quoted Devlin J in the case of Southport Corporation v Esso Petroleum Co [1954] EWCA Civ 5:

"It is clear that to give a cause of action for private nuisance the matter complained of must affect the property of the plaintiffs. But I know of no

principle that it must emanate from the land belonging to the defendant...I can see no reason why, if land or water belonging to the public or waste land is misused by the defendant, or if the defendant as a licensee or trespasser misuses someone else's land, he should not be liable for nuisance in the same way as an adjoining occupier would be."

36. *The claimants' evidence of noise and vibrations generated by the defendants' on their lands along Ali Rahaman Road and in the passage and re-passage of their vehicles over the said road, supports a finding by this court of an actionable nuisance. Before the first defendant built Shed No. 1 in 2001 for welding, fabrication and automotive repairs, he obtained no approval. The first defendant in cross examination indicated that he was aware that he needed to apply to the TCP for permission to change the use of land from residential/ agricultural to commercial/industrial. It seems to me that he knew that his conduct would lead to the discomfort of his neighbours and he was also aware, despite his evidence on this point (which I did not consider credible), that he needed planning permission for a change of use from the TCP.*

37. *The defendants' witness, Farisha Mohammed, conceded that, save for sandblasting, the impugned activities are carried out on the site. She further admitted in cross examination that in welding a grinding machine is used and in steel fabricating the metal must be knocked. The second defendant is a company involved in substantial industrial activities and large scale projects. The noise (grinding and knocking of metal) and fumes (whether generated by the spray painting or the repair of vehicles, or the operation of generators) is continuous and more than barely tolerable. I accept the evidence of the claimants' witnesses on this point.*

38. *The claimants have given evidence that the vibrations, noises and noxious fumes have adversely affected their use and enjoyment of their property, both inside and out. I accept the evidence of their discomfort and do not require their evidence to be corroborated by an expert's report. The activities have not been denied. It is self- evident that heavy vehicles and equipment will generate fumes and that welding and steel fabrication will generate noise, especially when the proximity of the activities to the claimants' home is taken into account. Even if it was not self-evident I would still have believed the claimants' witnesses. They provided direct testimony of the injurious extent of the noise and*

fumes. The evidence of the claimants' witnesses was convincing, credible and was not disturbed in cross-examination. I do not feel any assurance that the report obtained by the defendants (which suggests that the noise level is tolerable) is a sufficient ground, by itself, to disbelieve the claimants' sworn testimony. The writers of the report were not summoned by the defendants and questions have arisen (in the very report relied upon by the defendants) as to whether the equipment was operational when they visited.

40. I have addressed my mind to the time the acts complained of are committed, the locality of its commission, the manner in which it is committed and the effects on the claimants. I believe that to carry on such activities in the neighbourhood along Ali Rahaman Road clearly amounts to a nuisance. They amount to a substantial interference with the claimants' rights. This is an interference that would be injurious to any citizen of Trinidad and Tobago, living in such a neighbourhood, and the court has been careful to apply plain and sober standards in assessing the quality of the injury. Following Halsey v Esso Petroleum Co. Ltd I have accepted the claimant's evidence of noxious fumes without the need for medical reports.

Possession of a CEC is not a defence to a claim in nuisance as the common law remedy exists despite a party acting pursuant to a CEC.

Venture Production (Trinidad) Limited v Atlantic LNG Company of Trinidad and Tobago[123]

Facts: Venture Productions (Trinidad) Ltd is the owner of seabed mining rights over two blocks in the Gulf of Paria known as Guapo Bay/Brighton and Point Ligoure. Atlantic LNG Company of Trinidad and Tobago operates a liquefied natural gas (LNG) facility at Point Fortin. Atlantic is expanding its facility. It is building an additional jetty and loading facility for tankers. This requires dredging in the area of the seabed near to the new jetty. The dredged material also has to be disposed of. The dredging is in an area adjacent to the Point Ligoure block and the dredged material is being dumped in the Brighton Block. Atlantic has been given official permission to do this. Venture fears that the dredging operations will cause increased siltation at Point Ligoure, which will make the finding and exploitation of oil and natural gas reserves more difficult. It also

---

123 HCA No. 1947 of 2003

fears that dumping of dredged material at Brighton will endanger its existing wells, platforms and pipelines and make future oil and gas recovery economically unfeasible. Not surprisingly, conflict has arisen as both parties seek to assert their 'rights'. Venture now seeks injunctive relief to:

(i) Stop the dumping on the Brighton block;

(ii) Stop the dredging; or alternatively

(iii) Prohibit dredging and/or dumping in a manner that will cause a nuisance to its operations or interfere with its rights in the Brighton and Point Ligoure blocks.

Held: Archie J

33. The EMA does not own the Brighton block. It cannot permit activity thereon that is specifically prohibited. The fact that the EMA went ahead and granted the CEC in the terms that it did gives me little assurance that the impact on Venture's operations was given full consideration. That does not appear to have been the EMA's focus (To be fair to the EMA, when Venture made its comments on the EIA, it focused on Point Ligoure and only one paragraph addressed the proposed dumping at Guapo)

60. An injunction is hereby granted restraining the Defendant whether by itself, its servants or agents from performing any dumping operations within the plaintiffs Licensed Areas in the Guapo Bay/Brighton Marine Block comprising all those submarine areas containing approximately 6450 hectares the boundaries of which are set out in paragraph 1 of the summons herein.

It is clear that the *Environmental Management Act* did not curb the common law remedy of nuisance and so, possession of a permit, licence or approval by the EMA cannot act as a defence to an action founded on nuisance. Indeed *Rule 27 of the Noise Pollution Rules* states clearly:

Nothing in these Rules affects the operation of— (b) the common law regarding nuisance.

Use of Environmental Management Act Standards in Nuisance

An interesting development in the Court is the willingness to use standards set under the *Environmental Management Act* as a source of evidence to substantiate a claim for nuisance.

Ramdeo Seewah v Vishnu Siewah[124]

Facts: The Claimant, Ramdeo Seewah is the owner and occupier of a parcel of land situate at No. 37 Knaggs Street, Frederick Settlement, Caroni, in the Island of Trinidad. The Defendant is the owner and occupier of a parcel of land at No. 35 Knaggs Street, Frederick Settlement, Caroni. The Claimant and the Defendant are adjoining land owners/occupiers and the Defendant's premises abut the Claimant's premises. The Claimant claims against the Defendant with respect to damages for nuisance occasioned by excessive noise, noxious fumes and vibrations coming from the Defendant's premises situate at No. 35 Knaggs Street, Frederick Settlement, Caroni, by virtue of the manner of the use and operations of the aluminium pot smelting business of the Defendant at the said address which said excessive noise, noxious fumes and vibrations have come unto and about the Claimant's adjoining lands and buildings situate at No. 37 Knaggs Street, Frederick Settlement, Caroni.

Held: Rajkumar J

43. A private nuisance may be and usually is caused by a person doing, on his own land, something which he is lawfully entitled to do. His conduct only becomes a nuisance when the consequences of his act are not confined to his own land but extend to the land of his neighbour by:

(1) causing an encroachment on his neighbour's land, when it closely resembles trespass;

(2) causing physical damage to his neighbour's land or building or works or vegetation upon it; or

(3) unduly interfering with his neighbour in the comfortable and convenient enjoyment of his land.

---

124 CV 2009-2498.

44. It may be a nuisance when a person does something on his own property which interferes with his neighbour's ability to enjoy his property by putting it to profitable use: Clerk & Lindsell on Torts, 19th Ed, Paragraph 20-06.

Nuisance ....causing an interference with enjoyment of land, are, for example creating stenches by the carrying on of an offensive manufacture or otherwise, causing smoke or noxious fumes to pass on to the claimant's property, raising clouds of coal dust, making unreasonable noises, or vibration, using a building as a hospital for infectious diseases...: paragraph 20-09. No precise or universal formula is possible, but a useful test is what is reasonable according to ordinary usages of mankind living in a particular society.

45. Whether such an act does constitute a nuisance must be determined not merely by an abstract consideration of the act itself, but by reference to all the circumstances of the particular case, including, for example, the time of the commission of the act complained of; the place of its commission; the manner of committing it, that is, whether it is done wantonly or in the reasonable exercise of rights; and the effect of its commission, that is, whether those effects are transitory or permanent, occasional or continuous; so that the question of nuisance or no nuisance is one of fact: paragraph 20-10.

46. A nuisance of this kind, to be actionable, must be such as to be a real interference with the comfort or convenience of living according to the standards of the average man. An interference which alone causes harm to something of abnormal sensitiveness does not of itself constitute a nuisance. A man cannot increase the liabilities of his neighbour by applying his own property to special uses, whether for business or pleasure: paragraph 20-11

47. Private Nuisance is defined in Howard v Walker [1] by Lord Goddard as "an unlawful interference with a person's use or enjoyment of land, or some right over, or in connection with it".

Extent of the harm and the nature of the locality- This factor can be summarized in the words of Thesiger L.J in Sturges v Bridgeman (1879) L.R 11 Ch. 852 at 865, as follows - "what would be a nuisance in Belgrave Square would not necessarily be so in Bermondsey"

48. In the circumstances I find that the complaints have not been established on the evidence i. With respect to heat

ii. With respect to air quality – particulate matter

iii. With respect to noxious fumes

iv. With respect to Explosions.

49. With respect to noise I find that the complaint has been established on the evidence of the Claimant to the extent corroborated by the independent expert. I find that evidence of noncompliance with the standards set out in the noise pollution rules can be an important ingredient in determining whether a case of common law nuisance has been made out, although the common law of nuisance, and in particular, nuisance by noise, has not been eliminated or superseded by the standards set out in the Environmental Management Act. Apart from the fact that the prescribed standard has been exceeded I note that the expert's measurements demonstrate peaks of sound in excess of the background sound level, attributable to the defendant's operations, corroborating the claimant's complaint of noise nuisance at common law.

50. I find that scientific measurement of the noise levels prevailing at Mr. See-wah's home has confirmed his account of noise exceeding background levels that affects his use and enjoyment of his home, beyond the times attested to by the defendant. The defendant's light industrial/manufacturing activities are responsible for producing that noise. I do not believe that those activities are confined to the time periods attested to by the defendant. In any event I am persuaded he should, at the very least, be confined to those periods that he has attested to.

It is therefore ordered as follows: -

51. An injunction is granted restraining the Defendant, by himself his servants or agents from carrying out the following acts or any of them other than on Monday to Friday between the hours of 9:00 a.m. to 2:00 p.m. that is to say: -

Carrying out or permitting to be carried out upon those premises known as No. 35 Knaggs Street, Frederick Settlement, Caroni, in the island of Trinidad the business and activity of the melting of aluminium and in particular, the operation of the gas furnace thereon, and the conducting of that activity in such a manner as to permit or cause excessive noise, so as to cause a nuisance or injury to the Claim-

ant residing at No. 37 Knaggs Street, Frederick Settlement, Caroni, in the island of Trinidad. An injunction is granted restraining the Defendant, by himself his servants or agents from carrying out the following acts or any of them other than on Wednesdays between the hours of 11.30 a.m. to 2:00 p.m., namely the carrying out or permitting to be carried out upon those premises known as No. 35 Knaggs Street, Frederick Settlement, Caroni, in the island of Trinidad the business and activity of the grinding of aluminium pots.

Use of Environmental Management Act Civil Remedies in Nuisance

The High Court of TT has accepted that in an action for nuisance, there is no jurisdiction vested in the Supreme Court to utilise remedies provided for in the *Environmental Management Act*. Such remedies are only available to the Environmental Commission as also discussed in Chapter 10.

Karan Ramlal v Simon Maccoon[125]

Facts: Plaintiff's claim by writ in the High Court of Justice for, inter alia, damages for nuisance by noise caused by the playing of loud music pursuant to Section 66 of the Environmental Management Act ("the Act").

Held: Master Doyle

In summary, the plaintiff herein issued proceedings in the High Court of Justice on 22 October 2004 darning reliefs both within and outwit the jurisdiction of the High Court, obtained leave for a judge on 4th May 2005 to withdraw the claims within the jurisdiction of the High Court (save costs) and a purported default judgment for relief outwit the High Court's jurisdiction i.e. a proposed administrative civil assessment under Section 66 of the Act. In the premises this Court held that the High Court of Justice has no jurisdiction under the Environmental Management Act, 2000 and the Order for an assessment to be a nullity.

STATUTORY PRIVATE ACTION

Citizen suits are court proceedings brought by citizens who seek to enforce public rights. In the environmental arena, there are cases brought to enforce the rights or obligations created by environmental laws. These are

---

125 HCA No. 2812 of 2004

civil as opposed to criminal cases.[126]

Used effectively, citizen suits can foster concrete results and public benefits when governmental action is simply not working. As stated by the Sixth Circuit in the case of **Sierra Club v. Board of County Commissioners of Hamilton County, Ohio,** [127] *"...private citizens provide a second level of enforcement and can serve as a check to ensure the state and federal governments are diligent in prosecuting Clean Water Act violations."* In TT the equivalent of citizen suits is statutorily defined as direct private party action, as seen in *Section 69 of the Environmental Management Act.*

69 (1) Any private party may institute a civil action in the Commission against any other person for a claimed violation of any of the specified environmental requirements identified in section 62, other than paragraphs (c), (d) and (l), save where— (a) the complainant has given written notice of such claimed violation to the Managing Director of the Authority at least sixty days prior to the commencement of the civil action; (b) the complainant has served a copy of the complaint on the Managing Director within twenty-eight days of the date on which the complainant was first authorized to bring such an action. (c) the Authority has not commenced an enforcement action under sections 63 to 67 inclusive or through other appropriate means available to it under section 68 regarding such claimed violation; and (d) the Authority has not elected to assume responsibility for taking enforcement action under sections 63 to 68 inclusive within sixty days after the filing of a direct private party action by the complainant.

(2) For purposes of this section, any individual or group of individuals expressing a general interest in the environment or a specific concern with respect to the claimed violation shall be deemed to have standing to bring a direct private party action.

(3) In any such action under this section, the Authority or the Attorney General

---

126 David Mossop, *Citizen Suits ¾ Tools For Improving Compliance With Environmental Laws* <http://citeseerx.ist.psu.edu/viewdoc/download?doi=10.1.1.519.8696&rep= rep1&-type=pdf>

127 *Sierra Club v. Board of County Commissioners of Hamilton County, Ohio,* 2005 WL 2033708, at 15 (S.D. Ohio)(attached), affirmed, 504 F.3d 634 (6th Cir. 2007) http://www.environlaw.com/pdf/citizen_suits.pdf

may intervene at any time as a matter of right.

(4) This section shall come into force and effect on a date to be fixed by the President.

It is important to note that direct private action is limited to the breach of environmental requirements as stipulated in *Section 62 of the Environmental Management Act* [other than the environmental requirements contained in paragraphs (c), (d) and (l)] .

> *62. For the purposes of this Part and Part VIII, "environmental requirement" means the requirement upon a person to— (a) comply with the procedures for the registration of sources from which pollutants may be released into the environment; (b) comply with the procedures and standards with respect to permits or licenses required for any person to install or operate any process or source from which pollutants will be or may continue to be released into the environment; (c) provide in a timely manner complete and accurate information in any required submission to or communication with the Authority or in response to any inspection or request for information by the Authority; (d) refrain from any unauthorized activities impacting on the environment in an "environmentally sensitive area" or with respect to an "environmentally sensitive species"; (e) comply with the performance standards, procedures, licensing or permitting requirements established for the handling of hazardous substances; (f) apply for and obtain a Certificate of Environmental Clearance; (g) comply with the conditions and mitigation measures in any such certificate; Environmental requirements; (h) comply with the procedures and standards with respect to the periodic or continual monitoring of pollution or releases of pollutants or conditions required under a permit or license; (i) provide timely and accurate notification with respect to an accidental or unauthorized release of a pollutant or other incident with respect to a hazardous substance; (j) control the release of pollutants in such a manner as to comply with any permit or license granted under section 50(1), 53(1), 57(1) or 60(1); (k) submit timely payment of required fees or charges payable to the Authority; and (l) comply with all other procedures, standards, programmes and requirements in such a manner as may be prescribed by Rules or Regulations.*

Section 69 of the Environmental Management Act was interpreted in a case brought by Vijay Sookdeosingh as a result of claimed violation of the CEC granted to ALNG that was questioned by FFOS in ***Fishermen and Friends*** *of the Sea v Environmental Management Authority and Atlantic LNG Company of Trinidad and Tobago (Interested Party).*[128] In *Vijay Sookdeosingh v Atlantic LNG Company of Trinidad and Tobago, the Attorney General and the Environmental Management Authority,*[129] the Chairman of the Environmental Commission, Her Honour Sandra Paul, endorsed the entrenchment of direct party action in the *Environmental Management Act* where it was alleged that the EMA had failed to fulfil its statutory role of enforcement of provisions of the *Environmental Management Act* including compliance with a CEC.

Vijay Sookdeosingh filed a Notice of Direct Private Party Action against ALNG for breach of an environmental requirement, more particularly, a breach of a term at clause (ii) (j) of the Certificate of Environmental Clearance - CEC0114/2002 (CEC) dated June 6th 2003 that is, whereby Atlantic LNG was granted approval for the establishment of a Fourth Train (Train IV) for the liquefaction of natural gas (the Facility). (3) Clause (ii) (j) of the CEC provides that:

> *Atlantic LNG shall develop mechanisms to establish a buffer zone around the entire Facility if such is required to minimize impacts from the construction and operational phases of the activity, consistent with applicable international standards and guidelines and assessments of risk to neighbouring communities from the Trinidad LNG Facility; this plan shall be developed and forwarded to the EMA prior to the commencement of operations of Train IV.*

According to the Chairman of the Environmental Commission Her Honour Sandra Paul in *Vijay Sookdeosingh v. Atlantic LNG Company of Trinidad and Tobago, the Attorney General and Environmental Management Authority,*[130]

> *(20) Counsel for the Applicant submitted that he has locus standi to pursue this application in the Court. She submitted that section 69(2) means that once you are an individual or a group, and once you have a public interest in a violation or a private interest, an individual has locus standi to bring a Direct Private Party*

---

128 H.C.A. Cv. 2148 of 2003

129 EAA 003 of 2006

130 Ibid.

Action. In this particular matter, she submitted, the Applicant is an individual with a specific concern with respect to the claimed violation. He lives in close proximity to the Facility. Further, he lives just outside of the buffer zone and has concerns with respect to his health, safety and his quality of life. Consequently, he has standing as provided for under the Act to pursue the matter before the Court.

(21) However, Counsel for Atlantic LNG submitted to the Court that the Applicant lacked the necessary locus standi to bring a Direct Private Party Action to the Court. He submitted that what is meant by "specific concern" with respect to an individual meant more than just a passing interest or a theoretical or academic interest. He said that an individual must show a direct impact on him.

(22) He said that the violation complained of by the Applicant, that contrary to the terms in the CEC, Atlantic LNG had failed to establish the buffer zone in conformity with applicable international standards and guidelines and assessments of risk to neighbouring communities from the Facility, was sufficient to establish a nexus between that alleged violation and the health, safety and quality of life of the Applicant.

(23) Counsel for the Attorney General and the Authority did not challenge the locus standi of the Applicant. In fact, Counsel for the Attorney General submitted that the Applicant had locus standi before the Court, there being no evidence to contradict his assertion that he lives next to the buffer zone and that he has certain concerns relating to his health and safety.

(24) We note Counsel's for the Applicant referral to the position as it obtains to citizen enforcement of environmental laws in the United States of America. In an article published in the Southern California Law Review[131], the learned author observed: "Citizen enforcement has played an extremely valuable role in achieving compliance with environmental law ... Citizen enforcement has been especially instrumental in helping to bring government facilities into compliance. It also played a significant role in the private sector. Citizen groups are not dissuaded from enforcement by political pressure, nor are they subject to capture like regulatory staff. Citizen action thus provides an important deterrent to non-compliance when government agencies fail to act

---

131 Clifford Rechtschaffen, *Deterrence vs. Cooperation and the Evolving Theory of Environmental Enforcement* (1999) 71 S. Cal. L. Rev. 1181 at para.1231

...." *We agree with the observation of the learned author. It appears to the Court that Parliament contemplated a similar situation whereby private citizens can have an opportunity to participate in the policing of the environment by giving them an opportunity to bring a direct private party action when there is a claimed violation of an environmental requirement.*

(25) It is clear from section 69 that Parliament intended for a private party to be part of the enforcement mechanism where there is a claimed violation of an environmental requirement and where the Authority has failed to act.

(26) The complaint of the Applicant is that Atlantic LNG was in violation of a condition imposed in the CEC, in that they failed to comply with the establishment of a buffer zone using international guidelines and standards. If that is in fact so, we find that such non-compliance may well have consequences related to safety, health and quality of life of persons living in close proximity of the buffer zone. The Applicant is one such person.

(27) We therefore hold that he has a specific concern with respect to the claimed violation and consequently he has locus standi to bring this action.

(28) The Court in considering this issue will of necessity have to interpret section 69 of the Act.

(29) Counsel for the Applicant urged the Court to interpret section 69 literally. She submitted that section 69(1) sets out certain basic requirements, pre-conditions or conditions precedent that must be met before the Court has the jurisdiction to entertain a direct private party action. She said that section 69 provides for certain timelines to be observed before a private party can pursue a direct private party action before the Court.

(30) She pointed out that there were five statutory requirements that needed to be fulfilled.

1. The Authority must be given sixty days notice by the Applicant of the claimed violation before the Applicant can file his direct private party action;

2. The Applicant can file his direct private party action at any time between the sixty-first and eighty-eight day;

3. The Applicant must serve his direct private party action between the sixty-first and eighty-eight day;

4. The Authority must not have assumed enforcement action prior to the filing of the action; and

5. The Authority must not have assumed enforcement action within sixty days after the filing of a direct private party action.

(31) Counsel submitted that the Applicant met all the statutory requirements. On the question of notification, she said that this was done by letter to the Authority dated July 27ᵗʰ 2006 and captioned – "Notice of Direct Party Action Pursuant to section 69(1) (a) of the Environmental Management Act".

(32) She submitted that the Applicant was also in compliance with section 69(1) (b), because he served a copy of the complaint on the Managing Director within the twenty-eight days of the date when he was first authorized to bring the action. On October 6ᵗʰ, 2006, seventy-one days after notification, the Applicant filed the Notice of Direct Private Party Action. The Applicant had filed his complaint within the sixty-first and eighty-eighth day.

(33) In making this submission Counsel invited the Court to interpret first authorized as referring to the sixty-first day, being the day after the sixty day period of the notice. Hence a party is first authorized to bring a direct private party action on the sixty-first day and must serve a copy of the application not later than the eighty-eighth day.

(34) Counsel invited the Court, to consider in the alternative, if it did not agree that the Applicant had complied with section 69(1) (b), and that the Court had interpreted section 69(1) (b) as setting the time for filing the complaint on the sixty-first day, then it should grant the Applicant an extension of time for filing his complaint out of time pursuant to section 89(4) of the Act. She submitted that a twelve day delay was not an unreasonable one.

(35) In support of her submission that a twelve day delay was not an unreasonable one she drew the Court's attention to the history of the Applicant's efforts to obtain the information about the buffer zone stipulated in the CEC. Atlantic LNG made its decision to establish a buffer zone on January 13ᵗʰ 2006. Between that date and July 27ᵗʰ 2006 when the Authority was informed in writing of his intent to file a Direct Private Party Action, the Applicant through his

attorneys-at-law attempted to have the matter amicably resolved without having recourse to the Courts. She submitted that during the period of discussions with Atlantic LNG there was a change of Chief Executive Officer and there was forbearance on the Applicant's part to pursue any legal options without first giving the new incumbent an opportunity to respond to his concerns.

(36) Counsel for Atlantic LNG submitted that the Applicant has conceded that he is out of time for filing the substantive matter by the fact that he has filed an application for an extension of time for bringing a Direct Private Party Action. Consequently, this is not an interpretation application of section 69. He said that until an order is made by the Court there is no Direct Private Party Action before the Court.

(37) Further, Counsel for Atlantic LNG argued that the Applicant has failed to comply with the condition precedent that triggers his right to institute a third party action, namely compliance with the statutory regime of notification to the Authority within the context of sections 69 and 89 of the Act. The Direct Private Party Action was filed outside of the statutory time limit and ought not to have been instituted or proceeded with unless the Applicant applies for and obtains leave of the Court to institute its action pursuant to section 89(4).

(38) Counsel contended that the Applicant's delay in attempting to bring an action to the Commission was unreasonable having regard to the following facts:

(i) Atlantic LNG since on or about January 2006 commenced relocation of several persons in the buffer zone;

(ii) On December 21ˢᵗ 2003 Atlantic LNG had entered into contractual obligations with third parties to construct and maintain approximately 100 houses;

(iii) Atlantic LNG invested approximately TT$18 million in the construction of homes outside the zone for the relocation of those persons residing in the buffer zone;

(iv) Atlantic LNG in March 2004 entered into negotiations with several residents residing in the buffer zone who indicated their willingness to be relocated and/or compensated pursuant to the plan submitted to the Authority;

(v)Several persons residing in the buffer zone have entered into negotiations with

Atlantic LNG *to be relocated to houses built by Atlantic* LNG *outside of the buffer zone and/or distributed to such persons compensation in respect of their properties; and*

(vi) Atlantic LNG *negotiated with several landowners whose lands were within the buffer zone for the acquisition of these lands.*

(39) Having argued that the Applicant's delay in bringing an action to the Commission was unreasonable, Counsel for Atlantic LNG *went on to submit that section 69 of the Act created a new remedy for a private party or private citizen.*

(40) He said in order for a private citizen to bring an action to the Commission there are several "statutory triggers" identified in section 69(1) of the Act. He pointed out that the Applicant failed to give written notice of any claimed violation of a specified environmental requirement as required by section 69(a).

(41) He argued that there was no evidence of service of a copy of the filed complaint on the Managing Director of the Authority before the commencement of the action. Consequently the Applicant is in breach of section 69(1) (b). He further argued that section 69(1) (b) required the Applicant to serve a copy of the complaint on the Authority within twenty-eight days on which he was first authorized to bring the action.

(42) First authorized, he submitted, presumes actual knowledge that there has been a violation of an environmental requirement. In the present case it was February 2006. He submitted that if the Court did not agree with that interpretation of first authorized then the alternative submission to that would be that the only person to authorize enforcement action would have to be the Authority under the Act.

(43) He contended that section 69(1) (d) has not been complied with, in that the Authority has sixty days after the filing of the action to elect to assume responsibility for taking enforcement action under sections 63 and 68 of the Act.

(44) Counsel for the Attorney General submitted that it is accepted that the main body charged with the protection of the environment and the enforcement of action is the Authority. Sections 69 and 89 of the Act provide for private citizens to bring enforcement action in certain cases. However, there are safeguards which will allow the Authority to assume enforcement action.

(45) Counsel for the Attorney General invited the Court to interpret section 69 (1) as applying to actions brought only with respect to claimed violations at paragraphs (c), (d) and (l). He submitted that the words save where in section 69(1) meant that the Commission has jurisdiction to solely hear complaints with respect to violations at section 62 (c), (d) and (l) once the complainant has observed the steps set out at sections 69(1)(a) to (d). He went on to submit that with respect to the other violations of environmental requirements referred to in section 62, the Commission's jurisdiction is provided for by section 89 (2) of the Act which provides:

"The Commission shall not have jurisdiction over any private party action unless the complainant has given proper notice to the Authority of not less than sixty days before bringing such an action as required under section 69."

(46) Consequently, Counsel submitted, there are two categories of potential Direct Private Party Actions. The first category encompasses violations provided for in section 62 apart from violations under section 69(c), (d) and (l), the Commission's jurisdiction thereto is provided for under section 89(2). The second category of violations under section 62 (c), (d) and (l); the Commission's jurisdiction is derived from section 69(1).

(47) In discussing the meaning of the words first authorized he argued that once the complainant has given written notice of the claimed violation the Authority has sixty days within wish to act. If the Authority has failed to act, then the complainant is now authorized to act.

(48) He submitted that the Applicant by his attorney's letter of July 27th 2006 gave notice to the Authority. This was so despite the fact that it was captioned Notice of Direct Private Party Action. He said that it would have been better if it had been captioned Notice of Violation to fit the language of section 69(1) (a); however, he submitted, the language used went more to form than to substance.

(49) Counsel for the Authority submitted that in interpreting section 69(1) when regard is had to the words save where, in the ordinary meaning of those words they mean except and if read that way in section 69, the section does not make sense. She submitted that save where should be read in relations to sections 69(1) (c) and (d), so that the effect of those sub-sections would be that if the Authority has not commenced an action, the private party may not proceed to bring a complaint and conversely where the Authority decides

to take enforcement action the private party may also proceed to take action. If the Authority decides there is no merit in the allegation by the private party's claim of violation of an environmental requirement then it would be wrong for the private party to go off on a frolic of his own and decide that there is merit. At the end of the day she submitted the private party and the Authority must always work together.

(50) Counsel for the Authority submitted an interpretation of first authorized that is in agreement with the alternative interpretation submitted by Counsel for Atlantic LNG, that is, the Authority is the only person tasked with authorizing enforcement.

(51) She contended that in interpreting section 69 the philosophy of the Act which is contained in the Preamble must be borne in mind. The Preamble states inter alia -

"And whereas, management and conservation of the environment and the impact of environmental conditions on human health constitute a shared responsibility and benefit for everyone in the society requiring co-operation and co-ordination of public and private sector activities:

And whereas, in furtherance of its commitment, the Government is undertaking the establishment and operation of an Environmental Management Authority to co-ordinate, facilitate and oversee execution of the national strategy and programmes, to promote public awareness of environmental concerns, and to establish an effective regulatory regime which will protect, enhance and conserve the environment:"

(52) She submitted that a private party cannot go far on its own in any enforcement action. It is necessary for the Authority to play a supporting role in any enforcement procedure. Under section 69 the private party merely acts as a notifier. It is the Authority which is the specialist in the field of environmental management and conservation and has the best understanding of what is required. It is the Authority which ultimately decides on the course of action to be taken. Where the Authority does not elect to proceed to enforcement the private party cannot do so.

(53) Consequently, she submitted, first authorized means that the Authority within sixty days after it received the written notice of the claimed violation can authorize the private party to proceed to lay a private complaint against the al-

leged violator.

(54) The sole object in statutory interpretation is to arrive at the legislative intention. Parliament entrusts the Courts with the task of spelling out its intent.

(55) The Act makes provision for private parties to bring a complaint to the Environmental Commission for a violation of an environmental requirement. Section 69(1) and section 89 provides for the manner in which the jurisdiction of the Commission is to be invoked. Section 69(1) states -

"Any private party may institute a civil action in the Commission against any other person for a claimed violation of any of the specified environmental requirements identified in section 62, other than paragraphs (c), (d) and (l), save where —

a. the complainant has given written notice of such claimed violation to the Managing Director of the Authority at least sixty days prior to the commencement of the civil action;

b. the complainant has served a copy of the complaint on the Managing Director within twenty-eight days of the date on which the complainant was first authorized to bring such an action.

c. the Authority has not commenced an enforcement action under sections 63 to 67 inclusive or through other appropriate means available to it under section 68 regarding such claimed violation; and

d. the Authority has not elected to assume responsibility for taking enforcement action under sections 63 to 68 inclusive within sixty days after the filing of a direct private party action by the complainant."

Section 89 provides inter alia:

"89 (1) This section shall apply to every direct private party action brought pursuant to section 69.

(2) The Commission shall not have jurisdiction over any private party action unless the complainant has given proper notice to the Authority of not less than sixty days before bringing such an action as required under section 69.

(3) A direct private party action shall be instituted by filing a complaint with the Registrar of the Commission and serving a copy thereof on the respondent and

the secretary of the Authority, within twenty-eight days of the date on which the complainant is first authorized to bring such an action.

(4) Notwithstanding subsection (3), a complaint may be instituted out of time if the Commission is satisfied that there was a reasonable cause for not bringing the complaint within the time limit and that the complaint was filed thereafter, without unreasonable delay.

(7) At any time within sixty days after the filing of a direct private party action, the authority may assume responsibility for taking enforcement action against the respondent by - ….."

(56) The Court noted with interest Counsel's for the Applicant reference to the article Deterrence vs. Cooperation and the Evolving Theory of Environmental Enforcement where the author made the following observation about what obtains in the United States of America where ordinary citizens have been given the power to ensure that there is compliance with environmental laws. The learned author of that article opined that – "Citizen enforcement has played an extremely valuable role in achieving compliance with environmental law … Citizen enforcement has been especially instrumental in helping to bring government facilities into compliance. It also played a significant role in the private sector. Citizen groups are not dissuaded from enforcement by political pressure, nor are they subject to capture like regulatory staff. Citizen action thus provides an important deterrent to non-compliance when government agencies fail to act …."

(57) The Court also noted the submission of Counsel for Atlantic LNG and agreed with his submission when he contended that to police the environment can be a very extensive and difficult task. There may be people in areas that are being directly affected and the only way that the Authority can be made aware of this is by being informed by the people who are being affected. We reject his submission when he states that the private party simply acts only as a notifier to the Authority when there is a breach of an environmental requirement. (58) Having regard to the foregoing reference and submission, the Court is of the opinion that it was Parliament's intention to give to an individual the power to ensure compliance with environmental requirements when it enacted section 69 of the Act. As a consequence the Court is of the opinion that since Parliament intended to give the citizens the power to ensure compliance with environmental requirements, the use of the words save where in section 69(1) is to be interpreted as introducing

pre-conditions to be observed before an individual can bring a direct private party action to the Commission. (59) The Court finds that the Applicant has complied, in all material particulars, with the requirement of section 69 in instituting a civil action at the Commission. We so find for the following reasons -

(i) section 69 (1) (a) which required the complainant to give written notice of the claimed violation to the Managing Director was complied with. The Court accepts the letter dated July 27th 2006 as giving the necessary notice of the claimed violation. We so find despite the caption "Notice of Direct Private Party Action Pursuant to Section 69(1) (a) of Environmental Management Act, 2000". We agree with Counsel for the Attorney General when he submitted that the language used in the letter went more to form than to substance.

(ii) We find that the pre-condition for instituting an action as set out in section 69 (1) (a) has been complied with. We note in the caption to the above reproduced correspondence that section 69(1) (a) was referenced, and further in the body of the correspondence, the claimed violation was identified in the penultimate paragraph.

(iii) We find that section 69(1) (b) was complied with. In arriving at this finding the Court accepted the submission of Counsel for the Applicant and the Attorney General when they submitted that first authorized meant the complainant could institute an action between the sixty-first and eighty-eighth day when notification of the claimed violation was given to the Managing Director of the Authority. In making this determination we reject the submission of Counsel for the Authority and Atlantic LNG when they submitted that it is the Authority which is empowered to authorize the complainant to bring a complaint to the Commission. We do not believe that that was the intent of Parliament. We are of the opinion that it was Parliament's intention to empower citizens to ensure that there was compliance with environmental requirements where the Authority has failed to do so.

(iv) We find that section 69 (i) (b) has been complied with when the Applicant filed the Notice of Direct Private Action on October 6th 2006, a date between the sixty-first and eighty-eighth day as is required by the Act, and served a copy of it on the Authority.

(v)Finally, we find that the pre-condition set out under section 69(1)(c) has been complied with in that the Applicant filed his Direct Private Party Action only after the Authority had failed to take action against Atlantic LNG as provided

for in the Act.

The High Court of TT, as discussed in Chapter 10 on jurisdiction of the Environmental Commission, has ruled that it cannot exercise jurisdiction over a pure breach of an environmental requirement due to the fact that when such a claimed violation is being made by a private party, it must be done through the mechanism of direct private party action.

The complication in direct private party action is that the EMA must be served with a written notice by the private party of a claimed violation of an environmental requirement. Upon being served such a notice, the EMA can issue a Notice of Violation on the alleged offender and assume enforcement of the claimed violation. Upon service of the Notice of Violation, the role of the private party ends. This has led to questioning what happens if the EMA resolves the Notice of Violation in a manner that is not agreeable to the private party initially bringing attention to the claimed violation by means of written notice to the EMA. The EMA can also choose to take no action after serving the Notice of Violation on the alleged offender. FFOS sought to have this matter clarified at the Environmental Commission and the EMA objected on the basis that the Environmental Commission had no jurisdiction to question the actions of the EMA after it assumed responsibility for enforcing a claimed violation of an environmental requirement. The Environmental Commission ruled that it had such jurisdiction but the decision was ultimately overruled at the Court of Appeal of TT.[132]

Fishermen and Friends of the Sea v Environmental Management Authority[133]

Facts: FFOS in the substantive matter brought an appeal pursuant to sections 81 (5) (a) and 81 (5) (i) of the Environmental Management Act (the Environmental Management Act). FFOS claimed therein that after they notified the EMA that Atlantic LNG was in breach of an environmental requirement, the EMA served a Notice of Violation (NOV) on Atlantic LNG Company of Trinidad and Tobago (Atlantic LNG). They further

---

132 Further discussion on the jurisdiction of the Environmental Commission is contained in Chapter 10.

133 EAP 005 of 2007.

claimed that the EMA refused and/or failed and/or neglected to enforce or resolve the NOV within a reasonable time and was therefore in breach of its statutory duty as required by section 63 (2) of the Environmental Management Act. FFOS asked the court as a consequence of the EMA's breach of statutory duty, to make certain declarations and orders for certiorari and mandamus.

Held: 37.The court finds that FFOS had a legitimate expectation that the EMA would have pursued the enforcement of the NOV to its finality. The EMA's inaction in pursuing this enforcement has frustrated FFOS's right under the law to bring a complaint to the court by way of a civil action. 38. The court will not stand by and allow the EMA's inaction to fetter the ability of an individual to bring an action to it. Parliament gave the citizens of the Republic of Trinidad and Tobago the ability to participate in the protection, conservation and management of the environment by providing for individuals or a group of individuals expressing a general interest in the environment to have standing before the Environmental Commission to take action against those who are perceived as being in breach of environmental requirements. 39. The court therefore finds that FFOS had a legitimate expectation that the EMA would enforce the NOV. Having failed to do so FFOS has locus standi to appeal the EMA's decision not to pursue the enforcement of its NOV.

This decision, as seen in Chapter 10, was overruled by the Court of Appeal in *Environmental Management Authority v Fishermen and Friends of the Sea,*[134] heard together with *Environmental Management Authority v South West Tobago Fisherman's Association.*[135] The law as it now stands would require an aggrieved party to proceed by way of judicial review to the Supreme Court.

THE ROLE OF THE STATE

In TT, like many developing countries, the State is a major economic player and not merely a regulator of business activities. Thus, when the State decides to pursue a particular economic activity with much social opposition, and the State must apply to a State agency for approval, there is a clear con-

---

134 Civil Appeal No. 199 of 2008.
135 Civil Appeal No. 219 of 2009.

flict of interest that undermines the public perception of the transparency and objectivity of the approval process.

An example of the role of the State in economic activities can be found in the decision of the TT Government to construct and operate an aluminium smelter. ALUTRINT was originally established as a joint venture between wholly State-owned National Energy Corporation ("NEC") and Sural, a Venezuelan aluminium concern with NEC owning 60 per cent of ALU-TRINT's equity and Sural 40 per cent.[136] A former Prime Minister of TT, Patrick Mannning, made this project a personal and powerful crusade and it was difficult to see how a State agency could have resisted the inevitable push towards the establishment of a State majority owned smelter.

> *According to Mr. Patrick Manning "You will not be surprised, therefore, that there has been a rise in objections to one of the projects and in fact that is just the beginning of it. The project is the aluminium smelter and particularly the one that is carded for Cedros. You notice that we have not had those objections over the aluminium smelter that is carded for La Brea - don't have those objections there and that should tell you a story. And we have also seen that particular projects acting as a catalyst and a rallying point for those who have issues other than aluminium or the environment, a point around which civil society organizations can rally - we saw it in a demonstration in Cedros quite recently. And we have also seen a lot being said in the public domain about what aluminium smelters can or cannot do. And by and large, the more vocal among us - the voices that are being heard the loudest - voices that are suggesting that it is not in the national interest and that aluminium smelters do great damage to the flora and fauna surrounding it and these are things that ought not be pursued. But I would like to just remind of a biblical saying that you see in the book of proverbs, "There is gold and there are precious stones but the lips informed by knowledge are a precious jewel." Many of the lips that are speaking on this matter are not by any means informed by knowledge.[137]*

---

136 It was announced in early 2009 that Sural had pulled out of the joint venture and in December 2009, the Government announced that a Brazilian industrial group Votorantim Metais, will join the Government of Trinidad and Tobago as its equity partner in the smelter. See Metal Bulletin at http://www.metalbulletin.co.uk/Article/2352384/NonFerrous/Votorantim-to-invest-in-Alutrint-smelter-in-Trinidad-UPDATE.html

137 Feature Address Delivered By Honourable Patrick Manning, Prime Minister of Trinidad & Tobago at The Powergen Sod Turning Ceremony, Point Lisas, Office of the

The strident and aggressive tone of the former Prime Minister made it clear that little resistance would have been tolerated to this smelter project and it certainly placed EMA charged with responsibility for environmental clearance of this project in an invidious position.[138]

Another example of the State engaging in major developmental activities can be found in the construction sector. With the high oil prices and increased revenues in the first decade of the 21st century, there was a major construction drive by the Government. To the chagrin of the Government, this led to a shortage in the supply of construction raw materials. Quarrying, at that time, and still continues to be, a major environmental problem in TT, particularly affecting the water resources of the country. Quarrying is one of the activities listed under the *Certificate of Environmental Clearance (Designated Activities) Order, 2001*[139] as requiring environmental clearance from the EMA. The emerging practice is that all applications for CECs for quarrying are subject to the EIA process imposed by the EMA. This in turn provides the avenue for public participation and the opportunity for the public to express its views on the adverse effects quarrying has on its communities. The Government in 2007 responded by passing the, *Certificate of Environmental Clearance (Designated Activities) Amendment Order* 2007,[140] an amendment stating that a CEC was only required to establish a quarry in excess of 150 acres. The reality is that it is unusual in TT to have a quarry in excess of 150 acres - so the amendment was really intended to remove the EMA's power to regulate quarrying. A newspaper article has quoted the Chairman of the EMA as stating:

They want the sand and gravel for construction. The problem is there's a boom in

---

Prime Minister, 29 March 2006. Available from Internet: http://opm.gov.tt/news/index.php?pid=2001&nid=sp060329.

138 Several court challenges were successfully launched with respect to the grant of the CEC for the establishment of the aluminium smelter.

139 L.N. No. 103 of 2001.

140 L.N. No. 164 and L.N. No. 186 of 2008. Fortunately, the situation was reversed in 2012, when the *Certificate of Environmental Clearance (Designated Activities) Amendment Order 2012 (L.N. No. 52 of 2012)* returned quarries of all sizes to the oversight of the EMA.

construction and there is a shortage of aggregate. You know the background on quarries, you wrote about it.[141]

As with many developing countries, the State is not only an active participant in economic activities but understandably sees itself as having a major role in facilitating economic development. Very often the Government would lay out its economic blueprint and identify the projects on which it is basing its developmental thrust. Similarly, when the State is a direct economic player it is not likely to be easily deterred by a State agency in its thrust to promote specific economic activities. This is quite apparent in TT where heavy industrialisation is being promoted in light of the perceived abundance of natural gas as a source of energy. One example was the promotion by the Government of a massive steel plant in the face of strong opposition by environmentalists and communities near the proposed plant. The former Prime Minister Patrick Manning stated that the USD$1.2 billion steel unit proposed in the country by the Mumbai-based Essar group will proceed:

> *The construction of the steel plant proposed by the Ruias-led Essar group will begin shortly... This is an emotional issue (for) many. But when you examine the facts of the case they are not borne out by the emotion you're seeing. In fact people are shedding heat on it, not light.*[142]

Another project that saw strong support from Patrick Manning and which proceeded despite much opposition was the Atlantic LNG Train IV project.[143] This project generated tremendous public interest and opposition due to the public perception of negative environmental impacts associated with the earlier trains. The CEC process experienced some delays due to public pressure to have several critical issues properly examined before the CEC was granted to ALNG. ALNG was growing impatient with the process and the then Prime Minister was a strong advocate of the Train IV project. A chronology of reported facts make for an interesting read-

---

141 Anne Hilton, 'Construction boom, aggregate shortage' *Trinidad Newsday* (23 April 2008)

142 Paras Ramoutar, 'No stopping $1.2 bn Essar steel unit: Trinidad PM' *India News* (2008) http://www.indiaenews.com/america/20080423/113203.htm.

143 H.C.A. CV 2148 of 2003

ing. Patrick Manning was reported on 07 June 2003 to have said at a post Cabinet news conference held on 05 June 2003:

> ..*that he expected the Cabinet to give final approval for the project next Thursday... he expected the certificate of environmental clearance to be granted shortly since, as far as he was aware, the partners had gone a long way towards satisfying the requirements of the EMA.*[144]

It is somewhat unusual for a Prime Minister to announce that he expected a CEC to be granted shortly and that the requirements of the EMA had been met. What became even more perplexing is that the same newspaper article indicated that the Chairman of the EMA was far from satisfied with the status of the application.

> *...even if Cabinet gives approval to Atlantic LNG for the construction of its billion dollar Train Four, it would not be built unless Atlantic LNG meets the EMA's environmental standards... the EMA had set clear requirements for the Atlantic LNG partners and this would not be changed, even if the project was sanctioned by Government... Unusually exhaustive time has already been spent working with the company in an attempt to bring it up to standard ... specialist consultants from around the world had been brought in by the EMA to look into the matter... Atlantic LNG had not met the 'mitigated standard' which was lower than the normal standard for projects of that nature... the organization [EMA] was dispassionate about the issue and had an obligation to ensure that environmental laws were adhered to... the EMA would not be forced into anything...*[145]

Thus, the role of the state as an active player in economic activities and a facilitator of economic activities have understandably created concern with respect to the ability to nurture genuine State oversight in the environmental decision making process. This situation is not helped by the governance structure of the EMA which lends itself to suspicion that it is easily manipulated and controlled by whichever political party holds the reign of power as the EMA is managed by a Board of Directors appointed by the

---

144 Carol Quash, *Atlantic LNG's Train Four must meet EMA standards, Trinidad Express* (07 June 2003)

145 Ibid.

President.

Section 6 of the Environmental Management Act

6(1) There is hereby established a body corporate to be known as the Environmental Management Authority, which shall be governed by a Board of Directors consisting of the persons appointed in accordance with this section.

(2) The President shall appoint - (a) a Chairman; (b) nine other members drawn from the following disciplines or groups, namely, environmental management, ecology, environmental health, engineering, labour, community-based, organisations, business, economics, public administration, law and non-profit environmental nongovernmental organisations.

In TT, the Office of the President is largely ceremonial with the President being appointed by the Parliament. The vote for the appointment of a President has always gone in favour of the nominee of the political party with the majority of members in Parliament. This is the same political party that forms the Cabinet that governs the country. The convention is that when the President is given the statutory power to appoint a Board of Directors, this is done on the advice of the Cabinet. Effectively, therefore, the Cabinet receives the recommendation from the Minister with responsibility for the environment and then ratifies that decision and forwards same to the President whereby the President inevitably makes the appointments that are recommended. In a developing country, where the tradition of objectivity and transparency in public appointments is certainly underdeveloped, there is a fair degree of scepticism whether the EMA is serving the interest of the entire society, as the interests of the Government may be of paramount concern.

A second aspect of the *Environmental Management Act* that undermines the independence of the EMA is the power of the Minister over the actions of the EMA.

Section 5 of the Environmental Management Act

(5) The Minister may from time to time give the Authority directions of a special or general character in the exercise of the powers conferred and the duties imposed on the Authority by or under this Act

This power to issue directions of a special or general character that is vested in the Minister has created suspicion that the EMA can be manipulated and forced to act contrary to the public interest in the face of Ministerial directives. Having regard to the power of the State in appointing the Board of Directors of the EMA and the right vested in the Minister to give special and general directions to the EMA, there is an obvious conflict created when the State is seeking to obtain an approval from the EMA.

In ***People United Respecting the Environment and Rights Action Group v Environmental Management Authority, Alutrint Limited (Interested Party) and the Attorney General of Trinidad and Tobago***,[146] it was argued that when the State was a participator in a developmental project for which environmental approval was sought from the EMA, the EMA should engage in a higher level of scrutiny. This argument was rejected by the Court. As per Mira Deen-Armour at p.115:

> *Saskatchewan Action Foundation for the Environment v. Saskatchewan Minister of Environment and Public Safety (1992 97 Sask. R. 1354 was cited by Dr. Ramlogan in support of his submission that greater public participation was required where the developer was partly owned by Government. Dr. Ramlogan relied, in particular, on paragraph 37 of Saskatchewan: "Public participation in the process is all the more important because the government of Saskatchewan may have an interest direct or indirect in the advancement of a development… Accordingly, the minister being the person charged under the Act with granting approval and at the same time being a member of the government is placed in a position of potential conflict. Public participation … is important to avoid the appearance of partiality." Saskatchewan is distinguishable from the Trinidad and Tobago situation, since the Environmental Management Act creates an independent body for the purpose of deciding whether a certificate of environmental clearance ought to be granted. Even if members of the Authority are appointed by government, the Authority is in no way comparable to a Minister, who is a member of government. Accordingly, the government involvement in the project is not a ground, under the Environmental Management Act, for demanding more intense public participation.*

A clear example of the challenges with the role of the State is seen in that

---

146 CV 2007-02263

of the proposed highway alongside the Aripo Savannas. The Ministry of Works and Transport (MOWT) touted a major infrastructural project to run south of the Aripo Savannas, a designated sensitive area to be executed in segments. MOWT applied for a CEC for the phase of the highway adjacent to the sensitive area. A CEC was granted on 22 June, 2017 and a sod turning ceremony was held on 26 September, 2017 announcing the commencement of the project. On 29 September, 2017, FFOS filed for judicial review of the decision of the EMA to grant a CEC to MOWT for the highway project, on grounds that included the failure to properly consider the biological diversity of the Aripo Savannas with its unique ecosystems and rich diversity of flora and fauna. This highway was clearly a project in which the government had a significant interest. On 25 October, 2017, Mr. Rohan Sinanan, Minister of Works and Transport in the Senate spoke about the highway project that included the phase passing alongside the Aripo Savannas.

Mr. Vice-President, another major project at the Ministry of Works and Transport is the Valencia to Toco highway. In March of 2017, the route alignment and conceptual designs were undertaken for the construction of a first-class road from Valencia to Toco. At this time, they are being reviewed and the best route will be presented to the infrastructure committee very shortly and that highway, that first-class road to Toco will be a reality. But Mr. Vice-President, there has been so much talk about why is the Government building a road like that in Toco? Well, the first thing I want to say, the people of Toco are part of Trinidad and Tobago and it is time that part of the island gets its development. However, having said that, what the Government plans for that area is a fast ferry port in Toco. Mr. Vice-President, Toco is a village where you can find craft, tourism projects, a small folk museum and the Toco Composite School, good bathing, and it is a popular surfing spot between the months of October and April. However, Mr. Vice-President, the fast-ferry port in Toco is what will bring Trinidad and Tobago much closer than where it is now. The savings alone, with a port in Toco, in terms of energy, is significant. And what we see happening into Toco is the entire eastern seaboard of Trinidad will be opened up for serious commercial activities. So, when this Government decides to do a project, we "doh" just get up in the morning and say: Let us go and do this and let us go and do that. Everything has to do with commercial development. Yes, I think Mr. Watson Duke made a case for this port.

Mr. Vice-President, I am happy to announce that in July 2017, a consultant was engaged for that port in Toco and very soon we will have the conceptual designs, the layout designs and the tender document for that port. Mr. Vice-president, another major project, and these are projects that we are working on in 2017. 2.30 p.m. A lot of work has been going on in the Ministry of Works and Transport. Mr. Vice-President, the construction of the Wallerfield to Manzanilla Highway. The total length of this highway is approximately 34 kilometres to be done in three phases: the Cumuto to Toco Main Road, the Toco Main Road to Manzanilla and the Cumuto Link Road to the Churchill Roosevelt Highway….I also want to draw the attention, Mr. Vice-President, of the House, there have been some concerns about the location of the highway passing through the protected Aripo Savannas. This project is passing almost 150 metres away from the Aripo Savannas, so this is not interfering with the protected area of the Aripo Savannas.[147]

The support for this project reflects the robust approach that government tends to take when faced with judicial opposition to projects it has embraced. The Prime Minister of TT, the Honourable Dr. Keith Rowley launched a scathing attack on persons for opposing the highway project and exhorted his followers to raise their voices in opposition to the actions of FFOS.

One particular one, my mother and her friends buy so much cloth from him that he and he children eh have to work again in life but he know that you must not get this and that from here. And lie…Tonight I want to say to the people, where is your voice when this is happening to you…. You remain silent and they prevail.

The reference is clearly to Jimmy Aboud, popularly dubbed the "Textile King," the father of Gary Aboud, the Secretary of FFOS.

One of the challenges confronting TT is a political desire to obtain developed world status by 2030, propelled by the energy sector. This raised the issue of whether the developmental thrust of TT is sustainable. The State assumed the role of definer and implementer of the concept of sustainable development and this eschewed any role for the public to have a voice in

---

147 Appropriation (Financial Year 2018) Bill, 2017 [Second Day] October 25, 2017 <http://www.ttparliament.org/hansards/hs20171025.pdf>

determining the level of sustainability. The then Prime Minister in 2006, quite succinctly explained the challenge of balancing the environment and development:

> *For us, therefore it has to be a question of sustainable development, that is to say, a balance between the requirements of development and the need to preserve as far as possible the sanctity of the environment in which we operate. It is neither one extreme nor the next. It is a judicious balance designed to improve our standard of living.*[148]

The emerging issue is who determines the balance and by what means the balance is established. In a country where the notion of environmental democracy is emerging in the face of strong opposition from the State, there are questions being posed as to the role of the state in facilitating dialogue on sustainable development. The situation is not helped by a scathing denunciation by Prime Minister in 2006 where he described environmentalists as "right-wing environmentalists".

> *Within recent times we have experienced a phenomenon - we have begun to experience a phenomenon - that we see in the more developed countries of the world, which is the rise of the environmental lobby. In the classic sense, the right-wing environmentalists, they are of the view that any development that disturbs the environment in any significant way, and significant is to be defined, is development that should not be pursued.*[149]

It is difficult to see how the State would show the fortitude to address environmental concerns when it stands as a regulator, facilitator and a participant in the developmental thrust of TT. TT is at the cross roads of its environmental democratic process. The EMA was established to promote environmental management and embedded in its statutory remit were several instruments designed to promote public participation in the environmental decision-making process. Yet, it would appear that the EMA is pursuing its mandate in a manner that suggests a minimalist approach. Civil society is en-

---

148 Feature Address Delivered By Honourable Patrick Manning Prime Minister of Trinidad & Tobago at The Powergen Sod Turning Ceremony, Point Lisas, Office of the Prime Minister, 29 March 2006.

149 Ibid.

gaged in an uphill battle to ensure that environmental democracy is respected by the EMA. What is clear is that the State is perhaps the inspiration behind the approach of the EMA. Political will exercised in furtherance of economic imperatives may be influencing the attitude of EMA and the wider State machinery towards public participation in the environmental decision-making process. The challenge is to break the hegemony of State domination in the environmental decision-making process but unfortunately, the portents are not yet right for confronting such State domination and this therefore effectively diminishes the much vaunted ideological adherence to democracy that is the bedrock of the society.

CHAPTER 3

THE EMERGING ROLE OF PUBLIC
PARTICIPATION

INTRODUCTION

Governments make decisions that affect communities each and every day; however, most of these said decisions are not known by the communities which these leaders represent.[150] Within an environmental context, an environmental decision-maker, in rendering decisions pursuant to environmental legislation, is inevitably responsible for specifically taking into account the public interest.[151] It is on this foundation that the uprising of a call for greater public participation has occurred. Public participation is a process by which interested and affected individuals, organisations, and government entities are consulted and included in the decision-making process.[152] The public consists of a number of people reacting to a perceived interest.[153] Although environmental agencies may claim to consider all factors involved, in reality, a greater emphasis is placed on the scientific 'facts' that they would have gleaned from their research.[154] The public is the most affected segment by the consequences of environmental decisions and as such should be able to effectively influence the outcome of environmental

---

150 Sarah Pirk, *Expanding Public Participation in Environmental Justice: Methods, Legislation, Litigation and Beyond* [2002] 17 J. Envtl. L. & Litig. 207, 1

151 Michael Jeffery, *Intervenor Funding as the Key to Citizen Participation in Environmental Decision Making: Putting People Back into the Picture* [2002] 19 Ariz. J. Int'l & Comp. L. 643, 2

152 Adam Bran, *Public Participation Provisions Need Not Contribute To Environmental Injustice* [1996] Temp. Pol. & Civ. Rts. L. Rev5, 3

153 Ibid at [2]

154 Stephanie Tai, *Three Asymmetries of Informed Environmental Decision-making* [2005] 78 Temp. L. Rev. 659, 4

decisions.[155] Indeed, it is arguable that the environment is a public good[156] and therefore the public should ideally be able to participate in any decision-making process that would affect the environment, and consequently, the public. The issue should no longer be seen as a discountable factor in assessing environmental risks but that of an urgent and uncompromisable one.

Effective participation requires, at a minimum: (1) education about the environment and things that might affect it; (2) access to information (including the fact that information exists and is available); (3) a voice in decision-making; (4) transparency of decisional processes (by formal consideration of public input and explanation of how that input affected the decision at issue); (5) post-project analysis and monitoring, as well as access to pertinent information; (6) enforcement structures; and (7) recourse to independent tribunals for redress. For each of these elements, the public also needs protection against retaliation by the government or by the non-governmental proponents of the activity.[157]

The public will not participate in deliberative, consensus-building politics if it is not truly empowered in the process.[158] However, the manner and degree of inclusion in any decisional process will vary depending on the subject, the legal framework, and the political and social context of a decision. Participation should thus be understood to include the full range of options that engage and integrate the public into the process of making or implementing a policy choice.[159] There are many different theories that have arisen based on different forms of public participation. The pluralist model, with predominant regulatory ideals of inter-

---

155 Adam Bran, *Public Participation Provisions Need Not Contribute To Environmental Injustice* [1996] Temp. Pol. & Civ. Rts. L. Rev5, 12

156 Eileen Jones,, *Risky Assessments: Uncertainty in Science and the Human Dimensions of Environmental Decision-making* [1997] 22 Wm . & Mary Envtl. : & Pol'y Rev. 1, 1

157 Neil Popovic, *The Right To Participate in Decisions that affect The Environment* [1993] 10 Pace Envtl. L. Rev. 683, 4

158 Eileen Jones, *Risky Assessments: Uncertainty in Science and the Human Dimensions of Environmental Decisionmaking* [1997] 22 Wm . & Mary Envtl. : & Pol'y Rev. 1, 9

159 Eric Dannenmaier, *Sustainable Development Symposium: Democracy in Development: Toward a Legal framework For the Americas* [1997-1998] 11 Tul. Envtl. L.J. [iii], 11

est group inclusion and agency neutrality, rests on a foundation of utilitarianism.[160] The recently proposed civic republican model rejects utilitarianism in favour of a belief in true civic virtue.[161] Under this model, citizen inclusion is a regulatory ideal but is employed to achieve a form of deliberation focusing on true public good solutions rather than utility maximization. In this model, the public interest is an expression of a common good grounded in values people pursue not as individuals but as a community. This common good is the product of the deliberative process, not its discovery. The form and efficacy of citizen participation may vary depending upon which model predominates in agency proceedings and the institutional mechanisms that might favour one approach over another.[162]

Experts increasingly recognize that even technical and scientific solutions to environmental problems involve value judgments.[163] Is science premised on ambiguous data and possibly erroneous assumptions? How is uncertain science to be translated into a concrete regulatory decision? How, and to what extent, should these uncertainties be conveyed to the public?[164] In light of the answers to these and many further questions, science can no longer be seen as superior to the opinions of the public and as such, the current trend of limited public or no public participation needs to be curtailed. The "step up to the microphone and have your say in less than fifteen minutes" approach of many such public consultations resembles more of a crude preference tally rather than meaningful deliberation.[165] It would require agency officials to deliberately contemplate the limitations inherent in formal expertise.[166]

---

160 Eileen Guana, *The Environmental Justice Misfit: Public Participation and the Paradigm Paradox* [1998] 17 Standford Environmental Law Journal 3, 4

161 Ibid at [4]

162 Ibid.

163 Ibid at [6]

164 Stephanie Tai, *Three Asymmetries of Informed Environmental Decision-making* [2005] 78 Temp. L. Rev. 659, 4, 1

165 Eileen Guana, *The Environmental Justice Misfit: Public Participation and the Paradigm Paradox* [1998] 17 Standford Environmental Law Journal 3, 17

166 Ibid at [18]

It goes without saying that responsible public participation should be employed. Responsible participation can be enabled through education and training, management support, access to information and availability of technical services, through a regulatory framework that facilitates the establishment and operation of non-governmental organizations.[167] This promotes fiscal responsibility, transparency and accountability to society. Responsible participation includes processes by which citizen organizations are established and operated in a transparent and accountable manner, and engage in public deliberation effectively and with technical competence.[168] A good example of this can be found in the consensus-building approach. The consensus-building approach requires that all interested parties develop implementation proposals for the initiation of a project affecting the environment or the resolution of an environmental issue. The merits of the proposals are discussed and debated in a series of round table sessions moderated by neutral facilitators, and a final solution is only accepted when consensus, not total agreement, is reached. Every participant must agree that the negotiations were conducted in good faith and that all issues were heard and resolved within the limits imposed by law and economic feasibility.[169]

Another alternative to direct public participation is citizen advisory boards, chosen by a sponsoring agency. The agency chooses citizens who are affected by the decision or who are interested in it to serve on the board. The board investigates and recommends solutions to community controversies. Community Working Groups are also a way that public participation can increase as these groups are formed when citizens feel that a working group is needed to evaluate an upcoming proposal or facility. Community monitoring of pollutants is also a form of public participation that is sometimes overlooked. Although seemingly insignificant, this could put pressure on large companies to act in an environmentally friendly way towards their respective communities. Another deviation from

---

167 Eric Dannenmaier, *Sustainable Development Symposium: Democracy in Development: Toward a Legal framework For the Americas* [1998] 11 Tul. Envtl. L.J. [iii], 1

168 Ibid at [6]

169 Thomas Mulliken, Nancy Smith, and Michael Champion, *Inextricably Intertwined- Environmental Management and the Public* [2005] 17 Geo. Int'l Envtl. L. Rev. [vii]

traditional participation is regulatory negotiation which was developed to form dialogue among regulators, regulated parties, and interested parties.[170] It is used in rule-making and is considered an efficient way to form rules with which everyone can live.[171]

Perhaps the most advanced of all forms of public participation currently available is found through the internet. It has given the public and policy-makers access to information that was not even remotely available ten years ago. The internet, and other factors, have facilitated the creation of new "networks" of organizations, individuals and experts devoted to finding new ways to do work in the field - whether in conjunction with or wholly apart from work by government officials. This new capability helps bring to the international setting the possibility of decentralized, grassroots style communication and action that can aid in effective public participation.[172]

The participation of representatives of NGOs has been another important element of public participation. The participation by non-state actors in the international legal system enhances accountability because it can give a voice to citizens who would otherwise be unrepresented, ensure that actions taken meet local needs, counter effects of high-level governmental corruption, and therefore produce outcomes that maximize human welfare, efficiently.[173]

At the level of the individual citizen, public participation serves a variety of important roles. It is able to create feelings of self-confidence and shared control of government or a greater sense of control over one's life.[174] This feeling of political efficacy can also lead individuals to perceive the decision

---

170 Sarah Pirk, *Expanding Public Participation in Environmental Justice: Methods, Legislation, Litigation and Beyond* [2002] 17 J. Envtl. L. & Litig. 207, 4

171 Ibid.

172 Peter Lallas, *The Role of Process and Participation in the Development of Effective International Environmental Agreements: A Study of the Global Treaty on Persistent Organic Pollutants (POPs)* [2000] UCLA Journal of Environmental Law and Policy 19(1), 3

173 Ibid at [17]

174 Nancy Spike, *Public Participation in Environmental Decision-making at the New Millennium: Structuring New Spheres of Public Influence* [1999] 26 B.C. Envtl. Aff. L. Rev. 263, 4

making process as more democratic.[175] It is anchored by the democratic values of political equality and popular sovereignty which are thrust upon the republican form of government.[176] Since government is derived from the people, all citizens have the right to influence governmental decisions, and the government should respond to them.[177] The people therefore act as watchdogs of the government.[178]

In the absence of public participation, judgments about the distribution of environmental amenities or effects do not reside with those individuals and communities that will be affected most directly by the state of the environment. These putative decision-makers are not elected representatives responsive or accountable to the public, but bureaucrats or agency employees. In turn, the public may feel the loss of its right to govern, either directly through deliberative means or indirectly through elected representatives.[179] Private rights are even more important than any of a nation's current laws and policies as they are classified as "fundamental" and are protected by the highest law of the land, that is, constitutions.[180] Consequently, the right to participate becomes particularly important with regard to those regulatory decisions that could affect one's life or the security of the person[181] which can be interpreted, by extension, to include their environment. Public participation is also able to run against the tide of public mistrust and increase transparency.[182] Meaningfully implemented, citizen participation encourages government accountability, ensures continuation of a participatory de-

---

175 Ibid at [4]

176 Ibid at [3]

177 Nancy Spike, *Public Participation in Environmental Decision-making at the New Millennium: Structuring New Spheres of Public Influence* [1999] 26 B.C. Envtl. Aff. L. Rev. 263, 3

178 John Duncan Jr., *Multicultural Participation In The Public Hearing Process: Some Theoretical, Pragmatical and Analeptical Considerations* [1999] Colum. J. Envtl. L. 169, 5.

179 Eileen Jones, *Risky Assessments: Uncertainty in Science and the Human Dimensions of Environmental Decision-making* [1997] 22 Wm . & Mary Envtl.: & Pol'y Rev. 1,3

180 William Tileman, *Participation in the Environmental Impact Assessment Process: A Comparative Study of Impact Assessment in Canada, the United States and the European Community* [1995] Vol. 33, 7

181 Ibid at [22]

182 Julie Lemmer, *Cleaning up Development: EIA in Two of the World's Largest and Most Rapidly Developing Countries* [2007] 19 Geo. Int'l Envtl. L. Rev. 275, 2

mocracy and can even, in an environmental context, stimulate inventive and socially acceptable answers to environmental problems.[183]

The most ineffective public participation technique is the public hearing.[184] To be meaningful, the opportunity to participate should be genuine, commensurate with the importance of the issue, open, equally available to competing interests, and sufficiently early in the process.[185] Private and unsophisticated people speak to values rather than clouded issues lost in technical evidence.[186] Participation is essentially able to avoid the intellectual vacuum of closed door thinking.[187]

The constitutional right to participation, as it exists in most countries, has two components which would form part of fundamental justice.[188] First, and most important, people need a right of access to the decision-maker which includes timely notice. Second, people need access to information, including background information held by the regulators, submissions made by any party, opinions or recommendations by government, reasons for earlier decisions and information about the law and procedures followed by the administrative body in reaching a decision. Broader participation creates more information and alternatives to be presented to decision-makers, enhancing the opportunity to mesh public values and government policy.[189]

The new status quo is no longer to "announce and defend"[190] but rath-

---

183 Michael Jeffrey, *Intervenor Funding as the Key to Effective Citizen Participation in Environmental Decision Making: Putting the People Back into the Picture* Arizona Journal of International and Comparative Law 19 [2002], 3

184 Le Roy Paddock, *Environmental Accountability and Public Involvement* [2001] 21 Pace Envtl. L. Rev. 243 (2004), 1

185 William Tileman, *Participation in the Environmental Impact Assessment Process: A Comparative Study of Impact Assessment in Canada, the United States and the European Community* [1995] Vol. 33, 22

186 Ibid at [3]

187 Ibid at [3]

188 Ibid at [23]

189 Ibid at [1]

190 Eileen Jones, *Knights at the Roundtable: Public Participation Joins The Battle to Clean Up Cold War Waste* [1997] 8 Fordham Envtl. L.J. 277, 2

er it is "open and participatory".[191] Open and participatory environmental decision-making allows an informed citizenry to contribute to the efforts of a transparent and accountable government in producing higher quality decisions concerning the environment.[192] The limiting factor to growth and progress is no longer the ability to raise capital or increase production but the ability to achieve economically sustainable development.[193]

Increasingly, throughout the community of nations, at individual and regional levels, public participation is pervading the course of governance. Chinese citizens experienced unprecedented change with respect to their legal right to participate in decisions affecting the environment when, in 2003, the National People's Congress of the People's Republic of China enacted the *Environmental Impact Assessment Law of the People's Republic of China (EIA Law)*. Although the concept of Environmental Impact Assessments (EIA) had existed in China since 1973, prior to 2003, the public had been effectively absent from the process. The enactment of the EIA Law marked a watershed moment for public participation in China, as public involvement became a required component of the environmental decision-making process.[194]

Traditionally, Canada has been known to be a pro-environmental nation and, of late, it has been a leader in the inclusion of public participation in its environmental laws. The *Canadian Environmental Assessment Act, Section* 4(d) ensures that there are opportunities for timely and meaningful public participation throughout the environmental assessment process.[195] In fact, the Province of Ontario, Canada went a step further and, in 1998, introduced 'The *Intervenor Funding Project Act*' to remove any deterrent that the public may face in pursuing environmental justice. The Act does not assess costs against unsuccessful public interest litigants because of the "chilling effect" that awarding costs against them might have on public interest rep-

---

191 Jesse Moorman. *Promoting and Strengthening Public Participation in China's Environmental Impact Assessment Process* [2007] 8 Vt. J. Envtl. L. 281

192 Ibid at [13]

193 Ibid at [12]

194 Ibid at [1]

195 Ryan Fritsch '*The Joyous Environmentalism: Fostering Creative Democratic Discourses in Law and Community*' [2004] 18 W.R.L.S.I. 1, 5

resentation. In their view, for a private citizen or public interest intervener, the financial liability for an unsuccessful claim may constitute a significant deterrent.[196]

The Canadian trend has influenced the decisions of their neighbours in the USA who themselves have been enacting certain legislation empowering "the people" to participate in environmental protection through both administrative and adjudicative proceedings.[197] Citizens may have the opportunity to participate in two types of environmental administrative proceedings: rule making and adjudication. Rule making is an agency action that creates a regulation intended to implement, interpret, and prescribe a statute or policy. In other words, rule making is the process of making rules that apply prospectively to relevant parties. Adjudication is the process of resolving disputes between an agency and a particular party. Adjudications result in orders that resolve the matter in dispute.[198]

Within Latin America and the Caribbean, the concept of public participation in environmental decision-making is gaining some momentum but in its own unique way through non-governmental organisations. Most NGOs in the Latin American and Caribbean region are not membership or constituency based. Instead, they are "expert" organizations that derive their credibility from their academic knowledge of a subject rather than their representation of a specific group of citizens.[199] They also often receive funding (or partial funding) from foreign or international sources, leading to the occasional charge that they have even less of a voice in domestic affairs than they might otherwise be entitled to have. These organisations are, however, a legitimate part of the public, and provide representative voices for the same. Many of them share the view that while trade, treasury, and *hacienda* ministries focus on opening markets [FTAA-Free Trade Area of the Americas] and securing new economic pacts, progress towards meaningful participatory democracy must continue on a parallel and equal path

---

196 Michael Jeffrey, *Intervenor Funding as the Key to Effective Citizen Participation in Environmental Decision Making: Putting the People Back into the Picture* [2007] Arizona Journal of International and Comparative Law 19 [2002], 7

197 Ibid at [4]

198 Ibid at [4]

199 Eric Dannenmaier, *Sustainable Development Symposium* [1998] 11 Tul. Envtl. L.J. [iii], 3

if the region's growth is to be sustained.[200]

Further to this, the Organisation of American States (OAS) has initiated the *Inter-American Program of Action for Environmental Protection*. This resolution of the General Assembly of the OAS places a high priority on public awareness and participation. It directs its members to promote greater education and information access to the general public and NGOs so that such groups can participate in efforts to improve and protect the environment in the region.[201]

The European region is by no means lagging behind and, with the aid of the United Nations Economic Committee for Europe (UNECE) since 1998; it began its move towards greater public participation. From June 23 to 25, 1998, the Fourth Conference of the Parties met at Aarhus, Denmark where they formulated the *Convention on Access to Information, Public Participation in Decision-Making, and Access to Justice in Environmental Matters (the Aarhus Convention)*.[202] The *Aarhus Convention* opened for signature on June 25, 1998 to the fifty-five members of the UNECE, which includes most European countries, the former Soviet Union, the United States, and Canada. By the closing of the signature period on December 21, 1998, thirty-five countries and the European Union, excluding Germany, had signed the Convention.[203]

The *Aarhus Convention* allows the public to participate in certain governmental decisions regarding the granting of permits for various activities. The comprehensive list of governmental decisions covered by the Convention is similar to the activities subject to the environmental impact assessment requirements of the *Convention on Environmental Impact Assessment in a Transboundary Context*.

---

200 Ibid at [1]

201 Thomas Mulliken, Nancy Smith, and Michael Champion, *Inextricably Intertwined- Environmental Management and the Public* [2005] 17 Geo. Int'l Envtl. L. Rev. [vii], 16

202 *Convention on Access To Information, Public Participation in Decision-Making and Access to Justice in Environmental Matters,* 1998

203 Sean McAllister, *Human Rights and the Environment: The Convention on Access to Information, Public Participation in Decision-making and Access to Justice in Environmental Matters* [1998] 9 Colorado Journal of Environmental International Law and Policy 187, 5.

Annex I of the Convention sets out the covered activities, which include: "(1) energy production, (2) metal production and processing, (3) mineral and chemical production activities, (4) waste management activities, (5) paper and pulp production, (6) transportation infrastructure development, (7) animal-based food production activities, (8) water resources transfers, and (9) other activities that could have a significant effect on the environment".[204]

Signatories to the *Aarhus Convention* must inform their citizens of certain potential governmental decisions either by public or individual notice, where appropriate, and further, they must be informed early in the decision-making process. Notification must include the proposed activity, the nature of the possible decision, the public agency responsible, and the projected procedure for allowing the public to effectively participate in the process. Moreover, the *Aarhus Convention* requires signatories to allow the public to submit "any comments, information, analyses or opinions that it considers relevant to the proposed activity."[205]

The *Aarhus Convention* is the first multinational environmental agreement that focuses exclusively on obligations of nations to their citizens and NGOs. The *Aarhus Convention's* compliance mechanism includes several significant features including; (1) the ability of NGOs to nominate experts for possible election to the Compliance Committee; (2) the requirement that all Committee members be independent experts rather than representatives of state Parties to the Convention; and (3) the right of any member of the public and any NGO to file a "communication" with the Committee alleging a Party's non-compliance.[206] In fact, the Convention makes explicit mention of the term "public participation":

Article 6 - Each Party shall provide for early public participation, when all options are open and effective public participation can take place.[207]

---

204 Ibid at [3] and [4]

205 Ibid at [4]

206 Svitlana Kravchenko, *The Aarhus Convention and Innovations in Compliance with Multilateral Environmental Agreements* [2007] 18 Colo. J. Int'l Envtl. L. & Pol'y 1, 1

207 Le Roy Paddock, *Environmental Accountability and Public Involvement* [2004] 21 Pace Envtl. L. Rev. 243

Other examples of regional initiatives include the *Asia Europe Meeting* (ASEM) partners who have developed both binding and non-binding regional agreements focusing on environmental conservation and sustainability. These agreements contain provisions that promote the enhancement of public environmental awareness by developing and implementing educational programs and facilitating the sharing of environmental information among government, industry, and citizen groups. Further, ASEM has embarked, at the ministerial level, on a non-binding Asian initiative that would seek to implement public involvement in environmental issues at the same level as that sought by Europeans under the Aarhus Convention.

Likewise, the *Arab Ministerial Conference on Environment and Development has issued an Arab Declaration on Environment and Development and Future Perspectives (Arab Declaration).* The *Arab Declaration,* among other things, stresses that environmental protection and sustainable development require that States give support to individuals, local organisations and NGOs. The Arab Declaration views these groups as representative of popular participation, a concept which must be given due attention. Under this view, individuals and organisations shall have the "right to acquire information about environmental issues...access to data...and to participate in the formulation and implementation of decisions that may affect their environment".[208]

The importance of public participation goes beyond a mere "silencing" of environmental activists and other NGOs. In fact, it can also help to overcome deficiencies in regulatory oversight associated with limited government resources.[209] Citizens must have an intimate understanding of local environmental threats and violations of applicable laws, and can offer this knowledge to broaden government consideration and heighten awareness of these local issues. In addition, citizens can supplement potentially scarce government resources for monitoring and enforcement, ultimately saving the government time and money.[210] Meaningful citizen participation is essential to a democratic society because it promotes legitimacy and account-

---

208 Thomas Mulliken, Nancy Smith, and Michael Champion, *Inextricably Intertwined- Environmental Management and the Public* [2005] 17 Geo. Int'l Envtl. L. Rev. [vii], 16

209 Jesse Moorman, *Promoting and Strengthening Public Participation in China's Environmental Impact Assessment Process* [2007] 8 Vt. J. Envtl. L. 281, 3

210 Ibid.

ability in governmental decision-making processes and may drive the development of more innovative and socially acceptable solutions.[211] To further emphasize these benefits, in 1990, then President Clinton received a report from The Sustainable Communities Task Force stating that-

> *Lasting solutions [to environmental problems] are best identified when people from every part of a community - business, citizens, economic development and environmental groups, elected officials, civic organizations, religious institutions, and so forth - are brought together in a spirit of cooperation and respect to identify solutions to community problems.* [212]

Implementing public participation ideologies and theories into national policies and laws takes on greater significance when it is considered that most nations are signatories to international conventions endorsing such policies. The *Universal Declaration of Human Rights*, for example, provides that "everyone has the right to take part in the government of his country, directly or through chosen representatives". *Article 19 of the Declaration* provides also that "everyone has the right to freedom of opinion and expression; this right includes freedom to...seek, receive, and impart information and ideas through any media".[213] Another such example can be found within the *World Charter for Nature*, approved as a resolution of the United Nations General Assembly, which recommends that "all persons, in accordance with their national legislation, shall have the opportunity to participate, individually or with others, in the formulation of decisions of direct concern to their environment, and shall have access to means of redress when their environment has suffered damage or degradation".[214] In 1992, the *Rio Declaration on Environmental Development* was also added to the list of international treaties encouraging public participation;

---

211 Adam Bran, *Public Participation Provisions Need Not Contribute To Environmental Injustice* [1996] Temp. Pol. & Civ. Rts. L. Rev 5, 3

212 Lee Roy Paddock, *Environmental Accountability and Public Involvement* [2004] 21 Pace Envtl. L. Rev. 243.

213 Thomas Mulliken, Nancy Smith, and Michael Champion, *Inextricably Intertwined- Environmental Management and the Public* [2005] 17 Geo. Int'l Envtl. L. Rev. [vii], 14

214 Neil Popovic, *The Right To Participate in Decisions that affect The Environment* [1993] 10 Pace Envtl. L. Rev. 683, 3

Principle 10 of the Rio Declaration states: Environmental issues are best han-
dled with the participation of all concerned citizens, at the relevant level. At the
national level, each shall have appropriate access to information concerning the
environment that is held by public authorities, including information on hazard-
ous materials and activities in their communities, and the opportunity to partic-
ipate in decision-making processes. States shall facilitate and encourage public
awareness and participation by making information widely available. Effective
access to judicial administrative proceedings, including redress and remedy, shall
be provided.[215]

The *Rio Declaration* essentially codified the basic and familiar concepts underlying effective public participation; (1) access to information; (2) right
to participate in decision-making; (3) right to judicial enforcement; and (4)
remedy.[216] The *Rio Declaration* states that "environmental issues are best handled with the participation of all concerned citizens at the relevant level".[217]

Global trends also highlight a positive correlation between public participation and economic growth. This "nexus" between public participation
and successful economic growth is reflected in the historical experiences
of developed and heavily industrialised States such as the USA and the
countries that make up the European Union.[218] It is no coincidence that
these countries have created elaborate mechanisms for environmental public participation rights and have been the most successful at injecting those
rights into broad, far-reaching environmental legislation.[219]

Public participation in environmental decision-making is at the cornerstone
of democracy which echoes the phrase "by the people for the people", by
which the political leaders in a democratic country are elected. This principle is embodied in most of the constitutions of the countries of the world,

---

215 Thomas Mulliken, Nancy Smith, and Michael Champion, *Inextricably Intertwined- Envi-*
     ronmental Management and the Public [2005] 17 Geo. Int'l Envtl. L. Rev. [vii], 15

216 Ibid.

217 Julie Lemmer, *Cleaning up Development: EIA in Two of the World's Largest and Most Rapidly*
     Developing Countries [2007] 19 Geo. Int'l Envtl. L. Rev. 275, 5

218 Thomas Mulliken, Nancy Smith, and Michael Champion, *Inextricably Intertwined- Envi-*
     ronmental Management and the Public [2005] 17 Geo. Int'l Envtl. L. Rev. [vii], 1

219 Ibid at [2]

whereby the nation's policies are founded upon the duty of the State to protect and serve its citizens and by extension provide a safe and secure environment.[220] Although, for the most part, this duty has been overlooked in the past due to the short term vision of most governments whose focus lie in immediate economic gain, the tides of political pressure from pro-participation groups have led many governments to reconsider the foundations by which they operate. The people and what they value the most are now beginning to take greater priority for leaders around the world.

JUDICIAL SUPPORT OF PUBLIC PARTICIPATION IN THE ENVIRONMENTAL DECISION MAKING PROCESS

The system of planning approval with the requirement to assess environmental impacts of a proposed activity has been scrutinized by the Courts of most countries that have introduced an EIA process. Almost all EIA systems make provision for some type of public involvement. This term includes public consultation (or dialogue) and public participation, which is a more interactive and intensive process of stakeholder engagement. At a minimum, public involvement must provide an opportunity for those directly affected by a proposal to express their views regarding the proposal and its environmental and social impacts.

Moreover, there has been judicial recognition of the role of the public consultation and participation and as per Justice Sykes:

> It is now safe to say that consultation of citizens by public bodies and authorities is now a well-established feature of modern governance.[221]

In the United States Supreme Court, Justice Stevens delivering the judgment of the Court recognized the importance of public involvement in

---

220 William Tileman. *Participation in the Environmental Impact Assessment Process: A Comparative Study of Impact Assessment in Canada, the United States and the European Community* [1995] Vol. 33, 7

221 **Northern Jamaica Conservation Association and Others v National Resources Conservation Authority and Other, HCV 3022 of 2005 [38]**. See also, **Belize Tourism Industry Association v, National Environmental Appraisal Committee, Department of Environment and Belize Island Holdings Limited, CN. 223 of 2014**

the EIA process. As stated by Justice Stevens, the significance of the public consultation in the EIA process was highlighted.

The statutory requirement that an...agency contemplating a major action prepare an environmental impact statement ensures that the agency, in reaching its decision, will have available, and will carefully consider, detailed information concerning significant environmental impacts. It also guarantees that the relevant information will be made available to the larger audience that may also play a role in both the decision making process and the implementation of that decision.

Publication of an EIS, both in draft and final form, also serves a larger informational role. It gives the public the assurance that the agency "has indeed considered environmental concerns in its decision making process," Baltimore Gas & Electric Co., supra, at 97, and, perhaps more significantly, provides a springboard for public comment Strycker's Bay Neighbourhood Council, Inc., supra, at 227-228.[222]

Again in Australia, it was stated by SA Forgie:

There can be little doubt that the public does have a real and legitimate interest in the environmental consequences of proposed projects. Furthermore, there can be little doubt that it has an interest in the proper assessment of those consequences and, if the project proceeds, the management of those consequences. It follows that the public has an interest in having relevant information to assess these matters. The desirability of public disclosure is recognized...[223]

The highest Court in the United Kingdom has also joined the public participation bandwagon. As stated by Lord Hoffman:

And an essential element in this procedure is that what the Regulations call the environmental statement by the developer should have been made available to the public and that the public should have been given the opportunity to express an opinion in accordance with article 6.2 of the Directive.[224]

Indeed, it can be argued that the willingness by Courts to embrace public

---

222 **Robertson v. Methow Valley Citizens Council, [1989] 490 U.S. 332**

223 **The Environment Centre NT Inc v. Department of the Environment Sport and Territories No. D93/27 AAT No. 9781**, Paragraph 114

224 **Berkeley v. Secretary of State for the Environment [2001] ELR 303** paras. 7-9.

participation as a critical feature of the EIA process lies in the common law duty of fairness so often imposed on Government agencies. It is understandable therefore, why the courts have stated that there is a duty that public consultation and/or participation must be fair, genuine and meaningful, has been fully endorsed by the Courts.

The classic statement of the basic requirements of consultation is that formulated by Mr. Stephen Sedley Q.C. (as he then was) in the case of *Regina v Brent London Borough Council, Ex Parte Gunning and others*[225] and applied in *Northern Jamaica Conservation Association and Others v National Resources Conservation Authority and Other.*[226]

> *It is common ground that, whether or not consultation of interested parties and the public is a legal requirement, if it is embarked upon it must be carried out properly. To be proper, consultation must be undertaken at a time when proposals are still at a formative stage; it must include sufficient reasons for particular proposals to allow those consulted to give intelligent consideration and an intelligent response; adequate time must be given for this purpose; and the product of consultation must be conscientiously taken into account when the ultimate decision is taken.*

The issue of consultation and fairness was re-visited by Lord Woolf MR in 2001 in the United Kingdom when he articulated and stated the limitations of the principle of fairness and public consultation in the following terms:

> *... consultation is not litigation: the consulting authority is not required to publicize every submission it receives or (absent some statutory obligation) to disclose all its advice. Its obligation is to let those who have a potential interest in the subject matter know in clear terms what the proposal is and exactly why it is under positive consideration, telling them enough (which may be a good deal) to enable them to make an intelligent response. The obligation, although it may be quite onerous, goes no further than this.*[227]

Maurice Kay J in 2002 followed Lord Woolf MR and rejected the submission that fairness had ceased to be an aspect of a lawful consultation

---

225 [1985] 84 L.G.R. 168, 189

226 HCV 3022 of 2005 [38]

227 ***R. v North Devon HA Ex p. Coughlan [2001] Q.B.213 [112]***

process:

> *It is an aspect of what is 'proper' -- the word used in Coughlan (para 108). ... it is axiomatic that consultation, whether it is a matter of obligation or undertaken voluntarily, requires fairness." (paragraph 28): The Queen on the Application of Greenpeace Limited v. Secretary of State for Trade and Industry CO/8197/2006, [2007] EWHC 311 (Admin).*[228]

The issue of fairness received stirring endorsement in 2006 by Lord Justice Auld who stated that:

> *It is an accepted general principle of administrative law that a public body undertaking consultation must do so fairly as required by the circumstances of the case... "consultation must be fair to those who have an interest in it ...: what is fair depends on the nature of the subject matter..." and that "fairness requires that objectors should be given sufficient information to enable them to challenge the accuracy of any facts and the validity of any argument which can be seen by the decision-making body as truly likely to be influential in its decision-making process.*[229]

The English Courts in determining that there is a common law duty of fairness has had to derive judicial criteria for determining when such a common law duty has been breached. According to Mr. Justice Sullivan:

> *The overriding requirement that any consultation must be fair is not in doubt...A consultation exercise which is flawed in one, or even in a number of respects, is not necessarily so procedurally unfair as to be unlawful. With the benefit of hindsight, it will almost invariably be possible to suggest ways in which a consultation exercise might have been improved upon. That is most emphatically not the test. It must also be recognized that a decision-maker will usually have a broad discretion as to how a consultation exercise should be carried out. This applies with particular force to a consultation with the whole of the adult population of the United Kingdom. The defendant had a very broad discretion as to how best to carry out such a far-reaching consultation exercise. In reality, a conclusion that*

---

228 **R (Medway Council and others) v Secretary of State for Transport [2002] EWHC 2516 [28]**

229 **R (Edwards and others) v Environment Agency and others [2006] EWCA Civ 877 [93]**

a consultation exercise was unlawful on the ground of unfairness will be based upon a finding by the court, not merely that something went wrong, but that something went "clearly and radically" wrong.[230]

PUBLIC PARTICIPATION IN THE NEW ENVIRONMENTAL LEGAL REGIME OF TRINIDAD AND TOBAGO

The Environmental Management Act

Prior to 1995, there was no specialist agency dealing with environmental protection in TT. It was hardly surprising, therefore, in light of the environmental challenges facing TT, that civil society looked on with much anticipation at the establishment of the EMA in 1995, with the promulgation of an entirely new legal regime for the protection of the environment.[231] This legal regime recognised the importance of public participation.

The Preamble to the Environmental Management Act[232] sets out the spirit of the legislation and its intended objectives. The preamble makes it quite pellucid that public concerns are critical to the development of an effective legal regime for the protection of the environment. *The Preamble to the Environmental Management Act* states:

> *Whereas, the Government of the Republic of Trinidad and Tobago (hereinafter called "the Government") is committed to developing a national strategy for sustainable development, being the balance of economic growth with environmentally sound practices, in order to enhance the quality of life and meet the needs of present and future generations;... And Whereas, management and conservation of the environment and the impact of environmental conditions on human health constitute a shared responsibility and benefit for everyone in the society requiring*

---

230 *R (on the Application of Greenpeace Limited) v. Secretary of State for Trade and Industry [2007] EWHC 311*

231 *Environmental Management Act, Chap 35:05*

232 The *Environmental Management Act* was simply a replacement of the *Environmental Management Act No. 3 of 1995* without any substantial changes. The replacement arose out of constitutional questions and the *Environmental Management Act* was passed to facilitate the legislation being the beneficiary of a special majority rather than a simple majority.

co-operation and co-ordination of public and private sector activities;... And whereas, in furtherance of its commitment, the Government is undertaking the establishment and operation of an Environmental Management Authority to co-ordinate, facilitate and oversee execution of the national environmental strategy and programmes, to promote public awareness of environmental concerns, and to establish an effective regulatory regime which will protect, enhance and conserve the environment...

The *Environmental Management Act* continues to define the general principles articulated in the preamble and the objects of the *Environmental Management Act* def the public role in terms of awareness and participation.

Section 4 of the Environmental Management Act

(4) Objects of the Act (a) promote and encourage among all persons a better understanding and appreciation of the environment;... (c) ensure the establishment of an integrated environmental management system in which the Authority, in consultation with other persons, determines priorities and facilitates coordination among Governmental entities to effectively harmonise activities designed to protect, enhance and conserve the environment..."

The general functions of the EMA also include the role of fostering public awareness and public participation.

Section 6 of the Environmental Management Act

6(1) The general functions of the Authority are to - e) promote educational and public awareness programmes on the environment;

(2) In performing its functions, the Authority shall facilitate co-operation among persons and manage the environment in a manner which fosters participation and promotes consensus, including the encouragement and use of appropriate means to avoid or expeditiously resolve disputes through mechanism for alternative dispute resolution."

National Environmental Policy

An important aspect of the statutory regime for public participation in the decision making process is the NEP 2018 which enshrines public participation as part of the environmental management system.

Section 1.05 - Public participation is critical to sustainable development and is a prerequisite for responsive, transparent and accountable governmental entities and civil society organisations. It is also acknowledged that meaningful public participation can only be attained where there are transparent public processes, and access to appropriate, timely and comprehensible information concerning the environment held by public authorities. Such information must be made widely available without imposing undue financial burdens on the applicant and with adequate protection of privacy and business confidentiality. Consequently, all governmental entities of Trinidad and Tobago shall, in accordance with Principle 10 of the Rio Declaration, facilitate and encourage public awareness and participation in environmental and developmental matters by making information widely available, and ensuring effective access to judicial and administrative proceedings, including redress and remedy.

Section 2.20 Communication, Education and Public Participation The GoRTT recognises that empowering individuals to undertake environmentally responsible behaviour also requires systemic reinforcement of pro-environmental behaviours and knowledge. This entails continuous environmental education and public participation in environmental decision-making. It is the Government's policy that all environmental education in Trinidad and Tobago is in keeping with the goals, objectives and characterisations contained in the Belgrade Charter (1975), the Tbilisi Declaration (1977) and Chapter 36 or Agenda 21 (1992). To this end, and in keeping with SDG 4, the GoRTT will: a) Continue to introduce environmental education from pre-school school age to adulthood, for both formal and informal sectors, with the goal of providing knowledge of both local and global environmental issues as well as the skills required to enable effective public participation, decision-making and action; b) Further the integration of sustainable development concepts and the principles of this NEP into all education programmes and curricula; c) Mobilise resources and encourage partnerships among national, regional and international entities towards building public awareness and behavioural change; d) Coordinate environmental education and awareness programmes initiated by the public, private and non-governmental sectors at the national level; e) Empower public agencies to undertake environmental communication, awareness and education programmes based on local environmental issues in a manner appropriate for the target community; f) Support the development and promotion of mechanisms that provide viable solutions to environmental problems in communities; g) Ensure that mechanisms established for meaningful participation in decision-making regarding environmental and/or development issues are appropriately promoted, and made available to the public; and h) Ensure that all efforts at education, awareness-building and meaningful participation in decision-making regarding environmental and/or development issues encourage and facilitate the inclusion of marginalised groups such as indigenous peoples, the rural poor, children, youth, women, sick, disabled and elderly.

The courts have now sanctioned the binding statutory power of the NEP in *Fishermen and Friends of the Sea v The Minister of Planning, Housing and the Environment.*[233]

It is necessary now to see how the environmental legal regime has emerged with respect to public participation in the two main areas of regulatory concern, namely the regulation of new and significantly modified activities through the CEC process and the reduction of the pollution inventory of TT through the use of the permitting mechanism.

Making of Rules

The Minister with responsibility for the *Environmental Management Act* is empowered to make rules to give effect to the objectives of the legislation. According to *Section 26 of the Environmental Management Act*:

(26) The Minister may, in accordance with section 27, make Rules subject to negative resolution of Parliament, for the following: (a) procedures for the registration of sources from which pollutants may be released into the environment and the characterisation of such sources; (b) the quantity, condition or concentration of pollutants or substances containing pollutants that may be released into the environment generally or by specific sources or categories of sources; (c) procedures and standards with respect to permits or licences required for a person to install or operate any process or other source from which pollutants will be or may continue to be released into the environment; (d) the form and manner of — (i) applying

---

233 PCA No. 0028 of 2016

for any licence, permit or certification that may be required or granted by the Authority; (ii) revoking, suspending, varying or cancelling a permit or licence or a condition in that permit or licence; (e) procedures, standards and guidelines for the formal designation and protection of "environmentally sensitive areas" or "environmentally sensitive species" under section 41; (f) incentive programmes or mechanisms which encourage the use of effective environmental systems and the achievement of improvements in environmental quality, as provided in section 34; (g) designation of hazardous substances or categories of hazardous substances under section 59, and the performance standards, procedures, safeguards and licensing or permitting requirements in accordance with which such hazardous substances shall be handled; (h) the procedure to be followed by any person required to apply for and receive a certificate of environmental clearance, and the standards for preparation and submission of any environmental impact assessment which may be required under sections 35 to 38 inclusive; (i) the definition of various categories of waste under sections 55 to 57 inclusive, the requirements with respect to the handling and disposal of such categories of waste, and the licensing of facilities at which such wastes are handled or disposed; (j) procedures and standards for the periodic or continual monitoring of pollutant releases in conjunction with any process, activity, vehicle or premises; (k) the establishment of ambient environmental quality criteria and standards which may be taken into account in setting any general, categorical or source-specific limitations under paragraph (b) for any new or continued release of pollutants into the environment; (l) the design, construction, operation, maintenance and monitoring of facilities or processes for the control of pollution and the handling of wastes; and (m) any other matter required to be, or which may be prescribed by the Authority.

Public participation is embedded in the rule making process.

Sections 27-28 of the Environmental Management Act

27(1) In the course of developing Rules, the Minister shall— (a) submit draft Rules for public comment in accordance with section 28; (b) consider the public comments received and revise the Rules as he thinks fit; (c) cause the Rules to be published in the Gazette and laid thereafter in Parliament.

(2) Any Rules made by the Minister shall become effective when the Rules are published in the Gazette or at such later time as may be specified in the Rules.

28(1) Where a provision of this Act specifically requires compliance with this section, the Authority shall— (a) publish a notice of the proposed action in the Gazette and at least one daily newspaper of general circulation— (i) advising of the matter being submitted for public comment, including a general description of the matter under consideration; (ii) identifying the location or locations where the administrative record is being maintained; (iii) stating the length of the public comment period; and (iv) advising where the comments are to be sent; (b) establish and maintain an administrative record regarding the proposed action and make such administrative record available to the public at one or more locations.

(2) The administrative record required under subsection (1) shall include a written description of the proposed action, the major environmental issues involved in the matter under consideration, copies of documents or other supporting materials which the Authority believes would assist the public in developing a reasonable understanding of those issues, and a statement of the Authority's reasons for the proposed action.

(3) The Authority shall receive written comments for not less than thirty days from the date of notice in the Gazette and, if the Authority determines there is sufficient public interest, it may hold a public hearing for discussing the proposed action and receiving verbal comments.

The *Environmental Management Act*, therefore, built into its statutory regime the need for public participation on rules that would vest power in the EMA to grant permits to facilitate continuing pollution within a legal framework. However, it must be observed that the *Environmental Management Act* makes no provision for public participation in the granting of permits. Rules have been made to deal with water pollution, sensitive areas and sensitive species; however, these rules fail to provide any avenue for the public to comment on the grant of a permit to any particular entity. This is of much concern as TT follows a pattern of mixed development and it is not unusual for a heavy polluting industry to be in close proximity to residential communities. Despite this, the public has no means of expressing its view on the grant of a permit during the permit application process and must resort to judicial review if there is disagreement with the terms and conditions of the permit granted by the EMA. It is noteworthy however that with respect to noise and air, there is provision for public participation in the granting of a permit for the emission of noise and air pollutants.

> *Rule 10 of the Noise Pollution Control Rules 2001[234] states:*
>
> *(1) an application for a variation with respect to an event or activity shall... (d) be placed in one national daily newspaper in a form prescribed by the Authority for a period of at least two (2) consecutive days and at least one calendar week before the submission of the application for a variation;*
>
> *(2) An application for a variation with respect to a facility shall: (b) be placed in one national daily newspaper in a form prescribed by the Authority for a period of at least two (2) consecutive days and at least one calendar week before the submission of the application for a variation;...*
>
> *Rule 11 provides for affected person.*
>
> *(1) The Authority may, during the determination of an application under these Rules, request oral information or additional written information from - (b) a person who is directly affected by the application...*

The vesting of the right in the public to comment on the issuance of permits for the emission of noise and air pollutants is commendable but somewhat strange in light of the refusal to provide a similar right with respect to a permit for water pollution.

Environmental Approval

The CEC process allows the EMA to control the environmental impacts associated with new developments or environmental impacts associated with the significant modification of existing developments. The CEC is intended to ensure that there is limited or no environmental consequences of development activities occurring in the post *Environmental Management Act* era. As expected, the CEC process has been placed under more intense judicial scrutiny than any other aspect of the *Environmental Management Act*. While the issue of public participation in the CEC process has been a key component of the judicial examination, there are other important aspects that must be examined. Therefore, the CEC process and its judicial interpretation includ-

---

234 L.N. No. 60 of 2001.

ing public participation in the decision making process shall be dealt with in a chapter of its own.

CHAPTER 4

THE CERTIFICATE OF ENVIRONMENTAL CLEARANCE PROCESS

APPLICATION FOR A CEC

The CEC process allows the EMA to control the environmental impacts associated with new developments or with significant modification of existing developments. The CEC is intended to ensure that there is limited or no environmental consequences of developmental activities occurring in the post *Environmental Management Act* era.

Implementing the CEC process starts with engaging in a new or significantly modified construction, process, works or other activity with respect to an activity identified in the *CEC (Designated Activities) Order*[235].

> *Section 35 of the Environmental Management Act*
>
> *35(1) For the purpose of determining the environmental impact which might arise out of any new or significantly modified construction, process, works or other activity, the Minister may by Order subject to negative resolution of Parliament designate a list of activities requiring a certificate of environmental clearance (hereinafter called "Certificate").*
>
> *(2) No person shall proceed with any activity which the Minister has designated as requiring a Certificate unless such person applies for and receives a Certificate from the Authority.*

---

235 L.N. No. 103 of 2001

(3) An application made under this section shall be made in accordance with the manner prescribed.

The *CEC (Designated Activities) Order* identified forty-four activities as requiring a CEC. Accordingly, once a person believes that a CEC is required, such a person is required to submit an application for a CEC pursuant to *Rule 3 of the CEC Rules*. Upon receipt of the application, there are four options available to the EMA, as set out below.

CEC Not Required

According to *Rule 4(1) (a) of the CEC Rules*, the EMA can notify an applicant that a CEC is not required under the *Environmental Management Act*, which consequently means that the applicant can proceed with the activity subject to the requirements of other relevant legislation.

> *Section 39 of the Environmental Management Act*
>
> *(39) Sections 35 to 38 inclusive shall not apply to—(a) any activity with respect to which, prior to the date on which review under this section first became applicable, all final approvals necessary to proceed already had been obtained from all other governmental entities requiring such approvals;*

The relationship between a CEC from the EMA and approval from other governmental entities was explored in ***Charlotteville Beachfront Movement v Tobago House of Assembly***.[236] As per Rajkumar J:

> *51. It was further contended that the Defendant has been bestowed with the legal authority to proceed with the project in the form of the CEC. Again this is a misunderstanding of the evidence and the purpose of a CEC. (a) The CEC itself makes it clear that its grant does not absolve the defendant from compliance with other statutory requirements. (b) Further a certificate of environmental clearance is simply a certificate that the environmental requirements for such activity specified therein have been complied with. The activity specified in that CEC was construction of a waste water treatment plant. The project itself is wider in scope – namely development of land comprising 15,000 plus square*

---

236 CV 2013-01738

meters in accordance with plans and amended plans submitted to the Town and Country Planning Division.

Similarly, a separate governmental entity such as the Town and Country Planning Division cannot rely on actions of the EMA to justify its planning decision on the basis of being a separate legal entity.

Maharaj and Concerned Residents of Cunupia v Minister of Planning and R.P.N. Enterprises Limited[237]

Held: Dean-Armorer J

I considered whether this constituted a change of circumstances. In my view, the opinion and actions of the EMA, as a separate entity could not constitute a change in circumstances. Whether or not the conditions imposed by the EMA would achieve their objective was a matter to be determined in the future and could not constitute a change at the time of the review. Whether or not the imposed condition would achieve their objective, depended on many variables, not the least of which, was whether the Interested Party would comply. It seems unacceptable that the Minister would reverse his decision on the basis of a hope of compliance, whose enforcement lay in the hands of a separate legal entity.

Further Information Required to Process CEC Application

The EMA may inform an applicant for a CEC that it requires further information to process an application for a CEC pursuant to *Rule 4(1) (b) of the CEC Rules*. This however, has to be construed together with *Rule 4(1) (a) of the CEC Rules* that the application lacks sufficient information to determine whether or not a CEC is required.

---

237 TT 2016 HC 70

Application Does Not Require an Environmental Impact Assessment (EIA)

The applicant, after submitting information required pursuant to *Rule 4(1) (a) and (b) of the CEC Rules*, may be informed by the EMA in accordance with *Rule 4(1) (c) of the CEC Rules* that the application requires a CEC but not an EIA.

The danger inherent in giving the EMA discretion to dispose of an application on the basis of information contained therein must be properly understood. It is correct that an application may be straightforward and on the face of it there may be no adverse environmental effects so that a CEC may be granted. A problem may arise however, when an applicant submits a detailed document (essentially an EIA) together with the application form and the EMA makes a determination that no further information is required and thereby grants a CEC to the applicant. Imagine a situation where a person is living in a highly residential area and then noticing an industrial facility being constructed. The affected person visits the EMA to complain and is told that a CEC was granted for the construction and operation of a hazardous waste disposal unit in his/her neighbourhood. He/she is enraged but is told that the application was complete and there was sufficient information attached to the application, resulting in no need for an EIA. This consequently amounts to a perversion of the spirit and intent of the *Environmental Management Act*. The entire EIA process can be circumvented by an unfortunate exercise of discretion by the EMA to summarily deal with an application. This is critical as statutory public consultation only arises when an EIA is required.

This raises the important issue as to how the EMA ought to exercise its discretion to grant a CEC for certain activities, without the benefit of an EIA. *Bhadase Sooknanan and Friends of the Sea v Environmental Man-agement Authority and the Ministry of Energy,*[238] explored the discretion of the EMA to grant a CEC for a seismic survey without the benefit of an EIA. In this case, judicial review was sought with respect to the decision of the EMA to grant a CEC without an EIA, thereby allowing PETROTRIN, in carrying out a

---

238 CV 2014-00813

3-Dimensional Seismic Survey to cover an area of approximately five hundred and ten (510) kilometres within Soldado Fields and North Marine Field located in the Gulf of Paria off the West Coast of Trinidad.

According to Kangaloo J:

> 26. *The preamble to the EMA Act envisions a collaborative approach, with the EMA working in tandem with the public to protect the environment. In the instant case, conversely, this has turned into a battle between two self-styled heroes of the environment who are at loggerheads, with the Interested Party supporting the EMA.*

> 27. *The EMA on an application by Petrotrin granted a CEC to Petrotrin to conduct a 3- Dimensional Seismic Survey to cover an area of approximately 510 kilometres within Soldado Fields and North Marine Field located in the Gulf of Paria. This CEC was granted without an EIA. Section 35(4) of the EMA provides for an EIA if required. The use of 'if required' by the legislative drafters left it open to the expert body to determine whether one is indeed necessary upon consideration of the specific application. This discretionary power afforded to the EMA is one that allows that authoritative body to decide whether an EIA is needed having regard to the specific detail of the application.*

> 28. *The Applicants say that they do not challenge the issue of the CEC, but rather that the CEC was issued without an EIA. The EMA contends that an EIA was not required, based on the information the EMA had available to it, both from its own resources and from Petrotrin. Consequently, the EMA also submits, that in accordance with its statutory framework, no consultation was required if no EIA was needed.*

> 29. *In arriving at its decision to grant the CEC, the EMA considered various factors. According to Mr. Travis Sooknanan to whom the file was first assigned, he looked at three factors; nature, scale and location of the proposed activity, all of which are instrumental in understanding the type of activity that was to be performed.*

> 30. *With respect to the nature and location of the activity he noted that the area in question was a mature seismic survey field upon which numerous surveys had been conducted previously. The scale of the activity was confined to only 510 km of the Gulf of Paria and it was not intended to last for an extensive period*

of time.

31. He stated that he also considered the proposed mitigation factors of Petrotrin which would include dissemination of information on the survey, proper disposal of solid waste, notices, visual observers who will be on the lookout for marine mammals and compensation to fishermen, all in his assessment of the application. This coupled with his personal knowledge and experience as it relates to CECs, compelled him to recommend that it be granted without needing an EIA.

32. His superiors were also of the opinion based on the evidence before them and their own personal knowledge that an EIA was not necessary. Thus the initial recommendation of Mr. Sooknanan was approved.

33. The Applicants contend that the EMA ought to have had regard to the following reports annexed to the Aboud affidavit – the Kishore, Mangal, Hutchinson and Fisheries Division Reports. The Applicants say these reports contain relevant considerations which the Respondent failed to take into account.

34. Paragraph 4 of the original Aboud affidavit also details the literature and the other communications which have been recorded as well as publications in the media which the he says the Respondent ought to have taken into consideration but did not prior to making its decision.

35. The Applicants also contend that in so far as the Respondent made reference to mitigation measures in the Persadie report in its response to the pre-action protocol correspondence, the EMA nonetheless failed to acknowledge which mitigation measures it was taking into consideration such as seasonal access restrictions, avoidance of spawning and feeding areas and avoidance of nursery areas and migratory paths.

36. The submission of the Applicants is that this is essential to note as it does not auger well for the assessment made by the Respondent that the risks were minor to moderate without referring to any known mitigation measures.

37. In response, the Applicants contend that these reports do not demonstrate a direct correlation between seismic surveys and the degradation of the fishing beds

44. The well-known dicta of Lord Diplock in the case of Council of Civil Service Unions and Others v Minister for the Civil Service [1985] A.C 374

("GCHQ") provides the three prong test for unlawfulness upon which adminis-trative action is subject to control by judicial review; illegality, irrationality, and procedural impropriety.

45. Taking irrationality first, Lord Diplock in GCHQ had this to say:

"By "irrationality" I mean ... a decision which is so outrageous in its defiance of logic or of accepted moral standards that no sensible person who had applied his mind to the question to be decided could have arrived at it. (Associated Provincial Picture Houses Ltd. v. Wednesbury Corporation [1948] 1 K.B. 223)."

46. Senior Counsel for the Respondent submits that taking a holistic approach to the evidence and factors that were considered prior to granting the CEC, it cannot be said that the Respondent acted irrationally or that the decision was so outrageous so as to defy logic.

47. Rather, the Respondents say, what they have done is clearly within the band of possible rational action whereby a decision was taken. More so, anyone raising the question of irrationality has to surmount great obstacles to prove irrationality on the part of the Respondent, such obstacles being compared to a mountain.

48. The Applicants reiterate that the Respondent failed to take into account ger-mane information that would have assisted in its decision and that rather the Respondent had regard to archaic material by looking at reports some twenty years old when there existed more recent documentation in relation to the issue.

49. This Court finds that the Respondent considered relevant factors in coming to its decision to granted Petrotrin a CEC without requiring an EIA. The Respondent considered the nature, location and scale of the activity. The Respondent considered the mitigation measures in place to counter the potential risks. The Respondent considered those who would be affected.

Thus, in the opinion of the High Court of TT, Parliament, by way of the *Environmental Management Act* and its subsidiary legislation, has vested dis-cretion in the EMA to determine whether or not an EIA is required for a particular application. The judge felt that based on the evidence, the EMA had acted rationally in deciding not to require an EIA for an application for a CEC to conduct an offshore seismic survey.

Consultation in Non-EIA Required CEC Approval

The position of statutory public consultation as exclusively part of the EIA process is underscored by several decisions of the Courts on public consultations in the non-EIA required approval process for a CEC.

In one instance, the High Court took the view that when an EIA is not required as part of the CEC approval process, there is no statutory requirement for public consultation but the Court noted favourably, public consultations done voluntarily by an applicant.

In ***Bhadase Sooknanan and Fishermen and Friends of the Sea v Environmental Management Authority and the Ministry of Energy***,[239] Kangaloo J indicated:

> *56. The requirement of public consultation in Trinidad and Tobago is borne out in section 35(5) of the EMA Act. This is only activated and enforced when the EMA has commissioned the preparation of an EIA in relation to the application before it.*

> *57. The Respondent is of the view that there was no express duty on the part of the EMA to consult when considering whether an EIA is required but rather, it is only when an EIA is required that such a duty arises. The case of R (on the application of Hillingdon London Borough Council) v Lord Chancellor (2008) EWHC 2683 suggests that the Respondent had no legal obligation to consult with the Applicants.*

> *58. In response to this the Applicants, relying on the case of Ulric 'Buggy' Haynes Coaching School v The Minister of Planning and Sustainable Development CV2013-05227, submit that the Court is not prevented from imposing such a duty of consultation on a decision maker. Further, the Applicants have lamented throughout their evidence and submissions about the lack of "meaningful" consultation with "meaningful" effect on the part of the EMA. The question that this Court is therefore obliged to pose is - what is meaningful in whose eyes and to whose standards?*

> *59. The Applicants on the one hand contend that the EMA ought itself*

---

239 Ibid.

to have conducted consultation but then on the other hand submit that the EMA ought to have insisted that rather Petrotrin engage in "meaningful" consultation with those persons potentially affected by the activities of Petrotrin.

60. The evidence of the Respondent clearly demonstrates that Petrotrin had three consultation meetings in July 2013 with the fishing community. On a reading of the Atlantic LNG case per Stollmeyer J. this court is satisfied that any such consultation would have been adequately carried either by Petrotrin or by the EMA in more serious cases, in particular where an EIA was required. In that case Stollmeyer J. said: "EMA had a broad discretion in determining whether and when to hold public hearings. There is no express provision requiring follow up public hearings before granting the CEC. That is left up to its discretion ..."

61. Stollmeyer J. goes on: "... section 28 attempts to remedy this by allowing affected communities more meaningful participation in decisions that affect them. It also provides communities with valuable information about the potential health and environmental effects of the project. It affords persons who may be affected the opportunity to voice their concerns ... and correspondingly places EMA under a duty to consider what they say. These persons are given a fair hearing."

62. In the Atlantic LNG case Stollmeyer J found that the consultation process had been accomplished in three stages by virtue of three meetings and so concluded that there was consultation, going further to say that the EMA had not exercised its discretion unreasonably.

63. This court is satisfied that meetings held by Petrotrin with the fishing community demonstrated sufficient consultation in all of the circumstances of this case; particularly in light of this Court's finding that such consultation was not mandated by the legislation, no EIA having been required by the EMA.

64. Even in the absence of the requirement for an EIA, this court finds that, as per Berkeley v Sec of State for the Environment [2001] 2 AC 603, the Applicants were given "an opportunity to express [their] opinion on the environmental issues" by virtue of the three (3) consultative sessions held by Petrotrin.

65. As per Stollmeyer J in the Atlantic LNG case;

"It is sufficient if those affected, or likely to be affected, are put into a position

that allows their views and opinions to be heard, to be ventilated fully, and that those views and opinions be considered properly in the decision making process. There is no requirement for ongoing public debate."

66. This Court agrees with the submission of the Respondent that consultations cannot go on forever. There must be an end at some point. Therefore, the Court finds that those affected persons were indeed given an opportunity to have their concerns addressed and as such there was consultation although not mandated by legislation in this instance.

The High Court has also taken the view that the issue of public consultations outside of the EIA process is largely irrelevant as it is not statutorily required. In ***Charlotteville Beachfront Movement v Tobago House of Assembly***,[240] Rajkumar J stated:

66. The authorities on consultation were considered at length in— the People United Respecting the Environment and Anor v The Environmental Management Authority And Anor (the Alutrint Case) CV2007-02263 per the Honourable Justice Dean-Armorer at pages 103 -104, including:

(i) R v Secretary of State for Social Services, ex parte Association of Metropolitan Authorities [1986] 1 All ER 164, where Webster J stated- "There is no general principle to be extracted from the case law as to what kind or amount of consultation is required before delegated legislation, of which consultation is a precondition, can validly be made. But in any context the essence of consultation is the communication of a genuine invitation to give advice and a genuine consideration of that advice. In my view it must go without saying that to achieve consultation sufficient information must be supplied by the consulting to the consulted party to enable it to tender helpful advice. Sufficient time must be given by the consulting to the consulted party to enable it to do that, and sufficient time must be available for such advice to be considered by the consulting party. Sufficient, in that context, does not mean ample, but at least enough to enable the relevant purpose to be fulfilled. By helpful advice, in this context, I mean sufficiently informed and considered information or advice about aspects of the form or substance of the proposals, or their implications for the consulted party, being aspects material to the implementation of the proposal as

---

240 CV 2013-01738

to which the Secretary of State might not be fully informed or advised and as to which the party consulted might have relevant information or advice to offer."

(ii) Also cited was the case of R v North and East Devon Health Authority, ex parte Coughlan [2000] 3 All ER 850, where Lord Woolf at para 108 stated:

"It is common ground that, whether or not consultation of interested parties and the public is a legal requirement, if it is embarked upon it must be carried out properly. To be proper, consultation must be undertaken at a time when proposals are still at a formative stage; it must include sufficient reasons for particular proposals to allow those consulted to give intelligent consideration and an intelligent response; adequate time must be given for this purpose; and the product of consultation must be conscientiously taken into account when the ultimate decision is taken: R v Brent London Borough Council, Ex p Gunning (1985) 84 LGR 168."

At page 887 paragraph 112 - It has to be remembered that consultation is not litigation: the consulting authority is not required to publicize every submission it receives or (absent from statutory obligation) to disclose all its advice. Its obligation is to let those who have a potential interest in the subject matter know in clear terms what the proposal is and exactly why it is under consideration, telling them enough (which may be a good deal) to enable them to make an intelligent response". The obligation, although it may be quite onerous, goes no further than this".

71. In Fishermen and Friends of the Sea v The Environment Management Authority and Another [2006] 2 LRC 384, Lord Walker at paragraph 28, emphasizing the need for public consultations, indicated that-

"Public consultation and involvement in decisions on environmental issues are matters of high importance in a democracy."

72. It is clear that even on the evidence of the applicants there was consultation. In this case the adequacy of consultation would make no difference to its outcome. The outcome is the quashing of the decisions challenged, on the basis of illegality and unreasonableness.

73. It is therefore not necessary to consider or even comment upon whether there was adequate consultation or whether such consultation as there was is reviewa-

ble by a court on the evidence presented by the applicants, save that in the event that the EMA were to require an EIA in respect of any other activity related to the project, (a matter entirely within its sole discretion), the issue of the adequacy and content of consultation may assume relevance.

In *Talisman (Trinidad) Petroleum Limited v. The Environmental Management Authority*,[241] the case did not involve public consultation in the context of an EIA process but the Environmental Commission emphasised the importance generally of public consultation.

Chairman Hosein

Quite apart from the Rules, there is in conformity with the need for participation under Section 16(2) of the Act, the provision relating to Public comment and the procedure thereunder, (See Section 28 of the Act). The general advantages of public participation are, inter alia, that it:

- *improves the understanding of issues among all parties;*

- *finds common ground and determines whether agreement can be reached on some of the issues*

- *highlights trade-offs that must be addressed in reaching decisions; and*

- *improves the general understanding of the problems associated with a project, as well as the overall decision-making process.*

(See Columbia Journal of Transnational Law Vol. 33, 1995 No. 2 at page 344 by Dr. William A. Tilleman) .... And among the justifications for allowing public participation into EIA's at page 345 the Author states: -

"Environmental assessments are intended to generate higher quality information about potential environmental impacts. In other words, it is a process designed to assist the proponent and the regulators with decisions regarding approvals. Public input therefore enhances a policy of consultation, one designed to improve the quality of development decisions. The public has access to decision-makers

---

241 No. EA003 of 2002.

to advise them of concerns, issues and values."

In the case of ***Fishermen and Friends of the Sea v Environmental Management Authority and BP Trinidad and Tobago LLC (Interested Party),***[242] the dissenting judge in the Court of Appeal explored the importance of public consultation

> *Lucky JA*
>
> *The crucial question is whether the EMA followed the procedure set out in the above sections before granting the certificate. It seems to me that the judge did not address this issue because he had pre-empted the determination of those issues by refusing to grant an extension of time. I think that if he had he may not have exercised his discretion as he did without hearing the substantive matter because the following questions inter alia would have arisen: what specifically are the list of activities? What is the environmental impact assessment (the EIA)? Was the EIA submitted for public comment? (section 28 of the EMA Act). What was the public response? Were their comments or representations made during the public comment period?*

However, at the Privy Council in ***Fishermen and Friends of the Sea v Environmental Management Authority and BP Trinidad and Tobago LLC (Interested Party),***[243] while the Court endorsed the importance of public consultations, it was inclined to take the view that the substance rather than the form was critical. However, the PC made it clear that dispensation with public consultations would be inimical to the EIA achieving substantial compliance.

> *Lord Walker of Gestingthorpe*
>
> *28. In their Lordships' view there is only one significant criticism to be made of the judge's careful and thorough judgment. In the penultimate paragraph of his judgment (set out in paragraph 26 above) the judge emphasised that the Authority had taken an informed decision, but the judge paid insufficient attention to the need for public consultation and involvement in the decision-making process (his reference to "consultation by technocrats" does not seem to refer to public*

---

242 Civ Appeal No. 106 of 2002
243 PCA No. 30 of 2004

consultation). Public consultation and involvement in decisions on environmental issues are matters of high importance in a democracy. In Berkeley v Secretary of State for the Environment [2001] 2 AC 603, 615, 616, Lord Hoffmann said,

"The directly enforceable right of the citizen which is accorded by the Directive is not merely a right to a fully informed decision on the substantive issue. It must have been adopted on an appropriate basis and that requires the inclusive and democratic procedure prescribed by the Directive in which the public, however misguided or wrong-headed its views may be, is given an opportunity to express its opinion on the environmental issues.

A court is therefore not entitled retrospectively to dispense with the requirement of an ELA on the ground that the outcome would have been the same or that the local planning authority or Secretary of State had all the information necessary to enable them to reach a proper decision on the environmental issues."

29. These passages refer to the requirements of legislation of the European Union. But similar principles underlie the EMA 2000, as appears from the detailed requirements of section 28. The doctrine of "substantial compliance" must therefore be treated with considerable caution in environmental cases of this sort: see Berkeley at pp616-7.

30. Before their Lordships, Mr Herberg (for BPTT) accepted that there was an arguable case that the Authority had not fully complied with the requirements of the EMA 2000 and the secondary legislation made under it. Mr Daly SC (for the Authority), while rejecting the submission of Mr Maharaj SC as to "clear" or "naked" illegality, did not contend that there had been no procedural irregularity. Had the irregularity significantly affected the process of public consultation it is very doubtful whether it would be right, in a case of so much public interest, to treat the Authority as having substantially complied with its obligations.

31. In this case, however, the procedural irregularities arose primarily from shortcomings in the transitional provisions of the EMA 2000. The Authority's human and financial resources were no doubt limited and its officers were understandably reluctant to spend time and money in reconsidering ELAs which had already been carefully considered after their submission to the TCPD and the Ministry of Energy. But any shortcuts which were taken did not interfere with the processes of public consultation. A lengthy and detailed ELA on the Bombax project, including the risk assessment in section 8, was delivered to Mr Aboud of FFS on or about 26 July 2001, and at the same time it was made available for public inspection at various locations, and public comment was invited. The same ELA, shorn of section 8, was republished on or about 15 October 2001, and again public comment was invited. FFS responded on 5 November 2001, during the statutory consultation period. The omission (which dealt specifically with the safety of the 36-inch pipeline) was ill-advised. But Mr Aboud already had that information, and he used the full ELA to obtain advice at the end of August 2001. The concerns about the 36-inch pipeline were fully aired.

EIA Required to Process CEC Application

Rule 4(1)(d) of the CEC Rules provide that the applicant may be required to conduct an EIA in compliance with a Terms of Reference (TOR) as a condition to the determination of an application for a CEC by the EMA.

> *Rule 4(1)(d) of the CEC Rules states: The Authority shall, within 10 working days after receipt of an application under rule 3(1) or 3(3) issue to the applicant a notice acknowledging receipt of the application and it shall —(d) notify the applicant that an ELA is required in compliance with a TOR;*

This is a critical component of the environmental approval process and the emerging legal concerns centres around public participation and adequacy of the EIA so as to facilitate the issuing of a CEC by the EMA in accordance with existing legal principles used in judicial review to assess the decisions of a governmental entity.

> *Section 35 of the Environmental Management Act*
>
> *(4) The Authority in considering the application may ask for further information including, if required, an environmental impact assessment, in accordance with the procedure prescribed. (5) Any application which requires the preparation of an environmental impact assessment shall be submitted for public comment in accordance with section 28 before any Certificate is issued by the Authority.*

Terms of Reference (TOR)

The first stage in the CEC process, as it applies to the requirement for an

EIA, deals with the TOR for the EIA. The EMA prepares the draft TOR and forwards same to the applicant who is then made responsible for obtaining comments from stakeholders and other members of the public. This is a critical function as the quality of the TOR often determines the quality of the EIA.

> *Rule 5(2) of the CEC Rules provides that (2) the applicant shall, where appropriate, conduct consultations with relevant agencies, non-Governmental organisations and other members of the public on the draft TOR and may, within 28 days after notification under sub rule (1)(c), submit written representations to the Authority requesting that the draft TOR be modified and setting out*

> *a. the manner in which he proposes that the TOR should be modified;*

> *b. a reasoned justification for the proposed modifications; and*

> *c. a report of the consultations with relevant agencies, non-Governmental organisations and other members of the public on the draft TOR*

The EMA has interpreted *Rule 5(2) of the CEC Rules* of placing full responsibility on the applicant in determining who are the appropriate stakeholders and the manner of the consultations. The result has been varied with some stakeholders being invited to comment on TORs while others seeming to have equal standing are ignored. Additionally, some applicants have opted for public meetings where comments can be offered on the draft TOR while others elect to receive comments only in writing. By not laying down a set procedure for facilitating public comments on draft TORs, the EMA has unwittingly allowed a system to emerge that is totally dependent on the integrity and willingness of the applicant to engage in the widest possible public consultation in the review of draft TORs. The matter was articulated in ***People United Respecting the Environment and Rights Action Group v Environmental Management Authority, Alutrint Limited (Interested Party) and the Attorney General of Trinidad and Tobago.***[244]

> *Facts: In 2005, the Government of the Republic of Trinidad and Tobago (GORTT) approved the establishment of an aluminium complex capable of producing 125,000 metric tonnes per annum. Part of the proposed complex,*

---

244 CV 2007- 02263

that is, the aluminium smelter, anode plant and rod mill, wire and cable plant and associated infrastructure, is to be sited on approximately 100 hectares of land at Main Site North, Union Industrial Estate in La Brea. A local joint venture company, Alutrint Limited, was formed to manage the project development and ownership of this complex. Alutrint's equity ownership is 60% National Energy Corporation (NEC) and 40% Sural, a Venezuelan based company that specializes in the manufacture and retail of aluminium products. The establishment of the proposed aluminium complex falls under activity 21 of the CEC Order, 2001, that is, "the establishment of a facility for the production or reforming of metals or related products". Issues raised in opposition of the CEC included violation of the precautionary principle, failure to deal adequately with air pollution and the disposal of spent pot liner and non-compliance with the requirements for public consultations.

Held: Dean-Armorer J

56. The consultation undertaken by the developer towards the preparation of the final TOR consisted of the full page advertisement, the provision of packages to thirty-five (35) stakeholders and forwarding flyers to residents of the surrounding communities. The rule places the method and the extent of pre-TOR consultation within the discretion of the developer. The EMA's actions become relevant in so far as it could be established that the decision of the EMA to accept the consultations was so unreasonable that no reasonable Authority would have accepted them. Recalling that the threshold for establishing irrationality is notoriously high, in my view the Authority could not be so faulted. The pre- TOR consultation was extensive targeting government ministries, non-governmental organizations and individuals (through flyers). These consultations may not have been perfect. According to judicial precedent, they were not required to be perfect; however, they are not so defective so as to tarnish the Authority with irrationality for having accepted them.

While in ***People United Respecting the Environment v Environmental Management Authority, Alutrint Limited (Interested Party) and the Attorney General of Trinidad and Tobago,***[245] the High Court upheld the public participation on the draft TOR, the court did acknowledge that public consultation can be defective as to tarnish the EMA with irrationality for accepting the adequacy of the mechanisms employed by an applicant to

---

245 CV 2007- 02263

satisfy the requirements of *Rule 5(2) of the CEC Rules.*

The issue of public consultations on the draft TOR returned to the Court in the matter of ***Fishermen and Friends of the Sea v Environmental Management Authority, Ministry of Works and Transport (First Interested Party) and KALL Company Limited (Second Interested Party).***[246] The High Court and the full Court of Appeal dismissed the application for leave to apply for judicial review. However, Justice Smith, in a separate judgement found merit in the argument that the failure to have public consultations on the draft TOR raised the prospect of a good arguable case but this was outweighed by the delay on the part of FFOS in launching the judicial challenge. This position was not adopted by the other two justices hearing the appeal. The position adopted by the majority judges in the Court of Appeal of TT that consultations with the public on the draft TOR was not mandatory and was at the discretion of an applicant for a CEC was endorsed by the Privy Council.

Fishermen and Friends of the Sea (Appellant) v Environmental Management Authority and others (Respondents), [2018] UKPC 24

Lord Carnwath:

6. Given the importance attached by the appellants to rule 5(2), it is worth noting at this stage its relatively limited place in the procedure. The TOR is not a requirement of the Act. It appears to be no more than a preparatory step under the rules, designed to set the parameters of the ELA as between the Authority and the applicant. Although the implication is that the ELA will be prepared "in compliance with" the TOR, there is nothing in terms in the Act or the Rules to limit the consideration of the final decision on the CEC by reference to it. The requirement to consult other agencies and members of the public "where appropriate" shows that this is not a mandatory requirement in all cases; nor does it grant any general right to the public to be consulted at that stage. The implication seems to be that there may be agencies or individuals with a special interest in, or able to make a particular contribution to, setting the parameters of the ELA at an early stage. It is left to the applicant, at least in the first instance, to determine whom to consult. The responses if any are reported to the authority by the applicant; the

---

246 Civ Appeal No P050 of 2018

consultees have no independent right to make representations on the draft TOR. *On the other hand, the* TOR *process does not pre-empt in any way the rights of the public to take part in the statutory public comment procedure under sections 28 and 35(5), and to have their comments taken into account in the Authority's final decision.*

34. Comment has already been made on the limited role of rule 5(2) in the EIA procedure. The Board finds it hard to envisage a case where a failure at that preliminary stage should be held to invalidate the final certificate, given the extensive statutory provisions for public consultation on the terms of the EIA at a later stage. If it is alleged that lack of consultation on the draft TOR *led to some matter being inadequately considered, this can no doubt be raised by way of objection to the EIA. There is in any event no evidence in this case that those who took part in the later consultation were dissatisfied in any way with earlier procedures.*

35. It is particularly difficult for the appellant to complain, given its unexplained failure to take any part in the statutory consultation process, or to raise any complaint about the scope of the TOR *(which was finalised in December 2016) at an earlier stage. Further, even at this late stage, the appellant has failed to identify which other agencies, public or private, should "appropriately" have been consulted on the draft* TOR *and why. More importantly it has failed to identify any defect in the draft* TOR *which might have been corrected by such consultations. Indeed, the emphasis of its complaints has been, not that the* TOR *was deficient, but that some of its requirements (on matters such as cumulative impacts) were relaxed in the final decision.*

Non-Statutory Required Public Consultations on the Basis of the TOR

Rule 5(3) of the CEC Rules provide for the preparation of the final TOR.

Rule 5(3) of the CEC Rules -The Authority shall consider any written representations and the prescribed information submitted by the applicant pursuant to sub rule (2) and shall finalise the TOR *as it sees fit, and issue the final* TOR *to the applicant within 10 working days after the expiry of the period specified for the submission of written representations in sub rule (2).*

Having regard to the statutory requirement contained in *Rule 4(1) (d) of the CEC Rules* that the EIA be prepared in conformity with the TOR, the

TOR is imbued with statutory strength. The EMA has used the TOR to introduce two new components of public participation in the EIA process.

The first public hearing is to be conducted as soon as the final TOR is issued by the EMA to the applicant requiring a CEC, and its main purpose is to sensitize stakeholders to a project and gather stakeholders concerns, ideas and perceptions prior to conducting actual studies for the preparation of the EIA. The second public hearing requires a developer to return to the stakeholders to provide information on its findings and proposed management plans. The need for compliance with these hearings were underscored in *People United Respecting the Environment v Environmental Management Authority, Alutrint Limited (Interested Party) and the Attorney General of Trinidad and Tobago*[247] and the Court made it clear that having regard to the importance of public participation in the CEC process, it would be fatal not to engage properly in these public hearings.

Dean-Armorer J

56. Another aspect of developer consultation has been queried by the Claimant that is to say, the admitted failure of the developer to conduct consultations at the formative stage of the EIA.

While conceding that in fact there had been a failure on the part of the developer to comply with this very clear guideline, learned Senior Counsel for both the EMA and the Interested Party have sought to minimise the admitted flaw.

57. In my view, the stipulate on in the TOR for public consultation prior to the preparation of the EIA is reminiscent of the Sedly principle that consultations must be taken when the project is at a formative stage. Moreover, it is no answer to contend that this was not a requirement of statute but of the TOR which is merely a guide. According to the Sedly principles consultation, as long as it is undertaken, must be carried out properly.

58. On the face of the facts therefore this aspect of the consultation process was flawed.

59. The next step would be to consider whether this flaw in the consultation process

---

'CV 2007- 02263

means that the decision should be quashed. According to Justice Sykes in the Jamaican Case, the Court is required to consider the : "seriousness of the flaw and the impact that it had or might have had on the consultation process…" See page 40 of the judgment of Justice Sykes. Justice Sykes urged further, that the Court is required to make a "qualitative decision…" The Court is required to examine "… what took place and make a judgment on whether those flaws were serious enough to deprive the process of efficacy…"

60. In assessing whether the admitted flaw deprived the process of efficacy, the flaw may be tested by considering what difference would have resulted had the developer complied with this requirement of the TOR. In that hypothetical situation, the developer would have received public comments prior to embarking on the preparation of the EIA. This in my view was substantially achieved by the use of questionnaires and the smaller cottage meetings. The failure of the developer to hold the public consultation prior to preparing the TOR in itself does not deprive the process of efficacy.

61. However, the Claimants have also complained of the proximity of the first and the second public consultation meetings, the first having been held on the 9th November, 2005 and the Second on the 14th November, 2005.

62. The compound effect of the developer's failure to hold the meeting at the start of the EIA process and the proximity of the two meetings in my view would have operated to escape and therefore to frustrate the provisions of the TOR, which required the first meeting at an early stage to "sensitize stakeholders to the project and gather stakeholders concerns, ideas and perceptions…." Having done so, time must be allotted to allow stakeholder concerns to inform the data collection phase, after which the developer is required to return to the stakeholders to provide information on its findings and proposed management plans. The time was not allowed. It may very well be the case that strict compliance would have yielded no different result. However, in this regard the TOR places the stakeholder centre stage. The stakeholder must be sensitized; the developer must take into account stakeholder concerns and then return, reporting on its findings and proposed management plans. In my view, this was no minor flaw. The omission to comply with this aspect of the TOR deprived the developer of the time envisaged to take stakeholder views into account. This was a flaw which diminished the quality of public consultation.

63. This Court is obligated to implement the caveat of Lord Walker in

FFOS v. EMA that the Court should approach the doctrine of substantial compliance with caution, when public consultations are affected. Even if it could be argued that there may have been substantial compliance, in my view, it would have been procedurally irregular for the EMA to issue the CEC on the basis of flawed public consultation.

Written Public Comment Period

Once the EIA is completed and submitted to the EMA, it is placed into the public domain for written comments from the public. There are two issues associated with the written public comment period, namely the duration of the period and the documents that are made available for public comment.

With respect to the duration of the written public comment period, the *Environmental Management Act* establishes a minimum period but sets no outer limit for such period.

Section 28 of the Environmental Management Act

28(3) The Authority shall receive written comments for not less than thirty days from the date of notice in the Gazette…

It would appear to be the trend for the EMA to set the time for receipt of written public comment at the minimum of thirty (30) days. Given the fact that many of the projects in TT are energy based (petroleum and petrochemicals), it is difficult to have large and complex EIAs reviewed within thirty (30) days. Further, there is a paucity of technical expertise in TT available and willing to review these EIAs and therefore significant time is spent trying to obtain such resources. Additionally, the EMA often adopts the position that EIAs are copyright material and therefore must be read at the Library of the EMA thereby only allowing 10 percent of the EIA to be photocopied according to copyrighted legislation. The situation is exacerbated by the fact that the review period is 30 calendar days as opposed to 30 working days, therefore reducing the number of days that the public may access said documents.

The issue of the duration of the written public comment period was raised in ***Fishermen and Friends of the Sea v Environmental Management Au-***

thority and BP Trinidad and Tobago LLC (Interested Party),[248] the first environmental public interest litigation launched in TT by FFOS.

This case involved a decision by BPTT to expand its deliverability and transportation share in the ALNG liquefied natural gas project. The main components of the project include the installation of two new drilling plat-forms, upgrade of one existing platform (Cassia A), installation of two infield submarine pipelines (one 26" and one 6"), and installation of a 48" main trunk pipeline. Due to the perceived adverse environmental impacts on the lives of many residents of Trinidad and Tobago, there was an appli-cation for a CEC by BPTT but was opposed by FFOS, a local NGO.

It was argued on behalf of FFOS that, due to the complex nature of the proposed activities and the voluminous documents which the public was required to peruse in order to comment properly on the EIAs, the EMA owed a duty to the public to provide a longer period for public comment than the statutory minimum period of thirty (30) days. FFOS was not suc-cessful in their judicial review application as the matter was filed outside the date for submitting such an application. The Courts refused to exercise their discretion and extend time for filing of the application for judicial review outside of the statutory time frame.

The matter of the adequacy in the time provided by the EMA for receipt of written comments from the public on an EIA was explored in the *People United Respecting the Environment and Rights Action Group v Environ-mental Management Authority, Alutrint Limited (Interested Party) and the Attorney General of Trinidad and Tobago.*[249]

Dean-Armorer J

A number of issues targeted the brevity of different parts of the consultation process. At the third issue of his submissions, Learned Senior contended that the Defendant did not allow sufficient time for meaningful consultation. The Claimants contend that the two public comment periods were too short. No ground of illegality could be established because public comment periods were

---

248 Civ Appeal No. 106 of 2002
249 CV2007-02263

within the minimum time stipulated by s. 28(3) of the Environmental Management Act. While accepting that the issues canvassed by the proposed project were both deep and numerous, the time allotted in this case cannot be regarded as unreasonable, having regard to the timetable set by the Rules. The Authority finds itself in this unenviable predicament of having to balance environmental with economic considerations, or more specifically having to balance the need of the public for thorough consultation with the developer's need to press on with the project. In my view the EMA cannot be faulted for complying with the statutory timetable. The actions of the Authority are in stark contrast with the defendant in the Jamaican Case where only eight (8) days including a weekend was allowed for the claimant to study technical material.

The second issue that goes to the heart of the integrity of the written public comment period is the availability of all relevant information to allow for meaningful public participation. As stated in *Section 28(2)(1) of the Environmental Management Act, (2) The administrative record required under subsection (1) shall include…copies of documents or other supporting materials which the Authority believes would assist the public in developing a reasonable understanding of those issues…"* There is now accepted to be a clear duty on the part of a decision maker to provide sufficient information to allow for meaningful public participation.

In **Quebec (Attorney General) v Canada (National Energy Board), [1994] 1 S.C.R. 159,** referring to **Re Canadian Radio Television Commission and in Re London Cable TV Ltd. [1976] 2 F.C 621 (CA), at pp 624-25**, this duty was simply stated as follows:

In general, included in the requirements of procedural fairness is the right to disclosure by the administrative decision-maker of sufficient information to permit meaningful participation in the hearing process.

The issue of the adequacy of information made available for meaningful public participation has not been subject to any final litigation but was alluded to in **People United Respecting the Environment v Environmental Management Authority, Alutrint Limited (Interested Party) and the Attorney General of Trinidad and Tobago; Trinidad and Tobago Civil Rights Association v Environmental Management Authority, Alutrint Limited (Interested Party) and the Attorney General of Trinidad and**

Tobago; and *Smelta Karavan v Environmental Management Authority, Alutrint Limited (Interested Party) and the Attorney General of Trinidad and Tobago.*

In *People United Respecting the Environment and Rights Action Group v Environmental Management Authority, Alutrint Limited (Interested Party) and the Attorney General of Trinidad and Tobago*, Dean-Armorer J noted:

> 81. *In any event s. 28(2) requires the EMA to place on the Administrative Record such document as it "believes" would assist the public. The legislature has invested discretionary power in the Authority as to the documents which ought to be placed on the Administrative record. In my view the exercise of this discretion is reviewable only on Wednesbury grounds, which do not form part of the grounds on which this issue was raised. Accordingly, the second issue must be resolved in favour of the Defendant.*

Public Hearing

Perhaps the main and most significant pillar of the public participation process is the discretion vested in the EMA to hold a public hearing where there is sufficient public interest.

> *Section 28(3) of the Environmental Management Act states, …if the Authority determines there is sufficient public interest, it may hold a public hearing for discussing the proposed action and receiving verbal comments.*

The EMA has made sparing use of this power and it is certainly the exception for a public hearing to be held rather than the norm. The failure to hold a public hearing constituted one of the grounds for judicial review in *Fishermen and Friends of the Sea v Environmental Management Authority and BP Trinidad and Tobago LLC (Interested Party)*, but this was not addressed due to the dismissal of the application on the ground of undue delay as well as substantial prejudice and hardship to third parties.

The issue of the public hearing was also questioned in the second environmental public interest litigation to be filed in TT, that is, in the case of *Fishermen and Friends of the Sea v The Environmental Management Authority and Atlantic LNG Company of Trinidad and Tobago (Interested*

Party)[250] involving an appeal over the decision of the EMA to grant a CEC to ALNG for the construction and operation of a Fourth Train for the Liquefaction of Natural Gas. The EMA held a public hearing pursuant to *Section 28(3) of the Environmental Management Act* to receive verbal comments. The EMA, however, took the position that this section only required them to host a single meeting and hear the views of the public and that there was no requirement to have any further meetings to discuss with the public how their views were addressed by the EMA. Justice Stollmeyer in ***Fishermen and Friends of the Sea v The Environmental Management Authority and Atlantic LNG Company of Trinidad and Tobago (Interested Party)***[251] agreed with the views of the EMA and noted:

> *The EMA has a broad discretion in determining whether and when to hold public hearings. There is no express provision requiring follow up public hearings before granting the CEC. That is left up to its discretion, and will depend on the circumstances of the case and the severity of the concerns... The rules of natural justice do not necessarily require that there be a formal, oral, hearing in public. It is sufficient if those affected, or likely to be affected, are put into a position that allows their views and opinions to be heard, to be ventilated fully, and that those views and opinions be considered properly in the decision making process. There is no requirement for ongoing public debate.*

While the decision of Justice Stollmeyer is the current position of the law as it stands at the first instance level, it is hoped that this limited view of the public hearing, that by and large excludes any follow-up meeting to discuss how the public views were addressed prior to the taking of a decision, would not endure. Environmental democracy based on public participation and effective public consultation cannot be fulfilled with a single perfunctory meeting by an authority without engaging the public in a meaningful debate to demonstrate that their views were considered and addressed in any final decision.

---

250 H.C.A. Cv. 2148 of 2003
251 Ibid.

Defects in the EIA

An EIA is to be conducted in accordance with the TOR and the provisions of the *CEC Rules.*

> *According to Rule 10 of the CEC Rules- an EIA required by the Authority under section 35(4) of the Act shall be carried out by persons with expertise and experience in the specific areas for which information is required and may, where appropriate include the following information:*
>
> *(a) a non-technical summary of the findings of the assessment comprising the key issues, a brief evaluation of the potential effects and hazards of the proposed activity and the measures and recommendations proposed for addressing the findings of the evaluation;*
>
> *(b) a description of the existing ecological and other characteristics and conditions of the site and areas likely to be affected by the proposed activity, with relevant information about the land use requirements during the various phases of the activity;*
>
> *(c) illustrative materials where appropriate, including maps and photographs;*
>
> *(d) a description of the activity giving adequate and concise information on-*
>
> *(i) the characteristics of the processes and methods proposed;*
>
> *(ii) the design, size, scale and capacity;*
>
> *(iii) equipment and machinery to be involved;*
>
> *(iv) source, nature and quantity of materials to be used;*
>
> *(v) rates of extraction; and*
>
> *(vi) the estimated type and quantities of expected emissions, residues, wastes, noise, light, vibrations, heat, and radiation to air, water and soil during the various phases of the activity;*
>
> *(e) an identification and assessment of the main effects that the activity is likely to have on the components of the environment, including:*
>
> *(i) human beings;*

(ii) fauna;

(iii) flora;

(iv) soil;

(v) water- surface and ground;

(vi) air;

(vii) the coast and sea;

(viii) weather and climate;

(ix) the landscape;

(x) the interaction between any of the foregoing;

(xi) material assets;

(xii) the cultural heritage;

(f) an evaluation of the alternatives to the activity, giving consideration to concerns of environment, alternative sites, designs, approaches and processes;

(g) an account of the assessment of the methods used and the level of uncertainty of any predictions;

(h) an account of the measures proposed to avoid, reduce, mitigate or remedy any of the significant adverse effects identified;

(i) an identification of the potential hazards and an assessment of the level of risk that may be caused by the proposed activity and an account of the measures envisaged to address any environmental emergencies that may result from the activity;

(j) a description of the program proposed for monitoring actual impacts and the effects of the mitigation measures at the various stages of the activity;

(k) the data and methods used to obtain the information in paragraph (e).

The EIA must attain a level of substantial compliance with the TOR and the *CEC Rules* in order to be considered as a rational, reasonable and legal decision of the EMA. In the first decision to address this issue, *Fishermen and Friends of the Sea v Environmental Management Authority and BP Trinidad and Tobago LLC (Interested Party),*[252] the doctrine of substantial compliance was alluded to but caution was urged in environmental cases especially where it involved public consultations.

Lord Walker of Gestingthorpe

28. In their Lordships' view... Public consultation and involvement in decisions on environmental issues are matters of high importance in a democracy.... A court is therefore not entitled retrospectively to dispense with the requirement of an EIA on the ground that the outcome would have been the same or that the local planning authority or Secretary of State had all the information necessary to enable them to reach a proper decision on the environmental issues."

29. These passages refer to the requirements of legislation of the European Union. But similar principles underlie the EMA 2000, as appears from the detailed requirements of section 28. The doctrine of "substantial compliance" must therefore be treated with considerable caution in environmental cases of this sort: see Berkeley at pp616-7.

30. Before their Lordships, Mr Herberg (for BPTT) accepted that there was an arguable case that the Authority had not fully complied with the requirements of the EMA 2000 and the secondary legislation made under it. Mr Daly SC (for the Authority), while rejecting the submission of Mr Maharaj SC as to "clear" or "naked" illegality, did not contend that there had been no procedural irregularity. Had the irregularity significantly affected the process of public consultation it is very doubtful whether it would be right, in a case of so much public interest, to treat the Authority as having substantially complied with its obligations.

In the first case to be subjected to full judicial review that involved the issue of the adequacy of a CEC, there was an extensive treatment as to how such a judicial review should be undertaken. This case examined the judicial standard for an EIA as articulated in the USA through the judicial test known as the "hard look" doctrine. The EIA must contain such information as is necessary for the decision-maker to take a hard look at all

---

252 PCA No. 30 of 2004

the circumstances surrounding the decision. In *Fishermen and Friends of the Sea v The Environmental Management Authority and Atlantic LNG Company of Trinidad and Tobago (Interested Party)*[253] as per Stollmeyer J:

> *An analysis of the major Canadian and American authorities reveals that the court's role in judicial review of environmental assessment is clearly circumscribed. The scope of judicial review of the agency's discretion is narrow because of policy concerns which militate in favour of a more deferential approach, as recognised in Iverhuron & District Ratepayers Ass'n*

> *1. Canada (Minister of the Environment): (2001) 272 NR 62 para 53 "The extent to which certain factors are considered, and the weight given to the various factors on the overall assessment of environmental effects, are matters for those who have expertise to make such judgments, and not for the court."*

> *The court limits itself to mainly procedural review seeking to ensure that the statutory requirements have been complied with and the legislative purpose is achieved. Courts only intervene to overturn the agency's findings if they are arbitrary and capricious.*

> *It is clear from these decisions that the court's function in judicial review proceedings is not to act as an "academy of science" (see Steyn J. in Vancouver Island Peace Society v. Canada [1992] 3 F.C. 42, 51) or a "legislative upper chamber". To turn the reviewing court into an "academy of science" would be both inefficient and contrary to the scheme of the Act (see Sexton J.A. in Iverhuron). As long as the agency complies with the statutory process, the Court must defer to their substantive determinations, but this deference is not absolute. The Court of Appeal in Iverhuron made it clear that the Court's approach should not "be so deferential as to exclude all inquiry into the substantive adequacy of the environmental assessment. To adopt this approach would risk turning the right to judicial review of the decision into a hollow one."*

> *The approach to judicial review of cumulative impact assessment in these cases is referred to as the "hard look doctrine" and originated in the context of court review of administrative decisions. The approach adopted by these*

---

253 H.C.A. Cv. 2148 of 2003

courts does not in substance differ from the approach adopted in this jurisdiction when considering applications for judicial review of an administrative decision. The "hard look" requires the agency to take its statutory responsibilities seriously and take a "hard look" at all the relevant circumstances. It calls only for the Court "to ensure that the agency took a hard look at the cumulative environmental consequences"(see NRDC v. Morton 485 F 2d. 827). Once the agency has taken "a hard look" by complying procedurally and substantively with the legislative intent, the court cannot impose its views or interject into the agency's discretion as to the action to be taken. The court applies this doctrine by scrutinising the record to satisfy itself that the agency has exercised a reasoned discretion with reasons that do not deviate from or ignore the ascertainable legislative intent (see Greater Boston Television Corporation v. FCC 444 F2d. 841 (D.C. Cir 1970)). The agency's hard look must be supported by substantial evidence and the court should only set aside the agency's decision if it is not supported by substantial evidence (see Harold Leventhal, Environmental Decision making and the Role of the Courts)

Neighbours of Cuddy Mountain, Blue Mountains Biodiversity Project v. Blackwood 161 F.3d 1208 (9th Cir. 1998) and Muckleshoot Indian Tribe v. Forest Service 177 F.3d. 800 (9th cir. 1999) develop an approach to judicial review in which the court's mandate is to verify two things

procedural compliance- a demonstrated carrying- out of regulatory detail shows that the mechanics of the regulation have been followed by the agency.

substantive compliance- a sufficiently detailed regulatory compliance demonstrates fulfilment of the Act's mandate as a whole. Information supplied in response to these regulations succeeds only to the extent that it evidences a carrying out of the statutory goal.

The approach to judicial review of cumulative impact assessment in these cases is referred to as the "hard look doctrine" and originated in the context of court review of administrative decisions. The approach adopted by these courts does not in substance differ from the approach adopted in this jurisdiction when considering applications for judicial review of an administrative decision. The "hard look" requires the agency to take its statutory responsibilities seriously and take a "hard look" at all the relevant circumstances. It calls only for the Court "to ensure that the agency took a hard look at the cumulative environmental consequences"(see NRDC v. Morton 485 F 2d. 827). Once the agency has taken "a hard look" by complying procedurally and substantively with the legislative intent, the court cannot impose its views or interject into the agency's discretion as to the action to be taken. The court applies this doctrine by scrutinising the record to satisfy itself that the agency has exercised a reasoned discretion with reasons that do not deviate from or ignore the ascertainable legislative intent (see Greater Boston Television Corporation v. FCC 444 F2d. 841 (D.C. Cir 1970)). The agency's hard look must be supported by substantial evidence and the court should only set aside the agency's decision if it is not supported by substantial evidence (see Harold Leventhal, Environmental Decision making and the Role of the Courts).

The Act and the CEC Rules provide a process for environmental impact assessment which requires the EMA to consider procedurally and substantively the cumulative impacts of the project on the environment. The purpose of this is to ensure that the actions of the EMA are fully informed and well considered. Compliance with the Act is judged by the level of detail the data provides. The EMA's decision-making process must exhibit a transparency so that the decision is seen to depend on specific, detailed information collected in compliance with the Rules.

For the EMA to satisfy this requirement there must be evidence that "quantified and detailed information" was considered. This requirement was set out in Neighbours of Cuddy Mountain, where the Court found that the Forest Service failed to adequately assess the cumulative effects. The language offered by the Forest Service to assess the cumulative effects was extremely vague and the analysis was very general:

"To "consider" cumulative effects, some quantified or detailed information is required. Without such information, neither the courts nor the public, in reviewing the Forest Service's decisions, can be assured that the Forest Service provided the hard look that it is required to provide...General statements about "possible" effects and "some risk" do not constitute a "hard look" absent a justification regarding why more definitive information could not be provided."

The same point was reiterated in Blue Mountains Biodiversity Project where the plaintiffs challenged a post-fire salvage timber sale under NEPA, arguing that the Forest Service's failure to issue an EIS was a violation of that statute. The Court agreed with the plaintiffs, noting that the Forest Service's failure to discuss certain reports suggested a failure to take the hard look required. The Court rejected the Forest Service's use of broad generalities and irrelevant issues. The Court insisted that the Forest Service take a hard look at possible effects rather than offering generalities. The hard look had to be supported by hard data. Only with such data could the conclusions of the assessment be verified, evaluated, and accepted as compliance with NEPA's mandate.

This requirement of specific detail was also emphasised in Muckleshoot Indian Tribe, where the Court laid out the test as to whether an environmental impact survey is adequate as being: "whether there is a reasonably thorough discussion of the significant aspects of the probable environmental consequences."

As in Neighbours of Cuddy Mountain and Blue Mountains Biodiversity Project, the Court focused on the need for details: an environmental impact statement must "catalogue relevant past projects"; "it must include a useful analysis of the cumulative impacts of past, present and future projects"; it must discuss future projects, and it must analyse the total effects in sufficient detail to inform the decision maker in deciding whether to alter the project to avoid or lessen these impacts.

In my view, the EMA complied with the assessment procedures set out in the CEC rules. It insisted that a proper EIA was submitted. Not only did the EMA take a hard look at the EIA, but it took a long and detailed one before granting the CEC. As I have said, there were reports from a variety of external sources specifically for the EIA and the process of considering the CEC application. The Ministry of Energy was particularly comprehensive in its comments. This was all quite apart from the EMA's own internal appraisal. The consequence of all this was a long delay about which ALNG expressed concern to Dr. Ken Julien, Executive Chairman, Sub Committee- LNG Expansion. ALNG regarded the abundant caution exercised by the EMA and the independent reviews of the EIA conducted to be "excessive, unnecessary and time-consuming".

This detailed look extended to the cumulative impacts of the project. It is clear from the evidence that additional information and clarification was requested from ALNG on this issue. There is substantial evidence that cumulative impacts were considered. Indeed, the Ministry of Energy opined that the EIA failed to deal with cumulative impacts in any "meaningful manner", and required further detailed data. The additional information requested was very specific and detailed. The EMA subsequently obtained and considered this information.

It therefore cannot be said that the EMA merely rubber-stamped the cumulative impact assessment data contained in the EIA. The EMA sought independent expert assistance in evaluating the CEC application generally and the cumulative impacts in particular, and carried out appropriate analyses. There is detailed information verifying that the EMA's assessment of this issue complied with the Act's mandate of "sustainable development, balancing economic growth with environmentally sound practices in order to enhance the quality of life and meet the needs of present and future generations."

I have therefore come to the conclusion that the cumulative impact was considered. A "hard look" was taken, based on the information then available. That information was sufficient in all the circumstances. There was no good reason to defer the decision to a future date. The decision to issue the CEC was not irrational because of a failure to consider the cumulative impact, or to do so properly.

The High Court of TT returned to the question of the test for adequacy of an EIA in ***People United Respecting the Environment and Rights Action Group v Environmental Management Authority, Alutrint Limited (Interested Party) and the Attorney General of Trinidad and Tobago***[254] where the Commonwealth tests of substantial compliance was applied. This test acknowledges that an EIA need not be perfect but it must substantially comply with the requirements for preparation of an EIA as contained in the TOR and the environmental legal regime.

Dean-Armorer J

At paragraph 69, Lord Hoffman refers to the ground of irrationality as "... this demanding requirement ..."and indicated that their Lordships adopted the observations of Cripps J, sitting in the Land and Environment Court of New South Wales in Prineas v Forestry Commission Of New South Wales: "I do not think the statute......imposes on a determining authority

---

254 CV 2007-02263

when preparing an environmental impact statement, a standard of absolute per-fection... in my opinion there must be imported into the statutory obligation a concept of reasonableness... Provided an environmental impact statement is comprehensive in it treatment of the subject matter, objective in its approach and meets the requirement that it alerts the decision maker and members of the public to the affect of the activity on the environment and the consequences to the community inherent in carrying out or not carrying out the activity it meets the standard imposed by the Regulations...."

" The fact that the environmental impact statement does not cover every topic and explore every avenue advocated by the experts does not necessarily invalidate it or require a finding that it does not substantially comply with the statute and the Regulations."

87. The EIA is an information-gathering process. See Bell and Mc Gillivray Environmental Law (6th edition). It is a means to decision making and is not a decision-making end in itself. (Prineas). Its objective is to alert the decision-maker and members of the public to the effect of the activity on the environment.

88. When the Authority required the developer to conduct an environmental assessment both the developer and the Authority are governed by the provi-sions of the CEC Rules as to the contents of the EIA, the manner of its preparation and the timeline within which it should be prepared.

89. Rule 10 in particular provides standards for preparation of the EIA. In the claims before me, great emphasis has been placed on Rule 10 (e). Rule 10 (e) itemises a number of components of the environment in respect of which an activity is likely to have an effect, and which must be identified and assessed in the EIA. The timeline components are adequately rehearsed earlier in this judgement.

90. A number of authorities have addressed the issue of defects in the EIA and whether defects ought to invalidate the clearance certificates or planning permission granted on the basis of defective EIA.

91. The decision of the highest authority is BACONGO #2 from which the following principles may be extracted:

- The question of whether or not an EIA complies with the statute is a decision to be made by the Authority reviewable according to principles of administrative law (paragraph 68). In particular on the ground of irrationality or that the decision frustrated the purpose of the Act. In considering the adequacy of the EIA, the Court does not employ a standard of perfection.

- The EIS should be comprehensive in its treatment of the subject matter, objective in its approach and alert the decision-maker and the public as to effects on the environment (Prineas). To this list is added the quality of being substantial see FFOS v. ALNG per Stollmeyer J. The EIA process in Trinidad and Tobago as in Belize is iterative and is not the last opportunity of the Authority to exercise control.

92. The Court found the decision of Justice Stollmeyer in FFOS v ALNG to be very useful.

The following principles in respect of judicial review of cumulative impact assessment, may be extracted from FFOS v ALNG:

- The Court must ensure, by scrutinising the record that the agency took a "hard look" at all relevant circumstances.

- Once the agency has taken the hard look, the Court cannot impose its views.

93. The Court derived assistance from the block of English cases. In spite of the difference in the respective regimes, the following guidelines emerge from the English cases:

- There is no requirement of perfection in the preparation of an EIS. The Court will exercise its power of review in the rare case where an environmental statement is so deficient that is could not reasonably be described as an environmental statement. (See Blewett)

94. The Court will strike down environmental clearance if the Court can see clear differences in the evidence before it. See Viridor. Such a situation is to be distinguished from cases where it is possible for the Court to see some material on which the decision-maker could have relied on to reach a decision as to all relevant matters (Viridor).

The Court re-applied "hard look" test as applied to cumulative impacts of a development, in **Fishermen and Friends of the Sea v Environmental**

Management Authority, Ministry of Works and Transport (First Inter-ested Party) and KALL Company Limited (Second Interested Party).[255] In dismissing the application for leave to apply for judicial review, Justice Smith, in a separate judgement, found merit in the argument that there was not compliance with the requirement for a true cumulative impact assessment.

According to Smith JA:

I am of the view that the EMA did require a true cumulative impact assessment...Their decision to forego the same ought to have been based on a "hard look" based on a proper quantitative and qualitative assessment. Whether the facts reveal such a "hard look" is open to question in this case. Hence there is a case with some realistic prospect of success based on the rationality of the decision of the EMA to forego a true cumulative impact assessment."[256]

The views of Justice Smith, however, did not find favour with the other two justices of appeal hearing the matter and the Privy Council which also questioned the relevance of the "hard look" test to the jurisprudence of TT.

Fishermen and Friends of the Sea (Appellant) v Environmental Management Authority and others (Respondents), [2018] UKPC 24

Lord Carnwath:

Introduction

36. No reference was made to cumulative impacts in the four issues defined in the Pre-Action Protocol letter. However, two of the 14 grounds set in the application for leave ((vi) and (ix)) referred to a failure to consider cumulative effects, first of the CEC in respect of the 5,000 metre highway and secondly of the "proposed highway route". The judge (para 63) treated the second as a repetition of the first. This failure was alleged to be either "ultra vires rule 10 of the rules" or a failure to have regard to a relevant consideration.

---

255 CV 2017-03452

256 CA No. 050 of 2018, p. 19 of 39. See also, **Peninsula Citizens For Sustainable Development Ltd v. The Department of the Environment and Ara Macao Development Interested Party Ltd Claim No. 170 of 2007 (Belize).**

37. In spite of the apparently limited scope of these grounds as so pleaded, they were presented to the judge as raising a wider issue relating to the failure to consider the impact of future phases of the project (para 57). He thought that there would have been an arguable point with a reasonable prospect of success "if ... phase one could not have been considered a stand-alone project within itself", adding:

"In other words, if it were that the construction of phase one would not make sense without the construction of any of the future phases, then it would clearly be irrational for the EMA to grant a CEC without considering the effects of the other phases upon which usability of Phase one is dependant." (para 59)

However, as he understood it, the present proposal was not "a highway to no-where, whose sole usefulness depends on the construction of the other phases in the larger project". Accordingly, the Authority was not required to consider the cumulative effects of future phases (para 60).

38. In the Court of Appeal Smith JA (paras 70ff) identified the alleged failure by reference to the consideration of cumulative impacts in the EIA, which he took to be limited to Package 1, rather than to the entire Highway Extension, as requested in the Terms of Reference and the Review and Assessment Report. He thought that a decision to forego such consideration should have reflected "a 'hard look' based on a proper quantitative and qualitative assessment". Whether that had been done was "open to question" (para 78). Hence there was a case with some realistic prospects of success on the "rationality" of the decision to forego a true cumulative impact assessment. However, the merits of this argument were not sufficient to overcome "the discretionary time bars and/ or the third party and good administration considerations that negate the case for leave" (para 79).

39. On this point he was in the minority. J Jones JA (with whom Des Vignes JA agreed) noted and rejected the argument that the failure to consider cumulative effects was ultra vires rule 10 of the CEC Rules (para 135). She saw the real issue as being whether, in the face of its request in the TOR for information on the possible cumulative effects of future phases, the Authority acted unreasonably in accepting the Ministry's excuses for not providing it (para 136). She referred to the exchanges between the Ministry and the Authority on the failure to provide this information. She also referred (para 143) to the evidence of Mr Romano for the Authority responding to this allegation, and explaining that the Ministry's approach was acceptable in the light of the lack of adequate knowledge of the specific design and operation of any possible future packages, and that it was regarded as appropriate and not unreasonable for the Ministry to defer such assessment while the other stages were unapproved and in various stages of development.

40. In conclusion (paras 147-149) she accepted that the cumulative effects of other phases were a material consideration, having been accepted as such by the Authority. However, it was for the Authority alone to determine the weight to be given to it in the light of the reasons put forward by the Ministry. The allegation that the Authority had failed to have regard to this material consideration was not supported by the facts, and it had not been shown that their approach was irrational.

41. Before the Board there was some discussion whether the judge had correctly understood the nature of the 5,000 metre highway covered by the CEC itself. It does not in itself show any direct connection to the existing highway, and to that extent might be regarded as a "road to nowhere", if no account is taken of the short connecting roads which (it is said) will link it to the local villages and hence to the wider network. Given the limited way in which the issue was formulated in the original ground, the approach of the judge is understandable. However, it is unnecessary to consider that further, since, as has been seen, the issue as presented to the Court of Appeal and to the Board relates not to the impact of this limited stretch of highway, but to the impact of the other phases of the CRHE scheme.

42. In support of the view of G Smith JA that it was an argument with realistic prospects of success, Mr Wald relied on the judgment of Stollmeyer J in Fishermen and Friends of the Sea v Environmental Management Authority HCA Civ 2148 of 2003. (This appears also to be the source of the "hard look" approach favoured by G Smith JA.) Discussing the assessment of "cumulative impacts" (p 90) the judge said:

"Rule 10(e) of the CEC Rules requires the EMA to consider the cumulative effects but does not provide any specific guidelines or parameters for cumulative impact assessment. The EMA is given a broad discretion to determine the scope

and sufficiency of the assessment but is not provided with any guidance on how this discretion is to be exercised. The term 'cumulative effect' is not specifically defined, but its importance is well recognised as being one of the more important considerations in carrying out an environmental assessment.

The Act and the National Environmental Policy aim at achieving sustainable development and the EMA must consider development projects in a cumulative context. It must be given careful scrutiny because natural resources are seen as being under increasing pressure."

43. *He referred (p 91) to what he described as the "most comprehensive definition of cumulative effect" as formulated by the US Council on Environmental Quality (CEQ), created by the US National Environmental Policy Act 1969:*

"... the impact on the environment which results from the incremental impact of the action [being analysed] when added to other past, present, and reasonably foreseeable future actions regardless of what agency ... or person undertakes such other actions. ..." (CFR, Title 40, Ch V, Pt 1508, para 1508.7)

After reference to what he called "the major Canadian and American authorities" he continued (pp 92-93):

"The approach to judicial review of cumulative impact assessment in these cases is referred to as the 'hard look doctrine' and originated in the context of court review of administrative decisions. The approach adopted by these courts does not in substance differ from the approach adopted in this jurisdiction when considering applications for judicial review of an administrative decision. The 'hard look' requires the agency to take its statutory responsibilities seriously and take a 'hard look' at all the relevant circumstances. It calls only for the Court 'to ensure that the agency took a hard look at the cumulative environmental consequences' (see Natural Resources Defense Council Inc v Morton 458 F 2d 827). Once the agency has taken 'a hard look' by complying procedurally and substantively with the legislative intent, the court cannot impose its views or interject into the agency's discretion as to the action to be taken."

44. *Although the definition cited by Stollmeyer J is not in terms imported into the CEC Rules, the Board readily accepts its utility, and the importance of considering cumulative impacts as so defined in appropriate cases. However, it is to be noted that the "cumulative impacts" relied on in that case were quite different*

from the present. They related, not to future extensions, but to the additional impact of a proposed fourth installation (or "train") for liquid natural gas, when combined with the three existing trains (see p 73). There was therefore no uncertainty about what was involved.

45. The Board is not persuaded that the "hard look" doctrine, familiar in USA authorities, is a necessary addition to the administrative law of Trinidad and Tobago. In any event, the allegation in the present case was not that the authority had failed to take a "hard look", but that it had failed to have regard to this issue at all. It was to that allegation that Mr Romano was responding. As he explained in his affidavit, the Authority accepted that the cumulative impacts of possible future additional phases of the highway could be assessed when the details of any contemplated additional highway segments were known. He noted that any future extensions would lead away from the vicinity of the Aripo Savannas. He said:

"In the opinion of the EMA, NIDCO's response was acceptable when viewed in the light of the uncertainties due to lack of adequate knowledge of the specific design and operation of any possible future packages concerning any extensions to the highway."

46. On this issue the Board finds itself in full agreement with the majority of the Court of Appeal. There is no arguable breach of rule 10. Although the definition of "impacts" includes cumulative impacts, the reference is to the impact of the particular "activity". In itself the rule says nothing about the impact of future extensions. For that the case stands or falls on the requirement laid down by the Authority itself in its own TOR and repeated in the review. The Board understands the concerns of the Technical Staff at the Authority's change of position on this aspect. However, in the light of Mr Romano's explanation of the Authority's reasons for not pressing this point (the good faith of which is not questioned), it is impossible to say that the Authority failed to have regard to this issue, or that its response was irrational.

Refusal to Issue a CEC

The *Environmental Management Act* vests in the EMA discretion to refuse or issue a CEC. However, this is not an unfettered right.

Section 36 of the Environmental Act

36(1) After considering all relevant matters, including the comments or representations made during the public comment Certificate of environmental clearance, the Authority may issue a Certificate subject to such terms and conditions as it thinks fit, including the requirement to undertake appropriate mitigation measures.

It is clear that when an EIA is required and there is refusal to grant a CEC, natural justice is statutorily present as the EMA is required to give reasons for its refusal to issue a CEC.

Section 36 of the Environmental Management Act - 36(2) Where the Authority refuses to issue a Certificate, it shall provide to the applicant in writing its reasons for such action.

The more complex situation is whether the EMA can refuse to grant a CEC without seeking information beyond that which is contained in the application. A reading of *Sections 35 and 36 of the Environmental Management Act* would suggest that the EMA can only refuse to issue a CEC when there are environmental impacts which cannot be mitigated in such a manner as to be rendered insignificant to the satisfaction of the EMA. Therefore, the EMA can only reach such a decision if the application contains sufficient details on environmental impacts and mitigation measures. The application form is derived from *Rule 3(5) of the CEC Rules* and only requires an overview of the activity for which there is an application for a CEC. Further, the application form currently used by the EMA goes beyond *Rule 3(5) of the CEC Rules* and requires information on proposed mitigation measures for adverse effects. Importantly, however, it fails to ask for specific information on the adverse effects. Accordingly, although it can be argued that the applicant must know of the adverse effects in order to determine the mitigation measures, there will have to be a presumption that the EMA can reason backwards from the stated mitigation measures to the adverse effects of a particular activity. This is certainly not a reasonable presumption. Second, the only area of the *CEC Rules* that specifically calls for effects and mitigation measures in detail is *Rule 10* which outlines the adverse effects as should be contained in an EIA. It can therefore be argued that the EMA can only refuse to grant a CEC after it has full knowledge of the environmental effects and the inadequacy of the mitigation measures. Third, there is a natural justice element to a decision of the EMA which is in the same position as other administrative bodies in TT. It would seem fair and just for the EMA to provide prior notice to an applicant that the EMA is considering the rejection of its application, informing the applicant as to why the EMA is proposing such a course of action, and providing the applicant with an opportunity to make representations. Thus, it is questionable whether the EMA can summarily terminate an application for a CEC on the basis of information contained in the application form.

The Environmental Commission has ruled that the EMA cannot refuse to issue a CEC without giving an applicant a right to establish that potentially adverse environmental impacts could be mitigated. The Environmental Commission felt that this was a basic tenet of natural justice and could only be properly exercised with the opportunity to conduct an EIA.

Talisman (Trinidad) Petroleum Limited v Environmental Management Authority,[257]

Chairman Hosein

The right to a fair hearing is a principle of natural justice and has been applied as a base on which to build a kind of code of fair administrative procedure.

"The courts took their stand several centuries ago on the broad principle that bodies entrusted with legal power could not validly exercise it without first hearing the person who was going to suffer. This principle was applied very widely to administrative as well as to judicial acts, and to the acts of individual Ministers and Officials as well as to the acts of collective bodies such as justices and committees. Even where an order or determination is unchallengeable as regards its substance, the court can at best control the preliminary procedure so as to require fair consideration of both sides of the case. Thus, the law makes its contribution to good administration......overlooking it is one of the most common legal errors to which human nature is prone. When a Lord Chief Justice, an Archbishop of Canterbury, and a three judge Court of Appeal have strayed from the path of rectitude, it is not surprising that it is one of the

---

257 No EA3 of 2002

more frequent mistakes of ordinary mortals."

See page 469-470, Administrative Law by Wade & Forsyth, 8th Ed.

It is important to note that the significance and universality of the principle "make it applicable to almost the whole range of administrative powers, however silent about it the statute may be." (See page P. 474 op cit.)The duty to act fairly and to observe the rules of natural justice involves "giving to the person whose activities are being investigated a reasonable opportunity to put forward facts and arguments in justification of his conduct of these activities before they reach a conclusion which may affect him adversely" per Lord Diplock in Hoffman La Roche (f) & Co. vs. Secretary of State for Trade and Industry (1975) A.C. 295 (368 D-E).

That a decision-making body should not see relevant material without giving those affected a chance to comment on it and, if they wish, to controvert it is fundamental to the principle of law (which governs public administration as much as it does adjudication) ...see Sedley J., R London Borough of Camden ec p Paddock (1995) COD 130. See also Judicial Review Handbook 3rd Ed. By Michael Fordham at Para 60 5.5. Indeed, the Appellant complains that he did not see or know of the material or documents upon which the Respondent had based its decision until the hearing of the Appeal.

In A.G. vs. Ryan (PC) [1980] ac 718 at page 730, per Lord Diplock at P. 730:

"It has long been settled that a decision affecting the legal rights of an individual which is arrived at by a procedure which offends against the principles of natural justice is outside the jurisdiction of the decision-making authority."

These principles mutatis mutandis may be applied to the method by which the Respondent arrived at its decision to issue the Refusal.

When these principles of fairness are taken into account, it is clear that the Appellant, having been denied the opportunity to persuade or to show how it would be able to carry out the proposed activity without damaging the Swamp (especially in the absence of a prohibition against such activity), the decision to refuse in the circumstances would be fundamentally flawed.

Mrs. Badri-Maharaj in her address referred to Lloyd v. Mc Mahon (1987)

1 A.C. 625 per Lord Bridge at page 702 where he said:

"The so-called rules of natural justice are not engraved on tablets of stone. To use the phrase which better expressed the underlying concept, what the requirements of fairness demand when anybody, domestic, administrative or judicial, has to make a decision which will affect the right of individuals depends on the character of the decision-making body, the kind of decision it has to make and the statutory or other framework in which it operates."

As Supperstone and Goudie in their work Judicial Review at chapter 8, para. 8.16 under the rubric scope and application of the principles of natural justice, state:

"...since whether those rules apply and the extent of the duty depend upon the particular type of case concerned, it is often difficult to predict with confidence what fairness will be considered to require in any particular context. ....the courts have emphasized that the normal assumption is that the rules will apply"

and at para. 8.17 continues –

"They have been stated indeed to apply 'to all powers of decision unless the circumstances suffice to exclude them.' These circumstances may be found in the person or body making the decision, the nature of the decision to be made, the gravity of the matter in issue, the terms of any contract or other provisions governing the powers to decide and so on."

Per Megarry J. in Gaiman vs. National Association for Mental Health (1971) Ch. 317 at 333.

In Lloyd vs. Mc Mahon, the Councillors had misconducted themselves in failing to make a rate thereby incurring a loss of some £106,103. The District Auditor had already pointed out possible consequences for individual Councillors. When the Auditor issued an "unless" notice, in which he indicated that he would commence action to recover any losses incurred by the failure to make a rate from the Councillors responsible for incurring them, the Councillors were notified that they might make representations in writing to the Auditor before he reached a decision, and the Auditor enclosed a note of the various matters to which he had had regard in issuing the notice. The note identified specific losses resulting from the delay totalling £106,103 including the loss of interest on sums that would, but for the delay, have been paid earlier than had been the case. The Appellant Councillors were identified as persons who by their voting or absence might have failed to discharge their duty as members of the Council and might, therefore, be guilty of wilful misconduct resulting in the losses in question. The note also showed that there was no lawful justification for the delay in making the rate.

Of great importance was the fact there that the Appellant Councillors made a collective written and fully documented response to the Auditor's notice with the assistance of the Council's Chief Executive. And at page 708 Lord Bridge noted that the Auditor had "asserted his sincere belief in what had been said in the collective written response" and therefore to give an individual oral hearing "w o u l d have been a departure from the collective stance which the Appellants were given and had deliberately adopted." So it is clear that the Councillors had an opportunity to make their freely documented and collective representations in writing, after having been given a note of the various matters to which the Auditor had had regard in issuing the notice. That is a far cry from being asked to supply further information as was the case in the instant matter. As Lord Bridge indicated at page 702-703 "It is well established that where a Statute has conferred on anybody, the power to make decisions affecting individuals, the Courts will not only require the procedure prescribed by the Statute to be followed, but will readily imply so much and no more to be introduced by way of additional procedural safeguards as will assure the attainment of fairness."

While the procedure under Rule 4 does not specifically provide for an oral hearing by the Respondent, it is required by Section 16(2) of the Act in the discharge of its obligation to facilitate cooperation among persons and manage the environment in a manner which fosters participation and promotes consensus. And under Rule 4 1 (c) and (d) there is provision for the issue of a CEC without an EIA or requiring an EIA. The requirement for an EIA involves a full assessment of the likely impact of the proposed activity and how, by proposed or other mitigating measures any risks of harm to the environment may be eliminated or reduced to a level that is acceptable. Further, Rule 5 provides an opportunity for consultation with the Appellant in respect of a TOR as well as, where appropriate, with relevant agencies (which would include the Forestry Division) and NGOs and having exhausted the available procedures as may be applicable, by Rule 7 it is empowered to either issue or refuse a CEC. So Rules 4 and 5 do involve in accordance with Section 16(2) the application of rules of fairness, before the decision to issue or refuse the CEC under Rule 7 is ultimately made.

The Government of Trinidad and Tobago has stipulated in the preamble to the Environmental Management Act, its commitment to developing a strategy for sustainable development, being the balance of economic growth with environmentally sound practices, in order to enhance the quality of life and meeting the needs of present and future generations. That commitment must not be lost sight of especially as it has been given effect in the objects of the Act (See Section 4(d) (i) (ii) (iii) and has been provided for under Section 16(1) (b) as one of the functions of the Respondent.

I am indebted to Mr. Morgan and Mrs. Badri-Maharaj for their painstaking erudition and researches but I mean no disrespect to Counsel if I did not refer to all of their various citations but only to some in this judgement. I accept the general propositions of law which they establish in relation to the facts of each respective case. As I see it, the instant matter requires an answer to two questions: -

First, whether the Respondent's reliance on the Ramsar convention, the prohibitions in the Forests Act, the Conservation of Wildlife Act, and the Wetland Policy was right in law as a basis to support its decision to refuse to issue a CEC to the Appellant and secondly whether at the time of its refusal to issue a CEC and having regard to the information before it, there was a breach of the Appellant's right to a fair hearing and/or a procedural irregularity under Rule 4 of the CEC Rules.

For the reasons given and in the light of the foregoing, I have come to the conclusion that the first question must be answered in the negative and the second question must be answered in the affirmative.

At the end of the day, therefore, the order which we make is that the Appeal be and is hereby allowed, the refusal is set aside, and the application is referred back to the Respondent for reconsideration in accordance with the principles of natural justice set out herein and also with particular reference to Rule 4 (1) (c) and/or (d) of the CEC Rules.

Post-CEC Approval Consultations

It is accepted that in making a decision to grant a CEC in the event that an EIA is required, the EMA must have substantial information before it, to take a "hard look" at the application for a CEC. Put another way, the EIA must be in substantial compliance with the TOR and the relevant rules guiding the preparation of an EIA. Where there is substantial evidence to facilitate a 'hard look" or substantial compliance with the TOR and the *CEC Rules*, the EMA may grant the CEC and issue it with conditions that must be complied with for a particular project to proceed.

Section 36 of the Environmental Management Act

36(1) After considering all relevant matters, including the comments or representations made during the public comment period, the Authority may issue a Certificate subject to such terms and conditions as it thinks fit, including the requirement to undertake appropriate mitigation measures.

What the EMA cannot do is to put as a condition, an issue that negates substantial compliance of an EIA with the TOR and the *CEC Rules* or which undermines the requirement of substantial information to permit the EMA to take a "hard look" at the adequacy of the EIA. In **People United Respecting the Environment and Rights Action Group v Environmental Management Authority, Alutrint Limited (Interested Party) and the Attorney General of Trinidad and Tobago,**[258] the absence of a detailed plan for the disposal of spent pot liners from the proposed smelter meant that there could not have been substantial compliance with the TOR and the *CEC Rules*. This is particularly significant as there is no statutory basis for public consultation in the post-CEC approval process and therefore fulfilment of conditions in a CEC would not attract public participation. This was proposed to the High Court in **People United Respecting the Environment and Rights Action Group v Environmental Management Authority, Alutrint Limited (Interested Party) and the Attorney General**

---

258 CV 2007-02263

of Trinidad and Tobago.[259]

Dean-Amorer J

Whether the deferral of the following key issues such as the Buffer Zone Management and Monitoring Plan (Clause (ii) (a) of the CEC); Medical Monitoring Plan intended to establish a baseline and periodically monitor employee and community health in consultation with the Ministry of Health (Clause (ii) (ff) of the CEC); Electromagnetic Radiation Monitoring Plan (Clause (ii) (nn) of the CEC); Spent Pot Lining Management Plan (Clause (ii) (vv) of the CEC); and Decommissioning Plan (Clause (ii) (ccc) of the CEC); Community Awareness and Emergency Response (CAER) (Clause (iii) (e) of the CEC) to the post CEC period is contrary to Section 28 (2) and 28 (3) of the Environmental Management Act and breaches the legitimate expectations of the public as there is no opportunity for public consultations in the post CEC period and these documents are critical for the proper assessment of the Smelter project by the public.

It must be emphasised that the Privy Council has upheld the right vested in the EMA to issue conditions as part of a CEC so as to address issues that may have not been dealt with in the EIA. This decision cannot be interpreted however to be judicial sanction to accept a totally defective EIA and remedy same through the use of conditions. The decision to grant a CEC on the basis of a substantially non-compliant EIA may be deemed irrational and/or unreasonable.

Fishermen and Friends of the Sea (Appellant) v Environmental Management Authority and others (Respondents), [2018] UKPC 24

Lord Carnwath

36. No reference was made to cumulative impacts in the four issues defined in the Pre-Action Protocol letter. However, two of the 14 grounds set in the application for leave ((vi) and (ix)) referred to a failure to consider cumulative effects, first of the CEC in respect of the 5,000 metre highway and secondly of the "proposed highway route". The judge (para 63) treated the second as a repetition of the

---

259 Ibid.

first. This failure was alleged to be either "ultra vires rule 10 of the rules" or a failure to have regard to a relevant consideration.

37. In spite of the apparently limited scope of these grounds as so pleaded, they were presented to the judge as raising a wider issue relating to the failure to consider the impact of future phases of the project (para 57). He thought that there would have been an arguable point with a reasonable prospect of success "if ... phase one could not have been considered a stand-alone project within itself", adding:

"In other words, if it were that the construction of phase one would not make sense without the construction of any of the future phases, then it would clearly be irrational for the EMA to grant a CEC without considering the effects of the other phases upon which usability of Phase one is dependant." (para 59)

However, as he understood it, the present proposal was not "a highway to no-where, whose sole usefulness depends on the construction of the other phases in the larger project". Accordingly, the Authority was not required to consider the cumulative effects of future phases (para 60).

38. In the Court of Appeal Smith JA (paras 70ff) identified the alleged failure by reference to the consideration of cumulative impacts in the ELA, which he took to be limited to Package 1, rather than to the entire Highway Extension, as requested in the Terms of Reference and the Review and Assessment Report. He thought that a decision to forego such consideration should have reflected "a 'hard look' based on a proper quantitative and qualitative assessment". Whether that had been done was "open to question" (para 78). Hence there was a case with some realistic prospects of success on the "rationality" of the decision to forego a true cumulative impact assessment. However, the merits of this argument were not sufficient to overcome "the discretionary time bars and/or the third party and good administration considerations that negate the case for leave" (para 79).

39. On this point he was in the minority. J Jones JA (with whom Des Vignes JA agreed) noted and rejected the argument that the failure to consider cumulative effects was ultra vires rule 10 of the CEC Rules (para 135). She saw the real issue as being whether, in the face of its request in the TOR for information on the possible cumulative effects of future phases, the Authority acted unreasonably in accepting the Ministry's excuses for not providing it (para 136). She referred to the exchanges between the Ministry and the Authority on the failure to provide this information. She also referred (para 143) to the evidence of Mr Romano for the Authority responding to this allegation, and explaining that the Ministry's approach was acceptable in the light of the lack of adequate knowledge of the specific design and operation of any possible future packages, and that it was regarded as appropriate and not unreasonable for the Ministry to defer such assessment while the other stages were unapproved and in various stages of development.

40. In conclusion (paras 147-149) she accepted that the cumulative effects of other phases were a material consideration, having been accepted as such by the Authority. However, it was for the Authority alone to determine the weight to be given to it in the light of the reasons put forward by the Ministry. The allegation that the Authority had failed to have regard to this material consideration was not supported by the facts, and it had not been shown that their approach was irrational.

41. Before the Board there was some discussion whether the judge had correctly understood the nature of the 5,000 metre highway covered by the CEC itself. It does not in itself show any direct connection to the existing highway, and to that extent might be regarded as a "road to nowhere", if no account is taken of the short connecting roads which (it is said) will link it to the local villages and hence to the wider network. Given the limited way in which the issue was formulated in the original ground, the approach of the judge is understandable. However, it is unnecessary to consider that further, since, as has been seen, the issue as presented to the Court of Appeal and to the Board relates not to the impact of this limited stretch of highway, but to the impact of the other phases of the CRHE scheme.

42. In support of the view of G Smith JA that it was an argument with realistic prospects of success, Mr Wald relied on the judgment of Stollmeyer J in Fishermen and Friends of the Sea v Environmental Management Authority HCA Civ 2148 of 2003. (This appears also to be the source of the "hard look" approach favoured by G Smith JA.) Discussing the assessment of "cumulative impacts" (p 90) the judge said:

"Rule 10(e) of the CEC Rules requires the EMA to consider the cumulative effects but does not provide any specific guidelines or parameters for cumulative impact assessment. The EMA is given a broad discretion to determine the scope and sufficiency of the assessment but is not provided with any guidance on how

this discretion is to be exercised. The term 'cumulative effect' is not specifically defined, but its importance is well recognised as being one of the more important considerations in carrying out an environmental assessment. The Act and the National Environmental Policy aim at achieving sustainable development and the EMA must consider development projects in a cumulative context. It must be given careful scrutiny because natural resources are seen as being under increasing pressure."

43. He referred (p 91) to what he described as the "most comprehensive definition of cumulative effect" as formulated by the US Council on Environmental Quality (CEQ), created by the US National Environmental Policy Act 1969:

"... the impact on the environment which results from the incremental impact of the action [being analysed] when added to other past, present, and reasonably foreseeable future actions regardless of what agency ... or person undertakes such other actions. ..." (CFR, Title 40, Ch V, Pt 1508, para 1508.7)

After reference to what he called "the major Canadian and American authorities" he continued (pp 92-93):

"The approach to judicial review of cumulative impact assessment in these cases is referred to as the 'hard look doctrine' and originated in the context of court review of administrative decisions. The approach adopted by these courts does not in substance differ from the approach adopted in this jurisdiction when considering applications for judicial review of an administrative decision.

The 'hard look' requires the agency to take its statutory responsibilities seriously and take a 'hard look' at all the relevant circumstances. It calls only for the Court 'to ensure that the agency took a hard look at the cumulative environmental consequences' (see Natural Resources Defense Council Inc v Morton 458 F 2d 827). Once the agency has taken 'a hard look' by complying procedurally and substantively with the legislative intent, the court cannot impose its views or interject into the agency's discretion as to the action to be taken."

44. Although the definition cited by Stollmeyer J is not in terms imported into the CEC Rules, the Board readily accepts its utility, and the importance of considering cumulative impacts as so defined in appropriate cases. However, it is to be noted that the "cumulative impacts" relied on in that case were quite different from the present. They related, not to future extensions, but to the additional impact of a proposed fourth installation (or "train") for liquid natural gas, when combined with the three existing trains (see p 73). There was therefore no uncertainty about what was involved.

45. The Board is not persuaded that the "hard look" doctrine, familiar in USA authorities, is a necessary addition to the administrative law of Trinidad and Tobago. In any event, the allegation in the present case was not that the authority had failed to take a "hard look", but that it had failed to have regard to this issue at all. It was to that allegation that Mr Romano was responding. As he explained in his affidavit, the Authority accepted that the cumulative impacts of possible future additional phases of the highway could be assessed when the details of any contemplated additional highway segments were known. He noted that any future extensions would lead away from the vicinity of the Aripo Savannas. He said:

"In the opinion of the EMA, NIDCO's response was acceptable when viewed in the light of the uncertainties due to lack of adequate knowledge of the specific design and operation of any possible future packages concerning any extensions to the highway."

46. On this issue the Board finds itself in full agreement with the majority of the Court of Appeal. There is no arguable breach of rule 10. Although the definition of "impacts" includes cumulative impacts, the reference is to the impact of the particular "activity". In itself the rule says nothing about the impact of future extensions. For that the case stands or falls on the requirement laid down by the Authority itself in its own TOR and repeated in the review. The Board understands the concerns of the Technical Staff at the Authority's change of position on this aspect. However, in the light of Mr Romano's explanation of the Authority's reasons for not pressing this point (the good faith of which is not questioned), it is impossible to say that the Authority failed to have regard to this issue, or that its response was irrational.

USE OF CONSENT AGREEMENTS

A disturbing trend that had emerged in the environmental approval process is the engaging of a designated activity by a party without a CEC and subsequent ratification by the EMA through the process of the service of a Notice of Violation pursuant to *Section 63(1) of the Environmental Management Act* and execution of a consent agreement under *Section 63(2) of the Environmental Management Act*. The use of a consent agreement in these circumstances could be used to circumvent the CEC process as it did in many instances. One of the underlying concerns is while the CEC process under certain circumstances contemplates public participation; there is no statutory basis for such participation in the negotiation and execution of a consent agreement. Indeed, while there are statutory provisions for displaying of a CEC in accordance with *Rule 7(2) of the CEC Rules* and having information pertinent to a CEC stored in a National Register of Certificates of Environmental Clearance as per *Rule 8 of the CEC Rules*, these are not applicable to consent agreements. Further, *Rule 9(1) of the CEC Rules* provides for public viewing of the National Register of Certificates of Environmental Clearance.

The matter involving the circumventing of the CEC process by means of a consent agreement was pronounced upon in **Concerned Residents of Cunupia v Environmental Management Authority**,[260] overruling the first instance judgment in **Concerned Residents of Cunupia v Environmental Management Authority**.[261] Consequently, the Court of Appeal of TT has now indicated that a CEC is not interchangeable with a consent agreement.

Pemberton JA (Majority judgment)

29. The Act sets out in plain, ordinary and unambiguous language that for the purpose of determining the environmental impact that may arise that the Minister may designate a list of activities as requiring CEC's. These activities are clearly spelt out in the Order. In this particular case we can extrapolate from section 35(1) and (2) and Article 18, that to establish a concrete batching plant a designated activity, a person must apply for and obtain a CEC. That is mandatory. That is the plain ordinary meaning to be derived from the words. That is the stated intention of Parliament. Since 'operation' is not mentioned, Mr Singh is of the view that that phase is not to be included as requiring a CEC. Mr Maharaj does not agree and has employed the contextual and purposive

---

260 Civ Appeal No. P195 of 2015
261 CV 2012-03024.

approach to buttress his conclusion that 'establishment' appearing in Activity 18, must include 'operation'.

30. I do not accept that there is any need to infer any meaning to arrive at the intention of Parliament as proffered by Mr Maharaj. To my mind, section 35 forms part of the Environmental Management regime. The conjoint effect of section 35(1) and (2) is that any person desirous of engaging in a designated activity shall not proceed with that activity, unless he/she applies for and obtains a CEC, authorising the activity. That is mandatory. The provisions of Activity 18 are clear and there is no need to repeat them. The fundamental omission by RPN's engaging in works towards the establishment and operation of the concrete batching plant, a designated activity put them in error from the start. The unvarnished fact is that RPN is a violator, not having its estab-lishment and operations sanction by a CEC. The fact that the violation was discovered by the EMA during the plant's operation is immaterial. That does not take it out of the mandatory requirements of section 35(2) as defined by Activity 18.

1. I must allude to the operation of the plant. Section 37 speaks to monitoring the performance of "the activity". A reading of the section reveals that it is concerned with the operations phase for which a CEC has been granted. If no CEC has been granted, the EMA cannot perform its statutory duty of monitoring. I do not accept Mr Singh's approach to the issue of seeking recourse to sections 41-47 of the Act. Further, recourse to the regime to which Mr Singh alluded, is still based on the application for and obtaining of a valid CEC for designated activities. Environmentally sensitive areas are jealously guarded by their own regimes of granting of permits. Those arguments will not apply and cannot justify an operation whose start-up was bedded in illegality, that is, when the persons proceeding with designated activities did not comply with the Act.

2. I say again, that the regime has been clearly provided for by Parliament. I would therefore conclude that when one looks at the statute as a whole and the purpose behind it, it is clear that 'operation' does not form part of the definition in Activity 18 and there is no need to make that inference[27]. Having said that, it does not mean that RPN is free from the mandatory provisions of section 35(2).

3. In answer to the question posed, given the context and purpose of the Act, the operation of the concrete batching plant does not fall within the category of "a designated activity" pursuant to section 35(2). The trial judge was not plainly wrong in her conclusion of this issue.

40. However the trial judge was of the view that the decision of the EMA's to avoid requiring a new CEC and to enter instead into a Consent Agreement compromised the policy of the public participation, which is reflected in the Act and enshrined in the National Environmental Policy. This was the basis for her striking down the decision; I do not agree that she needed to address that issue at all. It is my view that the Consent Agreement did not provide that the violator could have avoided the requirement of a new CEC and that is evident from the terms quoted above.

41. In so far as it was interpreted by the EMA that the Consent Agreement under section 63(2)(b) dispensed with the requirement of section 35(2), that interpretation was not only flawed but also incomprehensible given the patent terms of the Consent Agreement itself. Any decisions purported to be made in pursuance of that interpretation are therefore illegal.

Rajkumar JA (Agreeing with the Majority Decision but delivering a separate judgment):

87. Section 63(2) (b) of the Environmental Management Act does not authorize the EMA to override the provisions of Section 35(2) of that Act. The EMA therefore had no power to waive the application of Section 35(2), whether by entering into a Consent Agreement under Section 63 or otherwise. Its powers were to be exercised within the confines of the enabling statute. By entering into a Consent Agreement with RPN, without requiring RPN to first apply for and obtain a CEC for the operation of the concrete batching plant, as mandated by Section 35(2), the EMA acted without jurisdiction, and therefore illegally.

88. It was submitted that the consequences of the EMA's construction of s. 63(2) (b) of the Environmental Management Act would be as follows:

i. If a developer establishes or substantially constructs facilities associated with Activity 18 without first obtaining a CEC, it would not be issued a CEC. Instead, the Respondent may issue a negotiated Consent Agreement, not required to be placed on the National Register and therefore not being subject to any public scrutiny;

ii. No relevant environmental information, including operational information and mitigation measures, in relation to designated activities subject to a Consent Agreement, would be publicly accessible via the National Register;[6]

iii. Violators of Section 35 could potentially benefit by expediting construction of a facility for a Designated Activity in order to avoid delays and bureaucracy of the CEC process;

iv. It is also apparent that if no application is ever made for a CEC, in cases where otherwise an ELA might have been required, there would be a deprivation of the possibility of a right of public participation in environmental decision-making.

v. It was contended that the consequences of the Appellant's proposed construction identified by the Appellant would include the following

a. There will remain one major statutory regime for the regulation of significant environmental impacts in Trinidad and Tobago - CECs will regulate impacts accruing from pre-construction to abandonment/ decommissioning;

b. While Consent Agreements may be used to, inter alia, implement preventative and mitigatory measures commensurate with the environmental impact associated with establishing a facility for a Designated Activity without a CEC, they would still require applying for a CEC in respect of the establishment and operational phases of the designated activity; (All relevant environmental information, including operational information and mitigation measures, in relation to Designated Activities subject to CECs will be publicly accessible via the National Register);

c. Relevant environmental information would be open to public scrutiny if it affects the public, as such information would be contained in a CEC application in respect of a Designated Activity;

89. a. There was no factual basis for a finding of material non-disclosure on the part of the appellants.

b. However, even if there had been the nondisclosure alleged, it would not, as a matter of law, have been sufficiently material in the context of this case to justify the exercise of discretion to deny relief on that basis.

c. The EMA's decision to enter into a Consent Agreement without requiring that a CEC be obtained was based upon an incorrect construction of the Environmental Management Act and was therefore illegal because:

d. The establishment of a concrete batching plant is a Designated Activity under Activity 18 of the Certificate of Environmental Clearance (Designated Activities) Order, and therefore requires a CEC;

e. The operation of a concrete batching plant must be read as included in the definition of a Designated Activity under Activity 18 of the Certificate of Environmental Clearance (Designated Activities) Order, and it therefore requires a CEC;

f. Section 35 (2) of the Environmental Management Act, (the Environmental Management Act), establishes that a CEC must be obtained as a mandatory precondition before proceeding with a Designated Activity.

g. The EMA has no power, statutory or otherwise, to dispense with that mandatory precondition by entering into a Consent Agreement under s. 63(2) (b) of the Environmental Management Act.

90. *It is noted that RPN, having failed to obtain planning approval relocated the concrete batching plant. As to the order of Mandamus requested this relief is now of academic interest only. However, the orders sought for a declaration and for certiorari would not be academic even now, as they are the natural consequence of the determination by this court that the interpretation by of its powers under Section 63(2) (b) of the Environmental Management Act was erroneous.*

91. *The EMA's actions consequent upon that erroneous interpretation were therefore illegal. It remains the case therefore that the decision of the respondent to have permitted the operation of the concrete batching plant was unlawful, null and void, and of no effect. There remains the need for certainty with respect to the legality of its action in entering into the Consent Agreement. There remains the need for statutory construction with respect to this issue. It also remains necessary to quash that decision rather than letting it stand as a precedent that may in future be relied upon by the EMA. The relocation of RPN's plant does not affect any of these issues. Further, the CRC was entitled to have succeeded in the High Court and any orders for costs against it must be reversed.*

92. *I would allow the appeal and order that the EMA pay to the appellants their*

costs incurred in this appeal and in the court below. I would also have granted the orders set out below.

CHAPTER 5

THE POLLUTER PAYS PRINCIPLE

ORIGIN AND DEVELOPMENT OF THE POLLUTER PAYS PRINCIPLE

The polluter pays principle is regarded as a normative doctrine of environmental law and is considered to be one of the more salient aspects of sustainable development. The polluter pays system inherently results in a balance between ecology and development, a critical feature of sustainability. The principle is derived from the basic proposition that parties who generate pollution should bear the cost of abatement.[262] The general population should not be required to subsidize pollution. Indeed, polluters must assume full responsibility and internalize all appropriate costs to ensure that the state of the environment achieves acceptance by the wider society.[263] The main objectives of the polluter pays principle, therefore, are cost allocation and cost internalization. It is in effect an efficiency principle of allocating costs for domestic pollution which does not actually involve a reduction in pollution.[264] No doubt, however, placing the responsibility for assumption of the cost associated with its polluting activities must redound to the benefit of the environment as the private sector should rationally follow its natural instinct for cost reduction as one of the pillars of corporate success, thereby lowering its levels of pollution.

In the early 1970s, the Organization for Economic Cooperation and De-

---

262 Jonathan Remy Nash, *Too Much Market? Conflict Between Tradable Pollution Allowances and the "Polluter Pays" Principle* (2002) 24 Harvard Environmental Law Review, 465, 466.

263 Ibid at [468]

264 Candice Stevens, *Interpreting the Polluter Pays Principle in the Trade and Environment Context* Cornell International Law Journal (1994) Vol 27 Iss 3, Article 5, 577, 579.

velopment (OECD) countries, including the USA, began implementing increasingly stringent environmental policies; however, industries began to fear the cost of these measures and their effects on competition levels, resulting in governments becoming under much pressure to absorb the costs of regulatory compliance.[265] The polluter pays principle first originated in a legal context in a document prepared by the OECD. It recommended that:

> *The principle to be used for allocating costs of pollution prevention and control measures to encourage rational use of scarce environmental resources and to avoid distortions in international trade and investment is the so-called "Polluter Pays" principle.*[266]

The basis of the principle is that the polluter should bear the expenses of implementing measures imposed by public agencies to ensure that the environment is protected. This objective translated into the principle that the internalization of costs should be reflected in the cost of goods and services which cause pollution in production and/or consumption. Measures taken to ensure protection of the environment should eschew subsidies which may potentially create distortions in international trade and investment and place an unfair burden on the public to fund the profits of private enterprise.[267] Nevertheless, although the OECD consists of official government representation, the recommendation was never formally ratified by any government. Therefore, it merely functioned as a statement of environmental goals and principles for the international community and was only formalized in the OECD document.[268]

The polluter pays principle, however, has appeared in an increasing number of international legal documents addressing international environmental

---

265 OECD (1995), *Environmental Principles and Concepts,* at 12, OECD Doc. GD (95)124.

266 OECD (1972), *Environment and Economics: Guiding Principles Concerning International Economic Aspects of Environmental Policies, Annex P 1*, OECD Doc. C(72)128, (May 26, 1972), available at 1972 WL 24710.

267 Eric Larson *Why Environmental Liability Regimes in the United States, the European Community, and Japan Have Grown Synonymous With the Polluter Pays Principle* (2005) 38 Vanderbilt Journal of Transnational Law 541, 546.

268 Margaret Grossman *Agriculture and the Polluter Pays Principle: An Introduction* (2006) 59 OKLA L Rev 1, 3.

law issues. It has been referred to as an *"instrument of international jurisprudence [that] articulates policies and prescriptions directed at the achievement of worldwide sustainable development"*.[269] The inclusion of the polluter pays principle into some of the more important international declarations on the environment demonstrates its growing international significance and acceptability.

THE POLLUTER PAYS PRINCIPLE IN THE CARIBBEAN REGION

Although the EU leads the way in the regional development of the polluter pays principle, there is some development in other regional blocs that suggests its growing significance in the political consciousness of regional decision-makers. For example, the *Revised Treaty of Chaguaramas*,[270] that was intended to deepen the efforts of Caribbean nation states towards economic integration, expressly promotes the polluter pays principle.

> *Article 65 - Environmental Protection: 1. The policies of the Community shall be implemented in a manner that ensures the prudent and rational management of the resources of the Member States. In particular, the Community shall promote measures to ensure: 2. (e) the precautionary principle and those principles relating to preventive action, rectification of environmental damage at source and the principle that the polluter pays...*[271]

Unfortunately, actions in the Caribbean have not gone beyond the lofty regional pronouncement contained in the *Revised Treaty of Chaguaramas* and remain very much an elusive ideal.

THE POLLUTER PAYS PRINCIPLE IN TT

The polluter pays principle is entrenched in national legislation through the

---

269 J. Batt and D. Short, *The Jurisprudence of the 1992 Rio Declaration on Environment and Development: A Law, Science and Policy Explanation of Certain Aspects of the United Nations Conference on Environment and Development* (1993) Journal of Natural Resources and Environmental Law 8: 229, 230.

270 Caricom Secretariat [online].

271 Ibid.

NEP 2018. It is stated in Section 1.05:

The cost of preventing pollution, minimising environmental damage due to pollution, and/or compensation for damages due to pollution, shall be borne by those responsible for the pollution.

This principle may be applied through command-and-control measures (E.g. Pollution Standards) or market-based measures (E.g. Taxes). Important elements of the application of this principle using pollution standards are:

a) Charges are levied as:

i. An application or processing fee proportional to the cost of processing a license or permit; and

ii. A licence or permit operating fee proportional to: (1) the quantities/concentration/amount of pollutants which the holder is permitted to generate, or (2) to the best approximate of the total cost to society due to polluting activities undertaken;

b) Charges are levied for compensation and damages associated with pollution of the environment; and

c) Money collected will be used to correct environmental damages and improve pollution management.

This important environmental principle has travelled through the judicial system of TT and has been pronounced upon by the highest court of the land, that is, the Privy Council.

In *Fishermen and Friends of the Sea v. the Minister of Planning, Housing and the Environment,*[272] judicial review was sought with respect to the decision of the Minister to make regulations for granting of water pollution permits on the basis of a flat fixed fee. As noted, *Section 26 of the Environmental Management Act* allows the Minster to make rules for the procedures for the registration of polluters who may be allowed to release pollutants into the environment along with the quantity, condition or concentration of pollutants or substances containing pollutants that may be released into the

---

272 CV 2008-04593.

environment and for the procedures and standards with respect to permits or licenses required for polluters to install or operate any process or other source from which pollutants will be or may continue to be released into the environment. FFOS in its capacity as a public interest group brought an action to challenge the defendant's decision to institute the standardized permit fee under the provisions of the *Environmental Management Act*. The fee structure imposed a fixed fee for permits without regard to the differentiating aspects of a polluter's business and levels of pollution. FFOS raised the question as to whether such a fee structure was a proper application of the polluter pays principle. FFOS was successful at the High Court as seen in *Fishermen and Friends of the Sea v The Minister of Planning, Housing and the Environment*[273] but the decision was reversed at the Court of Appeal in *The Minister of Planning, Housing and the Environment v Fishermen and Friends of the Sea*.[274] FFOS successfully appealed the matter at the PC. In *Fishermen and Friends of the Sea v The Minister of Planning, Housing and the Environment*,[275] Lord Carnwath made it clear that the polluter pays principle was well enshrined in the legal landscape of TT and had to be complied with. As per Lord Carnwath:

> *2. The Polluter Pays Principle ("PPP" or "the Principle") is now firmly established as a basic principle of international and domestic environmental laws. It is designed to achieve the "internalization of environmental costs", by ensuring that the costs of pollution control and remediation are borne by those who cause the pollution, and thus reflected in the costs of their goods and services, rather than borne by the community at large (see e.g. OECD Council 1972 Recommendation of the Council on Guiding Principles concerning International Economic Aspects of Environmental Policies; Rio Declaration 1992 Principle 16). Most recently, the Principle has been simply expressed in the Draft Global Pact for the Environment, presented by President Macron to the United Nations Assembly on 19 September 2017: "Article 8 Polluter-Pays Parties shall ensure that prevention; mitigation and remediation costs for pollution, and other environmental disruptions and degradation are, to the greatest possible extent, borne by their originator."*

---

273 Ibid.
274 Civ Appeal No. 240 of 2012.
275 PCA No. 0028 of 2016.

3. Discussing the Principle (as it appeared in the EC Treaty, article 130r (2), now article 191(2) of the TFEU) Advocate General Léger identified "two aspects": Page 3 "93. It must be understood as requiring the person who causes the pollution, and that person alone, to bear not only the costs of remedying pollution …, but also those arising from the implementation of a policy of prevention …" (Case C-293/97) R v Secretary of State for the Environment, Ex p Stanley [1999] QB 1279, paras 92-95) Both aspects are relevant in the present case. He added (para 97) that the principle may take the form that "in return for the payment of a charge, the polluter is authorized to carry out a polluting activity".

4. Although the Principle is well-established, such statements have been criticized as lacking precision: "Despite the antiquity and strong ethical foundations of the polluter pays principle, its content is less easy to determine. Proclaiming that 'the polluter should pay' is a simple statement which is intuitively fair, but of necessity it requires an investigation into issues such as who is the polluter? For what should they be made to pay? How much should they be made to pay? And so on …" (Burnett-Hall on Environmental Law 3rd ed. (2012), p 91, para 2-121).

5. In Trinidad and Tobago an attempt has been made to tackle such questions in a more methodical way through the statutory National Environmental Policy ("the NEP") as applied to charges for licenses, and, in the context of water pollution, through the Water Pollution Management Programme ("the WPMP"). Paragraph 2.3 of the NEP includes the following: "Polluter Pays Principle A key principle of pollution control policy is that the cost of preventing pollution or of minimising environmental damage due to pollution will be borne by those responsible for pollution. The principle seeks to accomplish the optimal allocation of limited resources. Important elements of the principle are: (a) Charges are levied as an application or processing fee, purchase price of a license or permit, which entitle the holder to generate specific quantities of pollutants; and (b) Money collected will be used to correct environmental damage."

6. The central issue in this case is whether the Ministerial regulations by which charges were fixed were consistent with this aspect of the NEP (in particular subparagraph 2.3(b)). There is a further issue in any event as to whether the Minister, in formulating the regulations, gave proper consideration to the NEP and to the WPMP.

7. The appellants are a non-profit organization, concerned with the protection of the environment in Trinidad and Tobago. They have an impressive record of some ten years of giving advice, guidance and assistance to the national community. There is rightly no challenge to their standing to bring this case in the public interest. The statutory and policy background The Environmental Management Act

8. This statute ("the Act", it replacing an Act of 1995 in materially the same terms) provides the statutory framework for what is described in the preamble as the government's commitment to "developing a national strategy for sustainable development ..." The preamble also states that sustainable development is to be encouraged by use of economic and non-economic incentives, and that "polluters should be held responsible for the costs of their polluting activities".

9. Section 6 provides for the establishment of the Environmental Management Authority ("the Authority"). Section 16 defines the functions of the Authority, to include (inter alia) (a) making recommendations for a National Environmental Policy, (b) developing and implementing "policies and programmes for the effective management and wise use of the environment, consistent with the objects of this Act", (g) monitoring compliance with the standards criteria and programmes relating to the environment; and (h) taking "all appropriate action for the prevention and control of pollution and conservation of the environment". Section 20 gives the Authority power to do "all things necessary or convenient to be done" in the performance of its functions. Other provisions confer powers for specific activities, for example "Emergency response activities" (section 25) and "Environmental Incentive Programmes" (section 34).

10. Section 18 provides for the submission by the Authority's board, following public consultation, of a "comprehensive National Environmental Policy", to be approved by the Minister and laid before Parliament. Section 31 provides: "The Authority and all other governmental entities shall conduct their operations and programmes in accordance with the National Environmental Policy established under section 18." It is not in dispute that this section applies to the functions of the Minister in respect of the making of the relevant rules and regulations in the present case....

18. The NEP, under section 18 of the Act, was made and laid before Parliament on2 September 1998. A revised policy was made in 2006. Chapter 2 (unchanged in the revised version)... is headed "Goals, Objectives and Basic

Principles". It includes (under the general heading "2.3 Basic principles") the "Polluter Pays Principle"...

19. The Water Pollution Management Programme ("WPMP") was prepared by the Authority under section 52 and published in February 2005 (but see further para 24 below). The introduction noted that, while the Act dealt separately with pollution management in air, water and land, the Authority had chosen water pollution management as the area that required immediate attention. There followed a survey of the main categories of water, both freshwater and coastal and marine, and of sources of pollution actual and potential. This led to section 5, dealing with the creation of a Register of Water Pollutants (under section 52(2) of the Act), and section 6 "the Water Pollution Management Programme".

20. Section 6 began by noting that the starting point for the development of the WPMP was "an Environmental Quality Workshop held with personnel from the US based Environmental Law Institute and the Authority's staff", followed by discussions with a legal expert from the United States Environmental Protection Agency....

30. The grounds for judicial review included (ground 1) the claim that the fixed fee permit fee structure was in breach of PPP as expressed in paragraph 2.3 of the NEP (which was set out), and (grounds 3 and 4) contrary to the policies of the Ministry and the Authority. In the latter context, specific reference was made to the "Analysis of Various Permit Fee Models" in the WPMP....

34. Dr Mohammed's affidavit indicated that he had been the responsible Minister between 22 October 1999 and 10 December 2000. He confirmed his role as the then Minister in the approval of what became the 2001 rules and fees regulations. His "firm view" had been that "having regard to the state of economic development and the level of institutional development of the country" the most appropriate model would be the one which was "user friendly and the simplest to administer". He had given instructions accordingly. His affidavit makes no reference to the (1998) NEP, and gives no indication that he was aware of the six models later proposed in the WPMP or what other information he was given about the possible alternatives. The only other evidence for the Minister was the affidavit of Mr. Rajkumar, referred to above (para 25). That adds little information as to the process of approval of the Programme or the setting of fees. As already noted, it attributed the analysis of the models to Dr Ramlogan, who had left in 2001. ... The interpretation of the NEP 37. The first issue, as it has emerged from the submissions before the Board, comes down to a relatively narrow issue of interpretation of the "important elements" of the PPP as identified by paragraph 2.3 of the NEP...41. With respect to the Court of Appeal, the Board is unable to accept their interpretation of paragraph 2.3 of the NEP. even allowing for the fact that the paragraph is intended by way of "guidance" only, sub-paragraph (b) must be given separate effect in accordance with its natural meaning. It is in terms directed, not to the general purpose of the permitting system nor to the implementation of permit conditions, but to the use by the Authority itself of the "money collected" by way of fees for the correction of environmental damage. (Mr. Roe accepts that there is no other relevant source of "money collected" in this context.) Thus, it is not sufficient that the polluter will necessarily expend its own money in complying with the permit conditions, and so contribute to the "correction" of environmental damage. The fees are to be used to finance or contribute to correction activities by the Authority itself....There is no reference to this aspect of paragraph 2.3 in the evidence filed on behalf of the Minister, nor specifically in Mr. Goddard's account of the matters taken into account in setting the fees. The only Page 16 reasonable inference is that it was ignored. It follows that to this extent the regulations fail to comply with the NEP and are therefore in breach of the Minister's duty under section 31 of the Act...

47. The appellant's complaint is two-fold: first, that the Minister in 2006 exercised no judgement of her own on the application of PPP, but treated it as a matter delegated to the Authority; secondly, and in any event, that at that time the 2001 prescribed permit fee was re-adopted, without any reconsideration in the light of paragraph 2.3 of the NEP or of the analysis and recommendation of the 2005 WPMP...

52. The consequence is that, as far as relates to the prescribed fee for an application for a permit, the 2006 regulations are unlawful.

CHALLENGES TO THE POLLUTER PAYS PRINCIPLE

Originally an economic principle, the polluter pays principle has assumed legal status and is now considered a general principle of international environmental law and as noted before, the polluter pays principle has entered into the jurisprudence of TT. The polluter pays principle undoubtedly plays a positive role in the reduction of pollution and, in particular, pollution which occurs as a result of industrial activity. There are a number of factors which may be taken into consideration in deriving the fees/charges to be levied against a polluter as seen in cases from different jurisdictions. These include:

1. Facility Complexity

2. Flow Volume of Pollutants Released

3. Type of Pollutants Released

4. Receiving waters

5. Costs of abatement and remediation

6. Costs of monitoring and compliance

7. Administrative costs – fees should be based on the complexity of the permit which reflects the administrative effort required to get the permit in place.

8. No subsidy from Tax Payers

9. Potential Public Health Threat

10. Length of Permit

11. Disincentive to Pollute

The challenge that falls to be determined is how to implement the polluter pays principle while attempting to insert into the decision-making process the wide range of factors that ought to be considered. The complexity of deriving an appropriate formula for the implementation of the polluter pays principle has now attained critical importance in TT in light of its judicial sanction and there is now no room for reversal on its implementation.

CHAPTER 6

THE PRECAUTIONARY PRINCIPLE

HISTORICAL ARTICULATION OF THE PRECAUTIONARY PRINCIPLE

There have been several suggestions as to how the precautionary principle originated. Legal scholar Frank Cross claims that the phrase was initially coined by German bureaucrats in 1965. Others suggest that it was derived during the 1970s and the German articulation of *Vorsorgeprinzip*, which can be translated as the "precaution" or "foresight" principle.[276] Sonja Boehmer Christiansen claims that the precautionary principle evolved out of the German socio-legal tradition, during the era of democratic socialism, and centred on the concept of good household management where it was invested with a managerial or programmable quality and a purposeful role in guiding future political and regulatory action.[277]

An early version of the precautionary principle was introduced by the United Nations in 1982 in its *General Assembly Resolution on the World Charter for Nature*.[278] The precautionary principle was not quoted by name in the Resolution; however, two concepts were inserted into the Resolution:

1. Activities which are likely to cause irreversible damage to nature shall be

---

276 Julian Morris, *Rethinking Risk and the Precautionary Principle* (Oxford: Butterworth-Heinemann 2000), 1-21.

277 Timothy O'Riordan, and J. Cameron, *The History and Contemporary Significance of the Precautionary Principle*, in T. O'Riordan and J. Cameron (eds.) *Interpreting the Precautionary Principle* (London: Earthscan Publications Ltd. 1994), 16

278 S. La Franci, *Surveying the Precautionary Principle's Ongoing Global Development: The Evolution of an Emergent Environmental Management Tool* (2005) Boston College Environmental Affairs Law Review 32: 679, 682.

avoided.

2. Activities which are likely to pose a significant risk to nature shall be preceded by an exhaustive examination, their proponents shall demonstrate that expected benefits outweigh potential damage to nature, and where potential adverse effects are not fully understood, the activities should not proceed.[279]

In the Resolution, it is of significance to note that included in the two concepts relating to the precautionary principle, were the theories of irreversible damage and scientific uncertainty.[280] Early versions of the precautionary principle were used in situations of *"inadequate proof of a causal link, that is, in situations in which, potentially the cure would not affect the disease at all."*[281] In addition, the early versions did not state whether decisions made in light of uncertainty needed to be reviewed by the regulatory bodies after additional information became available.

In 1987, following the acceptance of the precautionary principle in *General Assembly Resolution on the World Charter for Nature in 1982,*[282] the *London Declaration of the Second International North Sea Conference*[283] made mention of the precautionary principle. This Declaration's concern was to safeguard marine ecosystems through the use of best available technology, *"even where there is no scientific evidence to prove a causal link between emissions and effects."*[284] The use of the precautionary principle in this Declaration heralded the start of its international recognition,[285] both in hard and soft

279 Ibid.

280 Ibid.

281 John S. Applegate, *The Taming of the Precautionary Principle* (2002) William and Mary Environmental Law and Policy Review 27: 13, 27.

282 UN General Assembly [online], "World Charter for Nature", A/RES/37/7, 28 October 1982. [accessed 10 November 2008]. Available from Internet: www.un.org/documents/ga/res/37/a37r007.htm.

283 Second International Conference on the Protection of the North Sea, London, 24-25 November 1987. [accessed 09 November 2008]. Available from Internet: www.seas-at-risk.org/1mages/1987%20London%20Declaration.pdf.

284 S. La Franci 'Surveying the Precautionary Principle's Ongoing Global Development: The Evolution of an Emergent Environmental Management Tool' (2005) Boston College Environmental Affairs Law Review 32: 679, 682

285 Ibid.

law instruments.[286] In addition, in 1987, the *Pollution Control Guidelines*,[287] authorized by Article 4(e) of the Agreement on the Protection of Lake Constance Against Pollution (Steckborn Agreement),[288] incorporated a precautionary approach into its guidelines.[289] These guidelines relate to Switzerland, Austria and Germany in respect of their duty to protect the drinking water and fishing supplies of Lake Constance. The principle states that their duties include *"integrated protection of waters"* and *"precautionary measures for the protection against accidents with water-contaminating substances."*[290]

In 1990, the Houston Economic Summit Declaration[291] included provisions for the precautionary principle. It inserted:

> *In the face of threats of irreversible environmental damage, lack of full scientific certainty is no excuse to postpone actions which are justified in their own right.*[292]

The European States, Canada and the United States, in 1990, made note of a precautionary approach in environmental policies in the *Bergen Ministerial Declaration on Sustainable Development in the Economic Commission for Europe Region*.[293] This Declaration stated:

> *In order to achieve sustainable development, policies must be based on the precautionary principle. Environmental measures must anticipate, prevent and attack the causes of environmental degradation. Where there are threats of serious or*

---

286 Ibid, pp. 682-683.

287 FAO, IUCN, UNEP [online], "Ecolex: The Gateway to Environmental Law". [accessed 11 November 2008]. Available from Internet: www.ecolex.org/ecolex/ledge/view/SearchResults?query=contre.

288 Ibid.

289 L. Coleman 'The European Union: An Appropriate Model for a Precautionary Approach?' (2002) *Seattle University Law Review* 25: 609, 614.

290 Ibid.

291 G8 Information Centre [online], "Houston Economic Declaration", 11 July 1990. [accessed 09 November 2008]. Available from Internet: www.g8.utoronto.ca/summit/1990houston/declaration.html.

292 Ibid.

293 "Bergen Ministerial Declaration on Sustainable Development in the Economic Commission for Europe Region", 1990, UN Doc. A/CONF.151/PC/10.

irreversible damage, lack of full scientific certainty should not be used as a reason for postponing measures to prevent environmental degradation.[294]

In 1992, the *Rio Declaration*, a non-binding document incorporating the precautionary principle was created on Environment and Development.[295] The Declaration was used by the *United Nations Conference on Environment and Development (UNCED)*. *Principle 15 of the Declaration* stated:

> *In order to protect the environment, the Precautionary approach shall be widely applied by states according to their capabilities. Where there are threats of serious or irreversible damage, lack of full scientific certainty shall not be used as a reason for postponing cost-effective measures to prevent environmental degradation.[296]*

Also, in this same year, the precautionary principle was incorporated into the *Framework Convention on Climate Change* by the United Nations, a binding international treaty, and it read:

> *The parties should take precautionary measures to anticipate, prevent or minimize the causes of climate change and mitigate its adverse effect. Where there are threats of serious or irreversible damage, lack of full scientific certainty shall not be used as a reason for postponing such measures, taking into account that policies and measures to deal with climate change should be cost-effective so as to ensure global benefits at the lowest possible cost.[297]*

The, United Nations, in its *Convention on Biological Diversity,*[298] more commonly known as the CBD, also made mention of the precautionary princi-

---

294 Ibid.

295 United Nations Environment Programme (UNEP) [online], "Rio Declaration on Environment and Development", adopted 14 June 1992. [accessed 15 October 2008]. Available from Internet: http://www.unep.org/Documents.multilingual/Default.asp?DocumentID=78&ArticleID=1163.

296 UNEP [online], "Rio Declaration on Environment and Development".

297 United Nations Framework Convention on Climate Change (UNFCCC) [online], "Essential Background: The Convention and the Protocol". [accessed 11 November 2008]. Available from Internet: http://unfccc.int/essential_background/items/2877.php.

298 UNEP [online], "Convention on Biological Diversity", 05 June 1992. [accessed 08 November 2008]. Available from Internet: http://www.cbd.int/doc/legal/cbd-un-en.pdf.

ple.[299] Within the convention is stated that:

Noting also that that where there is a threat of significant reduction or loss of biological diversity, lack of full scientific certainty should not be used as a reason for postponing measures to avoid or minimize such a threat.[300]

While, at the onset, the precautionary principle was mainly used in environmental and health issues, it is now emerging in a wide range of international documents and treaties ranging from species, air pollution, marine environment protection,[301] climate change, atmospheric emissions, fisheries, ocean dumping and mining, and the European Union wildlife protection.[302] The precautionary principle also plays a role in human rights, planetary defence, terrorist attacks, tourism, pesticide use, ozone layer depletion, hazardous waste, and genetically modified organisms (GMOs).[303]

The acceptance of the precautionary principle in many international treaties and documents has led to an acceptance by many that it is now part of customary international law. International courts refer to it when making environmental decisions which therefore reflects the belief of some judges' that the principle has gained international customary law acceptance.[304]

THE PRECAUTIONARY PRINCIPLE IN THE CARIBBEAN

The Caribbean has indicated its intention to have member countries pursue the adoption of the precautionary principle. The *Revised Treaty of Chaguar-*

---

299 S. La Franci, *Surveying the Precautionary Principle's Ongoing Global Development: The Evolution of an Emergent Environmental Management Tool* (2005) Boston College Environmental Affairs Law Review 32: 679, 686

300 Ibid.

301 Ibid.

302 R. Unger, *Student Article: Brandishing the Precautionary Principle through the Alien Tort Claims Act* (2001) New York University Environmental Law Journal 9: 638, 649.

303 S. Wood and R. Wood, *Constitutional and Administrative Law: Whither the Precautionary Principle? An Administrative Assessment from an Administrative Law Perspective* (2006) The American Journal of Comparative Law 54: 581, 582.

304 R. Unger, *Student Article: Brandishing the Precautionary Principle through the Alien Tort Claims Act* (2001) New York University Environmental Law Journal 9: 638, 649

amas[305] states:

> *Article 65 - Environmental Protection: 1. The policies of the Community shall be implemented in a manner that ensures the prudent and rational management of the resources of the Member States. In particular, the Community shall promote measures to ensure:*
>
> *2. (e) the precautionary principle...*[306]

To date, little progress has been made in the Caribbean to have member states implement the ideal stated in the *Revised Treaty of Chaguaramas* with respect to the precautionary principle.

THE PRECAUTIONARY PRINCIPLE IN TT

The precautionary principle is part of the legislative environmental framework of TT through the NEP 2018. It is stated in Section 1.05:

> *The finite nature of the earth's systems and processes dictate that there are limits to the amount of human activity tolerable before there is a risk of abrupt and irreversible environmental changes. The GoRTT will adhere to the principle that if there are threats of serious irreversible damage to humans or the environment, lack of full scientific certainty will not be used as a reason for postponing social and environmental safeguards. Furthermore, the GoRTT affirms:*
>
> *1. Scientific uncertainty will not be used as a reason not to act in respect to environmental concerns;*
>
> *2. Action will affirmatively be taken with respect to environmental concerns;*
>
> *3. Those engaging in potentially damaging activities will shoulder the burden of establishing the absence of significant environmental harm; and*
>
> *4. It may restrict imports based on a standard involving less than full scientific*

---

305 Caricom Secretariat [online], "Revised Treaty of Chaguaramas establishing the Caribbean Community including the Caricom Single Market and Economy", 2001. [accessed 07 November 2008]. Available from Internet: http://www.caricom.org/jsp/community/revised_treaty-text.pdf.

306 Ibid.

certainty of environmental harm.

As noted in *Fishermen and Friends of the Sea v The Minister of Planning, Housing and the Environment,*[307] the NEP 2006 is of statutory strength in TT and must be complied with by governmental entities including the EMA. It must also be observed that the precautionary principle as articulated in the NEP 2018 mentions threats of 'serious irreversible' environmental damage and not the usual 'serious or irreversible'. This would certainly create a higher judicial hurdle for a litigant to overcome in an effort to establish a breach of the precautionary principle.

TT became the first Caribbean country to judicially examine the precautionary principle. In *Fishermen and Friends of the Sea v The Environmental Management Authority and Atlantic LNG Company of Trinidad and Tobago (Interested Party),*[308] Justice Stollmeyer explored the precautionary principle.

> *The first specific references to the precautionary principle at the international level appears in the 1985 Vienna Convention on Ozone Depleting Substances and the Declaration of the Second International North Sea Conference on the Protection of the North Sea. The principle crystallized and achieved universal acceptance in international law at The United Nations Conference on Environment and Development in Rio, the Rio Declaration 1992 (see Tromans "High Talk and Low Cunning": Putting Environmental Principles Into Legal Practice [1995] J.P.L.779). There are varying opinions on the current status of the precautionary principle in international law. Some argue that it is still an emerging rule of customary international law, while others maintain that it is an established rule. The Supreme Court of India, for example, considers the principle to be "part of customary international law" (see A.P. Pollution Control Board v. Nayado 1999.S.O.L.Case No.53, para. 27). Page 51 of 103 The acceptance of the principle as a necessary consideration in environmental cases across the Commonwealth is evidence of its emergence as a common law doctrine. This was recognized by Stein J. in Leatch v. National Parks and Wildlife Service and Shoalhaven City Council (1993) 81 LGERA 270 at 279 (a decision of the New South Wales Land and Environmental Court): "In*

---

307 P.C.A No. 0028 of 2016

308 H.C.A. Cv. 2148 of 2003

my opinion the precautionary principle is a statement of common sense and has already been applied by decision-makers in appropriate circumstances prior to the principle being spelt out." Similarly in Vellore Citizens Welfare Forum v. Union of India [1996] S.C. 2715, 2720, 2721, it was recognized that the principle has its genesis in the common law right to a clean environment. The Court there referred to "Laws of England (Commentaries by Blackstone) Vol. III 4th ed. 1876, Chapter XIII - Nuisance" and concluded: "Our legal system having been founded on the British Common Law, the right of a person to pollution free environment is a part of the basic jurisprudence of the land." The principle is regarded as a new legal response to the scientific uncertainties surrounding the capacity of the environment to cope with the increasing demands placed upon it. Its objective is to "protect the environment, as well as human life and animal and plant life, when no concrete threat to those resources have yet been demonstrated but initial scientific findings indicate a possible risk." The principle therefore sets out a rule for action in situations of uncertain risk where there is an inseparable connection between that principle and a potential risk to objects of legal protection (see Monsanto page 8).

There is a further matter to be taken into account when application of the principle is being considered. Indeed, it is a factor falling for consideration whenever foreign law, statutory or otherwise, is being examined to see whether it can either be of assistance in the interpretation of domestic law, or if it is applicable in this jurisdiction at all. Page 52 of 103 It is that social and economic conditions vary- sometimes widely — between different countries and the norms, the mores, of one - far less its law — cannot be transported lock, stock and barrel from one to another. That law must always be looked at in the light of prevailing local circumstances and adapted suitably, assuming this to be possible at all. While Trinidad and Tobago may be regarded as socially and economically developed to a greater extent than some other countries, the conditions and resources here, whether, human, financial, physical or otherwise, cannot necessarily be equated with those existing in, say, Europe or North America. Consequently, the high standards set, and met, there may not be realistic in the context of conditions and resources here. This is reflected, or so it would appear, in the National Environmental Policy referring to threats of "serious irreversible" environmental damage, as opposed to "serious or irreversible". There are three stages in the application of the principle. First, before the precautionary principle is invoked, there must be a comprehensive scientific evaluation of any potential risk. The precautionary principle is usually invoked if, following this risk assessment, serious or irreversible threats of environmental damage are discovered. The risk assessment is a critical requirement as its purpose is to calculate the degree of probability of the threats of serious irreversible environmental damage. There must be an assessment of the severity of the impact on human health and the environment were the threat to occur, the extent to which there may be possible adverse effects, the reversibility of any adverse effects and the possibility of delayed effects (see Pfizer Animal Health SA v. Council of the European Union [2002] ECR 11- 3305 (T13/99) para 153). The National Environmental Policy of Trinidad & Tobago specifies that the risk or threat Page 53 of 103 must be "serious irreversible environmental damage", indicating that the threshold and the burden of risk demonstration is significantly higher in other jurisdictions where the risk is defined as serious or (my emphasis) irreversible environmental damage. Second, the precautionary principle is only invoked where scientific opinion conflicts on the potential threat. Scientific uncertainty on the nature and severity of the threat is the second condition for the application of the principle. The principle places the burden of proof on developers to prove that their actions will not cause serious or irreversible harm to the environment. It is therefore placed on the party who threatens the environmental status quo. Third, where there is scientific uncertainty as to the existence or extent of the threats to the environment the authority or agency (in this case the EMA) may, by reason of the precautionary principle, take protective measures without having to wait until the reality and the seriousness of those threats become fully apparent. Measures aimed at preventing or containing the threats may be adopted. There are no hard and fast rules on when to take action. Each case has to be considered on its own facts. The principle is not precise and I take note of the statements by Talbot J in Nicholls v. Director General of National Parks & Wildlife (1994) 84 LGERA 397 at 419 (another decision of the New South Wales Land and Environmental Court): "...the precautionary principle, while it may be framed appropriately for the purpose of a political aspiration, its implementation as a legal standard could have the potential to create indeterminable forensic argument. Taken literally in practice it might prove to be unworkable." Despite its imprecision, however, the principle remains a guiding one in our environmental policy. Page 54 of 103 The principle does not state clearly how strong a suspicion of a threat should before action is taken. To act on suspicion or doubt, however small, would amount to a requirement for full scientific certainty that there was no threat of serious irreversible damage. This would be just as unrealistic as requiring full scientific certainty of the existence of a threat. Therefore, a strict interpretation of the precautionary principle would appear unworkable and impractical. The generally accepted interpretation of the principle is to act prudently when there is sufficient scientific evidence and where inaction could lead to potential irreversibility or demonstrate harm to future generations. The European Court made this clear in Monsanto (at page 26 para 102). "According to the precautionary principle, there is no need to provide complete proof of a risk to the environment or to human health; rather, protective measures are already justified where a preliminary and objective scientific risk evaluation gives reasonable grounds for concern that the potentially dangerous effects on the environment, human health, animal and plant health may be inconsistent with the community's high level of protection." The European Court's interpretation of the level of scientific evidence is widely accepted and I agree with the statement in Monsanto (at para 138) that"…not every claim or scientifically unfounded presumption of potential risk to human health on the environment can justify the adoption of national protective measures. Rather, the risk must be adequately substantiated by scientific evidence"(my emphasis). The question is raised as to whether the threshold was crossed requiring the EMA to invoke the principle. While I would say that it does not appear that in all the circumstances of this case there was sufficient scientific evidence to Page 55 of 103 substantiate the risk of serious and irreversible threats to the environment, human health and life, so as to trigger application of the principle, I do not think it necessary for me to decide this question. This is because there is insufficient evidence to enable me to conclude that the EMA failed to apply the precautionary principle. It appears to me that it did so in any event. The CEC Rules and the procedure for environmental impact assessment involve all three aspects of the principle: risk assessment; scientific assessment of the risk; and risk management. The EMA identified the project as a potential threat to the environment and focused on areas of specific concern in settling the terms of reference. It considered the Environmental Impact Assessment, the Hazard Assessment Report and the Environmental Baseline Report. It sought independent analysis of these reports from a wide range of disciplines before granting the CEC. It obtained appropriate scientific evidence dealing with the concerns raised. It considered this evidence. The CEC was granted subject to the imposition of an extensive list of conditions. These conditions were both protective and preventative measures. They also included monitoring programmes which were designed to compel ALNG to forward scientific data relating to specific environmental impacts to the EMA. It therefore cannot be said that the EMA failed to take precautionary measures in light of the scientific uncertainties of the nature and extent of the serious irreversible threats to the environment. In my view, the principle was adhered to. The National Environmental Policy gives no express indication of what preventative measures should be taken. It is clear that the threat must be serious and irreversible and must be adequately substantiated by scientific evidence. The measures adopted are left to the discretion of the EMA. In the exercise of its discretion, the EMA considered the measures appropriate to the threats as identified by FFOS and by Dr. Page 56 of 103 Naraynsingh-Chang. Given the criticisms of the reliability of Dr. Naraynsingh-Chang's report, the EMA cannot be found to have ignored the principle nor to have acted illegally given the manner in which its discretion was exercised. The "...preliminary and objective scientific risk evaluation..." did not give "...reasonable grounds for concern that the potentially dangerous effects..." might be inconsistent with the required standards of protection. The precautionary principle having been applied, the arguments advanced that the decision was made in defiance of the precautionary principle, and that the failure to re-locate the residents constituted a failure to adhere to that principle must also fail In a recent decision, a first instance judge examined the application of the precautionary principle with respect to the disposal of spent pot liner and air pollution in a proposed smelter project.

The High Court of TT subsequently judicially examined the precautionary principle in ***People United Respecting the Environment and Rights Action Group v Environmental Management Authority, Alutrint Limited (Interested Party) and the Attorney General of Trinidad and Tobago.***[309]

Dean-Armorer J

I will consider the Precautionary principle first. This ground of challenge was made only on behalf of the Claimants, PURE. Learned Counsel, Dr. Ramlogan crafted the ground in this way: "Whether the decision to grant the CEC in the presence of scientific uncertainty with respect to air pollution and hazardous waste disposal violates the precautionary principle and was illegal and/or

---

309 CV 2007-02263

irrational..." *The precautionary principle is an emerging rule of customary international law which was incorporated into domestic law in this jurisdiction by the conjoint effect of s.31 of the Environmental Management Act and the National Environmental Policy. This principle, which was described by Stein J in Leatch v. National Parks and Wildlife Service as "a statement of common sense ..." is no longer merely a matter of political aspiration but must be applied in the decision making process which is the concern of the court in judicial review. See Murrumbidgee Ground water Preservation Association v Minister for National Resource. There are three hurdles to be crossed before the precautionary principle can be invoked:*

- *There must be a threat of serious and irreversible damage to the environment. The threats must be adequately sustained by scientific evidence (see paragraph 134 of the judgment in Telstra)*

- *There must be a lack of full scientific certainty.*

- *Where these two elements are present, the burden of proving that no threat exists is carried by the applicant/developer.*

In my view the first two elements are present in the instant Claim. In respect of the first element, the prevailing jurisprudence requires the existence of "scientific evidence..." The law will reject mere "...claims or scientifically unfounded presumptions...". The risk of serious and irreversible damage must be "adequately sustained by scientific evidence..." See reference to Monsanto v. Presidenza del Consiglio dei Ministri cited at paragraph 134 of Telstra. In the light of this learning, this Court considered whether there was scientific evidence or whether there were mere unsubstantiated claims. There could be no doubt that there was considerable scientific evidence before this Court of threats of both serious and irreversible damage to both the environment and human health. Experts of the highest calibre swore lengthy affidavits as testimony of the threat. Even if on a balance of probabilities and on account of the lack of cross-examination, the Court chose to accept the expert evidence on behalf of the Defendant, such a finding does not detract from the fact that the Claimant supplied scientific evidence. Such evidence would most certainly have come to the attention of the EMA, as decision-maker through the public hearings and during the written comment period. Accordingly, it is my view that in the instant Claim, the evidence suggests that the first stage has been passed for the precautionary principle to be triggered. The second stage is the presence of sci-

entific uncertainty. According to the learning in Telstra, the factor of uncertainty is a necessary precondition to the application of the precautionary principle. Certainty as to "serious and irreversible environmental damage" would require the application of preventative rather than precautionary measures. See Telstra paragraph 149. In my view, the second stage has also been passed in this case. The fact of conflicting scientific opinions as to the effect of the project in itself implies uncertainty. Uncertainty also surrounds the accuracy of the air dispersion predictions. Dr. Vine, who testified on behalf of the Claimant, PURE, stated that "the predictions of airborne emission" concentrations are so uncertain that there is a strong likelihood that actual concentrations would be found to be unmanageably deleterious to human health. The project also envisages the production of the spent pot liner some eight (8) years from the start of the project. Dr. Murphy, who testified on behalf of the EMA conceded in his affidavit that the "...risks associated with transportation of SPL from the site to the ships needed further research....". There is no finalised contract for the final disposal of SPL and no finalised method of over land transportation of the spent pot liner. Moreover, the project envisages decommissioning a half century, hence, with no real predictions as to the effect of decommissioning on the environment. The fact that decommissioning may require a separate CEC does not resolve the uncertainty as to the scientific effects of the decommissioning when it takes place. These factors themselves import uncertainty, with those in favour of the project urging that it will be innocuous and those in the opposing camp insisting that the concomitant result would be both serious and irreversible environmental damage. The burden therefore shifts and the developer, Alutrint, is required to prove that there is no threat. The learning suggests, however, that this is a burden to be discharged not before the reviewing Court but before the decision-maker. See paragraph 154 of Telsta. Moreover, a failure on behalf of the developer to discharge the burden does not lead inexorably to a refusal of the CEC. The decision-maker must now assume that the threat is a reality and take it into account together with other factors such as social and economic factors. See paragraph 154 of Telstra. This Court considered whether the decision-making process of the Defendant / EMA could be faulted. The decision-making process of the Defendant could be faulted if either or both of two situations are present. If the Claimant has proved on a balance of probabilities that the Defendant failed to apply the precautionary principle the Court would conclude that the ensuing decision was illegal. Secondly, the decision-making process would fail for irrationality if the Defendant, notwithstanding an absence of evidence as to what in fact transpired before the EMA, succeeds in proving that the result was so outrageous in its defiance of logic and accepted moral standards that no reasonable authority could have arrived at it. (per Lord Diplock in CCSU). There is no evidence before this Court to suggest that the EMA omitted to apply the precautionary principle in the process of deciding whether to grant a CEC. In order to prove that the decision was illegal on account of an omission to apply the precautionary principle, the Claimant ought to have produced or have sought the production of such records of the decision-maker which tended to prove that it failed to apply the precautionary principle. Irrationality is more elusive.

The Court may look at the final decision and find it so unreasonable that no reasonable decision-maker could have arrived at that decision. This finding however is by no means an exercise of the Court imposing its subjective view. The threshold is notoriously high. The decision must be "... outrageous in its defiance of logic or acceptable moral standards ...". See CCSU. In my view, in respect of the precautionary principle at least, the decision falls within the band of decisions that could be made by the reasonable decision-maker who employed the "calculus which decision-makers are instructed to apply..." and took into account all factors which were required to be considered, without giving overriding weight to the need for precaution. See Telstra.

The precautionary principle was further endorsed in ***Bhadase Sooknanan and Fishermen and Friends of the Sea v Environmental Management Authority and the Ministry of Energy***[310] by Justice Kangaloo.

43. The precautionary principle has been incorporated into the laws of this jurisdiction by virtue of Section 31 of the EMA Act and Chapter 2 of the National Environmental Policy under the rubric Goals, Objectives and Basic Principles which provides as follows: "Government policy will adhere to the principle that if there are threats of serious irreversible environmental damage, lack of full scientific certainty will not be used as a reason for postponing measures to prevent environmental degradation."

44. The Applicants contend that it is not sufficient, on a proper application of this principle, for the Respondent to say that it was incumbent on someone to persuade them that there was scientific certainty of the risk of degradation

45. The Applicants also submit that it was only through the EIA process that an accurate picture of the risks, mitigation measures and compensation could be

---

310 CV 2014-00813

calculated. For this the Applicants relied on the case of Telstra Corporation Limited v Hornsby Shire Council [2006] NSWLEC 133.

46. This Court finds that the EMA has satisfied the burden placed on it by such principle, as admirably traversed by Stollmeyer J. in the Atlantic LNG case, to ensure that the seismic surveys did not pose any threat of serious irreversible environmental damage.

47. The Respondent says the Gulf of Paria is a "mature seismic survey field" as previous seismic activities have been conducted there. Both Messrs. Rajkumar and De Souza set out in their affidavits the matters they took into account in arriving at the initial decision not to require an EIA and the Review and confirmation of that decision during the EMA's second tier of consideration.

48. In this Court's view, the EMA did the "hard work" required on the facts of the instant case, to satisfy itself that it could issue the CEC without an EIA. This Court considers therefore that the statutory requirements were complied with and the legislative purpose achieved.

AN OUNCE OF PREVENTION IS BETTER THAN A POUND OF CURE

The precautionary principle faces many challenges in seeking acceptance in TT as the establishment of conditions that trigger the application of the precautionary principle is difficult. The definition of the precautionary principle consistently references the presence of threats of serious irreversible damage to the environment rather than serious or irreversible. The issue that arises is what is the threshold for establishing the presence of such threats? Is there a requirement of scientific certainty that such threats exist before the trigger for the application of the precautionary principle? It is clear from the emerging case law, especially from Europe, that it cannot be mere speculation; however, the threshold for the consideration of the principle has not been established. Yet, despite uncertainties, the precautionary principle has certainly become part of the judicial range of modern environmental law principles that is permeating the environmental legal regime of TT.

CHAPTER 7

SUSTAINABLE DEVELOPMENT

DEFINING SUSTAINABLE DEVELOPMENT

Mary Somerville provided one of the earliest significant analyses of the problems that man could introduce into his natural environment by his undisciplined interference with its operation. She observed that there existed a delicate balance between man and nature, and commented on the need to understand such a balance before attempting to change it.

> *Man's necessities and enjoyments have been the cause of great changes in the animal creation, and his destructive propensity of still greater. Animals are intended for our use, and field sports are advantageous by encouraging a daring and active spirit in young men; but the utter destruction of some races, in order to protect those destined for his pleasure, is too selfish, and cruelty is unpardonable: But the ignorant are often cruel. A farmer sees the rooks pecking a little of his grain, or digging at the roots of the springing corn, and poisons all in his neighbourhood. A few years after he is surprised to find his crops destroyed by grubs. The works of the Creator are nicely balanced and man cannot infringe His laws with impunity.[311]*

It was George Perkins Marsh, however, whose comprehensive analysis of man and nature effected a turnaround in the assessment of the human impact on the environment.[312] Marsh provided penetrating insight into the disastrous toll which human intervention had taken on vegetables, plants, woods, animals, waters and sands. He noted that:

> *Man has too long forgotten that the earth was given to him for usufruct alone,*

311 Mary Somerville, *Physical Geography* [1862] London: John Murray, p. 535
312 G. P. Marsh, *Man and Nature* (Massachusetts: Belknap Press 1965)

not for consumption, still less for profligate waste. Nature has provided against the absolute destruction of her works... But she has left it within the power of man irreparably to derange the combinations of inorganic matter and of organic life...[313]

Scholars such as Marsh and Somerville realised the value of conservation and the implications which interference and abuse of the environment had for the general well-being of man. Their works provided the early foundation for the rise of conservationism as a philosophical underpinning of environmentalism. At the turn of the 20th century, with the advocacy of Gifford Pinchot, conservationism took its root in the pantheon of environmental philosophies. Pinchot, a high-ranking government bureaucrat, had the opportunity to influence and implement government policies on environmental conservation, in particular, those that affected forested areas. The basic principles of conservation, as articulated by Pinchot, are summarized in a quotation from his paper, "Conservation".

The central thing for which conservation stands is to make this country the best possible place to live in, both for us and our descendants. It stands against the waste of natural resources which cannot be renewed ... it stands for the perpetuation of the resources which can be renewed ... and most of all it stands for an equal opportunity for every American citizen to get his fair share of benefit from these resources, both now and hereafter. Conservation stands for the same kind of practical management of this country by the principles that every businessman stands for in the handling of his own business. It believes in prudence and foresight instead of reckless blindness ... and it demands the complete and orderly development of all our resources for the benefit of all the people... It recognizes fully the right of the present generation to use what it needs and all it needs of the natural resources now available, but it recognizes equally our obligation so to use what we need that our descendants shall not be deprived of what they need.[314]

Today, the conservation approach continues to be the dominant environmental philosophy of the 21st century, its current reincarnation being *"sus-*

---

313 Ibid at [36]

314 G. Pinchot, *Conservation*, in D. Wall, (Green History: A Reader in Environmental Literature, Philosophy and Politics, London: Routledge 1994), 136

tainable development". Over the course of history, many cultures and indigenous peoples have recognized the need for harmonization between the environment, society and economy.

It was only in 1987 that there was an attempt at a consensual definition of sustainable development with the World Commission on Environment and Development (WCED) in its report, *Our Common Future,* coining the phrase "*sustainable development*". Sustainable development was defined as "*development which meets the needs of the present without compromising the ability of future generations to meet their own needs*".[315] Two key concepts are contained within this definition; (1) Needs must be acknowledged, particularly those of the poor, and (2) The limitations imposed by the current state of technology and the organisation of society with respect to the environment's ability to meet present and future goals must also be recognised.[316] There is, therefore, an attempt to address the complexities of the association between environmental preservation and the development dimension. Essentially, this school of thought appears to be an amalgamation of conservation philosophy and environmental economics, albeit with some refinements. The most noticeable of these is the acknowledgement and endorsement of the concept of intergenerational equity. The notion of sustainable development seems to be based on a growing recognition that economic and environmental gains are not mutually exclusive. While economic growth may be a necessity, its quality may also be questionable.

As a philosophy of developmental and environmental management, sustainable development has received powerful endorsements from numerous world leaders, regional groups and international organizations. In 1988, at a G7 meeting in Canada, US President Ronald Reagan and British Prime Minister Margaret Thatcher both endorsed the concept of sustainable development; in 1992, the *Rio de Janeiro Earth Summit* declared that the right to develop should be fulfilled so as to equitably meet the developmental and environmental needs of present and future generations.

The concept of sustainable development encompasses the total quality of

---

315 World Commission on Environment and Development (WCED) (1987), *Our Common Future* (New York: Oxford University Press), 46
316 Ibid at [43]

life by attempting to achieve a balance between meeting the current needs of individuals while protecting the ability of future generations to meet their own needs.[317] These needs include the environment's ability to provide resources; recycle waste; and maintain a rich biodiversity, genetic diversity, and functional diversity on a sustainable basis.[318] These must occur without increasing the use of natural resources beyond the capacity of the environment to supply them indefinitely.

The World Commission equates sustainable development with *"rapid economic growth in both industrial and developing countries"* which it believes *"will help developing countries mitigate the strains on the rural environment, raise productivity, and consumption standards, and allow nations to move beyond dependence on one or two primary products for their export earnings"*.[319] This view is further supported by Mathews who claimed that it was critical to raise global economic output, if only to meet basic human needs, thus lifting billions out of poverty.[320] The main issue, therefore, appears to be how increased wealth can be achieved in an environmentally sound manner in order to redistribute income more equitably.

The definition of sustainable development was significantly modified in Johannesburg in 2002. To paraphrase part of the conference declaration:

> *We commit ourselves to undertaking concrete actions and measures at all levels and to enhancing international cooperation, taking into account the Rio principles, including, inter alia, the principle of common but differentiated responsibilities as set out in principle 7 of the Rio Declaration on Environment and Development. These efforts will also promote the integration of the three components of sustainable development - economic development, social development and environmental protection - as interdependent and mutually reinforcing pillars. Poverty eradication, changing unsustainable patterns of production and consumption and protecting and managing the natural resource base of economic*

---

317 C. Maser and O. Ukaga, *Evaluating Sustainable Development: Giving People a Voice in their Destiny* (Sterling, VA: Stylus Publishing, 2004), 1

318 Ibid.

319 World Commission on Environment and Development (WCED) (1987), *Our Common Future* (New York: Oxford University Press), 89

320 J. Mathews, *Environment, Development and Security* [1990] *Bulletin of the American Academy of Arts and Sciences*, p. XLIII.

and social development are overarching objectives of, and essential requirements for, sustainable development. We recognize that implementation of the outcomes of the Summit should benefit all, particularly women, youth, children and other vulnerable groups. Furthermore, the implementation should involve all relevant actors through partnerships, especially between Governments of the North and South, on the one hand, and between Governments and major groups, on the other, to achieve the widely shared goals of sustainable development.... Good governance within each country and at the international level is essential for sustainable development. At the domestic level, sound environmental, social and economic policies, democratic institutions responsive to the needs of the people, the rule of law, anti-corruption measures, gender equality and an enabling environment for investment are the basis for sustainable development. As a result of globalization, external factors have become critical in determining the success or failure of developing countries in their national effort. The gap between developed and developing countries points to the continued need for a dynamic and enabling international economic environment supportive of international cooperation, particularly in the areas of finance, technology transfer, debt and trade and full and effective participation of developing countries in global decision-making, if the momentum for global progress towards sustainable development is to be maintained and increased. Peace, security, stability and respect for human rights and fundamental freedoms, including the right to development as well as respect for cultural diversity, are essential for achieving sustainable development and ensuring that sustainable development benefits all. We acknowledge the importance of ethics for sustainable development and, therefore, emphasize the need to consider ethics the implementation of Agenda 21.[321]

Sustainable development no longer focuses solely on environmental issues. In 2005, the *United Nations World Summit Outcome* document referred to *"the interdependent and mutually reinforcing pillars"* of sustainable development as economic development, social development and environmental protection.[322] Additionally, there have been increased calls for a fourth pillar of sustain-

---

321 United Nations Department for Economic and Social Affairs, "Plan of Implementation of the World Summit on Sustainable Development", last updated 24 March 2009. [cited 12 March 2009]. http://www.un.org/esa/sustdev/documents/WSSD_POI_PD/English/WSSD_PlanImpl.pdf.

322 General Assembly (2005), 2005 World Summit Outcome, A/RES/60/1, para. 48.

able development to be included, namely, culture. Nevertheless, all must be considered within the constraints of the earth's resources. Hasan refers to sustainability as a process which develops all aspects of human life affecting sustenance and means resolving the conflicts between competing goals and interests, while simultaneously pursuing economic prosperity, environmental quality and social equity.[323]

While economic and environmental gurus are locked in a key battle trying to arrive at a meaning of sustainable development that would satisfy their respective agendas, there is the emergence of several key principles in both the legislative and judicial fora of nation states that offer some hope for sustainable development during this period of uncertainty as the philosophy attempts to take shape in the shifting sands of the current global, regional and national debate. The International Court of Justice (ICJ) has already examined the acceptability of sustainable development and it has been endorsed in a powerful dissenting judgement by Justice Weeramantry in *Hungary v. Slovakia (Gabcikovo-Nagymaros Project)*.[324] In 1993, Hungary and Slovakia began proceedings before the ICJ on the basis of a special agreement signed in Brussels in 1993. The ICJ held that the both countries had violated their obligations under a special bilateral treaty on the Construction and Operation of the Gabcikovo-Nagymaros System of Locks Treaty signed in 1977. The treaty was originally concluded between Hungary and Czechoslovakia for the construction and joint operation of a large, integrated complex of structures and installations on certain parts of the territories of the two countries along the Danube. The objectives were the generation of hydroelectric power, improved navigation and flood control. Work commenced in 1978; however, in response to domestic pressure, the Hungarian government decided to abandon the work at Nagymaros in 1989 stating economic and environmental reasons. In 1991, Czechoslovakia proceeded to develop an alternative solution which included the unilateral diversion of the Danube on its territory and the construction of an overflow dam, a levee linking the dam to a bypass

---

323 *Abdallah M. Hasna, 'Dimensions of sustainability' [2007] Journal of Engineering for Sustainable Development: Energy, Environment, and Health, Vol 2, Number 1, 47,51*

324 37 ILM 162 (1998). Slovakia was part of the nation known as Czechoslovakia and attained separate nationhood on 01 January 1993.

canal and ancillary works. Hungary responded by stating that its access to the water of the Danube would be adversely affected while Czechoslovakia proceeded to dam the Danube. Hungary's unilateral suspension and subsequent abandonment of the project as well as Slovakia's unilateral diversion of the Danube were found to be unlawful. The ICJ concluded that the treaty was still in force and must be executed *pacta sunt servanda*. In a separate dissenting statement, Vice-President Weeramantry discussed the principle of sustainable development. He stated that:

> *The principle of sustainable development is thus a part of modern international law by reason not only of its inescapable logical necessity, but also by reason of its wide and general acceptance by the global community.*

> *The concept has a significant role to play in the resolution of environmentally related disputes. The components of the principle come from well-established areas of international law - human rights, State responsibility, environmental law, economic and industrial law, equity, territorial sovereignty, abuse of rights, good neighbourliness - to mention a few. It has also been expressly incorporated into a number of binding and far-reaching international agreements, thus giving it binding force in the context of those agreements. It offers an important principle for the resolution of tensions between two established rights. It reaffirms in the arena of international law that there must be both development and environmental protection, and that neither of these rights can be neglected.*

> *The general support of the international community does not of course mean that each and every member of the community of nations has given its express and specific support to the principle- nor is this a requirement for the establishment of a principle of customary international law.*

SUSTAINABLE DEVELOPMENT IN TT

In TT, a useful starting point on the issue of sustainable development is the *Environmental Management Act*. As stated in the recitals of the *Environmental Management Act*:

> *Whereas, the Government of the Republic of Trinidad and Tobago (hereinafter called "the Government") is committed to developing a national strategy for sustainable development, being the balance of economic growth with environmentally sound*

practices, in order to enhance the quality of life and meet the needs of present and future generations:.... And whereas, sustainable development should be encouraged through the use of economic and non-economic incentives, and polluters should be held responsible for the costs of their polluting activities:

Section 16 of the Environmental Management Act:

16(1) The general functions of the Authority are to— ...(b) develops and implement policies and programmes for the effective management and wise use of the environment, consistent with the objects of this Act;

Rules made under the *Environmental Management Act* also seek to capture the philosophy of sustainable development. The *Environmentally Sensitive Species Rules,*[325] *Schedule II, Rule 3(1)(d), Guidelines for Environmentally Sensitive Species*:

29. The designation of species as "environmentally sensitive" is to meet one or more of three general categories of objectives: (a) conservation of biological diversity and protection of the environment; (b) sustainable economic and human development;...

Similarly the *Environmentally Sensitive Areas Rules,*[326] *Schedule II, Guidelines for Environmentally Sensitive Areas States*:

The designation of an area, as "environmentally sensitive" is to meet one or more of three categories of general objectives: (a) Conservation of natural resources and protection of the environment. (b) Sustainable economic and human development....

The NEP 2018 also seeks to embody the philosophy of sustainable development. In Section 1.05, it is stated:

Sustainable development, defined in the Brundtland Report as "development that meets the needs of the present without compromising the ability of future generations to meet their own needs,", is recognised as the overarching model for improving the quality of life for the citizens of Trinidad and Tobago. It is understood that economic development, social development and environmental management are interdependent, indivisible and mutually reinforcing components of sustaina-

---

325 L.N. No 63 of 2001

326 L.N. No. 64 of 2001

ble development. Moreover, the attainment of peace and sustainability can only be done when environmental concerns are integrated across all spheres, at the policy, planning, programme and project levels. Thus, development and the pursuit of peace, justice and strong institutions in Trinidad and Tobago must be done in a manner that strives to balance social, economic and environmental considerations.

The courts have already started exploring the principle of sustainable development. Perhaps the first case to consider sustainable development in TT pre-dated the *Environmental Management Act.*

Goolcharan Jabar and Parbatee Jabar v The Minister of Agriculture, Land and Marine Resources[327] as per Lucky J

As I alluded to earlier, the Applicants' expert Balliram Seepersad agrees with Professor Kenny that there can be sustainable agricultural development associated with the wetlands in Nariva Swamp. "However, such development can only be effected after careful scientific study, detailed planning and with careful monitoring of the process. There is no evidence, as I said earlier, of anything to this effect being done. "The FAO- Report, BS-1, indicates a need for an overall development and management policy which should encompass environmental protection and should ensure the development does not create a negative impact on the swamp's ecosystem. There is no development and management policy. Recommendations have been made, papers written and presented, but there has been no implementation.

The principle of sustainable development appeared in the post *Environmental Management Act* era in the ***Talisman (Trinidad) Petroleum Limited v Environmental Management Authority,***[328] where Justice Hosein observed:

The Government of Trinidad and Tobago has stipulated in the preamble to the Environmental Management Act, its commitment to developing a strategy for sustainable development, being the balance of economic growth with environmentally sound practices, in order to enhance the quality of life and meeting the needs of present and future generations. That commitment must not be lost sight of....

---

327 HC No. 630 of 1993
328 No. EA3 of 2002

In *Fishermen and Friends of the Sea v Environmental Management Authority and BP Trinidad and Tobago LLC (Interested Party)*[329] (Court of Appeal) in a dissenting judgment, Justice Lucky noted:

> *It seems to me that citizens should prevent destruction of the environment for industrial development which involves the extraction of the non-renewable resources of the country or if for sustained economic development necessary safeguards and guarantees should be put in place with the necessary check and balances to protect the environment. Necessary Legislation has been passed to ensure the foregoing. Hence the establishment of the EMA.*

It may be fair to conclude that the concept of sustainable development is part of the environmental legal regime of TT and may play an increasingly important role in future jurisprudence.

---

329 Civ Appeal No. 106 of 2002

CHAPTER 8

RIGHT TO A HEALTHY
ENVIRONMENT

The debate on the right to a healthy environment resonated throughout the jurisprudence of the late 20th century and is still, to date, the subject of much debate. The human rights debate initially emerged post-World War II, in a period were environmental concerns were of little priority; hence, the *Universal Declaration of Human Rights (UDHR)* adopted in 1948 failed to make reference to environmental protection and preservation. In 1966, the *International Covenant of Economic, Social and Cultural Rights (ICESCR)* provided the first platform upon which a right to a healthy environment could be constructed. It mandated that every man, woman and child has an inherent right to the "*highest attainable standard of physical and mental health*".[330] Arguably, this right to health is dependent on a sustainable and healthy environment. Human rights groups originally interpreted the "right to a healthy environment" as a right which would protect the health of individuals by imposing specific obligations to protect the environment as a prerequisite to the right to health.[331]

The movement to expressly construct a right to a healthy environment began in the late 1960s and culminated in its articulation at UNCHE. The initial concept of a human right to a clean and healthy environment was proposed in the *UN Stockholm Declaration of 1972* which issued from the UN Conference on the Human Environment.

The Declaration provides, *inter alia*, in Principle 1 that:

---

330 International Covenant on Economic, Social, and Cultural Rights, Article 12

331 J. McClymonds, *The Human Right to a Healthy Environment: an international legal perspective* [1992] 37 New York Law School Law Review 583

Man has the fundamental right to freedom, equality and adequate conditions of life, in an environment of a quality that permits a life of dignity and well-being...[332]

The next major statement in defence of a right to a healthy environment came in 1987 by virtue of *Principle 1 of the Proposed Legal Principles for Environmental Protection and Sustainable Development* adopted by the World Commission on Environment and Development (WCED) which states:

All human beings have the fundamental right to an environment adequate for their health and well-being.

An interesting development that took place after the issuance of the report of the World Commission on Environment and Development had its genesis in the emerging international debate on the status of children. Children have been known to suffer the greatest impact from the environment, while playing the smallest role in contributing to environmental degradation. Furthermore, children have little power to effect change.[333] The Convention on the Rights of the Child states that "*a child has the right to enjoy the highest attainable standard of health...*"[334] States are mandated to implement this right through measures such as combating "*disease and malnutrition...through, inter alia... the provision of adequate foods and clean drinking water, taking into consideration the danger and risks of environmental pollution*".[335] This represented the first time that there was explicit recognition of the connection between the health of an individual and the condition of the environment in a human rights treaty.[336]

The decade of the 1980s saw an accelerated debate concerning the right to a healthy environment as a recognized principle of international human

---

332 UNEP, "Declaration of the United Nations Conference on the Human Environment" http://www.unep.org/Documents.Multilingual/Default.asp?DocumentID=97&ArticleID=1503.

333 UNICEF (1992), *State of the World's Children* (New York: UNICEF), 8-9

334 Convention on the Rights of the Child, 20 November 1989, 1577 U.N.T.S. 3, *28 I.L.M. 1457*

335 Ibid, Art. 24, P 2(c).

336 Prudence Taylor, *From Environmental to Ecological Human Rights: A New Dynamic in International Law?* [1998] 10 Georgetown International Environmental Law Review *309*, 339-40

rights law.[337] In 1992, the *Rio Declaration,* placed the issue of human rights in relation to a clean and healthy environment within the context of sustainable development. *Principle 1 of the Rio Declaration* provides that:

> *Human beings are at the centre of concerns for sustainable development. They are entitled to a healthy and productive life in harmony with nature.*[338]

However, the *Rio Declaration* is criticized for avoiding the use of "rights" in its language.[339] In 1994, the "rights" based concept was presented at a UN meeting of Experts on Human Rights and the Environment. The *UN Draft Declaration of Principles on Human Rights and the Environment* stated that "*all persons have the right to a secure, healthy and ecologically sound environment*".[340] This draft declaration, however, did not find the necessary support of UN members for its translation into a legally binding instrument. Notwithstanding this lack of support, by the turn of the 21st century, the realization that environmental problems pose serious problems for human health and could even potentially threaten the continued existence of mankind accentuated the debate on the right to a healthy environment. The right to life can be rendered somewhat nugatory if the environment in which a person is living is in a degraded state. In 2000, the Committee on Economic, Social and Cultural Rights which constitutes the main implementation body of the ICESCR explicitly recognized the correlation between the right to health and the right to a healthy environment. General Comment No. 14 states:

> *The Committee interprets the right to health, as defined in article 12.1, as an inclusive right extending not only to timely and appropriate health care but also to the determinants of health, such as access to safe and potable water and adequate sanitation, an adequate supply of safe food, nutrition and housing, healthy occupational and environmental conditions, and access to health-related education*

---

337 Dinah Shelton, *Human Rights, Environmental Rights, and the Right to Environment'* [1991] 28 Stanford Journal of International Law 103, 125-129

338 UNEP, "Rio Declaration on Environment and Development".

339 S. Atapattu (2002), *The Right to a Healthy Life or the Right To Die Polluted? The Emergence of a Human Right to a Healthy Environment Under International Law,* Tulane Environmental Law Journal, Vol 16(1); 65, 74

340 Draft Declaration of Principles on Human Rights and the Environment, U.N. Hum. Rights Committee. (16 May 1994)

and information, including on sexual and reproductive health.[341]

In 2002, the UN Committee on Economic, Social and Cultural Rights is-sued a comment based on *Article 11 of the ICESCR* stating that:

> *The human right to water is indispensable for leading a healthy life in human dignity. It is a pre-requisite to the realization of all other human rights.[342]*

Furthermore, former Director General of the World Health Organization (WHO), Dr. Gro Brundtland, noted that this development *"is a major boost in efforts to achieve the Millennium Development Goals of halving the number of people without access to water and sanitation by 2015- two prerequisites for health, and it was also expressed that the recognition of water as a basic human right will provide an effec-tive tool to make a real difference at the country level".[343]*

Recently, there have been attempts to facilitate a convergence between sus-tainable development and the right to a healthy environment. In 1987, it was proposed by the WCED that there be a reconciliation between economic development and environmental protection. Sustainable development is known to have human rights implications since it inherently implies the right of the present and future generations to develop in a sustainable man-ner.[344] The Plan of Action issued in the 2002 World Summit on Sustainable Development, although somewhat lukewarm, provides a framework for consideration of the human right to a clean and healthy environment. It recommends that States:

> *Acknowledge the consideration being given to the possible relationship between environment and human rights, including the right to development...[345]*

---

341 U.N. Econ. & Soc. Council [ECOSOC], Committee on Economic Social. and Cultur-al Rights, General Comment No. 14: "The Right to the Highest Attainable Standard of Health", P 11, U.N. Doc E/C.12/2000/4 (Aug. 11, 2000).

342 U.N. Committee on Economic, Social and Cultural Rights, *"Substantive Issues Arising in the Implementation of the International Covenant on Economic, Social and Cultural Right"*, 29th Sess., U.N. Doc. E/C.12/2002/11.

343 World Health Organization, *Water for Health Enshrined as a Human Right*, 27 November 2002 (Press Release).

344 WCED (1987), p. 330.

345 "Report of the World Summit on Sustainable Development, Plan of Implementa-

The Plan of Action recognises the complexities of sustainable development and the myriad challenges which must be addressed in order for sustainable development to be achieved. Additionally, the Plan of Action recognizes the crucial role which must be played by governments nationally and internationally. The importance of public participation and the subsequent governmental responses leading to a positive correlation between human rights and a healthy environment is also highlighted.

The concept of environmental human rights is not new. Worsening environmental problems has increased the call for strengthening environmental human rights. It is, therefore, now increasingly practical to link human rights to the concept of sustainable development since the right to life cannot be realized without basic rights to safe water, air and land.

The link between human rights and the environment is more frequently demonstrated in regional, rather than global, instruments. The *Additional Protocol to the American Convention on Human Rights and the Right to Life* provides that *"everyone shall have the right to live in a healthy environment and to have access to basic public services"*.[346] It further states that *"The States parties shall promote the protection, preservation and improvement of the environment."* The American Convention has led to the establishment of the Inter-American Commission on Human Rights which has dedicated special attention to the environment, human health and human rights in studies conducted in several countries. In a report devoted to Ecuador, it was noted that environmental degradation poses a threat to the realization of the right to life and physical security and integrity as a result of pollution particularly from oil extracting activities.[347] Such pollution was linked to the denial of basic human dignity and it was noted that:

> *Conditions of severe environmental pollution which may cause serious physical illness, impairment and suffering on the part of the local populace, are inconsist-*

---

tion", 04 September 2002, annex, U.N. Doc. A/CONF 199/20.

346 *Art. 11, Additional Protocol to the American Convention on Human Rights, 17 November 1988, 28 I.L.M. 156, 161.*

347 Inter-American. C.H.R., *Report on the Situation of Human Rights in Ecuador*, OEA/Ser.L/V/II.96, doc. 10 rev. 1, at 89-92 (1997).

ent with the right to be respected as a human being.[348]

The issue of a right to a healthy environment was raised in TT in *Fishermen and Friends of the Sea v The Environmental Management Authority and Atlantic LNG Company of Trinidad and Tobago (Interested Party)*[349] where the court was asked to imply a right to a healthy environment from existing constitutional rights to life, protection of law, respect for family and private life and the right not to be subjected to cruel and unusual punishment. Justice Stollmeyer took a conservative view to the expansion of constitutional rights to incorporate a right to a healthy environment.

> *The EMA acted illegally by granting the CEC and in so doing infringed the rights of residents to life, protection of law, respect for family and private life, and the right not to be subjected to cruel and unusual punishment. FFOS contends that the EMA erred in law by granting the CEC. Its decision amounted to an infringement of the fundamental human right to life, to be entitled to such procedural provisions as are necessary to give effect to the rights of individuals, to respect for the private and family life of individuals as guaranteed by Sections 4 and 5 of the Constitution of Trinidad and Tobago. I was referred to the judgment in the Matter of an Application for Judicial Review Right Honourable Lord Saville of Newdigate Sir Edward Somers Justice William Hoyt (Sitting as Saville Inquiry) (Ex Parte A and Ors), RV. [1999] EWHC Admin 747 (28th July, 1999) at pg. 14 para.37 of the transcript. It was also submitted that the options available to the reasonable decision maker are curtailed when a fundamental right such as the right to life is engaged. It is not open to the decision maker to risk interfering with fundamental rights in the absence of compelling justification. Even the broadest discretion is constrained by the need for there to be countervailing circumstances justifying interference with human rights. The courts will anxiously scrutinise the strength of the countervailing circumstances and the degree of interference with the human right involved. FFOS also contended that an integral part of the right to life is the right to a healthy environment; that it is impossible for human life to survive without a healthy environment, and that Section 2(1) of the National Environmental Policy supports this submission. I was referred to Francis Coralie v. Union Territory of Delhi A.I.R. (SC*

---

348 Ibid at [92]

349 HCA CV 2148 of 2003

1981) 746 where Bhagwati J. said (at para 7): "But the question which arises is whether the right to life is limited only to protection of limb or faculty or does it go further and embrace something more. We think that the right to life include the right to live with human dignity and all that goes along with it, namely, the bare necessaries of life such as adequate nutrition, clothing and shelter over the head and facilities for reading, writing and expressing oneself in the diverse forms, freely moving about and mixing commingling with fellow human beings." FFOS also relied on the decision in Rural Litigation and Entitlement Kendra v State of U.P. A.I.R (SC 1985) 652 where Bhagwati J. (at p.656) said "This would undoubtedly cause hardship to them but it is a price that has to be paid for protecting and safeguarding the right of the people to live in healthy environment with minimal disturbance of ecological balance and without avoidable hazard to them and to their cattle, homes and agricultural land and undue affection of air, water and environment." FFOS also submitted that Section 5(2)(b) of the Constitution prohibits cruel and unusual treatment, and the facts and circumstances of this case show that the impugned decisions and/or actions of the EMA amount to a contravention of this right. It was submitted that where the facts show that the lack and/or absence of appropriate environmental measures and/or safeguards which results in threats and/or risks to human life and/or health and/or public safety, the Court is entitled to find that this fundamental right has been contravened. The European Court of Human Rights has entertained arguments on this issue but on the facts of the cases before it, it did not find in favour of the party putting forward the arguments. In support of this submission I was referred to the decisions in Noel Narvii v. France, ECHR 28204/95 (Judgment of December 4th, 1995); In the case of Lopez Ostra v. Spain, ECHR 00016798/90 (1994); and LCB v. United Kingdom France, ECHR (Judgment of June 9th, 1998) FFOS also submitted that the EMA, in the exercise of its powers to grant the CEC, had a duty to effect such procedural measures as are necessary to give effect to the rights to individuals. The failure and/or omission of the EMA to take the necessary steps to ensure that there were no significant threats to the lives, health and safety of individuals and to the environment generally amount to a contravention of this right. I was referred to the decision in Attorney General v Wayne Whiteman (1991) 39 WIR 397. It was further submitted that environmental degradation and circumstances which pose threats to human life, human health, public safety and the environmental generally, and which have the effect or can have the effect of preventing persons from enjoying their homes, or contravene their right to respect of private and family life. Senior Counsel relied on the European Court on Human Rights' decision in Lopez Ostra v. Spain ECHR 00016798/90 (1994). It was recognised there that severe environmental pollution may affect individuals' well-being and prevent them from enjoying their homes in such a way to affect their private and family life, even though it does not seriously endanger their health. Mr. Maharaj submitted that where the activity impacts upon the fundamental rights of persons, there is a special obligation for the authority to specially consider that issue. Therefore, in its decision-making process the EMA had to consider the fact that this matter impacted upon the rights of the individuals in the community. Unless they could show that they gave consideration to that, there is an overriding weight for the decision to be set aside. It was submitted on behalf of the EMA that the Applicant had not been given locus standi to allege a breach of the constitutional rights of others. Section 14 of the Constitution prescribes the procedure to be adopted where a person alleges that any provision of Chapter 1 of the Constitution has been, is being, or is likely to be, contravened in relation him. The inclusion of these grounds by FFOS is therefore misconceived. In any event, there is no evidence to support and contravention of the fundamental right to life under Section 4 (a) of the Constitution or any of the fundamental rights in Section 4(b), (c) or Section 5(2) or 5(2)(h) of the Constitution. It is well accepted that if there has been, or may be, a breach of a constitutional right, the remedy lies against the State, not a private individual or corporation. There can therefore be no remedy obtained in these proceedings against the EMA for breach of a constitutional right. That is sufficient to dispose of this ground. FFOS, however, also advances the argument that these rights constitute standards or benchmarks that are to be met when the EMA is considering an application for a certificate of environmental clearance. I agree that these rights should provide some basis for guiding decision makers. Indeed, the philosophy underlying the legislative regime is to some extent at least predicated upon them. The legislation is there, in effect, to protect those rights, even if not to the fullest extent claimed by FFOS and the residents. The Act, for example, provides procedural steps that allow concerns and objections to be heard and considered; provides protection of the law; respect for family and private life; protection against cruel and inhumane punishment; and the right to enjoy a healthy environment. While I accept the existence of certain common law environmental rights (to which I have already referred), I am reluctant to elevate them or categorise them together with those rights entrenched in the Constitution, despite also accepting that the latter is a living document which should be interpreted generously. The position remains, however, as acknowledged in Europe and India, for example that these "rights" are subject to other considerations. I do not wish to embark here on an investigation as to whether the rights of an individual should prevail over those of the society generally, or vice versa. It is sufficient to say that issues of environmental control often involve the delicate balancing of competing social and economic interests, as well as the application of specialised expertise. Furthermore, the inevitable trade-off between economic and ecological values is a subject matter which is inherently political. It is not for a court to rewrite the Constitution. I am not persuaded that I should attempt to do so in this instance. This is best left to the legislature. Finally, the law in its existing state, quite apart from the Constitution, provides safeguards for the individual and his, or her, rights. In the event, I am not satisfied that the decision made by the EMA ignored the common law rights of FFOS or the residents; nor that it was, or is, properly to be regarded as illegal. I am not persuaded that the EMA failed to understand correctly the law regulating its decision-making process, or that it failed to give effect to that law.

It should be noted that when ***Fishermen and Friends of the Sea v The Environmental Management Authority and Atlantic LNG Company of Trinidad and Tobago (Interested Party)***[350] was filed, the NEP 1998 was in force. At Chapter 2 Goals, Objectives and Basic Principles, 2.1 Introduction, it was stated:

Article 4 of The Constitution of Trinidad and Tobago declares that every person in Trinidad and Tobago has the fundamental rights of -- life and the enjoyment of property. Further, the Government of Trinidad and Tobago recognizes that humans influence and are influenced by their environment and that the natural and built environments affect their well-being. Government therefore accepts the responsibility to adopt policies and measures with a view to improving human health and the quality of life. Government and also acknowledges that following basic environmental, health and development principles are interdependent and in harmony with the Constitution of the Nation.

Despite a clear statement in the NEP 1998, that there is a right to a healthy environment implicit in the existing constitutional rights to life and enjoyment of property, the court rejected this in the ***Fishermen and Friends of the Sea v The Environmental Management Authority and Atlantic LNG***

350 Ibid.

Company of Trinidad and Tobago (Interested Party[351] and the EMA even argued against the interpretation contained in the NEP 1998 that it was responsible for preparing. Interestingly, the alluding to an implied constitutional right to a healthy environment as part of the Goals, Objectives and Basic Principles of NEP 1998 was removed and placed in the foreword of the NEP 2006. Even more noteworthy is the removal from the NEP 2018, of the reference to a right to a healthy environment implicit in the existing constitutional rights to life and enjoyment of property.

An interesting consent agreement on the relationship between the right to health and the environment was agreed upon by the State and a victim of lead poisoning, in the case of *Soodeen v Attorney General of Trinidad and Tobago*[352] where the consent agreement raised eyebrows and demonstrated the growing environment awareness. This matter was a constitutional action brought by the Soodeen family against the State as a result of harm-suffered by members of the Soodeen family in violation of Section 4 of the Constitution of TT. The action arose out of the dumping of lead waste at Demerara Road, Trinidad. It would appear that in the 1980s a practice arose where lead waste was transported by a truck and dumped on a piece of State land occupied by squatters. In a supporting affidavit, Albert Soodeen, the father of three children affected in different degrees by lead poisoning, claimed that he moved to Demerara Road in 1990 as a squatter on State land. He claimed to have noticed trucks dumping what he later found out to be battery waste on Demerara Road and adjoining areas. Soodeen observed that the trucks appeared to be operated by private contractors who may have been working for a company. Soodeen said that the villagers in Demerara Road used the lead waste to pave the roadway and floors of their homes. Children even played with the lead waste but he never received any warning about the dangers of lead waste or saw any action being taken to prevent the dumping of lead waste in the area. This dumping was taking place between 1990 and 1992 when he moved with his family into the area. The first time Soodeen found out about lead poisoning was when one of his children became ill in 1993. Soodeen's other children were later tested and diagnosed as suffering from lead poisoning. Subsequently,

---

351 Ibid.

352 S-839 of 1996

some 25 children were hospitalized with lead poisoning.

In June of 1993, the Ministry of Health issued a press release indicating that residents of Demerara Road had been exposed to lead poisoning and that the residents would be relocated. Soodeen indicated that no efforts were made to relocate anyone between June 1993 to March 1994. As a result of the announcement of lead contamination, the Soodeens moved to about a mile away from Demerara Road. One of the Soodeen children had been mentally affected, one died and the third would appear to have recovered substantially from the lead poisoning. A consent order was entered into by parties to the action and the terms of the consent order are instructive. First, it was accepted by the State that the Soodeens had certain fundamental human rights contravened by the State, namely their rights to life and the enjoyment of property and the right not to be deprived thereof except by due process of law. Second, it was stated that the failure of the State to safeguard the Soodeens from contamination by lead poisoning and from the risks of contamination was unconstitutional and illegal. Third, it was stated that the failure of the State to warn the Soodeens of the existence of lead contamination and the effects of lead poisoning was unconstitutional and illegal. Fourth, it was stated that the failure of the State to offer to pay prompt and adequate compensation for their deprivation of the use and enjoyment of their property was unconstitutional and illegal.

This consent agreement by the State has caused some concern. The fact is that there was no evidence that the State was responsible for the dumping of lead waste in the area or that the State knew of the dumping of lead waste in the area. Further, the Soodeens were squatters living illegally on State land and the State may not have known of their presence. The consent agreement may be justice for the Soodeens but nothing has transpired with respect to those responsible for creating the danger of lead poisoning in Demerara Road.

CHAPTER 9

ENVIRONMENTAL JUSTICE, ECOLOGICAL JUSTICE, INTRAGENERATIONAL EQUITY, INTERGENERATIONAL EQUITY, COMMON HERITAGE AND COMMON CONCERNS

ENVIRONMENTAL JUSTICE

The environmental justice movement began in the USA and is today a complex creature. In the 1970s, in the USA, the environmental justice movement began to mobilize in response to specific cases of exposure by less fortunate groups to environmental hazards, discrimination in housing, land use, health care, sanitation services etc. It sought to sensitize the world to and to change the correlation between race and poverty and industrial waste and pollution facilities and sites.[353] Decisions to situate hazardous waste facilities, industrial activities and landfills in African American communities enraged activists. Robert Bullard is one of its key activists and intellectual leaders[354]. It critiqued

---

353 Luke W., Foster, Sheila R. Cole, *From the Ground Up: Environmental Racism and the Rise of the Environmental Justice Movement (Critical America (New York University Paperback)) by Cole, Luke W., Foster, Sheila R. Published by NYU Press (2000)* (NYU Press).

354 Robert D. Bullard, *Dumping in Dixie: Race, Class and Environmental Quality* (Boulder, Colo: Westview Press 2000). Robert D. Bullard, '*Leveling the Playing Field Through Environmental Justice*' [1999] 23 Vt. L. Rev. 453

traditional post-industrial and post-materialist concern[355] for the environment that focused on the environmental needs of the wealthy to the detriment of those less privileged. Rev. Benjamin Chavis, the Executive Director of the United Church for Christ Commission on Racial Justice, condemned what he termed "environmental racism" in the 1987 Commission study[356] on toxic wastes that confirmed that race was the key factor for locating hazardous waste facilities in the USA[357]. President Clinton's administration was responsible for the Executive Order 12898 which ruled that every federal agency must incorporate environmental justice as part of its mission. The Order was a victory for the environmental justice activists and the industrial lobby has sought to limit its impact. The Office of Environmental Justice was established within the Environmental Protection Agency.

In the USA, environmental justice groups tend to have a strong human rights and social justice identity. To date, the literature has distilled over 50 environmental themes within the environmental justice movement in the USA[358]. Activists lobby against inequality on many fronts: waste landfills and wind farm locations, land reform, the impact of forest fires, access to sanitation, drinking water quality, hazards related to mineral extraction, the lack of greenspace, wildlife reservations, access to urban agricultural land, environmentally safe housing, noise and air pollution, placement of transport infrastructure, flooding, access to quality food, toxic waste management etc.

The principle of environmental justice which has found itself in the environmental legal regime of countries such as the USA, has embedded itself,

---

355 Ramachandra Guha and Juan Martínez Alier, *Varieties of Environmentalism: Essays North and South* (London: Earthscan Publications, 1997),16

356 United Church for Christ Commission on Racial Justice, *Toxic Waste and Race in the United Sates: A National Report on the Racial and Socioeconomic Characteristics of Communities with Hazardous Wastes Sites* (New York: Public Data Access, 1987)

357 Richard J. Lazarus, '*Environmental Racism! That's What It Is.*' 2000 U. Ill. L. Rev. 255-274

358 Robert Benford. *The half-life of the environmental justice frame: Innovation, diffusion and stagnation.* In David Pellow and Robert Bruille (eds), *Power, Justice, and the Environment: A Critical Appraisal of the Environmental Justice Movement* . (Cambridge, MA: MIT Press. 2005).

in the environmental legal regime of TT through the NEP 2018. As already pointed out in *Fishermen and Friends of the Sea v The Minister of Planning, Housing and the Environment*,[359] the NEP is of statutory strength in TT and must be complied with by governmental entities including the EMA.

Section 1.05 Furthermore, the GoRTT, all subnational actors and international actors operating within the State's boundaries shall adopt/maintain, where appropriate, the features of good governance required to galvanise environmental sustainability, including but not limited to:

11. Effective process to redress past and present environmental justice;

Section 2.22 The GoRTT understands that the meaningful involvement of all persons in the development, implementation and enforcement of environmental laws and policies fosters a society of environmental stewards. More so, providing access to effective redress for environmental disputes and issues empowers individuals to take personal responsibility for an environmentally sustainable future. Accordingly, the GoRTT will: a) Encourage public participation in the development, implementation and enforcement of environmental laws, regulations, policies, management plans and programmes as far as practicably possible; b) Empower government entities with responsibility for the environment to adopt proactive measures for discovering and responding to environmental issues in a timely manner; c) Support the development of ADR mechanisms for addressing environmental and natural resource conflicts; d) Amend or develop new legislation, as appropriate, to facilitate expedient civil action on environmental issues; e) Empower community groups and non-governmental organisations to seek redress through litigative or ADR mechanisms; f) Support education and awareness campaigns that promote avenues for environmental redress and remedies; g) Encourage the mainstreaming of environmental laws, regulations and policies among all stakeholders with critical roles in dispensing environmental justice including but not limited to, the police service and the judiciary; h) Amend or develop new legislation, as appropriate, to establish courts dedicated to addressing environmental issues across Trinidad and Tobago; and i) ,Revise, as appropriate, environmental regulations to maintain effective financial disincentives and mechanisms for appropriate financial compensation for environmental losses.

---

359 P.C.A No. 0028 of 2016

The principle of environmental justice has already made its way into the jurisprudence of TT. In ***Fishermen and Friends of the Sea v The Environmental Management Authority and Atlantic LNG Company of Trinidad and Tobago (Interested Party),*** Stollmeyer J accepted the role of environmental justice in the development, implementation and enforcement of environmental laws and policies.

> *The EMA has a broad discretion in determining whether and when to hold public hearings. There is no express provision requiring follow up public hearings before granting the CEC. That is left up to its discretion, and will depend on the circumstances of the case and the severity of the concerns. Follow-up procedures may be considered necessary to fulfil the intention of the section, which is to incorporate the affected community in the decision- making process by way of having this concerns and opinions. Community involvement is one manifestation of the holistic approach adopted by the Act. Environmental degradation has a human face as well; it is not limited to merely land, water and air. Communities frequently face the most severe impacts but are often the least involved in making environmental decisions that affect their well-being.*

> *Section 28 attempts to remedy this by allowing affected communities more meaningful participation in decisions that affect them. It also provides communities with valuable information about the potential health and environmental effects of the project. It affords persons who may be affected the opportunity to voice their concerns, views, comments and recommendations and, correspondingly, places the EMA under a duty to consider what they say. These persons are, in essence, given a fair hearing.*

> *In essence, it aims to achieve environmental justice, which is "the fair treatment and meaningful involvement of all people regardless of race, colour, national origin, or income with respect to the development, implementation and enforcement of environmental laws, regulations and policies.*

ECOLOGICAL JUSTICE

Ecological justice is a relatively new concept and has been argued to be based on the premise of "treating species besides homo sapiens as having claim in justice to share of the Earth's resources. It explores the nature of

286

justice claims as applied to organisms of various degrees of complexity and describes the institutional arrangements necessary to integrate the claims of ecological justice into human decision making."[360]

Ecological justice was a guiding principle of the NEP 2006 where it was referenced together with environmental justice as seen in Section 2.3.

> *NEP 2006, 2.3 Basic Principles Government's environmental policy will be guided by the following basic principles: Respect and Care for the Community of Life - The ethic of ecological justice based on respect for one another and for nature is the foundation of sustainable development. Development therefore, should not be at the expense of other groups, nor threaten the existence of other species.*

The inclusion of ecological justice in NEP 2018 is now less precise and is contained within general language espousing protection of biological diversity.

> *Section 2.08 Trinidad and Tobago has some of the highest levels of biodiversity globally, being home to a diverse array of ecosystems and native species. The GoRTT recognises its responsibility to be diligent stewards of all forms of life based on intrinsic value...Thus, in continuing its efforts to achieve SDG 14 and 15, which aim to protect, restore and promote the sustainable use of biological resources and halt biodiversity loss, the GoRTT, will...*

Having regard to the fact that the principle of environmental justice has already made its way into the jurisprudence of TT in ***Fishermen and Friends of the Sea v. Environmental Management Authority and Atlantic LNG Company of Trinidad and Tobago (Interested Party),*** it is arguable therefore, ecological justice is part of the body of legal principles shaping the development of environmental law in TT.

INTRAGENERATIONAL EQUITY

Two major goals of modern society and sustainable development are poverty eradication and equity. As such, these principles have been consistently mentioned in international instruments in the fields of social, economic and environmental law. The principles of equity and the eradication of

---

360 Brian Baxter, *A Theory of Ecological Justice* (Routledge, 2014)

poverty find their basis in *Chapter IX of the Charter of the United Nations* where the UN adopts the role of, *inter alia,* promoting higher standards of living, full employment, conditions of economic and social progress and development, and respect for human rights.[361] Within a nation state, aspirations of poverty alleviation are critical. The relationship between poverty and the environment was made clear during the first attempt at articulating an international policy on environmental protection. In 1972, the world leaders gathered in Stockholm for UNCHE, the first major conference on the environment. This conference saw the expression of concerns by many developing countries on the problem of poverty and its impact on efforts to ensure that the human environment was maintained at acceptable levels. One report to the conference prepared by the Afghanistan delegation, noted that *"the world's ills involve the three P's - pollution, population and poverty."*[362] A similar theme was echoed in the Indian report where it was asserted that *"on account partly, of dire poverty of the masses, the lack of education, the extreme pre-occupation with the urgent demands of sheer existence, there is often an apathy, a general lack of popular concern about the quality of the environment in India."*[363]

It is clear from available evidence that poverty continues to stalk the developing world with devastating effects. Today, the issue of poverty is still as strong as in 1972 when the international community met for the first time to discuss issues of poverty. At UNCED, in 1992, the second major international conference on the environment held 20 years after UNCHE, poverty once again assumed a dominant role. A joint report submitted by the Asian and Pacific Regions stated *"that the need for poverty alleviation is most urgent. The interaction between poverty and the environment sets off a downward spiral of ecological deterioration that threatens the physical security, well-being and health of many of the region's poorest people."*[364]

---

361 United Nations, "Charter of the United Nations", adopted 26 June 1945. [accessed 10 November 2008]. http://www.un.org/aboutun/charter/.

362 United Nations (1972), *Environmental Problems of Afghanistan* (New York: United Nations).

363 United Nations (1972), *Some Aspects of Environmental Degradation and its Control in India,* Report submitted to the United Nations Conference on the Human Environment.

364 Economic and Social Commission for Asia and the Pacific, *The Asian and Pacific Input to the United Nations Conference on Environment and Development Brazil, 1992* (UN: New York), p. 7.

Concerns with poverty and the interlocking issue of development, and their impact on the environment, have been recurring themes from 1972 onwards in the speeches of national leaders on environmental protection. There is the oft-quoted remark by the late Indian Prime Minister, Indira Ghandi, that *"poverty is the greatest pollutant in the case of the developing world."*[365] Even leaders that have pushed their people into the embrace of poverty through untrammelled despotism have sought to link poverty with environmental degradation. In echoing the words of Indira Ghandi, Robert Mugabe, the former President of Zimbabwe said:

> *preventable poverty is one of the major causes of environmental degradation today. Poverty pollutes our environment. Those who are poor and hungry will often destroy their immediate environment in order to survive. Their livestock will overgraze the grasslands and in growing numbers will crowd congested cities. They will overuse marginal lands. This explains why the greatest environmental change is occurring in developing countries. These countries are poor.*[366]

Achieving poverty alleviation can only be done with the adoption of a measure of equity in the distribution of the bounties of a society. The WCED defines equity as:

> *Our inability to promote the common interest in sustainable development is often a product of the relative neglect of economic and social justice within and amongst nations.*[367]

Intragenerational equity is concerned with equality within the present generation, such that each member has an equal right to access the earth's natural and cultural resources. Weiss argues that members of the present generation have a right of *"equitable access to use and benefit from the planet's resources, which derives from the underlying equality all generations have with each other in relation to their use of the natural system"*.[368] At a basic level, intragenerational

---

365 Sanjoy Hazarika, *Bhopal - The Lessons of A Tragedy* (New Delhi: Penguin,1987)

366 Robert Mugabe, *Environmental Concerns in the Third World,* in *Earth and Us: Population-Resources-Environment and Development* (Oxford: Butterworth-Heinemann, 1991)

367 World Commission on Environment and Development (WCED) (1987), *Our Common Future* (New York: Oxford University Press, 1987), 49

368 Edith Weiss, (1990) *Agora: What Obligation Does Our Generation Owe to the Next? An Approach to Global Environmental Responsibility: Our Rights and Obligations to Future Generations*

equity can be interpreted to mean *"that everyone is entitled to the necessities of life: food, shelter, health care, education, and the essential infrastructure for social organization".*[369] Intragenerational equity can also be referred to as the obligation to *"ensure a just allocation of the utilization of resources among human members of the present generation, both at the domestic and global levels."*[370]

The principle of intragenerational equity has found itself in the environmental legal regime of TT through the NEP 2018. As already pointed out, the NEP 2018 is of statutory strength in TT and must be complied with by governmental entities including the EMA.

> *NEP 2018 Section 1.05 Equity is the cornerstone of achieving sustainable development. It is recognised that all citizens of Trinidad and Tobago within the current generation have the right of fair access to their generation's entitlement of natural resources...Thus, each generation has the duty of ensuring that pursuit of development does not impede the ability of each citizen, or successive generations of citizens, from meeting their needs. In addition, the GoRTT assumes responsibility for fairly allocating and regulating scarce resources to ensure that all benefits and burdens are equitably shared amongst all members of society.*

In turn, the *Preamble to the Environmental Management Act* reflects a link between sustainable development and intragenerational equity.

> *Whereas, the Government of the Republic of Trinidad and Tobago (hereinafter called "the Government") is committed to developing a national strategy for sustainable development, being the balance of economic growth with environmentally sound practices, in order to enhance the quality of life and meet the needs of present...generations....*

INTERGENERATIONAL EQUITY

Intergenerational equity is a value concept which focuses on the rights of

---

for the Environment' [1990] 190 American Journal of International Law 84, 397

369 Oscar Schachter, (1977) *Sharing the World's Resources* (Bangalore: Allied Press, 1977), 11-12

370 Marie-Claire Cordonier Segger and Ashfaq Khalfan, *Sustainable Development Law: Principles, Practices, and Prospects* (Oxford, UK: Oxford University Press, 2004)

future generations and is implicit in the concept of sustainable development. While intergenerational equity is often presented within the philosophical framework of how actions in the present may directly or indirectly degrade the environment in the future, it is based on the premise that each generation has a right to inherit the same diversity in natural and cultural resources enjoyed by previous generations, as well as a right to equitable access to the use and benefits of these resources. The present generation, therefore, is regarded as a custodian of the planet for future generations, extending the scope of social justice into the future.

Intergenerational equity constitutes a link for the realisation of mutual interests between environmental protection, socio-economic development, and human rights law. It is currently evolving and is considered to be a relatively new phenomenon as suggested by proponents of environmental justice and the rights of indigenous persons in particular.[371] Intergenerational equity, also known as the future generation trust, represents a call for equality between generations. That is, each generation is entitled to inherit a planet which is at least as good as that of the previous generation.[372] Each generation, therefore, should be entitled to the environment enjoyed by the previous generation.[373] According to Edith Brown Weiss, in her book, *In Fairness to Future Generations*:

> *At any given time, each generation is both a custodian and trustee of the planet for future generations and a beneficiary of its fruits. This imposes obligations upon us to care for the planet and gives us certain rights to use it... The proposed theory of intergenerational equity postulates that all countries have an intergenerational obligation to future generations as a class, regardless of nationality. This is necessary because the condition of the planet will have a profound impact on the welfare of our descendants. There is increasing recognition that while we may be able to*

371 Gregory Maggio, *Inter/intra-generational Equity: Current Applications under International Law for Promoting the Sustainable Development of Natural Resources* [1997] *Buffalo Environmental Law Journal* 4, 161, 166

372 Edith Weiss, (1990). *'gora: What Obligation Does Our Generation Owe to the Next? An Approach to Global Environmental Responsibility: Our Rights and Obligations to Future Generations for the Environment* [1990] 190 American Journal of International Law 84

373 Bruce Ackerman, *Social Injustice in the Liberal State* (New Haven: Yale University Press, 1980)

maximize the welfare of a few immediate successors, we will be able to do so only at the expense of our more remote descendants, who will inherit a despoiled natural and cultural environment. Our planet is finite, and we are becoming increasingly interdependent in using it. Our rapid technological growth ensures that this interdependence will increase. Thus our concern for our own country must, as we extend our concerns into longer time horizons and broader geographic scales, focus on protecting the planetary quality of our natural and cultural environment. This means that, even to protect our own future nationals, we must cooperate in the conservation of natural and cultural resources for all future generations.[374]

Weiss identifies three basic principles composing intergenerational equity; (1) conservation of options; (2) conservation of quality; and (3) the conservation of access.[375] First, the conservation of options obliges the present generation to act in a manner which would conserve the diversity of the natural resource base. Second, the conservation of quality deals with the maintenance of the quality of the planet in order to leave it in no worse condition for future generations and finally, the conservation of access deals with the preservation of the legacy of past generations. Weiss contends that these three principles can serve as the foundation for an international framework protecting the rights of future generations from present day rapacity.[376]

Unsurprisingly, the principle of intergenerational equity is also one of the four distinct legal principles comprising the sustainable development paradigm. According to Philippe Sands,[377] the principles comprising the concept of sustainable development include equitable use, sustainable use, and the integration of environmental concerns with development strategies. If the concept of intergenerational equity is predicated on maintaining the diversity of the natural resource base while ensuring no diminution in the

---

374 Edith Weiss, (1990). *Agora: What Obligation Does Our Generation Owe to the Next? An Approach to Global Environmental Responsibility: Our Rights and Obligations to Future Generations for the Environment* [1990] 190 American Journal of International Law 84, 17

375 Ibid at [38]

376 Ibid at [38-39]

377 M. Civic, *Prospects for the Respect and Promotion of Internationally Recognized Sustainable Development Practices: A Case Study of the World Bank Environmental Guidelines and Procedures* [1998] Fordham Environmental Law Review 9, 231, 237

quality of the planet and proper acknowledgement of the legacy of past generations, then there must be a proper balance between the environment and development. The unsustainable exploitation of natural resources may very well leave a deficit for future generations and a poorer planet in terms of the rich legacy of our ancestors. There can be no disputing that consideration of the notion of intergenerational equity is irretrievably woven into the fabric of sustainable development and a necessary notion for jurisprudential considerations.

The principle of intergenerational equity convincingly articulated in international environmental law is also entrenched in the environmental legal regime of TT through the NEP 2018. Case law has established that the NEP 2018 possesses statutory power in TT and must be complied with by governmental entities including the EMA.

> *NEP 2018 Section 1.05 Equity is the cornerstone of achieving sustainable development...In addition, future generations are entitled to enjoy a fair level of the common patrimony. Thus, each generation has the duty of ensuring that pursuit of development does not impede the ability of each citizen, or successive generations of citizens, from meeting their needs. In addition, the GoRTT assumes responsibility for fairly allocating and regulating scarce resources to ensure that all benefits and burdens are equitably shared amongst all members of society.*

This accurately reflects the *preamble of the Environmental Management Act* with respect to intergenerational equity.

> *Whereas, the Government of the Republic of Trinidad and Tobago (hereinafter called "the Government") is committed to developing a national strategy for sustainable development, being the balance of economic growth with environmentally sound practices, in order to enhance the quality of life and meet the needs of...future generations....*

COMMON HERITAGE AND COMMON CONCERNS

The NEP 2018 introduced into the jurisprudence of TT, the ethical responsibility in international environmental law that dealt with common heritage and common concern of humankind. The global interest in the common heritage of mankind started appearing in the 1960s and has steadily gained in importance. By 1972, the international community agreed the text on the first international treaty to deal with the common heritage of mankind, the *Convention concerning the Protection of the World Cultural and Natural Heritage 1972*. *Section 6(1) of the Convention concerning the Protection of the World Cultural and Natural Heritage 1972*, recognises state sovereignty over its natural resources but emphasised the need for taking steps to ensure that acts or omissions within territorial jurisdiction contemplate the impact on the common heritage of mankind. It remains to be seen how TT would deal with the common heritage and common concerns of humankind, in light of the entrenchment of a duty of care in the NEP 2018.

> *NEP 2018 Section 1.05 The GoRTT recognises that the management of the climate system and biodiversity of the Earth are common concerns for humankind. Moreover, resources of outer space, celestial bodies, the sea-bed, ocean floor and subsoil thereof beyond the limits of national jurisdiction are considered the common heritage of humankind. The GoRTT, sub-national actors, and transnational organisations within its boundaries shall share responsibility for addressing common concerns, minimising harm to issues of common concern and safeguarding the common heritage of humankind*

CHAPTER 10

THE ENVIRONMENTAL
COMMISSION

APPOINTMENT TO THE ENVIRONMENTAL COMMISSION

One of the main features of the *Environmental Management Act* is the establishment of an Environmental Commission as a specialized tribunal servicing the needs of the environment. Having such a specialized tribunal is intended to ensure swift and efficient justice in environmental matters. In addition, the inclusion of legal and technical experts in the environmental field as Commissioners is intended to ensure an improved decision-making process.

Section 81 of the Environmental Management Act establishes the Environmental Commission and its jurisdiction.

81(1) A tribunal to be known as the Environmental Commission is hereby established for the purpose of exercising the jurisdiction conferred upon it by this Act or by any other written law

(2) The Commission shall consist of a Chairman and such other members, including a Deputy Chairman, as may be appointed under or in pursuance of Section 82.

(3) The Commission shall be a superior court of record and have an official seal which shall be judicially noticed, and shall have in addition to the jurisdiction and powers conferred on it by this Act all the powers inherent in such a court.

(4) The Commission shall have the power to enforce its own orders and judgments, and the same power to punish contempt as the High Court of Justice.

Section 82 of the Environmental Management Act

82(1) The Commission shall be comprised of a full-time Chairman, and five other members including a Deputy Chairman, each of whom may be appointed to serve in a full-time, part-time or periodic capacity as may be required to fulfil the objects of this Act.

(2) The Chairman and Deputy Chairman of the Commission shall each be an attorney-at-law of not less than ten years standing, and shall be appointed by the President.

(3) The members of the Commission, other than the Chairman and Deputy Chairman, shall be appointed by the President from among such persons as appear to the President to be qualified by virtue of their knowledge of or experience in environmental issues, engineering, the natural sciences, or the social sciences.

(4) All members of the Commission shall hold office under such requirements and conditions of service and for such term, not less than three years, as may be determined by the President and set forth in the terms of reference at the time of their appointment, and shall be eligible for reappointment.

(5) Notwithstanding that his term of office has expired, any member of the Commission may, with the permission of the President acting on the advice of the Chairman of the Commission, continue in office for such a period after the expiry of his term as may be necessary to deliver judgment, or to do any other thing in relation to proceedings that were commenced before such member prior to the expiry of his term of office.

(6) Any member of the Commission may, at any time by notice in writing to the President, resign his office.

(7) The President may remove from office any member of the Commission for inability, misbehaviour, or on the ground of any employment or interest which is incompatible with the functions of a member of the Commission.

(8) Where any member of the Commission is ill, or otherwise unable to act, or where his office is vacant, the President may appoint a person to act in the stead of such member during his illness, or incapability, or until the office is filled, as the case may be.

(9) No defect in the qualification or appointment of any member of the Commis-

sion shall vitiate any proceedings thereof.

The disturbing aspect of the appointment of the Environmental Commissioners is the scope for political interference. The Commissioners are all appointed by the President who is a political appointee, appointed by the Electoral College which comprises both Houses of Parliament. While members of the judiciary are appointed by the constitutionally established Judicial and Legal Services Commission, the Environmental Commission, which is to serve as an important tribunal on environmental matters, is appointed by a different route.

The first panel of the Environmental Commission were appointed through advertisements in the national press by the then Ministry of the Environment based on recommendations by an interview committee. This interview committee, according to the draft Cabinet Note, recommended the appointment to the President. The facts surrounding the appointment of the first panel of the Environmental Commission illustrate the danger of having it executed through the political process. Cabinet Note, dated 17 May 2000, indicated that an interview committee was established and included a retired judge who later became the first Chairman of the Environmental Commission. The interview committee, according to the draft Cabinet Note, recommended the appointment of a sitting judge, Mr. Justice Ibrahim, who was due to retire from the Supreme Court of TT, as Chairman of the Environmental Commission. This matter became embroiled in public debate and no Chairman was confirmed. Subsequently, another advertisement was placed for a Chairman of the Environmental Commission and the first Chairman was appointed. It is important to note that in the second advertisement for a Chairman of the Environmental Commission it was stated that special consideration would be given to retired High Court Judges, a requirement not stated in the *Environmental Management Act* or in the first advertisement for a Chairman. In addition, a member of the interview panel that interviewed the first set of candidates for positions on the Environmental Commission, including the position of Chairman, was appointed as the first Chairman of the Environmental Commission pursuant to the second advertisement to recruit a Chairman for the Environmental Commission.

The facts surrounding the appointment of the first Chairman of the Environmental Commission are in no way intended to question the person's competence or sense of impartiality. However, the nature of the appointment process could inadvertently cast unnecessary and unwarranted aspersions on the integrity of the Environmental Commission.

The matter had a disturbing post-script when with a change in government, the first Chairman of the Environmental Commission was not re-appointed. The matter was taken to the Supreme Court by the TTCRA in *Trinidad and Tobago Civil Rights Association v Patrick Augustus Mervyn Manning Prime Minister and Head of Cabinet (for and on behalf of himself and all other members of Cabinet).*[378]

> *Facts: The residents of Tortuga claim that they are distressed by the dumping of garbage at the Forres Park Dump near to their homes. It is their desire to approach the Environmental Management Authority and possibly the Environmental Commission, ("the Commission"). Having heard, however that the first Chairman, Justice Hosein had not been re-appointed, and they fear that the Commission, in the manner in which it is constituted at present, will not be able to give them a fair and impartial hearing. This application canvasses issues of the doctrine of the separation of powers and the power of Parliament to alter the method by which a judicial officer could be appointed and removed. The Applicant claims as well that the residents of Tortuga are aggrieved by the alleged breach of natural justice, irrationality and bad faith, meted out to the rejected former Chairman. This case also canvasses issues of locus standi in the context of the Judicial Review Act. The facts relating to this application for Judicial Review occur in three (3) strata. At the most superficial, one encounters the Applicant, whose role is to file the application under s. 5(6) on behalf of the residents of Tortuga. At the second level are the persons who are truly aggrieved by the existence of a garbage dump near to their homes, but whose grievance, for the purpose of this application, is that they fear that they will be denied a fair and impartial hearing by the Commission. At the deepest level, are the facts concerning Justice Hosein who although he is the alleged victim of alleged breaches of natural justice and maladministration, has made no complaint.*

> *Held: Dean-Armorer J*

---

378 HCA No. 477 of 2004

5(i) Breach of Natural Justice:

In my view, Justice Hosein's case falls squarely within the category of the expectation cases as formulated by Megarry, V.C. in Mc Innis v Onslow-Fane [1978] 1 W.L.R. 1520. In my respectful view the words of Megarry, V.C. are directly applicable to the refusal by the executive to re-appoint Justice Hosein. Borrowing the words of Justice Megarry, it is in my view accurate to say that " although there is no forfeiture in form but merely an attempt at acquisition that fails, the legitimate expectation of the renewal of the (appointment)..... is one which raises the question of what it is that has happened to make the Applicant unsuitable for the membership or license for which he was previously thought suitable......." *Justice Hosein, according to the terms of S.82(4) was aware that he was eligible to be re-appointed, following the expiry of his first term of five (5) years. He took the necessary steps to ensure that the line Minister was apprised of his willingness to serve for another term. He was neither notified of the possibility of being replaced nor was he allowed in any form to advance reasons against his replacement. Learned Senior Counsel , Mr. Hamel-Smith argued by reference to s. 20 of the Judicial Review Act that Justice Hosein was entitled only to be treated in a fair manner. In my view, the words Lord Mustill in R v Secretary for State Exp. Doody (1994) A.C. 531, 560 are apt in elucidating the meaning of fairness in this case: "Fairness requires that a person who may be adversely affected by the decision will have an opportunity to make representations on his own behalf either before the decision is taken, with a view to producing a favourable result; or after it is taken, with a view to procuring its modification; or both." See supra. Justice Hosein was entitled to be treated in a fair manner which required at least that he be given an opportunity to be heard. He was never afforded this opportunity.*

(ii) Bad Faith

It has been argued on behalf of the Applicant that the executive acted in bad faith in refusing to re-appoint Justice Hosein. On behalf of the Applicant, learned Senior Counsel Mr. Maharaj relied on two (2) complaints which had been made by Justice Hosein first to the Prime Minister and secondly to Minister Dumas. Both complaints concerned the requirement of judicial independence, which should be accorded to the Commission. Learned Senior Counsel Mr. Maharaj commended to the Court the learning contained in Fordham, Judicial Re-

view Handbook (3rd ed.) and contended that this case was really one of abuse of power. Learned Senior Counsel Mr. Maharaj submitted that in order to decide this issue the Court should look to see if the decision was made in good faith. In my view this method of assessment will result in reversing the burden on the Applicant and placing it on the administrative authority. Moreover, the available learning on this area suggests that the threshold is high and asserts that it ought not lightly to be alleged and is difficult to prove. In Rees v. Crane, their Lordships dismissed Justice Crane's cross-appeal on the ground of bias notwithstanding a finding of personal hostility on the part of the incumbent Chief Justice. Their Lordships' words bear repetition "...it is not lightly to be assumed that he (the Chief Justice) would allow personal hostility to colour his decision to suspend the Respondent." See supra. I am also guided by learning in P.S.C. v Hayde C.A. 12/99 where the learned Chief Justice ruled that it was unlikely that bad faith would be found to have infected the decision of a group rather than an individual and that if bad faith is so alleged; the allegation should be supported by cogent evidence.

In the instant case the impugned decision was made by a group of persons, that is to say, the Cabinet. There is no cogent evidence of bad faith. The Court is required to infer the presence of bad faith and bias from the fact that the complaints of Justice Hosein were eventually followed by his replacement. In my view such an inference would be contrary to the preponderance of authority on bad faith and I am constrained to refuse to make it.

(iii) Irrationality

Learned Senior Counsel Mr. Maharaj submitted that in deciding whether a decision is irrational the Court should apply the test of whether that the decision does not "add up." This phrase in the words reported in R v Parliamentary Commissioner ex. P Balchin means "an error in reasoning which robs the decision of logic...". I cannot however ignore the reality that other formulated tests of the irrational decision have been authoritatively set at dizzying heights. They range from "perversity" in Pulhofer (see supra) to a finding that "the consequences of his guidance were so absurd that he (the decision-maker) must have taken leave of his senses" in Rv Secretary for State for the Environment ex p Nottinghamshire County Council [1986] A.C. 240 at 248. No less stringent is the test of Lord Diplock in CCSU v. Minister for the civil Service : a decision "so outra-

geous in its defiance of logic and accepted moral standards..." In my view the Applicant has fallen short of proving that the decision of Cabinet satisfies the tests. One may disagree with the decision and the reasoning provided by the Minister. Both decision and reason may be susceptible to justifiable criticism. That does not however render the decision reviewable on the ground of irrationality. I am therefore constrained to find against the Applicant on this ground as well.

(iv) Irrelevancy

Learned Senior Counsel Mr. Maharaj argued that the decision of Cabinet to appoint the incumbent Chairman instead of Justice Hosein was defective in that Cabinet took into account the irrelevant consideration of Justice Hosein's age and failed to take into account the superior judicial experience of Justice Hosein when compared to the present Chairman. Learned Senior Counsel also suggested, quite convincingly, that the Cabinet should have sought the assistance of an expert in judicial assessment. In respect of this ground I am persuaded by the submission of Learned Senior Counsel, Mr. Hamel-Smith as to the applicability of the Credence principle. See supra. Where the empowering statute is silent as to relevant criteria it falls to the decision-maker to decide what is relevant. The Environmental Management Act, 2000 has identified two criteria for the office of Chairman. By s.82 of the Environmental Management Act, 2000 the Chairman must be an attorney-at-law of ten years standing. Aside from these two criteria of profession and seniority, other relevant criteria fall to be selected by Cabinet as decision-maker. I find this ground to be without merit.

(v) Equality of Treatment

I am also un-persuaded by an argument that the fundamental rights under ss.4(b) and (d) of the Constitution were contravened in relation to the former Chairman. His standing as Chairman places him in a position of superiority to rather than equality with the other members of the Commission. The element of similar circumstances is missing. Having held that Cabinet, acted in breach of natural justice in failing to afford Justice Hosein an opportunity to be heard either before or immediately after its decision not to re-appoint him, it is now necessary to consider whether the residents of Tortuga were invested with sufficient interest in respect of a breach of natural justice committed against Justice Hosein. In my view, the decision of their Lordships in Durayappah v Fernando [1967] 2 A.C.337 is helpful in this case : "......

although the Council should have been given the opportunity of being heard in it defence it chose not to complain and took no step to protest against its dissolution that accordingly the Appellant as Mayor did not have the right to interfere independently of the Council... In keeping with this authoritative ruling, I am of the view and I hold that although Justice Hosein should have been given the opportunity of being heard he chose not to complain and took no step to protest against Cabinet's decision to appoint another to replace him and accordingly the residents of Tortuga do not have the right to interfere independently of Justice Hosein.

The Application is therefore dismissed.

Although Dean-Armorer J found that there was a breach of natural justice with respect to the non-appointment of the Chairman whose term expired, the court found that the Chairman himself did not initiate any judicial proceedings to have the Supreme Court examine his non-appointment and the matter was dismissed on the basis of standing. This decision was approved by the Court of Appeal in ***Trinidad and Tobago Civil Rights Association v Patrick Augustus Mervyn Manning Prime Minister and Head of Cabinet (for and on behalf of himself and all other members of Cabinet).***[379]

JURISDICTION OF THE ENVIRONMENTAL COMMISSION

The jurisdiction of the Environmental Commission has been a contentious issue and there are important deficiencies arising in this area.

Section 81(5) of the Environmental Management Act

The Commission shall have jurisdiction to hear and determine-

a) appeals from decisions or actions of the Authority as specifically authorised under this Act;

b) applications for deferment of decisions made under Section 25 or deferment of designations made under Section 41;

c) applications by the Authority for the enforcement of any Consent Agreement or any

---

379 CV App. 88 of 2005.

final Administrative Order, as provided in Section 67;

d) administrative civil assessments under Section 66;

e) appeals from the designation of "environmentally sensitive areas" or "environmentally sensitive species" by the Authority pursuant to Section 41;

f) appeals from a decision by the Authority under Section 36 to refuse to issue a certificate of environmental clearance or to grant such a certificate with conditions;

g) appeals from any determination by the Authority to disclose information or materials claimed as a trade secret or confidential business information under Section 23(3);

h) complaints brought by persons pursuant to Section 69, otherwise known as the direct private party action provision; and

i) such other matters as may be prescribed by or arise under this Act or any other written law where jurisdiction in the Commission is specifically provided.

The issue that has arisen pertains to the interpretation of *Sections 81(5)(a) and 81(5)(i) of the Environmental Management Act. Sections 81(5)(b) to (h) of the Environmental Management Act* establishes specific areas of jurisdiction, however *Sections 81(5)(a) and 8(5)(i) of the Environmental Management Act* would appear to refer to general jurisdiction. The Environmental Commission has interpreted *Sections 81(5)(a) and 8(5)(i) of the Environmental Management Act* to provide jurisdiction over all decision or matters arising under the *Environmental Management Act.*[380]

Fishermen and Friends of the Sea v Environmental Management Authority[381]

Facts: FFOS *in the substantive matter brought an appeal pursuant to sections 81 (5) (a) and 81 (5) (i) of the Environmental Management Act (the Environmental Management Act).* FFOS *claimed therein that after they notified the EMA that Atlantic LNG was in breach of an environmental requirement, the*

---

380   The issue was first raised in ***Michelle Dove v. The Environmental Management Authority Respondent, EAP No. 003 of 2007***, but was not judicially determined.

381 EAP 005 of 2007

EMA served a Notice of Violation (NOV) on Atlantic LNG Company of Trinidad and Tobago (Atlantic LNG). They further claimed that the EMA refused and/or failed and/or neglected to enforce or resolve the NOV within a reasonable time and was therefore in breach of its statutory duty as required by section 63 (2) of the Environmental Management Act. FFOS asked the court as a consequence of the EMA's breach of statutory duty, to make certain declarations and orders for certiorari and mandamus.

It was contended by the EMA that the court has no jurisdiction to entertain the appeal either under sections 81 (5) (a) or 81 (5) (i). Sections 81 (5) (a) & (i) provide that:

The Commission shall have jurisdiction to hear and determine (a) Appeals from decisions or actions of the Authority as specifically authorized under this Act; (i) such other matters as may be prescribed by or are under this Act or any other written law where jurisdiction in the Commission is specifically provided."

Held: Environmental Commission

(11) The court was invited by FFOS to interpret the section as follows "The Commission has jurisdiction to hear appeals of all decisions and/or actions of the authority that are authorized by the Act".

(12) The judgment of Tindal CJ in the Sussex Peerage Case is instructive. He stated

"If the words of the Statute are in themselves precise and unambiguous, then no more can be necessary than to expound those words in their natural and ordinary sense. The words themselves alone do, in such a case, best declare the intention of the lawgiver."

(13) The sole object in statutory interpretation is to arrive at the legislative intention.

Parliament entrusts the courts with the task of spelling out its intent.

(14) The various texts on statutory interpretation are instructive. The learned author in Cross on Statutory Interpretation stated:

"The judge must give effect to the grammatical and ordinary or, where appropri-

ate the technical meaning of words in the general context of the statute; he must also determine the extent of the general words with reference to that context,"

(15) *In dealing with the grammatical meaning Bennion said:*

"The grammatical meaning of an enactment is its linguistic meaning taken in isolation from legal considerations, that is the meaning it bears when, as a piece of English prose, it is constructed according to the rules and usages of grammar, syntax and punctuation, and accepted linguistic canons of construction."

Bennion also identified several forms of ambiguity, one of which is syntactic ambiguity. Syntactic ambiguity, according to Bennion, arises from the grammatical relationship of words as they are chosen and arranged by the drafter.

(16) *When the literal rule of statutory interpretation is applied, the grammatical construction of section 81 (5) (a) is quite clear. The words "specifically authorized" qualify the words "decisions or actions", and as a consequence the court finds that it has jurisdiction to hear and determine, by way of appeal, any decision or action of the EMA.*

(17) *If, however, the court were to concede that there is an ambiguity in the wording of section 81 (5) (a), as evidenced by the submissions of counsel for both sides, then the ambiguity would be what Bennion describes as syntactic ambiguity, that is the grammatical relationship of the words as they are arranged by the drafter. In this instance, the positioning of the phrase "as specifically authorized" seems to have lent two different interpretations to the section.*

(18) *Bennion states that where an enactment is grammatically ambiguous, which may be a consequence of syntactic ambiguity, the legal meaning is the one to which on balancing the factors arising from the relevant interpretative criteria accord the greater weight. How does one then determine the legal meaning? The legal meaning, according to Bennion, corresponds to the grammatical meaning of the words, and the grammatical meaning of an enactment is its linguistic meaning taken in isolation from legal considerations. That is to say, "it is the meaning it bears when, as a piece of English prose, it is construed according to the rules and usage of grammar, syntax and punctuation, and the accepted canons of construction"*

(19) *In light of the above, when section 81 (5) (a) is examined, the proximity of the phrase "as specifically authorized" to the words "decisions and actions"*

has to be taken into consideration. The court finds that the words "specifically authorized" qualify the words "decisions or actions", and as a consequence the court concludes that it has jurisdiction to hear by way of appeal, any decision or action of the EMA.

(20) If it were the legislator's intent to limit the court's jurisdiction, then the phrase "as specifically authorized" would have been positioned after "appeals" in the section. In that instance the phrase "as specifically authorized" would have qualified "appeals" ,thus limiting the court's jurisdiction to hear and determine only those appeals specifically authorized by the Environmental Management Act of decisions or actions of the EMA.

(21) Dr. Ramlogan invited the court to use the purposive approach to interpret section 81(5) (a). This approach calls for the court to look to the debate as recorded in Hansard to glean what Parliament intended when it passed the Environmental Management Act. The House of Lords case of: -

Pepper v. Hart' is instructive; in that case Lord Browne-Wilkinson said that:

"...there is a general rule that references to parliamentary material as an aid to statutory construction is not permissible."

He went on to state that:

"...as a matter of law, there are sound reasons for making a limited modification to the existing rule....

parliamentary material should [only] be permitted as an as an aid to construction of legislation which is ambiguous or obscure or the literal meaning of which leads to an absurdity."

(22) The court holds that the words of section 81 (5) (a) are not obscure and even if there exists a syntactic ambiguity, there is no absurdity when the literal rule of interpretation is applied to the section. Consequently, we reject the submission of Dr. Ramlogan that the purposive approach to interpreting section 81 (5) (a) should be applied.

(23)The court having regard to the foregoing, finds that on the application of the literal rule of interpretation, the grammatical construction of section 81 (5) (a) is quite clear the court has the jurisdiction to hear appeals of any decisions or

actions of the EMA which the Environmental Management Act has specifically authorized.

(24) *Hamel-Smith J.A. in Commercial Finance Company Limited v. Indira Ramsingh-Mahabir said:*

"I am fully aware that it is not the function of the Court to "legislate" but it certainly is its function to interpret fully the provisions of the Act to give effect to the intention of the legislature where this is manifest from the provisions of the Act as a whole.";

It is to be noted that the preamble of a written law shall be construed as a part thereof intended to assist in explaining the purport and object of the written law." When one looks at the preamble of the Environmental Management Act it states inter alia:

"...the Government is undertaking the establishment and operation of an Environmental Management Authority to co-ordinate , facilitate and oversee execution of the national environmental strategy and programmes, to promote public awareness of environmental concerns, and to establish an effective regulatory regime which will protect, enhance and conserve the environment:"

When one looks at the words "to establish an effective regulatory regime which will protect, enhance and conserve the environment", one sees that the EMA will of necessity be called upon, in furtherance of this mandate, to make decisions and take actions which would affect the environment. However, Parliament does not give the EMA unfettered authority to make these decisions or take actions; instead, it provided a check on the EMA's power by allowing appeals to the Commission from its decisions and actions which were authorized under the Environmental Management Act. It would be imprudent to construe those only certain decisions or actions were subject to appeal, to do so would create a situation where the EMA can act unfettered. There is no indication in the legislation that this was the intent of Parliament.

(26) *Consequently the Commission has the jurisdiction to hear an appeal against the decisions or actions of the EMA with respect to its:*

decision to stay a Notice of Violation; decision not to inform a complainant whether any subsequent/investigative/enforcement or other action had been taken in respect of the Notice of Violation; inaction or failure to make information requested by the Appellant available or to respond to a request for information in a timely manner; and iv*inaction or failure to hear and determine the said Notice of Violation in a timely manner.*

(27) *Dr. Ramlogan, counsel for FFOS argued in the alternative that the Commission has jurisdiction to hear and determine the decisions and actions of the EMA by the jurisdiction vested in it by section 81 (5) (i). Ms. Sharma, the counsel for the EMA was not of that view. Since it has already been determined that the court has jurisdiction pursuant to section 81 (5) (a) there is no need to go into those submissions at this time.*

Issue 2 - Does FFOS have locus standi before the court?

(28) *The court now has to consider whether or not FFOS has any locus standi. It is not in contention that FFOS brought to the attention of the EMA the fact that Atlantic LNG was in breach of an environmental requirement as provided for under section 62 of the Environmental Management Act, and as a consequence of this complaint the EMA issued a NOV.*

(29) *It is FFOS's contention that as the complainant which informed the EMA of the breach of the environmental requirement which resulted in the issuance of a NOV, it has a direct interest and a legitimate expectation that the NOV would be resolved according to law.*

(30) *It is further contended that the EMA having issued the NOV has deprived FFOS of the opportunity to bring any enforcement action such as a direct private action pursuant to section 69(1) of the Environmental Management Act against the violator. It is contended that the onus is on the EMA to carry out its duties in accordance with the law.*

FINDINGS

(36) *It is not in contention that FFOS in compliance with 69 (1) (a) gave written notice of a claimed violation of an environmental requirement to the Managing Director of the EMA. The EMA exercised its discretion under section 69(l) (c) and took action, in compliance with section 63 of the Environmental Management Act, against the claimed violator by issuing a NOV. By taking this action the EMA assumed responsibility for fully enforcing the NOV, and*

effectively precluded FFOS from pursuing any action before the Commission.

(37) *The court finds that FFOS had a legitimate expectation that the EMA would have pursued the enforcement of the NOV to its finality. The EMA's inaction in pursuing this enforcement has frustrated FFOS's right under the law to bring a complaint to the court by way of a civil action.*

(38) *The court will not stand by and allow the EMA's inaction to fetter the ability of an individual to bring an action to it. Parliament gave the citizens of the Republic of Trinidad and Tobago the ability to participate in the protection, conservation and management of the environment by providing for individuals or a group of individuals expressing a general interest in the environment to have standing before the Environmental Commission to take action against those who are perceived as being in breach of environmental requirements.*

(39) *The court therefore finds that FFOS had a legitimate expectation that the EMA would enforce the NOV. Having failed to do so FFOS has locus standi to appeal the EMA's decision not to pursue the enforcement of its NOV.*

The Environmental Commission returned to the matter of its jurisdiction and again ruled for a wider general jurisdiction.

South West Tobago Fisherman's Association v Environmental Management Authority[382]

Facts: (2) The EMA granted PGS Geophysical AS ("PGS") a certificate of environmental clearance ("The CEC"), Certificate Number 2224 of 2008, to carry out 2D Seismic Survey off the East, West and North Coast of Tobago for the exploration of crude oil or natural gas. The Authority granted this CEC subject to certain terms and conditions and stipulated that certain mitigation measures should be undertaken. (3)The Association, which represent a substantial number of fisher folk in Tobago, subsequently appealed to the Environmental Commission under Sections 81 (5) (a), (f) and (i) of the Act . The appeal includes several substantive grounds of appeal that do not need to be addressed in this ruling because the issues before us are one of locus standi and a request for a stay of the substantive proceedings.

---

382 EAP 004-2008.

Held: Environmental Commission- (8) Under the Act, the Association has locus standi to assert its claim against the t created the EMA and tasked it with, among other things, the establishment of an effective regulatory regime to protect, enhance and conserve the environment, the Act imbued the EMA with certain powers to make decisions and take actions in furtherance of this mandate. The Act also created a specialist superior court of record, the Commission, for the purpose of supporting and strengthening the role of the EMA. The EMA now has available to it the necessary institutional framework for enforcing its decisions, but the Act also created a mechanism for an aggrieved person to seek redress from a decision or action of the EMA, by way of appeal. To bring such an appeal, the aggrieved person, like the Association, must have proper locus standi. (9) Here, the Commission has locus standi under three sections of the Act: (i) Under Sections 81 (5) (a) of the Act because the Association is appealing a decision of action of the EMA; (ii) Under Sections 81 (5) (f) of the Act because the Association is appealing a decision made under 36 of the Act, and; (iii) Under Sections 81 (5) (i) because the Association is alleging that the EMA breached its duties and responsibilities arising under the Act at Sections 35, 36 and 37.

SECTIONS 81 (5) (A) OF THE ACT

(10) Under Sections 81 (5) (a), the Association has locus standi to assert its claim. The Commission has already interpreted section 81 (5) (a) as giving it the jurisdiction to hear and determine all appeals against decisions or actions of the EMA.

(11) Having regard to the foregoing, Counsel for the Association submitted that the EMA failed to act as it was required to do under Sections 35 and 36 of the Act and consequently an appeal for failure to act would lie with the Commission. These sections both make provision for how the EMA is to act when dealing with an application for a CEC. Section 35 (4) provides that:

The Authority in considering the application may ask for further information including, if required, an environmental impact assessment, in accordance with prescribed procedure.

Section 36(1) provides that:

After considering all relevant matters, including the comments or representations made during the public comment period, the Authority may issue a Certificate

310

subject to such terms and conditions as it thinks fit including the requirements to undertake appropriate mitigation measures.

(12) The Sections both require the EMA to take certain factors into consideration with respect to an application for a CEC and the issuance of a CEC respectively. Failure on the part of the EMA to act in accordance with the dictates of the section may well frustrate the interests of persons who may be affected by it action or lack of action. Certainly, these persons must have some legal recourse.

(13) The Commission, having determined in FFOS v EMA that it can hear appeals from any decision or action of the EMA, finds that the Association has locus standi to bring an appeal under Section 81 (5) (a) of the Act.

(14) Counsel for the EMA expressed the concern that by the assumption of jurisdiction by the Commission to hear appeals for all decisions or actions of the EMA was tantamount to authorizing the judicial review of decisions or actions of the EMA, through the back door. However, this concern is unwarranted, because the Commission on the hearing of an appeal can only dispose of it in a manner provided by the Act. The Commission has no power to give judicial review type relief. The Act at Section 86(3) provides that: -

.....The Commission may dispose of an appeal by –

a. *Dismissing it;*

b. *Allowing it;*

c. *Allowing it and modifying the decision or action of the Authority; or*

d. *Allowing it and referring the decision or action back to the Authority for reconsideration.*

The Association is not precluded from bringing a judicial review application to the High Court where the EMA may fail to take certain factors into consideration before it issues a CEC. However, Section 9 of the Judicial Review Act, Chapter 7:08 provides-

The court shall not grant leave to an applicant for judicial review of a decision where any other written law provides an alternative procedure to a question, review or appeal that decision, save in exceptional circumstances.

Having regard to the foregoing, the Association is entitled to challenge a decision or action of the EMA by way of appeal by the Commission.

(15) Counsel for the Association further submitted that the appealing to the Commission because the EMA failed in its obligation to monitor performance of the survey activity, which is required under Section 37 of the Act. Section 37 provides that the EMA must adequately monitor the performance of an approved activity:

The Authority shall monitor the performance of an activity to ensure compliance with any conditions in the Certificate, and to confirm that the performance of the activity is consistent with —

a. *The description provided in the application for a Certificate; and*

b. *The information provided in any environmental impact assessment*

(16) Under Section 37 of the Act if the EMA fails to monitor the performance of the activity to ensure compliance with the conditions in the CEC and a third party is affected what recourse does the third party have? It will not be in a position to enforce the terms of the CEC in the High Court because it is not a party to the CEC. It will not have any ground for relief by way of judicial review. Surely the third party must have some legal recourse. And that recourse is an appeal to the Commission.

(17) Here, the Commission holds that the Act imposed on obligation to monitor on the EMA. The EMA cannot shirk its responsibilities under the Act without consequences. The Act having created that unique responsibility for the EMA, also created a mechanism to ensure that the EMA upheld its responsibilities, that is, by way of appeal to the Commission under Section 81 (5) (a).

(18) Consequently, because the EMA failed to act properly when considering the CEC application and when monitoring the subsequent survey performance, the Association, based on the Commission's interpretation of Section 81 (5) (a), has locus standi to bring this claim.

SECTION 81 (5) (F) OF THE ACT

(19) Under Section 81(5) (f), the Association has locus standi to assert its claim. Counsel for the Association submitted that the Association can appeal a decision

of the EMA under Section 81 (5) (f) of the Act. The Commission considered this submission and finds that the provisions of Section 36 are quite clear in that the EMA must take certain actions prior to the grant of a CEC and the EMA may issue it subject to terms and conditions.

(20) Section 36 gives a discretionary power to the EMA. It may issue a CEC subject to terms and conditions including requirements to undertake appropriate mitigation methods. When exercising this discretion the EMA is required to act judiciously, prudently and fairly. If this discretion is improperly exercised, then the decision or action flowing there from will be subject to appeal to the Commission under Section 81 (5) (f). Consequently, the Association has locus standi to bring an appeal from a decision made under Section 36 of the Act by way of appeal under Section 81 (5) (f).

SECTION 81 (5) (I) OF THE ACT

(20) Under Section 81 (5) (i), the Association has locus standi to assert its claim. Section 81 (5) (i) provides another avenue for bringing an action to the Commission. This section states: -

The Commission shall have jurisdiction to hear and determine -

i. Such other matters that may be prescribed by or arise under this Act or any other written law where jurisdiction in the Commission is specifically provided.

(21) When the principles of sentence construction are applied to the wording above section, it is obvious that the Act describes three categories of matters that can be heard and determined, each category being separated by the word "or" which suggest that they are separate items over which jurisdiction is to be had. Therefore the Commission can hear and determine, firstly such other matters as may be prescribed by the Act, as for example under Rule 4(1) (b) the CEC Rules, secondly matters that arise under the Act , and thirdly, matters under any other written law where jurisdiction of the Commission is specifically provided. We will deal only with the issue of "matter arising" under the Act.

(22) In dealing with matters which arise under the Act, regard has been had to the High Court decision in the Australian case of The King v. The Commonwealth Court of Conciliation and Others, Ex parte Barrett

(23) In Ex parte Barrett, the court had to interpret the phrase "arising under" with respect to a provision in the Commonwealth Constitution which read:

The Parliament may make laws conferring original jurisdiction on the High Court in any matter -

i. Arising under this Constitution, or involving its interpretation.

ii. Arising under any laws made by the Parliament.

In interpreting the phrase "arising under", the Court held that a right or duty would arise under a law if that right or duty owed its existence to the particular law or depends on the law for its enforcement. Specifically, Latham CJ held the following:

[A] matter may arise under the Constitution without involving the interpretation, and that a case may involve the interpretation of the Constitution without arising under the Constitution. Paragraph (ii) is limited to matters arising under Federal statutes, and does not extend to matters involving the interpretation of such statutes if they do not arise there under. This variation in language supports the view that, in order to bring a matter within s 76 (ii) – which is the relevant provision in the present case – the inquiry to be made is not whether the determination of the matter involves the interpretation of a Federal law.

The relevant inquiry is whether the matter arises under the law. Thus one is compelled to the conclusion that a matter may properly be said to arise under a Federal law if the right or duty in question in the matter owes its existence to Federal law or depends upon Federal law for its enforcement, whether or not the determination for the controversy involves the interpretation (or validity) of the law.....If a right claim is conferred by or under a Federal statute, the claim arises under our stature (our emphasis).

(24) We accept this interpretation of "arising under" and apply it to "matters arise" in this case. We find therefore that, under Sections 35, 36 and 37, the Act gave rise to duties and obligations of the EMA that the EMA is required to discharge. Further, we find that the duties and obligations that the EMA must execute are enforceable against it under the Act.

(25) Therefore, the Commission holds that the Association has locus standi to as-

sert its claim under Sections 81(5) (i), as well as Sections 81(5) (a) and Sections 81(5)(f) and the EMA's contention to the contrary is rejected.

The Association, contrary to the EMA's submission, cannot initiate a direct private party action.

(26) Indeed an appeal is the only proper way for the Association to proceed in this case, because contrary to the EMA's position, it cannot initiate a direct private party action against the EMA.

(27) Counsel for the EMA submitted that the proper avenue for redress for the Association before the Commission would be by means of a direct private party action under Section 69 of the Act, alleging that the EMA has breached an environmental requirement.

(28) The Commission rejects this submission since the matters complained of do not fall within the ambit of Section 69. Section 69 provides, inter alia , that :

Any private party may institute a civil action in the Commission against any other person for a claimed violation of any of the specified environmental require-ments identified in Section 62, other than paragraphs (c), (d) and (l).....

It is obvious that what is contemplated at Section 69 is that a private party can bring an action against a person who is in breach of an environmental require-ment. However, the term "person" in Section 62 does not include the EMA. We say this based on the provisions in the Act that have vested the EMA with enforcement powers. Section 63 of the Act provides that where the EMA rea-sonably believes that a person is in violation of an environmental requirement, it can take certain actions. Sections 64 to 68 empower the EMA to take enforce-ment action against a person who has violated an environmental requirement, by issuing against the violators, Notices of Violation, Administrative Orders and Civil Assessments.

The Court of Appeal examined both decisions of the Environmental Commission on the issue of its general jurisdiction and has overruled the Environmental Commission by deciding to limit the general jurisdictional provisions of *Sections 81(5)(a) and 8(5)(i) of the Environmental Management Act* to decisions in the *Environmental Management Act* where there are specific references to appeals to the Environmental Commission in addition to jurisdictions in instances identified in Sections *81(5)(b) to 8(5)(h) of the Environmental Management Act.*

Environmental Management Authority v Fishermen and Friends of the Sea (Court of Appeal)[383] and Environmental Management Authority v. South West Tobago Fisherman's Association (Court of Appeal)[384]

Facts: In the first appeal, Atlantic LNG Company began construction work in furtherance of a liquification of natural gas project without having obtained a Certificate of Environmental Clearance as required by the law. This non-compliance was brought to the attention of the Authority by the Respondent in May 2003 by a formal complaint and the Authority then issued a Notice of Violation pursuant to section 63 of the Act to Atlantic LNG. Subsequently, in August 2004 at the request of Atlantic LNG the Authority stayed the NOV. The Respondent discovered that this stay had been granted and by Notice of Appeal filed in June 2007 appealed to the Commission against the decisions and/or actions of the Authority: (i) to stay the NOV, (ii) not to inform the Respondent of the actions taken by it with respect to the NOV, (iii) in a failure to supply the Respondent with information requested, and (iv) in a failure to deal with the NOV as prescribed by section 63 (2) of the Act. (h)5. In the second appeal, the Authority issued a CEC to Petroleum Geophysical A.S. in June 2008, to carry out a seismic survey off the coast of Tobago for the exploration of crude oil and natural gas. In July 2008 the Respondent wrote to the Authority complaining about PGS's noncompliance with parts of the CEC and an alleged breach by the Authority of its duty to monitor the performance of and ensure compliance with any conditions in the CEC (pursuant to section 37 of the Act). In December 2008 the Respondent brought an appeal before the Commission against the Authority pursuant to sub-sections 81 (5) (a), (f) and (i) of the Act. 6. In both appeals the issues raised concern mainly the jurisdiction of the Commission and the locus standi of the Respondents under three sub-sections of the Act.

Held: Jamadar JA (Unanimous Decision)

RULINGS OF THE COMMISSION

---

383 Civ Appeal No. 199 of 2008
384 Civ Appeal No. 219 of 2009

7. In the first appeal the Commission made the following rulings. On the issue of jurisdiction, the Commission interpreted sub-section 81 (5) (a) of the Act as conferring jurisdiction on it. The Commission came to this conclusion having relied on their interpretation of the ordinary meaning of the words read in the context of their grammatical meaning and the legislators' intentions as gleaned from the Act, and it determined that the words "specifically authorized" qualified the words "decisions or actions" in the sub-section. On the issue of locus standi, the Commission determined, that the Authority having assumed responsibility for issuing a NOV (against Atlantic LNG) upon complaint by the Respondent and having done so, that action created in the Respondent a legitimate expectation that the Authority would pursue this process in accordance with the provisions of the Act. And, that the alleged failure of the Authority to do so conferred in the Respondent the necessary locus standi to appeal to the Commission.

8. The Commission also determined that it did not have the jurisdiction to make prerogative orders and in particular orders for certiorari or mandamus. However, the Commission opined that matters filed in the High Court seeking judicial review of the decisions or actions of the Authority can properly be heard by the Commission by way of appeal (pursuant to the jurisdiction conferred on it by sub-section 81 (5) (a) of the Act), and went further to state that in any such matters "leave to an applicant for judicial review should be denied and the parties should be referred to the correct forum, the Environmental Commission".

9. In the second appeal the Commission ruled that the Commission had jurisdiction under any one and/or all of sub-sections 81 (5) (a), (f) and (i) of the Act, and that the Respondent had locus standi accordingly. That is, the Respondent had locus standi because, under sub-section 81 (5) (a) it was appealing a decision or action of the Authority, under sub-section 81 (5) (f) it was appealing a decision of the Authority under section 36 of the Act, and under sub-section 81 (5) (i) it was alleging that the Authority had breached its duties and responsibilities under sections 35, 36 and 37 of the Act (that is, in relation to matters prescribed by or arising under the Act).

THE FIRST APPEAL

(I) Section 81 (5) (a) of the Act

10. This issue raises for determination the proper interpretation to be given to sub-section 81 (5) (a) of the Act. Specifically, the question for determination is whether the words "as specifically authorized under this Act" qualify the word "appeals" or the words "from decisions or actions of the Authority", as they appear in sub-section 81 (5) (a) of the Act. The sub-section states as follows:

(5) The Commission shall have jurisdiction to hear and determine —

(a) Appeals from decisions or actions of the Authority as specifically authorized

under this Act;

11. In my opinion the words "as specifically authorized under this Act", qualify the word "appeals". Therefore, under sub-section 81 (5) (a) of the Act, the Commission has jurisdiction to hear and determine only appeals (from decisions or actions of the Authority) that are specifically authorized under the Act.

12. This is so for several reasons. On the basis of purely grammatical and textual considerations, this is the best construction to be given to sub-section 81 (5) (a) of the Act. It is accepted that on a purely literal interpretation, the sub-section permits a measure of ambiguity as evidenced by the competing arguments. However, I am of the view that the word "appeals" operates as the primary object noun in sub-section (5) (a) and as such is the object noun that is qualified by the words "as specifically authorized under this Act". The word "as" in the subsection functions as a preposition and therefore points to the relationship between the primary object noun ("appeals") and the rest of the sentence following the preposition "as" ("specifically authorized under this act").

13. Therefore, when one asks the question: Appeals from what? The sub-section answers: From decisions or actions of the Authority. But, when one asks the question: What does the Commission have jurisdiction to hear and determine? The answer is: "Appeals (from decisions and actions of the Authority) as specifically authorized under this Act".

14. In my opinion, the Commission was therefore wrong in law to construe sub-section 81 (5) (a) of the Act as conferring jurisdiction on the Commission to hear appeals from all or any decisions or actions of the Authority and/or any such decisions or actions as specifically authorized under the Act.

15. However, since I have accepted a reasonable measure of grammatical ambiguity in the sub-section, it is my view that the construction and interpretation that

I have adopted is to be preferred for several other and cumulatively reinforcing reasons.

16. *First, the interpretation given to the sub-section by the Commission could not likely have been the intention of Parliament when one considers the provision in its broader textual context. If the interpretation of the Commission is correct then sub-sections (5) (e), (f) and (g) would all be rendered superfluous. Further, when one reads sub-section (5) (a) in the context of sections 81 (1), 81 (3), 81 (5) (i) and also section 85 (1) and (3), and the consistently declared intention in the Act to limit the jurisdiction of the Commission to circumstances where that jurisdiction is "conferred upon it by this Act", "as specifically authorized under this act", and "specifically provided," and where every appeal "shall be filed within twenty-eight days of the service on the person seeking to appeal the decisions of the Authority ... or within such other time as may be prescribed ...", it is to my mind apparent that the intention of Parliament was to limit appeals to those which are specifically authorized by the Act. That is to say, for the time being, to those actions and decisions taken by the Authority under sections 23 (3), 30, 40, 46 48 (4), and 65 (2) of the Act.*

17. *It is to be noted that in all of the situations in which appeals are specifically authorized in the Act, except for an appeal pursuant to section 46 and sub-section 81 (5) (e), in every instance where the Act creates the right of appeal it also specifies who is entitled to appeal. In the case of section 46, I am of the view that because section 41 of the Act deals with the designation of certain portions of the environment as an "environmentally sensitive area" and with the designation of any plants or animals as an "environmentally sensitive species" requiring special protection, and because any such designation must be published in the Gazette (and would thereby be public notification of the particular designation), it is clear that by reason of the public notification of the designation it is intended that any member of the public is to be given the right to appeal. Therefore, in the case of section 46 there was obviously no need to specify who in particular is entitled to appeal. Any person is permitted to appeal to the Commission from designations made by the Authority pursuant to section 41 of the Act.*

18. *This understanding confirms, in the context of sub-section 81 (5) (a) and related provisions, that the intention of Parliament was to confer jurisdiction in the Commission in relation only to appeals in those circumstances specifically au-*

thorized under the Act. That is to say, sub-section 81 (5) (a) operates somewhat as an enabling section. It confers jurisdiction in the Commission where certain persons are granted the locus standi in the Act to appeal particular decisions or actions of the Authority.

19. Second, the interpretation given to this sub-section by the Commission can lead to absurdity, and Parliament is presumed to intend that legislation makes sense and is reasonable. In my opinion the interpretation given by the Commission to sub-section 81 (5) (a) can lead to results that are manifestly illogical, counter-productive and senseless.

20. The most obvious illustration of absurdity on the construction given by the Commission, is that appeals could only be entertained from decisions or actions that are "specifically authorized". The result is that there can be no appeal against decisions or actions taken by the Authority that are unauthorized! Such a result is illogical and senseless, because if jurisdiction was being conferred to hear appeals from all actions and decisions of the Authority, then surely Parliament would have intended that unauthorized actions or decisions be included.

21. Further, if the interpretation given by the Commission were to be followed, the result would be that every authorized action or decision of the Authority could be subject to an appeal to the Commission. This would therefore include every possible decision or action taken by the Authority. For example, decisions or actions taken under section 34 of the Act, which deals with the development, promotion and implementation of environmental incentive programmes. It would also include pure administrative decisions or actions, such as those taken under section 9 (delegation of functions or powers), section 11 (appointment of personnel), section 20 (general powers linked to performance of functions) and section 21 (appointment of inspectors). Finally, since the Authority is a body corporate governed by a Board of Directors (section 6 (1) of the Act), is it that all authorized decisions or actions of the Board are also subject to an appeal to the Commission? And if so, under the Freedom of Information Act, is it that all decision or actions of the Board are to be disclosed upon request according to law? In my opinion none of the above could have been the result intended by Parliament when it enacted sub-section 81 (5) (a) of the Act.

22. Third, the status of the Commission as a superior court of limited jurisdiction supports the interpretation given by this court to sub-section 81 (5) (a) of the Act. The Authority is clearly a public authority discharging a public function. It is also in this context an inferior tribunal for the purposes of public law. As such any decisions and/or actions taken by the Authority are potentially reviewable by way of judicial review proceedings in the usual manner. That is to say, any such review is governed by the Judicial Review Act, the relevant rules of procedure, the common law principles that inform this right of action and the constitutional mandate of the Supreme Court (as a court of unlimited jurisdiction with power to exercise judicial supervision and governance over all public authorities that are subject to public law). Any person who has the necessary standing and is not otherwise barred and who may not have access to the Commission to challenge decisions of the Authority, will be generally entitled to invoke the jurisdiction of the Supreme Court to judicially review the decisions or actions of the Authority. Such actions under the existing regime of the CPR, 1998 are generally heard in a timely and expeditious manner. In addition, in any such actions the courts enjoy the plenitude of powers that a court of unlimited jurisdiction is vested with, to make such orders and shape such remedies as are necessary to do justice in a particular case. And finally, all such proceedings are subject to the Constitutional and procedural safeguards and regimes that exist to ensure that the process of judicial review is fair and timely and in service of good public administration.

23. Therefore the construction and interpretation given in this judgment to sub-section 81 (5) (a) of the Act does not deprive any person of their constitutional rights to access to justice and the protection of the law. The assertion by the Commission that it is vested with the jurisdiction to deal with all reviews of the decisions and actions of the Authority and to claim this through sub-section 81 (5) (a) seems, with the greatest respect to its members, to be overreaching its limited jurisdiction.

24. In this regard I think the following comment of Baroness Hale in Suratt & Ors v The Attorney General of Trinidad and Tobago, in relation to the Equal Opportunity Tribunal established under the Equal Opportunity Act, 2000, is apt:

But the EOA clearly does not contemplate that the Tribunal should have an unlimited or inherent jurisdiction. Its jurisdiction is limited by section 41 (4) ... The powers in section 41 (4) (b) and (c) are clearly intended to be used, and used only, in connection with the jurisdiction conferred by section 41 (4) (a). If there were any doubt about that, these paragraphs should be interpreted so as to be in conformity with the Constitution. Their scope is in any event defined by the EOA in the circumstances prescribed by the EOA.

25. It is to be noted that the Equal Opportunity Tribunal, established by section 41 (1) of the Equal Opportunity Act, was established as a superior court of record using language almost identical to that used in section 81 (3) of the Act.

26. In my opinion the interpretation that I have given to sub-section 81 (5) (a) of the Act fits in with the general scheme of the Act and also with the establishment of the Commission as a superior court of record with limited jurisdiction. That is to say, and in so far as precedent is concerned and by way of analogy, the approach taken to the interpretation of sub-section 81 (5) (a) of the Act is consistent with the approach taken by the Privy Council to tribunals which are established by statute and are considered superior courts of limited jurisdiction.

27. Fourth, the effect of the interpretation given to sub-section 81 (5) (a) of the Act by this Court, appropriately limits the jurisdiction of the Commission without denying any person access to justice or the protection of the law. In this way the Authority is subject to both the general supervisory jurisdiction of the Supreme Court and also the limited jurisdiction of the Commission in relation to decisions and actions taken or omitted to be taken by it. The device which determines the appropriate course of action is section 9 of the Judicial Review Act. Generally speaking, matters which can properly be heard and determined by the Commission in the first instance are to be taken up before that court. And, again generally speaking, matters for which there are no alternative procedures available to question the impugned decisions or actions, may be reviewable by way of judicial review in the usual manner.

(II) LOCUS STANDI

28. In relation to the first appeal, it is noteworthy that the Respondent in this appeal has not been able to identify in its grounds of complaint (appeal) any decision or action of the Authority "specifically authorized under the Act". Therefore, in my opinion the Commission was wrong in law in its interpretation of sub-section 81 (5) (a) of the Act and in its application on this basis to the Respondent, so as to vest jurisdiction in itself to hear the appeal and/or locus standi in the Respondent to bring the appeal.

29. The first appeal is therefore allowed.

30. On the question of costs the Court will hear arguments from the parties before arriving at a decision.

THE SECOND APPEAL -

(I) SECTION 81 (5) (A) OF THE ACT

31. The discussion above also disposes of the first issue in relation to sub-section 81 (5) (a) in this appeal. That is to say, the Commission was wrong in its interpretation of sub-section 81 (5) (a) as to the jurisdiction that it conferred on the Commission and/or in its view that the subsection vested locus standi in the Respondent.

(II) SECTION 81 (5) (F) OF THE ACT

32. The sub- section states as follows:

5. The Commission shall have jurisdiction to hear and determine – (f) appeals from a decision by the Authority under section 36 to refuse to issue a Certificate of environmental clearance or to grant such a Certificate with conditions;

33. In light of the discussion in relation to sub-section 81 (5) (a) above, it is my opinion that the right of appeal under the Act is limited to those persons upon whom the right is specifically conferred. In relation to sub-section 81 (5) (f), a decision under section 36 to refuse to issue a CEC or to grant a CEC with conditions, the right of appeal is specifically given to "the person seeking such certificate", as provided for in section 40 of the Act. Therefore, in so far as this Respondent is attempting to appeal the Authority's decisions or actions in relation to the granting on conditions of a CEC, it has no such right of appeal and no locus standi to appeal to the Commission on this matter.

(III) SECTION 81 (5) (I) OF THE ACT

34. The sub-section states as follows:

5. The Commission shall have jurisdiction to hear and determine –

(i) such other matters as may be prescribed by or arise under this Act or any other written law where jurisdiction in the Commission is specifically provided.

35. In my opinion, the jurisdiction of the Commission that is conferred by this sub-section is limited to "such other matters ... where jurisdiction in the Commission is specifically provided". It is to be noted that this sub-section does not state that it provides access to the Commission by way of appeal. I am of the view that the word "matters" is the primary noun object of the subsection and is qualified by the phase "where jurisdiction in the Commission is specifically provided". This is so for the same and analogous textual and interpretative reasons that were articulated above in relation to sub-section 81 (5) (a).

36. When one asks the question: What other matters? The answer that the sub-section provides is: Such other matters "as may be prescribed by or arise under this Act or any other written law". However, when one asks about jurisdiction, that is, what jurisdiction is vested in the Commission? The answer is as stated above.

37. In my opinion the sub-section is conferring a jurisdiction in the Commission to hear and determine all or any matters which are prescribed by and/or arise under the Act or any other written law, but only where the jurisdiction in the Commission to hear such matters is specifically provided for. The discussion above in relation to sub-section 81 (5) (a) is apposite and will not be repeated, save to say that it applies in totality to the approach taken in interpreting this sub-section.

38. In my opinion the Commission was therefore wrong in law in its interpretation of subsection 81 (5) (i) of the Act and in its application on this basis to the Respondent, so as to vest jurisdiction in itself to hear the appeal and/or locus standi in the Respondent to bring the appeal. The matters challenged by the Respondent were simply not matters in which jurisdiction and/or locus standi can be vested in the Commission or the Respondent.

JURISDICTIONAL CONFLICT BETWEEN SUPREME COURT AND ENVIRONMENTAL COMMISSION

The High Court has ruled that it will not exercise jurisdiction in matters which fall exclusively within the remit of the Environmental Commission.

South West Tobago Fisherman's Association v The Attorney General of Trinidad & Tobago House of Assembly, Environmental Man-

agement Authority and Petroleum Geo-Services Limited[385]

*Facts: This case raises the question of the jurisdiction of the High Court with respect to liabilities created by the Environmental Management Act Chap.35:05. ("the Act"). The Claimant, the Southwest Fishing Association, is a limited liability company. Its members, described as "fisher folk", approximately 60 in number, are registered with the Fisheries Division of the Tobago House of Assembly. The Claimant alleges that its members are the users of and have an economic interest in the traditional fishing grounds off the Tobago coast ("the traditional fishing grounds"). PGS Ltd. intended to conduct seismic surveys in the traditional fishing grounds and for that purpose was required by the Act to apply for a Certificate of Environmental Clearance ("CEC") from the Authority. During the period the 1*st* to 6*th* June 2008 PGS Ltd. held meetings with Tobago fisher folk, some of whom were members of the Claimant. At those meetings PGS Ltd advised that as part of the requirements to obtain a CEC it was required to hold consultations with fisher folk, fishing communities and organisations. At those meetings PGS Ltd. made various presentations to the effect that the conduct of seismic surveys in the area would have no effect on the fishing in the area and that if it did compensation would be paid. The members of the Claimant were not satisfied with the representations made by PGS Ltd. and advised the meetings of their dissatisfaction. They were advised by PGS Ltd. that it would continue the discussions in an attempt to assuage their fears. The Claimant's case therefore is based on a breach by PGS Ltd. of a condition in their CEC; the failure of the Authority to properly monitor the licensed activities of PGS Ltd. and the negligence of the State and the THA in allowing the licensing of such activity. The Claimant also claims, as against the State and the THA that the grant of such a license is a wrongful interference with the business relations of it and its members. With respect to the relief sought by this action, declarations apart, the Claimant seeks damages and an injunction.*

Held: Jones J

19. In so far as the jurisdiction of the High Court is concerned the start must be the dicta of Willes J. in The Wolverhamptom New Waterworks Company v Hawkesford (1859) 6 C.B.(N.S.) 336 at 356:

---

385 CV 2008-02926

"There are three cases in which a liability may be established founded upon a statute. One is, where there is a liability existing at common law, and that liability is affirmed by a statute which gives a special and peculiar form of remedy different from the remedy which existed at common law: there, unless the statute contains words which expressly or by necessary implication exclude the common

—law remedy the party suing has his election to pursue either that or the statutory remedy. The second class of cases is, where the statute gives the right to sue, merely, but provides no form of remedy: there the party can only proceed by action at common law. But there is a third class viz. where a liability not existing at common law is created by a statute which at the same time gives a special and particular remedy for enforcing it. ....The remedy provided by the statute must be followed, and it is not competent to the party to pursue the course applicable to cases of the second class. The form given by the statute must be adopted and adhered to."

20. In my opinion this is the approach which ought to be adopted. Using this approach, it is necessary to examine the provisions of the Act as well as the nature of the relief sought by the Claimant to ascertain whether the liability sued upon was created by the Act and if so whether the Act creates a special and particular remedy for enforcing it. If the answer to both these questions is yes, then the Claimants are out of court at least with respect to those liabilities founded upon the Act.

21. To put the application in its proper context and prior to a detailed examination of the relevant sections it may be more appropriate to give a general overview of the Act. The Act establishes a regulatory framework for the management of the environment by the State. In this regard the Authority is designated the body to perform the function of environmental management on behalf of the State. To this end the Act mandates that the composition of the board of directors of the Authority reflect various disciplines which in the opinion of the legislators are necessary to ensure the proper management of the environment.

22. For the purposes of the Act environmental control is divided into six distinct categories: protection of natural resources; pollution and hazardous substances; air and noise pollution; water pollution; wastes and hazardous substances and spills. In addition, for the purpose of control and determining the impact of certain activities on the environment the Minister responsible for environmental management ("the Minister") is empowered by the Act to designate a list of activities which require a licence, termed in the Act, a certificate of environmental clearance. One of the duties of the Authority is to issue such licences and to monitor the performance of the licensed activity to ensure compliance with the terms and conditions of the CEC.

23. The Act also establishes a specialist tribunal, the Environmental Commission ("the Commission"), vested by the Act with the powers of a superior court of record and with all the powers inherent in such a court. Its function is to assist in the enforcement of the decisions of the Authority and to provide a forum whereby appeals from such decisions may be heard. The Commission is also empowered by the Act to deal with civil actions by private parties for the violation of certain specified environmental requirements. These civil actions are referred to in the Act as 'direct private party actions'. In addition, the Act authorises both the Authority and the Commission to make assessments of compensation, termed "administrative civil assessment", for certain of the damage suffered by virtue of breaches of the Act.

24. Section 81 of the Act establishes the Commission and delimits its jurisdiction. In particular section 81(5) states:

"(5) T h e Commission shall have the jurisdiction to hear and determine-

(a) appeals from decisions or actions of the Authority as specifically authorised by under this Act;

(b) applications for deferment of decisions made under section 2 or deferment of designations made under section 41;

(c) applications made by the Authority for the enforcement of any Consent Agreement of any final Administrative Order, as provided in section 67;

(d) administrative civil assessments under section 66;

(e) appeals from the designation of environmentally sensitive areas or environmentally sensitive species" by the Authority pursuant to section 41;

(f) appeals from a decision by the Authority under section 36 to refuse to issue a certificate of environmental clearance or to grant such a Certificate

327

with conditions;

(g) *appeals from any determination by the Authority to disclose information or materials claimed as a trade secret or confidential business information under section 23(3);*

(h) *complaints brought by persons pursuant to section 69 otherwise known as the direct private party action provision and*

(i) *such other matters as may be prescribed by or arise under this Act or any other written law where jurisdiction in the Commission is specifically provided.*

25. By section 82, the Chairman and Deputy Chairman apart, the members of the Commission shall "be qualified by virtue of their knowledge of, or experience in environmental issues, engineering, the natural sciences or the social sciences.": section 82(3). Both the Chairman and Deputy Chairman are required to be Attorneys at Law. With respect to the decisions of the Commission, the Act provides that such decisions shall be final on a question of fact and the amount of any administrative civil assessment. An appeal shall however lie on any question of law to the Court of Appeal: sections 86(5) and 89(11).

26. By section 37 of the Act the Authority is required to monitor the performance of the licensed activity to ensure compliance with the conditions of the CEC and the information provided in any environmental impact assessment. Sections 63 to 65 empower the Authority, by way of the issue of a notice of violation or an administrative order, to ensure compliance with its environmental requirements. The exercise of this power is triggered once the Authority reasonably believes that a person is in violation of an environmental requirement

27. The first step is a notice of violation: section 63. The notice of violation shall include a request that the person make modifications to the activity or representations to the Authority with respect to the violations. Upon a failure to resolve the violation at this stage the Authority may issue an Administrative Order with directions aimed at ensuring compliance with the terms and conditions of the CEC: section 65. These directions include the power to direct that the violation immediately cease or that the offender immediately remedy the damage: section 65 (1)(b)

28. The directions contained in the Administrative Order are deemed to be final

and conclusive after the expiry of 28 days unless (i) an extension of time for compliance is granted by the Authority; (ii) a consent agreement is arrived at or (iii) an appeal to the Commission is filed. An Administrative Order may also include a proposed administrative civil assessment.

29. In addition to its powers of enforcement by way of an Administrative Order, where it reasonably believes that a person is currently in violation of any environmental requirement, the EMA may seek a restraining order or other injunctive relief or an order for the closure of any facility: section 68 With respect to the payment of compensation for breaches of the Act, by section 66, both the Authority, for the purpose of an administrative order, and the Commission, pursuant to section 81(5)(d), may make an administrative civil assessment of:

• compensation for actual costs incurred by the Authority in responding to environmental conditions or circumstances arising out of violations referenced in the administrative order;

• compensation for damages to the environment associated with public lands or holdings which arise out of the violation referenced in the Administrative order;

• damages for any economic benefit or amount saved by any person through failure to comply with applicable environmental requirements and

• damages for the failure of a person to comply with applicable environmental requirements in an amount which shall not exceed (i) in the case of an individual $5,000.00 for each violation or in the case of a continuing violation $1,000.00 a day for each such instance, (ii) in the case of a person other than an individual, $10,000.00 for each violation or in the case of a continuing violation $5,000.00 a day for each such instance.

30. This compensation is only enforceable upon the Commission making an order determining the amount of such assessment: section 67(2).

31. Pursuant to section 67 therefore compensation for breaches of liabilities established by the Act are only enforceable if awarded by the Commission. Further, save insofar as section 66(d) may resemble damages properly so called, the compensation provided by section 66 is with respect to (i) compensation for the cost incurred by the Authority in responding to the damage caused by the breach or (ii) compensation for the damage to the environment with respect to public lands or holdings; or (iii) in the nature of a penalty quantified by refer-ence to the money saved by the offender in not complying with the environmental requirement. Insofar as section 66(d) may allow the payment of compensation

related to the actual damage suffered by a person it must be noted that in this instance the damages or compensation awardable is not at large but the Act provides an upper limit with respect to such compensation measurable by the character of the offender and the period of time the violation continues rather than the damage suffered.

(1) Section 69 of the Act deals with civil actions by private parties termed 'direct private party actions'. It provides: Any private party may institute a civil action in the Commission against any other person for a claimed violation of any of the specified environmental requirements identified in section 62, other than paragraphs (c), (d), and (l) save where:

a. the Complainant has given written notice of such claimed violation to the Managing Director of the Authority at least sixty days prior to the commence-ment of the civil action;

b. the complainant has served a copy of the complaint on the Managing Director within 28 days of the date of which the complainant was first authorised to bring such an action.

c. The Authority has not commenced an enforcement action under sections 63 to 67 inclusive or through other appropriate means available to it under section 68 regarding such claimed violation; and

d. The Authority has not elected to assume responsibility for taking enforce-ment action under sections 63 to 68 inclusive within sixty days after the filing of a direct private party action by the complainant.

32. While not a matter for me the drafting of the provisions dealing with the access to the Commission by the private citizen by way of direct private party action leaves much to be desired. It is clear however that by the use of the words "in the Commission" the civil action referred to by section 69 are complaints brought by private persons or bodies to the Commission referred to in section 81(5)(h) as 'direct private party actions'. With respect to direct private party actions section 89(2) provides: "The Commission shall not have jurisdiction over any private party action unless the complainant has given proper notice to the Authority of not less than sixty days before bringing such action as required under section 69".

33. It is clear therefore that the Act provides that the primary responsibility for ensuring compliance with the requirements of the Act lies with the Authority. In this regard it is the Authority which is endowed with certain coercive powers to ensure compliance with the Act. In addition, the Act vests the right to apply for a restraining or similar order in the Authority. In contrast while the Act allows for actions by private parties for claimed violations of certain environmental requirements such action is by the Act subject to certain constraints. In the first place the action must be brought in the Commission. In the second place the right of a private party to sue is limited to certain violations. Further, unlike damages awardable by the civil court, the compensation payable to the private party for the breach of an environmental requirement is limited with respect to the quantum allowable to a specific amount per day for each violation.

34. While section 69 of the Act is not the best drafted section it is clear that the intention is that in order to pursue such an action, the private party must give the Authority sufficient notice of the alleged violation, at least 60 days, so as to allow the Authority the opportunity to assume the responsibility for taking enforcement action. It is only if the Authority fails to take enforcement action that the civil action can be pursued.

35. It is undisputable that the Act creates new liabilities where none previously existed. It is equally indisputable that there is contained in the Act a means of enforcing these new liabilities and providing remedies for the breaches. Consistent with the intention of the Act some of these new liabilities are enforceable only by the Authority while others, subject to the right of the Authority to assume responsibility for the enforcement of these liabilities, are enforceable by private persons.

36. Further it is clear that while the intention of the legislature is to have all of the remedies established by the Act for a breach of the liabilities created by it available to the Authority the remedies available to private parties are limited notably with respect to the non-availability of the remedy of injunction and the limits to compensation awardable. Despite this it seems to me that the situation falls squarely under the third category identified by Willes J in the

Wolverhampton case. The Act creates new liabilities not existing at common law and at the same time gives special and particular remedies for enforcing same. In the instant case the remedies given by the Act must be followed. In this regard I note that this conclusion was also arrived at by Master Doyle with respect to the liabilities created by the Act in the case of Karan Ramlal v Simon Macoon and Indira Ramsanahie HCA No. 2812 of 2004.

37. Declarations apart the Claimant seeks injunctive relief, both restraining and mandatory, and damages. With respect to the liabilities created by the Act the remedy of injunction is by the Act limited to the Authority. Further by deeming the Commission a superior court of record, in my opinion, the power to grant such an injunction is with respect to the liabilities created by the Act limited to the Commission. Similarly, the ability to provide compensation or damages for breaches of the Act termed in the Act administrative civil assessments is, by section 67 vested in the Commission alone.

38. With respect to the declarations sought in this action, declarations 1 to 5 deal either with the economic interests of the Claimant in the traditional fishing grounds or the liability of the First and Second Defendants under other legislation, declarations 6 to 8 however, in my opinion, are based on liabilities created by the Act. In those circumstances I am of the opinion that this Court has no jurisdiction to make these declarations nor to award damages pursuant to such declarations. In my opinion even if the Court had the jurisdiction to make the declarations or award the damages sought given the fact that Parliament has in its wisdom by the Act established a specialist tribunal to deal with these very matters this Court would decline to exercise jurisdiction.

39. With respect to the declaration sought at paragraph 9, in my view, as drafted this declaration may apply equally to the liabilities created by the Act as well as the liabilities referred to in declarations 1 to 5. The position is the same with respect to the claim for damages and compensation made at paragraphs 12 and 13 of the Claim Form.

ALTERNATIVE REMEDY

When there are allegations of a breach of the *Environmental Management Act* and another statutory requirement, the High Court seems inclined to keep jurisdiction rather than defer to the specialist tribunal. This is similar to the situation as claims for nuisance that can reside in both the High Court and the Environmental Commission.

In ***Charlotteville Beachfront Movement v Tobago House of Assembly***[386] as per Rajkumar J:

> *56. It was contended that the court had no jurisdiction to consider the legality of the activities taken by the defendant as there existed the alternative remedy of an action before the Environmental Commission, which, as a specialized body set up to deal with environmental issues, allegedly had exclusive jurisdiction.*

> *57. This argument is rejected. The allegations of illegality do not relate solely to compliance by the defendant with requirements under the Environmental Management Act. They relate to the failure to obtain approvals from the Town and Country Planning Authority, and the need to ensure that this project in fact has received all necessary statutory approvals.*

> *58. In any event it does not require a specialized body such as the Commission to detect whether the defendant has complied with obligations to observe requirements imposed by the Authority under the Act, when*

> *a. the defendant itself acknowledges that it required a CEC for the waste water treatment plant associated with the project, and*

> *b. it is beyond dispute that it simply did not have the CEC for this at the time that it took the above decisions, or even by the time that leave to review those decisions was sought.*

> *59. Section 9 of the Judicial Review Act Chap 7:08 provides that "the Court shall not grant leave to an applicant for judicial review of a decision where any other written law provides an alternative procedure to question, review or appeal that decision, save in exceptional circumstances."*

> *60. It was submitted that: -*

> *a. The Claimants have contended that the Defendant has not obtained the necessary documentation, that is to say, the Certificate of Environmental Clearance*

---

386 CV 2013-01738

("CEC") before commencing works,

b. The Claimants have alleged therefore that there has been a breach of the provisions of the Environmental Management Act Chap 35:05,

c. Breaches of the Environmental Management Act should attract, firstly, the attention of the Environmental Commission.

61. Section 81(5) of the Environmental Management Act Chap 35:05 provides as follows:

"The Commission shall have jurisdiction to hear and determine—

h. complaints brought by persons pursuant to section 69, otherwise known as the direct private party action provision; and

62. Section 69 of the Environmental Management Act Chap 35:05 provides as follows: "(1) Any private party may institute a civil action in the Commission against any other person for a claimed violation of any of the specified environmental requirements identified in section 62, other than paragraphs (c), (d) and (l), save where—

(a-d – not applicable)

(2) For purposes of this section, any individual or group of individuals expressing general interest in the environment or a specific concern with respect to the claimed violation shall be deemed to have standing to bring a direct private party action.

Section 62 (f) includes among the "environmental requirements", "apply for and obtain a Certificate of Environmental Clearance."

63. The alternative remedy argument proceeds under the misconception that the applicants are merely challenging the failure to obtain a CEC. In fact, they are challenging the decision to embark upon construction and to incidentally demolish the booth occupied by the second named claimant on a basis wider than this – namely the failure to have first obtained a CEC, AND the failure to have first obtained planning permission before so doing.

64. It is alleged that the ensuing illegality rendered the demolition of the booth occupied by the second claimant/applicant an illegal trespass. While the Environmental

Commission may have jurisdiction to consider a claim by the applicants against the defendant in respect of a failure to have obtained a CEC, the matters other than that of enforcement of environmental laws – namely enforcement of Planning Permission requirements, and the instant claim for damages for trespass in respect of demolition of the booth occupied by the second claimant are beyond the scope of the Environmental Management Act. The jurisdiction of the High Court cannot therefore be considered to ousted, more so as such ouster of jurisdiction on the basis of an existing alternative remedy is on a discretionary basis. See the Alutrint case – supra paragraph 121.

If it were even necessary to so find, the instant circumstances would constitute exceptional circumstances, especially as leave was unopposed and the alternative remedy point only raised long after leave had been granted.

REMEDIES AVAILABLE TO THE ENVIRONMENTAL COMMISSION

Injunctions

An arising issue is the extent of the exclusive power of the Environmental Commission to grant certain remedies that are traditionally available in the pursuit of judicial review. It was held by the High Court of TT, that by being deemed a superior court of record, the Environmental Commission can only grant injunctive relief at the behest of the EMA.

South West Tobago Fisherman's Association v The Attorney General of Trinidad & Tobago House of Assembly, Environmental Management Authority and Petroleum Geo-Services Limited[387]

1. Declarations apart the Claimant seeks injunctive relief, both restraining and mandatory, and damages. With respect to the liabilities created by the Act the remedy of injunction is by the Act limited to the Authority. Further by deeming the Commission a superior court of record, in my opinion, the power to grant such an injunction is with respect to the liabilities created by the Act limited to the Commission. Similarly, the ability to provide compensation or damages for breaches of the Act termed in the Act administrative civil assessments is, by section 67 vested in the Commission alone.

---

387 CV 2008-02926

The power for the EMA to obtain prohibitory orders is specifically provided for in the *Environmental Management Act.*

Section 68 of the Environmental Management Act

68. Whenever the Authority reasonably believes that any person is currently in violation of any environmental requirement, or is engaged in any activity which is likely to result in a violation of any environmental requirement, the Authority may in addition to, or in lieu of, other actions authorized under this Act— (a) seek a restraining order or other injunctive or equitable relief, to prohibit the continued violation or prevent the activity which will likely lead to a violation; (b) seek an order for the closure of any facility or a prohibition against the continued operation of any processes or equipment at such facility in order to halt or prevent any violation; or (c) pursue any other remedy which may be provided by law.

The successful obtaining of injunctive relief by the EMA before the Environmental Commission pursuant to its power under *Section 68 of the Environmental Management Act* has already been demonstrated.

Environmental Management Authority v Michael Trestrail [388]

An injunction was sought by the EMA in this matter and the Environmental Commission granted an injunction and other interim measures due to the imminence of the rainy season and the potential additional negative impacts of the activities being undertaken by Michael Trestrail, particularly as the Environmental Commission found that Mr. Trestrail acted in a manner that demonstrated a lack of concern for the consequences of the activities on the environment. The Environmental Commission found that the activities of Mr. Trestrail were grave and disturbing in their disregard for the environmental impacts on Mal D. Estomac Bay.

Issuance of Prerogative Orders

It has also been conceded by the Environmental Commission that it lacks the power to make prerogative orders.

---

388 EAA 002 of 2011

Fishermen and Friends of the Sea v Environmental Management Authority[389]

(1) *Counsel for the EMA, Ms. Sharma, submitted that the Commission has no jurisdiction to make declarations and/or orders for certiorari governing the carrying on of its business and the practice and procedure in connection with appeals to the Commission and other proceedings.*

(45) *Under the inherent jurisdiction of a superior court of record there are three broad classifications of cases in which the court exercises its jurisdiction. These are:*

(i) *control over process,*

(ii) *control over persons and*

(iii) *control over powers of inferior courts and tribunals.*

(46) *It is instructive that Jacob in discussing the third grouping, control over inferior courts and tribunals, referred specifically to the control and superintendence of the High Court over inferior courts, stemming from the jurisdiction of the King's Bench in matters of contempt of court. He was deliberate when he said that it is the High Court, a court of general jurisdiction, which has power to control inferior courts and tribunals. It is further instructive that Jacob did not include this power as being applicable to a superior court of law under its inherent jurisdiction. He made the point that the jurisdiction of the High Court to review decisions of an inferior court cannot be said to form of part its inherent jurisdiction, for this jurisdiction is exercised by virtue of the prerogative orders.*

(47) *Prerogative orders derive from that part of the common law which is more particularly applicable to the King. Sir William Blackstone in his Commentaries defined a court as a place wherein justice is judicially administered. Historically the sole executive power of the law was vested in the person of the King and it followed that all courts of justice, which were the medium by which he administers the laws, were derived from the power of the crown. Historically, in all courts, the King is supposed, in contemplation of law to be always pres-*

---

389 EAP 005 of 2007

ent; but as that is in fact impossible, he is therefore represented by his judges, whose power is only an emanation of the royal prerogative.

(48) *Superior courts of law do not all have the power to exercise prerogative powers as was demonstrated by the case of R v. St. Edmundsbury. For a court to exercise those powers they must be specifically given, for example by an Act of Parliament. In the case of R v. St. Edmundsbury, Wrottesley L.J. in referring to the powers of courts of limited jurisdiction said:*

"...the true view is that the King's Bench, because it was the court in which the King sat, originally in fact and theory, was charged with the general duty of seeing that all courts of limited jurisdiction kept within those limits. At any rate, in early times it was the King in Council who set out limits of those jurisdictions, though later this was done by statute. Some of these courts were limited only by local boundaries...Sometimes the limits were extremely wide.... There were the various courts which administered the law merchant. There was the court of the admiral in the time of Edward Ill, followed by the court of admiralty in the 15th century. There was the court of the constable and the marshal, administering. martial law... . . . There was the court of heraldry which, in addition to its jurisdiction over the coat of arms, exercised at one time a jurisdiction as to slander upon men of noble blood. These are only some of the many courts of limited jurisdiction which existed and sometimes flourished side by side with the King's Bench, Common Pleas, Exchequer and later the Chancery courts, but all these limited jurisdictions were subject to the jurisdiction of the King's Bench court in this respect, that if they transgressed their limits the writ of prohibition would go to put an end to the proceedings, and to prohibit both judges and parties from taking any steps to enforce anything that had been done."...

(49) The above cited authority clearly demonstrates that historically courts of limited jurisdiction were subject to prerogative orders of the King's Bench courts. Consequently, these courts of limited jurisdiction did not have the inherent jurisdiction to make prerogative orders. The only manner in which those courts could be seized of those powers is if they were so vested by an Act of Parliament.

FINDING

(50) We therefore find that the Environmental Commission, a superior court

of record with limited jurisdiction, in the absence of statutory provision, does not have the power to make orders for certiorari and mandamus. However, the Environmental Commission by virtue of section 81 (5) (a) is in fact vested with the power to review decisions and actions of the EMA by way of appeal, thus achieving in the main the same purpose of judicial review. The Commission though it is not empowered to grant reliefs of certiorari and mandamus has the authority under section 86 (3) to make certain types of orders in disposing of an appeal brought before it.

The Environmental Commission has therefore held that its powers under the *Environmental Management Act* can extend to providing relief that achieves in essence, the main objective of judicial review.

Section 86 of the Environmental Management Act

86(2) In appeals involving the Authority, there shall be a presumption of regularity with regard to findings of fact by the Authority, and such findings shall not be reversed unless the appellant affirmatively demonstrates that there is no substantial evidence supporting such findings of fact.

(3) Subject to subsection (4), the Commission may dispose of an appeal by— (a) dismissing it; (b) allowing it; (c) allowing it and modifying the decision or action of the Authority; or (d) allowing it and referring the decision or action back to the Authority for reconsideration.

(4) Subject to Rules made under section 84(15), the Commission may make an Order for the payment of costs to the successful party in relation to the whole of the proceedings before it, or any part thereof, including costs incurred in the summoning and attendance of necessary witness.

(5) The decision of the commission is final on a question of fact and the amount of any administrative civil assessment under section 66; however, an appeal shall lie on any question of law to the Court of Appeal upon entry of a final judgment by the Commission

Administrative Civil Assessments

A major power vested in the EMA and the Environmental Commission to address a breach of an environmental requirement under the *Environmental*

Management Act is the ability to impose administrative civil assessments.

Sections 66-67 of the Environmental Management Act

66(1) For the purposes of sections 65 and 81(5)(d), the Authority or the Commission may make an administrative civil assessment of— (a) compensation for actual costs incurred by the Authority to respond to environmental conditions or other circumstances arising out of the violation referenced in the Administrative Order; (b) compensation for damages to the environment associated with public lands or holdings which arise out of the violation referenced in the Administrative Order; (c) damages for any economic benefit or amount saved by a person through failure to comply with applicable environmental requirements; and (d) damages for the failure of a person to comply with applicable environmental requirements, in an amount determined pursuant to subsections (2) and (3).

(2) In determining the amount of any damages to be assessed under subsections (1) (c) and (d), the Authority or the Commission shall take into account— (a) the nature, circumstances, extent and gravity of the violation; Administrative civil assessment. (b) any history of prior violations; and (c) the degree of wilfulness or culpability in committing the violation and any good faith efforts to co-operate with the Authority.

(3) The total amount of any damages under subsection (1)(d), shall not exceed— (a) for an individual, five thousand dollars for each violation and, in the case of continuing or recurrent violation, one thousand dollars per day for each such instance until the violation is remedied or abated; or (b) for a person other than an individual, ten thousand dollars for each violation and, in the case of continuing or recurrent violations, five thousand dollars per day for each such instance until the violation is remedied or abated.

67. (1) The Authority may file any Consent Agreement or final Administrative Order and an application for enforcement with the Commission.

(2) Where an Administrative Order contains a proposed administrative civil assessment, that assessment is not enforceable until such time as the Commission makes an Order determining the amount of such assessment.

The use of administrative civil assessments by the EMA in addressing the breach of an environmental requirement was extensively examined by the

Environmental Commission which has the power to impose an administrative civil assessment acting on its own or to approve an administrative civil assessment where imposed by the EMA.

Michael Trestrail v Environmental Management Authority[390]

Facts: On March 24th 2011, the Applicant, the Environmental Management Authority ("The EMA") filed an application for injunctive relief against the Respondent, Mr. Michael Trestrail ("Mr. Trestrail") to stop works on his property situate at Mal D'Estomac. The EMA alleged that the activities that were being carried out there were being executed without a Certificate of Environmental Clearance ("CEC") as provided for by the Certificate of Environmental Clearance (Designated Activities) Order, 2001 ("the Designated Activities Order"), more particularly Designated Activities 8(c), 8(b), 12, 13 and 41(c) respectively.

Held: Environmental Commission

THE AIM OF THE DAMAGES

9. The aim of awarding damages at common law is to place the plaintiff as far as possible in the position he would have been in had the wrongful act not occurred. However, when awarding damages where there is a failure to comply with applicable environmental requirements the Court is also concerned with deterrence. The purpose of deterrence, in this context, includes:

(a) Making clear that the overall penalty for a breach of the law is always likely to be more costly than any expense that should have been incurred in avoiding the breach in the first place;

(b) The need for the overall penalty to be such as to bring the necessary message home to the particular respondent (whether individual or corporate) before the Court, in order to deter future breaches, whether by that respondent or by other potential respondents.

THE LAW

10. According to Section 66 (1) of the Environmental Management Act, the EMA or the Commission may make an administrative civil assessment of —

---

390 EAA 002 of 2011.

(a) Compensation for actual costs incurred by the EMA to respond to environmental conditions or other circumstances arising out of the violation referenced in the Administrative Order;

(b) Compensation for damages to the environment associated with public land or holdings which arise out of the violation referenced in the Administrative Order;

(c) Damages for any economic benefit or amount saved by a person through failure to comply with applicable environmental requirements; and

(d) Damages for the failure of a person to comply with applicable environmental requirements, in an amount determined pursuant to subsections (2) and (3).

In determining the amount of damages to be assessed under subsections (1) (c) and (d), the EMA or the Commission shall take into account –

(a) The nature, circumstances, extent and gravity of the violation;

(b) Any history of prior violations, and

(c) The degree of wilfulness or culpability in committing the violation and any good faith efforts to co-operate with the EMA.

The total amount of any damages under subsection (1) (d), shall not exceed –

(a) For an individual, five thousand dollars ($5,000.00) for each violation and, in the case of continuing or recurrent violation, one thousand dollars ($1,000.00) per day for each such instance until the violation is remedied or abated; or

(b) For a person other than an individual, ten thousand dollars ($10,000.00) for each violation and, in the case of continuing or recurrent violations, five thousand dollars ($5,000.00) per day for each such instance until the violation is remedied or abated.

THE PROPOSED ADMINISTRATIVE CIVIL ASSESSMENT

11. On July 7th 2011, the EMA filed the Proposed Administrative Civil Assessment. The Assessment was amended and filed on October 5th 2011 and further amended and filed on March 8th 2012. The EMA stated therein that in assessing an administrative civil assessment pursuant to Section 66 of the Act, it was guided by its Draft Civil Assessment Policy (the Civil Assessment Policy) made pursuant to Section 66 (1) (c) and (d) of the Act as an in-house guide to calculate administrative civil assessment for breaches of Sections 62(f) and (g) of the Act. The EMA used the Civil Assessment Policy solely for the calculation of damages under Section 66 (1) (d).

12. The Court is mindful of the fact that a civil assessment policy generally has two components: a gravity – based component, which is tied to the seriousness of the violation and an economic benefit component. The gravity component factors the seriousness of the violation and the extent to which the violation deviates from statutory or regulatory requirements. The economic benefit component determines an amount that equals or exceeds the gains realized by an individual's or company's non-compliance.

13. The Court recognizes that the EMA's civil assessment policy deals solely with the gravity-based component.

14. The Court accepted the EMA's Civil Assessment Policy as a diligent methodology for assessing damages. The Court particularly recognizes the value of Base Figure Matrices as an acceptable method of taking several factors peculiar to individual cases into consideration for the fair and expedient calculation of damages. It does so by applying the weightings to the factors outline in Section 66(2) of the Environmental Management Act.

METHODOLOGY

15. The EMA in its Civil Assessment Policy devised a method whereby it assigned weightings to the factors at Section 66 (2). Each of the four factors was given a weight out of 10. The more serious the violation the higher the weight out of 10, with the factors, nature, circumstances, extent and gravity, and degree of wilfulness or culpability in committing the violation, being doubled, resulting in the maximum score of 60. The total assessment value would be an amount over 60 as the denominator. The total assessment value would then be multiplied by the maximum penalty of five thousand dollars ($5,000.00) thus giving the penalty which would be applicable for each failure to comply with the applicable environmental requirements. The formula will therefore be: -

TOTAL ASSESSMENT VALUE/60 x MAXIMUM PENALTY

16. The EMA, in its Civil Assessment Policy in quantifying the damages for the failure to apply and obtain a certificate of environmental clearance, developed a series of Base Figure Matrices, as seen in Figures 1 through 5 of the Civil Assessment Policy. These matrices were applied to the factors which must be taken into account when determining damages.

CHAPTER 11

ROLE OF MULTILATERAL AGREEMENTS AND THE DOMESTIC ENVIRONMENTAL LEGAL REGIME

T has signed many Multilateral Environmental Agreements (MEAs), giving rise to a positive sense of environmental well-being.[391] Being a country based on common law jurisprudence, however, MEAs are not enforceable although signed by the State except where they have been expressly incorporated into the national legal regime by parliamentary action.

In *Talisman (Trinidad) Petroleum Limited v. Environmental Management Authority,*[392] the EMA refused the grant of a CEC for the exploration of hydrocarbons in the Nariva Swamp, an area that is a designated wetland under the *Convention on Wetlands of International Importance Especially as Waterfowl Habitat (Ramsar Convention)*. Under the *Ramsar Convention*, the Nariva Swamp was designated as a protected area but it was not so designated under the *Sensitive Species Areas Rules* made pursuant to the *Environmental Management Act*. The EMA sought to use the protected area status of the Nariva Swamp under the *Ramsar Convention* as a justification for refusing to grant a CEC for hydrocarbons exploration in the Nariva Swamp. This was rejected in *Talisman (Trinidad) Petroleum Limited v Environmental*

---

391 Mitchell, R *International Environmental Agreement Database (2006)* https://iea.uoregon.edu/country-members/Trinidad%20and%20Tobago.

392 No. EA03 of 2002

Management Authority[393] on the basis that the *Ramsar Convention* was not part of the national legal regime as it had not been subjected to parliamentary action.

Chairman His Honour, Z. Hosein:

In "An Overview of the World's Ramsar Sites" by Scott Frazier the author refers to the Fifth Conference of the Contracting Parties to the Ramsar Convention (1993) held in Japan, and refers to the challenges and commitments of contracting parties in conserving and ensuring the sustainable use of wet lands. Wet lands are known to be important for a host of varied reasons. They are natural storehouses of biological diversity and provide the life-support systems for much of humanity. They play a vital role in sediment and erosion control, flood control, maintenance of water quality and abatement of pollution, maintenance of water supply, including ground water and support for fisheries.

Wetlands contribute to climatic stability through their roles in global water and carbon cycles, grazing and cultivated lands are often wet land- dependent. Educational, scientific and recreational opportunities abound in wet lands. The author also notes that the tide of wetland destruction and degradation flows on in most parts of the world as non-sustainable development and human population pressures continue to escalate.

The author postulates that humanity depends on the sustainable use of wet lands. As wet lands or wet land functions are lost so the opportunities for sustainable development disappear. It is therefore obligatory that contracting parties to this convention fulfil their two obligations, namely: -

75. to designate wet lands of international importance as Ramsar sites in order to assure their conservation in perpetuity, and

76. to make wise use of all wetlands in their territory through a wide range of interactive policies, programmes and activities.

And in "Implementation of the Ramsar Convention in Trinidad and Tobago", the RSPB (Royal Society for the Protection of Birds Sabbatical

---

393 Ibid.

*Report by Dave Pritchard, December 1977), Bill Phillips, the Deputy Sec-
retary General of the Ramsar Convention Bureau in his Foreword to the said
Report had this to say:*

*"In the few years since joining the Ramsar Convention, (April 1993), Trinidad
and Tobago has been a lesson in pro-activity which many other countries
could learn from and especially the other Small Island States. Dave
Prichard uses the words "enthusiasm" and "courageous" several times to describe
the actions of the Government of Trinidad and Tobago and this is well justified.
He also notes that they have "set a commendable example in a short space
of time, by making full use of some of the main measures which Ramsar
participation offers:*

*Regional and International collaboration, a National Wetland Committee, a
National Wetland Policy, the Montreux Record, the Management Guidance
Procedure and the Small Grants Fund".*

*In the summary of conclusions and recommendations of the Report, the au-
thor was able to perceive in relation to National Wetland Policies at page
5, among other things, that "even a seemingly comprehensive measure like the
Trinidad and Tobago Environmental Act is not a complete rationalization
of measures for nature conservation and protected areas, and the draft National Environmental Policy does not show linkages leaving this to other
documents. Policy and legislation should visibly and reasonably promptly be
followed by "real world" implementation and enforcement."...*

*Mr. Morgan did not say anything which may be construed as a derogation of the
status and importance of Nariva Swamp as a Ramsar site and its continued
designation as such, but submitted that although the Ramsar Convention was
subscribed to by the Government of Trinidad and Tobago, it was not embodied
into the laws of Trinidad and Tobago, since there was no Act of Parliament
incorporating it into the local laws. There is that unmistakeably serious lapse
and it is trite law that while the convention will be binding upon the Government
of Trinidad and Tobago as a signatory thereto, its terms cannot be enforced
unless they are brought locally into effect by local enactment.*

*It is to be noted that the Ramsar site is mentioned in Schedule I of the
Environmentally Sensitive Areas Rules (ESA Rules) 2001 and it is therefore*

to be taken into account as a Ramsar site, however, neither the Ramsar site nor the Nariva Swamp has been designated as an Environmentally Sensitive Area pursuant to the ESA Rules. Until so designated, the Respondent cannot say that there is an absolute prohibition under the ESA Rules to a 3-D seismic survey being conducted therein. Until designation of the Ramsar site as an environmentally sensitive area or one which includes terms prohibiting an activity such as that proposed, the refusal on the basis simpliciter that it is a Ramsar site, is in law untenable.

CHAPTER 12

CONCLUSION

TT has set a precedent in the English-speaking Caribbean. It is the first country in the region to pursue a consolidated and scientific approach to environmental management. While it is true that other countries do have environment-related legislation, this is scattered and sometimes based on non-scientific and even arbitrary principles. Since the establishment of the EMA in 1995, there has been an increase in public awareness in TT with regard to environmental matters. Suffice it to say, heightened public awareness must be accompanied by implementation and enforcement of effective legislation if environmental management is to succeed. The lack of political will to deal with environmental issues in a developing country, such as TT, can be arguably ascribed to the presence of the dominant concern of using economic development as a means of eradicating social inequities which characterise these countries. There are no signs in TT beyond attractive but empty statements to suggest a greening of government policy.

The NEP 2018 has introduced a strong section on governance. It is left to be seen whether this would transcend rhetoric.

NEP 2018 Section 1.05 It is recognised that sustainable development can only be achieved where public, private and nongovernmental institutions are transparent, accountable and honest in their governance of human, financial, environmental and natural resources. Good governance is a function of mutual trust and reciprocal relations between governmental agencies, civil society, and non-state actors including businesses and NGOs. This must be based on the fulfilment of constitutional, legislative and executive functions and the acceptance of authority, probity, transparency and accountability. It necessitates that appropriate institutions, institutional relationships and common targets are established and supported. In the pursuit of good governance, the GoRTT reaffirms its responsibility to respect the health and well-being of all citizens. Furthermore, the GoRTT, all subnational actors and international actors operating

349

within the State's boundaries shall adopt/maintain, where appropriate, the features of good governance required to galvanise environmental sustainability, including but not limited to: 1. Internal democratic and transparent decision-making procedures and financial accountability; 2. Effective measures to combat official or other corruption; 3. Respect for due process and observance of the rule of law; 4. Protection of human rights as enshrined in the Constitution; 5. Transparent and non-corrupt public procurement procedures; 6. Meaningful participation of women at all levels of decision-making; 7. Meaningful engagement and involvement of Trinidad and Tobago's youth; 8. Respect for all forms of knowledge systems inclusive of traditional knowledge held by indigenous and local communities; 9. Equitable representation and meaningful participation of the poor and other marginalised groups in decision-making; 10. A culture of accountability in their responsibilities pertaining to the development and implementation of environmental and development policies, laws and policy instruments; 11. Effective process to redress past and present environmental justice; 12. Corporate social responsibility and socially responsible investments towards the equitable distribution of wealth and benefits within communities; 13. The right of workers to refuse work that is injurious to human health or the environment; and 14. The right of every citizen to expose any environmental or health hazard without fear of reprisal.

An important facet of environmental management in developing countries is the cynical view of the environment as an economic advantage. This perception paints a lucid picture of the brutal conflict between the environment and development and the state-sponsored support for development. It is often the case that developing countries export their natural "comparative advantage" through the lax application of environmental regulations. Natural resource management is not a priority in the developing world, as it is the disposal of such resources that provides the developmental base of the economy. By so doing, governments not only destroy the environment, but also threaten the lives of the inhabitants of the country. Developing countries are now in a position to exploit their environmental comparative advantage as they have lenient practices in the enforcement of environmental legal regimes.

Current models of development in developing economies will not allow for the development of sound international environmental management. Developing countries now have to adopt a different economic developmental paradigm which will seek to include the environment. They should assume a more holistic and harmonious approach, seeking to achieve the Chinese principle of *feng shui*. In addition to self-sufficiency, there should also be an inherent appreciation for the value of nature, culture and the environment. There should also be the political empowerment of marginalized groups in society, such as women and indigenous groups. This will lead to a fully integrated society where there will be sustainability in the social, cultural, political economic and environmental realms. In the myopic approach of developing countries to development, natural resources are haphazardly harvested in an attempt to maximise revenues, which is mistakenly perceived as economic growth. This carries adverse consequences for any prospects of long-term economic growth and development.

Today, TT is at the cross-roads of environmental management. It has an emerging rich repository of environmental jurisprudence. Concepts such as the right to a healthy environment, the polluter pays principle, the precautionary principle, environmental democracy through public participation, environmental justice and sustainable development are already being explored by the judiciary. Judicial activism is mainly being achieved through NGOs and in particular FFOS, an NGO that has directly or indirectly participated in over 65% of the national cases touching on the *Environmental Management Act*. The reality is that if TT follows the legal environmental traditions of the past, the country may very well bestow on future generations the legacy of an environment scarred by anthropogenic exploits. The numerous developing countries that are still to forge their environmental management regimes must look closely at the environmental legal regime of TT to avoid the obvious deficiencies in an environmental management system that has raised a lot of expectations, but disappointed many. Significantly, however, nothing positive will transpire unless a political will emerges from the state apparatus with a commitment to ensuring sustainable development. The needs of future generations cannot be sacrificed on the altar of political expediency and the time to act is now, for to wait signals irreversible peril.

INDEX

G-I

N - U

www.ingramcontent.com/pod-product-compliance
Lightning Source LLC
Chambersburg PA
CBHW051623170526
45167CB00001B/39